UNANTICIPATED

FEEDBACK

A MOTE IT IS

TO TROUBLE

THE MIND'S EYE ....

BY: JOHN E. HUNT

"Life does not consist mainly, or even largely, of facts or happenings. It consists mainly of the storm of thoughts that is forever flowing through one's head." - Mark Twain

TABLE OF CONTENTS

FORWARD

'Planning' isn't just a set of tools that we pick up and put down. Planning, as defined in this book, is a life tool, a world frame and structure for thinking. Planning, a type of structured thinking, creates or destroys life.

There are a number of quotes (some quite long) from Guardians, Paul and Apocalypse (3rd edition) which are incorporated into this book. They are books 1, 2 and 3 of a trilogy, and are strange novels in a number of ways, but the reason that the quotes from those books are in this book is that those novels are (among many other things) an examination of decision making in increasingly complex situations. The quotes from those books are included in this book to flesh out the theory–to try and make page after page of theory, suggestions, warnings and cautions come alive for the reader. Rather than show the quotes in italics, which is very tiring for a full page of text, I've broken long quotes out by indenting the quotes and putting them in a slightly smaller font. If you don't find them useful, skip them, but one of the central thesis of this book is that we learn only through stories, and those are interesting stories.

Planning is an exciting activity, one that we are all involved in constantly. There is a vast difference, which we merrily jump over, between planning for normal life and planning for something different. Involved in normal life, making the same kind of decisions over and over, with slight modifications and fine-tuning, we generally use those same approaches to the non-daily life decisions.

For example, there are the classic non-normal decisions, such as what career to follow, picking a significant other, discarding prior significant other's, what school or future training programs to go to, where to move, whether to take that new job, and each new day with a teenager. Relying on our standard methods of decision-making, which is basically doing what we did yesterday doesn't work well for those kinds of decisions.

Pink Floyd expressed this beautifully:

"You are young and life is long and there is time to kill today.
And then one day you find ten years have got behind you.
No one told you when to run, you missed the starting gun."

Do what you have always done and you will be where you always are. The larger world, however is not so obliging, and it will move on.

Another approach that is different in this book from other planning books is the embrace of that which isn't quite (or marginally, or even at all) socially acceptable. You are going to plan a great many things, most of which are at least socially unacceptable to someone, and some of which will be unacceptable to almost everyone. Those still need to be planned, and

—
9

whereas most planning books simply ignore what's most important to you in life, preferring to focus on nice 'clean' problems that are essentially useless, this book is going to demand you consider your inspirations in planning. Your inspirations are obviously yours, and that's where planning is most important. Your inspiration, because it's focused, new and different, is often a conflict with your daily planning models. Inspirations clearly need pulling out of the daily planning model and into focused attention, or your inspirations will be chewed up in the daily grind, growing stale and empty, and you become just another of the living dead among us.

WHY WAS THIS BOOK WRITTEN?

So, why does this book exist, and what do you want out of it? There are two questions here: why are you reading this book, and why the book was written. With most books, those are two quite different things and that is certainly the case with this book.

WHY DID I WRITE THIS BOOK?

This book is an extended meditation on the following quote:

"In seeing victory, not going beyond what everyone knows is not skilled.

Victory in battle that all-under-heaven calls skilled is not skilled.

Thus lifting an autumn hair does not mean great strength.

Seeing the sun and the moon does not mean a clear eye.

Hearing thunder does not mean a keen ear.

So-called skill is to be victorious over the easily defeated."[1]

If you perceive the subtle before it ripens into form, then you win. If you do not, you lose. Every time, in every situation. Everything in your life will be better if you perceive the subtle while it is formless, even if you perceive only moments before it takes the form that all recognize. By the time you hear the noise of thunder, the lighting bolt has struck and is gone. Whether you seek by buy low and sell high; recognize romantic interest or lack thereof; or any other problem, it all comes down to seizing opportunity at that moment it smiles warmly at you, or a moment later grasping uselessly at Fortune's bald head as the Goddess laughingly flies by.

So, perceive how? How to grasp the real facts as they take shape in the mist? Actually, there's no such thing as sheer fact; it's the object for a subject. The attitude of the mind beholding the object is what creates the character and meaning of a 'fact'. So if the revealed truth were outside your door, blazing in golden Technicolor before you, by the process of turning that perception into small words and human stories, we've lost touch with the real nature of those events out there. A story may or may not grasp the key points, at least for the part of the real world that matters to your life, but necessarily you've only grabbed a small part of that big world out there. Can't be helped.

The importance of Figure 1 (in part 2) which is central to this book, is that the Figure drives home that we are grasp only portion of what's going on. That Figure 1 shows the (dis)connects between the real world, the self and the social world. This is critical to shake us loose from our customary easy and pleasant vision of what we want to believe is out there, jarring us to an alert and ready mental state of at least being doubtful about what we perceive is out there. In life, it's the false assumption that we know to be true that is going to hurt. Visually: what you think you know, that you really don't know, has its teeth bared.

It's important to accept that no one can see the future by Force of Will. You wake up from a good night's sleep, roll over, stretch, smile, and decide you will know the future today. No. Fail. We hear what we want to hear, see what we want to see. So that blazing Technicolor future laid out before you in an earlier paragraph? You only see, generally, what you are expecting to see. Captain Jack Sparrow in the "Pirates of the Caribbean" had a compass that pointed the way to what he most desired-but what was it is that it pointed to? What was it that he desired in his heart? We know what we think we desire, but we often to not know what we really want.

"It would not be better if things happened to people just as they wish." Heraclitus

And wouldn't it be boring if life unfolded just as you had planned? Life has a whimsical sense of humor (to put it politely) and wants to keep you interested and engaged. So we don't need to worry about boredom.

This book is a set of ideas and tools to use to make decisions that work for you, decisions that make you happy, keep you alive and prosperous in the real world and in the social world. It's an ambitious goal, I know. It isn't that the rules for effective action in life are unknown, as the Art of War has an extensive set of concepts and suggestions that work, and that is one of many books that lays out the ground rules.

It is more that the ground rules for life and decisions are so different from the way that our minds ache to believe the world to be that we need a tool to translate between the world rules and our minds. That rather ambitious goal is what this book seeks to do. This book will present and argue for ideas that are shocking and quite different, but please give the ideas a chance: play and experiment with them. Caveat: playing with the ideas in legally forbidden contexts is your choice, not mine.

To God all things may be good, but a plan based on a bad idea and/or the wrong idea; or a poorly designed plan; or a poorly executed plan, is pretty much an absolute evil in all regards in all system of ethics, morality, philosophy and theology. And you won't get a bonus at work, either. A failed plan is certainly evil if you have a goal you wanted to accomplish, because you are not going to reach that goal. Even if the plan succeeds despite itself, accidentally creating something that is good; it is still a fail. Why? First, random results aren't acceptable design criteria for next actions. This is gambling, technically, not planning. A mighty (accidental) success under your belt, you'll use the same planning tools for the next, bigger and ultimately unsuccessful project. That is, you will accidently have climbed the small hill, to then confidently use the same tools to go off the larger cliff.

"The man who has planned badly, if fortune is on his side, may have had a stroke of luck; but his plan was a bad one nonetheless."
Herodotus

WHY ARE YOU READING THIS BOOK?

You are reading this book because you want something and you want it when you want it. Fair enough, that's certainly a valid goal! No one, outside of academics, really cares about planning except as the means to an end: to get what you care about what you want, sooner rather than later. So why can't the world just do what you want when you want it? As Brad Majors demanded (in the Rocky Horror picture Show): "a reasonable request which you have chosen to ignore!" And ignore his request the world did, beyond anything Brad could have imagined. The world just likes that kind of stuff.

Let's go back to experts and their opinions, which is where most planning books dwell. The experts have analyzed the planning process and labored over it until it's almost impossible to recognize original goal, which is getting what you want. Now, that's a general problem with experts, because:

"Now, we have been taught to go to experts for specialized problems. The problem with experts is this: if you go to your doctor with a broken leg, they can fix that. If you go in with a vague itch, which occurs at random intervals in different spots, you might as well stay home. Problems that can be solved have clear borders, such as a broken leg. Problems without clear boundaries, the itches, the occasional rattle in your car, those problems usually can't be solved. But a failure to solve some problems makes people doubt the experts. That's bad, because then the experts don't get paid. So, to preserve their claim of expertise, experts wall off the important stuff for the detail they can control. Authoritative and learned people create categories, they 'platonify' to define what's important as what they can control. What you think is important is pushed away, because anyone with a mind and a tongue can discourse about what is important to each of us. But, if you focus on petty details, bury what matters under a layer of jargon, and look serious, then the experts can make a living whether they can solve the problem of not. Making a living is important, because we all have to feed our children.

"So like dung beetles, they pile up esoteric knowledge in a ball and push it before them, proving their expertise. Professors, psychologists, theologians, among others. All the same process in the end. And the writings that the church so reverently venerates, all the cracked parchment written in ancient dead languages that they pore over? Who knows what the writings were before they were edited, revised, and simply re-written? Who knows what the authors really meant by their words? You do know that what is written in the official text is what works for those in power, and that's about all one can be sure of. There's a concept called negative evidence. Who can say what came from what, and what is missing that is important? The water on the floor—was it from an ice cube melting, or something completely different? There is no way of knowing what was lost or destroyed in the past ....."[2]

Which is why a lot of the planning literature doesn't seem (and isn't) all that relevant to your rather focused goals. A final stab at experts:

"Experts, the Cardinal thought glumly. Experts are far worse than a coin toss, because they believe in themselves. Overconfidence, refusal to look outside their own opinion. it's selective ignorance of the facts as they happily explain and wish away dissonant facts and contradictory data. We're all prisoners of our preconceptions, and our wishes are not the world."[3]

Finally, a cheerful thought: the cruelest lies are often told in silence, with no outward sign. You are boxed into something without even realizing it happened, which is a topic this book looks at over and over.

So, what we may want, why and when, outside of absolutely simple and clear problems such as starvation and/or a cold rain falling on us, is more complex than we often think. That is why many of our plans, perhaps most, just don't work. There's more to the problem than drawing a straight line between where you are and where you want to be, and then pulling on your hiking books.

WHERE IS THE OVERLAP?

Where is the overlap between why I wrote the book and why you are reading the book?

For anything beyond the problem of the cold rain falling on you, determining what you want, when and how, is complex. And even the cold rain problem, if you then run into a handy cave, isn't solved if that is where hungry bear has been hiding, it's stomach growling as it waits for the rain to stop. You can imagine the bears delight to find that take-out is being delivered, but you won't be as delighted. Surprised, yes-but not for long.

So, please bear with the diversions into why and wherefore, when you only want what and when. Your goals in reading the book and the author's goal in writing the book do converge. Let us step into that twilight zone where the mind and the world touch and embrace, a place where our hopes and desires fade into the fog of the future, just faintly glowing trails we follow. Let me take you, if I might, on a strange journey ...

By the way, all books have to warn against rash action. This book does not encourage or authorize you to take steps that violate criminal provisions – take some responsibility for your actions!

Unanticipated Feedback is the world trying to tell you something. Why is it unexpected?

The Famous Plan

This is a book on planning and so it has a plan.

The previous section talks about what you want from the book, and why the book was written, with the hope that those two will have some overlaps.

The key to planning is thinking!! Tools and toys are to be used after there is a goal, and it takes some time to get there. Almost all failures can be tied to not thinking about–and rethinking– what you want and are after. So Part 1 of this book starts with attitude and perspective. Perspective and worldview is presented from a rather different viewpoint, in an attempt to get people out of their boxes and into the bigger systems.

Then, we look at stories. Stories are the water we swim in, and we commonly don't grasp the weaknesses and limits of stories, a problem because we think exclusively in stories.

Part 2 starts with a quite different perspective on stories, which expands our view of stories to increase the breadth of our thinking. Then we look at feedback, because if we are going to think, we've got to have something useful to think with and about. Next we look at the OODA cycle, a model for effective action and that part concludes with the key question: what problems should I be solving? Which is NOT the same as the problems shouting at you right now.

Part 3 is getting what we want – or not. It starts with planning ideas and concepts, but spends most of the time on failure, because failure is both more interesting and more useful than success. Success is too often smoke and mirrors and moving the goalposts, whereas failure is that stinking mess sitting in front of you–or the best tuition you'll ever pay.

Part 4 looks at problem solving–if such a thing is possible. It talks about complex problems and systems and approaches to solving the unsolvable.

Finally, Part 5 is Dancing in the Storm–ideas for dealing with the chaos coming at you.

Like most plans, shouted proudly at the stars while standing on top of a mountaintop, I'm not sure it worked exactly as planned, but it's actually turned out better than I had anticipated.

PART 1. LOOKING AND LINKING

"What everyone knows is what has already happened or become obvious.
What the aware individual knows is what had not yet taken shape, what has not yet occurred.
Everyone says victory in battle is good, but if you see the subtle and notice the hidden so as to seize victory where there is no form, this is really good. Sun Tzu[4]

CHAPTER 1. LOOKING AT THE WORLD

CHAPTER 2. THIS IS AN AMORAL BOOK

CHAPTER 3. PARASITES RULE

CHAPTER 4. STORIES

CHAPTER 5. STORY FAILURES.

CHAPTER 1. LOOKING AT THE WORLD

ATTITUDE.

The first topic is attitude-your attitude. Not quite the same as 'altitude', but akin in many ways. Altitude is the height that you are above something, and attitude is how you view something. Getting some altitude when you want an overview is essential-it's a stepping back, and looking over, pulling yourself out of the swamp and looking down at why you are in the swamp. Attitude is how you are looking out at the world, how you are planning on engaging that world, whether to win or run. Perspective, which we cover later, is the mental model you use to sort that world into shape.

Why, in a book on planning, is attitude so important? We know what we want-let's get to it! That, actually, is the essential human error in all planning. We think a little (or not at all) and jump into the fray. It's key to think and then think again! Of course, it isn't that easy.

Attitude is absolutely critical because it is an invisible filter that results in you seeing only what you are looking for. That filter discards everything that you are not looking for and so you never actually see alternatives or conflicting information and/or unexpected issues. If you didn't define the filter carefully, you don't know what you missed. Now, perception is tricky. Each of us has a different sensory balance of what we pay attention to. One person may be more responsive to visual cues (shape and color) while touch has a harder time getting through. For another person, sound might be the first reference, while visual aspects of the world have a tougher time making an impression. Obviously our natural inclinations to notice some kinds of stimuli while remaining oblivious to others create blind spots. But regardless of our personal preferences, everything we do notice or discard starts with attitude. This is hardly a new idea:

> "If you do not the expect the unexpected you will not find it, for it is not to be reached by search or trail." (Heraclitus, approx. 500BC)

In truth, we mentally live in boxes in boxes. It's OK, because there has to be a structure in our minds. We often fail to notice the world outside, preferring to pay more attention to what's going on in our mind. But, blithely running down paths in our mind, we often don't notice how we think and what we are thinking about. That's especially true for wide and broad paths we run down over and over. The problem is that as we plan, we seek to look down into a structure, into a box (boxes). It's much harder to look outside the boxes that we live in, but the boxes in our mind that we use to define the world often guarantees plan failure because we start with flawed assumptions and/or define the box we are planning the wrong way. In other words, if the box we use to analyze the problem can't grasp the problem, our solution is going to be random.

> "I had a dream the other night that I was in jail. It was an odd dream, it wasn't so bad and then I realized that I shouldn't be in jail. There was no reason I should be there. I just hadn't taken the steps to not be there. I realized that I'd put myself in my own jail and I could let myself out."[5]

We must make our own decisions. From a negative point of view, we die alone. We live alone also-we are not hard wired into another's experiences. Perhaps technology will come up with a cable to plug between two people to actually share experiences, but it isn't happening now. We also take responsibility alone, so attitude is important to get it right. An old saying is 'never enough time to do it right, always enough time to do it over', and we don't want to be there.

We fail to think, caught up in our everyday lives. Immersed in our normal day-to-day activities, we don't stop to think about what we are doing. Most of the time, we don't have to. An old Chinese proverb says, "the fish is the last to know that it is in water." Being immersed caught up in the flow of daily life, we barely notice what we are immersed in. In professional speak, we are neurologically programmed to habituate to sensory stimulation so that we ignore the familiar but notice change-certain changes, that seem relevant to our normal life. We do not notice all changes, and especially changes that are not what we want to be.

Oh, eventually we notice big changes in the environment around us, but often too late. A classical example is that people in a shipwreck will stand by the rail, holding on tightly as the boat lists, waiting to be told what to do. And that's with the ship obviously going down, the people watching the water coming up! What about the less obvious events in life? What about the little hints, the small oil stain that might be our car's engine, might not be, or the bosses odd stare in our direction?

First, you have to be looking to see all the possibilities. 'See a penny, pick up, all the day you'll have good luck' has nothing to do with pennies or luck-it's that you're alert, aware and acting. There is the good luck right there.

The corollary to that is: a cowboy is telling another cowboy that he saw a shooting star while riding last night. The second cowboy mutters, 'I foresee that you will fall off your horse very soon'. 'You saw that from the stars?', the first cowboy stammered, amazed. 'No, I foresee it because you're not paying attention', the second cowboy drawled. Pulling back to look out at the larger world is demanded, but not while galloping.

Attitude is a cluster of behaviors and thoughts, and somewhat hard wired. Now, attitude can be changed, if we want to. That gets into a philosophical quandary-is it only those who want to change who can change? We'll assume not. There are simple behavior changes, small ones at first, to notice the unusual. We can identify our sensory handicaps and strengths, and try to listen to the other senses. We can seek fresh ways to experience the familiar, take new routes, talk to strangers, and experiment with our own learning style. We can realize that accepting what is appalling happens because we don't back up and think. But it's attitude that makes it possible to look for the new.

Now, we may be happy and sassy, which isn't so bad, except that we are really resistant to change then. Others can be amazed at our lack of self-awareness because we often hold beliefs about ourselves that we accept unquestioningly -beliefs that, to others, have little or no basis in reality. They may be right or wrong, but, it's better to have an inkling than not.

Sometimes we are not happy with our life. We may not always be aware of when we feel purpose and meaning, but we are nearly always aware of a sickening feeling when they are gone. It isn't an intellectual misapprehension, a casual reflection as we sit at an outdoor café studying the sky–it is a gut sense of disorientation and a loss of personal direction. Rarely are brute mental effort and self-help pep talks able to rekindle the missing feeling. All we can do is simply wait patiently, knowing from past experience that the feeling will return in its own sweet time. When purpose and meaning returns, we will be different, and the disorientation and distress we felt were an essential part of becoming someone new.

An idea that underlies much of this book is simple one, but complex in operation. We generally do well in the mundane choices of daily life. One does much the same thing over and over in daily life, and with repeated feedback, we do reasonably well. Eating, sleeping, working, socializing-we follow the same patterns over and over. Plans based on those patterns are generally (not always) at least functional, if for no other reason that if you do the same thing over and over, feedback from your actions will focus where it's working and where it's not.

It's using those routine mental models; the same planning patterns for the non-daily life problems where we slip up. Many planning books slide over this, probably because they think it is so obvious, but it is absolutely critical. Using the same problem solving patterns that you use for daily life isn't going to work if you unthinkingly use them for picking a career, a significant other, and/or the other major choices in life.

You have to start with some mental model, but recognizing that you have a different type of problem and so shifting gears is absolutely critical, and commonly disregarded. 'People don't plan to fail, but they fail to plan' is the easy slap on a failure, only part of the story. Almost always people do plan, using the last successful plan for a different problem. That's at best a random result and generally a fail.

"Whether you think you can, or think you can't, you're probably right."(Henry Ford)

19

PERSPECTIVE

Perspective is the model that we use to locate us in the world, so let's place things in perspective:

"Did you ever read the story about 'the last meeting place'?" Mary asked. "A short science fiction story; it had a tool, a time-travel gadget, so that great people from all ages could meet in a room. One day, one demands help from the others, and will not be denied. He's desperate, begging and then threatening. A quiet, hooded man in a corner looks at him, and says, 'I am the last.' All that you will all do leads to me, and then the end. There is silence in the room, and the man then understands. It is what you do that matters. The ultimate results are not yours to choose. But it's hard, isn't it? Giving up that part of the story— the meaning that they drive into you? That you always have to be doing something measured by their goals, not something measured inside yourself?"[6]

So don't take things so seriously. But don't take them too lightly either, because paying the mortgage and putting food on the table is pretty important, too, in the here and now.

The perspective we have on the world, the way that we define things to ourselves limits our attitude. The words we choose create our reality, not just describe it.

"Buddha said that the name of the object isn't the object. Our name for a thing pretends the name is the same as the thing, which is the basis for all magic, actually. When we use the name, we emotionally believe that we have control over the 'thing,' but that is just fantasy. When we accept others' names for things, we've given ourselves over to their pretend control of the greater world. The words I use bind me, not the world that I seek to bind with them. The words control only the human stories, not the real world that the words pretend they control."[7]

This idea is looked at in much greater detail later in the book, because it's far more important than we normally realize.

The following is a smorgasbord of ideas covered in and important to these books, all covered in greater detail later, but presented here to spark the mind.

One of the most dangerous, if not the most dangerous thing in life, is where you are sure you are right and on top of a situation. The danger is that one then doesn't carefully examine the situation, because you just know it's OK. The worst disasters and problems I've ever had arise from that situation, because occasionally, you're not even close to what the real situation is. It's a good way to lose weight and enjoy the beauty of the night sky since you can't sleep, but that gets long after a while. What you don't know can hurt you! The crucial-and-cruel-blind spot is where you didn't know that you didn't know. Eventually, you will find out, but the further along the track that train has run the worse (generally) the surprise will be.

Another aspect of perspective is missing the Big Picture. We can see part of the picture, but the part is out of context, and when it falls into context, it's then something really different from what we expected. An example of this is: (reviewing an e-mail sent)

> "Pay attention to your surroundings; you won't spot good luck unless you look for it, that's what we went over last night. Well, among other things. So, here is someone thanking me for helping them be alert to a problem, but it's a problem that shouldn't be. They spotted, solved and moved on, but they skipped the important step. Why did it pop up? That's the vague shape looming behind the anomaly. The real story isn't that surface problem, it's whether the problem's appearance is someone maneuvering to get inside from the outside. The problem existing, as described here, means, to me, that someone got something inside already. The next step, hiring a body to solve a computer problem, means opening up the network to access, which we completely forbid, or someone waltzing in the door and putting their dirty physical hands on the keyboards. He thought for a minute."[8]

Tied to the above, although it is an important idea in it's own, is that as you plan, predictable is dangerous. Sun Tzu harps on this incessantly. If your plans are the same each time, then people around you know something about you that they can manipulate. Embezzlement, for example, demands consistency in the rules, so that people can cheat the rules. If you are unpredictable, then often they will not embezzle-and if they do, they will get caught. Regardless of how certain you are that a process is tamper proof, if you do the same thing long enough, and there is value to someone to beat the rules, they will beat the rules and you won't even notice-at least for quite a while. Cows are stupid – but they escape from a fenced pasture.

Predicable also means that you are not thinking about the situation, that you are just doing the same things over and over.

People can freeze in thinking about situations for many reasons. One, surprisingly, is the danger of understanding the enemy too well. If you really, emotionally, understand your enemy/opposition, then what will you do if some of their ideas are correct? If you understand that there is something good about them can you still make the decision to destroy? Once we really see the world from a viewpoint that is poles apart from our own, if even the most repellent actions or lifestyles or beliefs become understandable to us, how can we judge them to be wrong? Do we lose the capacity to conclude that one position is more morally acceptable than another? If we live in the gray world of multiple perspectives, will we utterly lose our moral compass? On the other hand, just because we are agonizing, that doesn't mean that they are agonizing as they sight down their rifle sights at us. It's complex, but a decision must be made.

There are very good reasons that the enemy in wartime is

demonized. We look at the WW II posters of the participant countries, and are shocked/amused by the shallowness, the naked hatred and vicious stereotypes thrust in our face. But wartime isn't time for thought and reflection. If they are shooting at you, you can't reflect on their philosophies and their children-you shoot back, and intend to kill. In general, we handle ambiguity badly, and battle is a situation where we handle it very badly. Novel after novel published after major wars explore this disconnect between having to kill and suddenly understanding the human nature of the enemy. There is no all-embracing answer, by the way. You have to shoot back when people are shooting at you, and you may later have an unsettled feeling about having done so.

A researcher, experimenting with trying to get people to understand their enemy, found that people were uncomfortably aware that to really see the other side is dangerous, if not terrifying. The researcher typically assigned a traditional paper that discussed the pros and cons of an issue. By changing the assignment to a paper that was written from first one side and then from the other, the researcher discovered that people who could easily write a paper casually dissecting the pros and cons of a controversial issue were very hesitant about the poles-apart assignment. Reflecting, the researcher began to understand. If we succeed in understanding how someone else could believe, think, and live in ways that are deplorable or offensive to us, what will that do to our values that we used to pass judgment? If their perspective actually makes us realize that we have been perhaps inaccurate, perhaps completely wrong in how we are cutting up the world, what else would that discovery lead to? How will that change our lives? That's dangerous, and it moves us out of the us/them that we use to quiet our thoughts. If we understand both sides, and act, then we may or may not be morally superior, we may discover that we are doing what we want and believe. We may find we are choosing for ourselves, not for the higher good or a by the power of a writ from above. We are choosing might over right. That's hard, because regrets can set in.

But if we don't open our minds to different viewpoints, we can make terrible mistakes. Sometimes we are just really wrong. The following is an example of an error in thinking, a simple mistake that cost many people their lives in prior centuries. MIASMA was the theory that bad smells cause disease. Certainly bad smells cause discomfort, but the theory was that the smell was the disease. This was London, in the mid 1850's, when the lack of sewerage disposal facilities made the entire city reek. Reek, please note, by their standards, which were considerably lower than ours would be today. It wasn't considered a problem to have raw sewage in the river and in corners all over the poorer parts of the city, but the smell drove the city father's to do something. Surprisingly, public health greatly improved when sewage disposal improved, which had nothing to do with the smell.

"MIASMA TURNS OUT TO BE A CLASSIC CASE OF WHAT

FREUD, in another context, called "overdetermination." It was theory that drew its persuasive power not from any single fact but rather from its location at the intersection of so many separate but compatible elements, like a network of isolated streams that suddenly converges to form a river. The weight of tradition, the evolutionary history of disgust, technological limitations in microscopy, social prejudice-all these factors colluded to make it almost impossible for the Victorians to see miasma for the red herring that it was, however much they prided themselves on their Gradgrindian rationality. Every research paradigm, valuable or not, in the hjstory of ideas has been buttressed by a comparable mix of forces, and in this sense the deconstructionists and the cultural relativists-so often the subject of mockery lately-have it right to a certain extent, though they tend to place undue stress on purely ideological forces. (Miasma was as much a creature of biology as of politics.) The river of intellectual progress is not defined purely by the steady flow of good ideas begetting better ones; it follows the topography that has been carved out for it by external factors. Sometimes that topography throws up so many barricades that the river backs up for a while. Such was the case with miasma in the mid-nineteenth century. . . .

But most of these dams eventually burst. Yes, the path of science works within regimes of agreement and convention, and history is littered with past regimes that were overthrown. But some regimes are better than others, and the general tendency in science is for explanatory models to be overthrown in the name of better models. Oftentimes because their success sows the seeds of their destruction . Miasma became. so powerful that it inspired a massive, state-sponsored intervention in the daily lives of millions of people, clearing the air by draining the cesspools. That intervention, miscalculated as it was, had the paradoxical effect of making the patterns of the epidemic more visible, at least to eyes that were capable of seeing them. And seeing the patterns more clearly means progress, in the long run at least.. . .

If the dominance of the miasma model was itself shaped by multiple intersecting forces, so, too, was Snow's ability to see it for the illusion that it was. Miasma was the intellectual equivalent of a contagious disease; it had spread through the intelligentsia with an alarming infection rate. So why was John Snow immune?. . .

Snow couldn't say exactly what kind of element was behind cholera's catastrophic attack on the human body, but he knew from observation that it invariably launched that attack from one place: the gut. The respiratory system, on the other hand, was largely unaffected by cholera's ravages. For Snow, that suggested an obvious etiology: cholera was ingested, not inhaled.. . .

This is how great intellectual breakthroughs usually happen in practice. It is rarely the isolated genius having a eureka moment alone in the lab. Nor is it merely a question of building on precedent, of standing on the shoulders of giants, in Newton's famous phrase. Great breakthroughs are closer to what happens in a flood plain: a dozen separate tributaries converge, and the rising waters lift the genius high enough that he or she can see around the conceptual obstructions of the age."[9]

Truly ironically, what sparked this problem was a chorea epidemic, spread through contact of fecal material with drinking water. (You don't want to know the details) Fortunately, the epidemic ran it's course long before it was really understood what happened. The book suggested that:

> "But the most likely scenario is that the bacterium was itself in a life-or-death struggle with another organism: a viral phage that exploits V. cholerae for its own reproductive ends the way V. cholerae exploits the human small intestine. One phage injected into a bacterial cell yields about a hundred new viral particles, and kills off the bacterium in the process. After several days of that replication, the population of V. cholerae might have been replaced by phages that were harmless to humans."[10]

So not only did they miss that smell wasn't disease, they were saved by a battle in the bacterial world that they had no concept of. That was a completely random win, and sometimes you're luckier than you realize. That book argued:

> So often what is lacking in many of these explanations and prescriptions is some measure of humility, some sense that the theory being put forward is still unproven. It's not just that the authorities of the day were wrong about miasma, because people are wrong about most things most of the time. It's the tenacious, certainly without a doubt way they went about being wrong. Stepping back, there were holes in the theory everywhere. If nothing else, the canary in the miasma coal mine should have been the sewer-hunters, who spent their waking hours exposed to the most noxious--sometimes even explosive--air imaginable. And yet, bizarrely, the canary seemed to be doing just fine. But they knew it was the smell, and couldn't look outside.[11]

Another aspect of perspective is that:

> "Some days the statue, some days the pigeon," Cali declared. "You know, you've been good for me. I'm thinking about what I'm going to do to them, debating the temperature at which to sauté their private parts, for example, and I'm feeling better. . . . "[12]

You've got to want to fight back. You've got to recognize, in the chaos as it unfolds, that sometimes you win, sometimes you lose, and often it's pretty hard to tell the difference in the heat of the battle. Now, as chaos enfolds you, and people back away when they catch the scent of failure:

> "When something bad happens to you, you have three choices. You either let it define you, let it destroy you, or let it strengthen you," Grendeline announced, studying Cali. "You know, Cali, humans are literally crazy. They live in three worlds, all at the same time. World one; the external world interacting with the person inside you; World two; the social world's demands and structure interacting with the person

inside you; and World three; the person inside you interacting with yourself. Now, they've got you focused on you and the social world, and they have you tearing yourself apart. All that stuff about how people preach one lifestyle and practice another? They've got you practicing the life that they preach against. As long as you take the bait and live in their world, you've lost. You're filled with humiliation and contempt for yourself because you're filled with what others are thinking. You have to focus on the 'you' within you, and then focus on that real world that is banging into you. What the social world makes of all this is their problem, not yours, unless you bring it inside. The social world is a vampire. You have to invite them across the threshold and just like a vampire, the social world will suck the life out of you for its pleasure. For what it's worth, people who matter will realize what you were put through and understand. People hate posers, but embrace the real person fighting the good fight."[13]

It's our nature to act. Fashion, with it's ceaseless frothing, is clear proof of that. If you live long enough, you see the styles of your youth proudly worn by the young as symbols of their uniqueness. But just doing something isn't necessarily change or useful. Changing fashion is within the same rules and constraints, so it's literally surface change only.

How about the following as an approach to the remainder of the books?

"Replace the fear of the unknown with curiosity," Jose advised. Life's more interesting that way."[14]

CHAPTER 2. THIS IS AN IMMORAL BOOK

This is an immoral book (and damn proud of it) because the world is not what we would want/demand/hope/desire it to be. If you are going to be successful, you have to play and plan within the world we live in.

A classical - actually biblical - perspective is:

"The universe isn't a children's story, with bright colors, the good rewarded and the evil punished. For one thing, good and evil are far more complex than the child would want them to be," the old man advised. "The universe is events. The cosmic design has the sun rising on the evil as well as the good, and the rain falls on the desert as well as fertile soil. Natural laws govern the cosmic order. But natural law does not include a mechanically applied law of reward and retribution. There isn't an accounting department closing the books each night, posting the credits for the good and debits for the wicked. The natural order is amoral, by human ideas. The wicked may be restrained, because the dawn arrives and deprives them of the darkness where they hide. But the darkness was not there to hide the wicked, the darkness has a purpose of its own. The wicked are not struck down by the good each morning when an alarm rings at six a.m.; the dawn has other purposes. The food for the lion and the kill for the raven are innocent creatures that no more deserve to die than any others. Predator and prey are events, not stories. It is not true that the wicked will inevitably be punished or that the innocent will be immune from suffering.

"The universe is a paradoxical world because humans seek to impose their desires on the universe. In the universe, the regular, the unexpected, the good, the bad, the successful, and the sufferer coexist. Death and life are a cycle of growth and decay, pleasure and pain. The innocent do suffer, perhaps unjustly, perhaps not. Perhaps it's more complex than they can imagine. Those who do good and act righteously are not necessarily rewarded in this world. And should they be? Should people think God a piggy bank that they pump good deeds into and reward tokens pop out the bottom? It's more complex than that. But clearly, the principle of retributive justice as a mechanical law of the cosmos is repudiated in Job by the prologue, by the experience of Job, and by the answer of God. I'm not sure how much more clear I can make it."[15]

Or, from a different cultural perspective:

"Book XII is a part of the Indian Book of the Great War of the Sons of Bharata, Mahabharata," the Cardinal continued. "It asserted, to cut to some key excerpts: 'Without cutting the very vitals of others, without performing many cruel deeds, without killing living creatures, as fisherman kill fish, one cannot win prosperity...There are no special orders of creatures called enemies or friends...Persons become friends or enemies according to circumstance...Every work should be done completely...By killing its inhabitants, by destroying its roads, and by burning and pulling down its houses, a king should devastate his enemy's realms.' Finally: 'Might is above right; right proceeds from might; right has its support in might, as living beings in the soil. As smoke the wind, so right must follow might. Right in itself has no authority; it leans on might as the creeper on the tree.'"[16]

Might makes right. Not the way it perhaps should be, but the way it is. In the end, it is people with guns that enforce the system. Mao argued that "Political power grows out of the barrel of a gun", and he was right, like it or not. Just to be more difficult, it is a fact of life that human rights are a function of the resources available and the constraints in place. Inalienable rights, regardless of how desirable or 'right', don't exist unless the 'might', the resources, are actually possible.

If you doubt that might makes right in the little things, look at the cost constraints for the project that you are working on. Those are a 'might' and there is little point in arguing the ethical issues involved.

There are several troubling extensions of those thoughts: first, what is right now is based on might - so is it really right? If might changes, then how does the right change? And whatever you may believe is right, what is the might that is standing behind the right, holding it up? As Taleb said in AntiFragile;

It is painful to think about ruthlessness as an engine of improvement.[17]

Be that as it may, if you are going to plan, you have to work with the world as it is, not as you wish it to be. Note that planning for the world you wish it to be is dramatically different from wishing the world were as you define it and basing your plans on your wish world.

Much of the discomfort with "The Art of War" by Sun Tzu is tied to his cynical view of life, his non-moral view of the world, and those attacks are exactly correct. The attack, distilled into its essence, is that he denies that the world is the way we want it to be. A moral view of the world, stories that are good and evil and feature justice and injustice, are small human stories imposed on the world. The world is events. Humans must make stories about events, but the stories are not the events. We know that, but it's human nature to take the symbol as the reality and freeze with it. This book believes that the Art of War is right in it's practical approach. Now, what the ethics and morality you use to choose the actions you take based on the Art of War are subject to argument, but acting in this world requires focus on this world.

The same righteous distain is thrown at Machiavelli, who asserted in "The Prince" what should be done for certain results in the real world, not what should be done for moral comfort and conformity. The essence of Machiavelli's writings challenges that relationship between the social allowed world and the external world. The Prince is clear that the external isn't controlled by the social definitions but that, in the end, the larger world wins. This is terrifying in many ways, but that's that way it is.

We plan to get what we want in this world, here and now. If you plan based on what you should want according to others, or the world that they think you should want, then your plans will be unsatisfying, and rarely succeed. What others assure you is the 'Good' doesn't guarantee a win, at least in the larger world, so hoping and crossing our fingers isn't going to make out plans work.

We don't (rationally) expect a sheet of steel to have an ethical response to pressures and events. Given a certain strength and configuration of a steel beam, is will be capable of handling certain defined events in the real world. Hopefully, those are same events we are planning for. That's a rational analysis, based on experience and structural tables.

Rationality, as discussed later in the book, is a tool that we use when we have to, but it's not really us. Emotionally we hope and expect things to act in ways different than the real world allows them to act. We personify things. We name inanimate objects and expect them to act in accordance with their names, and when they don't we blame gremlins and stubbornness by the objects. We personify everything in the world around us, and we do it unconsciously, surrounding ourselves with a comfortable world structured in accordance with our wishes. We laugh at ourselves, but we knock on wood, carry lucky objects, and become furious at others who question or disrupt our luck.

This book denies the pretty view of the 'force'; all that torment about the light and the dark.

> "In your movies, the Light is the fancy city version of life, a pretty picture that avoids the hard questions, a story that makes no sense at a deeper level. But the stories make people feel good, like a Band-Aid covering an open sore. The dark is denied, but the dark is raw life. Life eating other life is what makes the world go around. Your anguish over your killing that worthless carbon-emitting pile of flesh is just wrong. The whole light/dark fantasy is the classic horns of a dilemma, maneuver warfare of the spirit that society created to keep people quiet. It can't be won, so you flop back and forth, and society, which really only wants you quiet, is content." . . . . What other creatures feel and think, that is Life. Life is far more than this elaborate facade humans have created to hide in. [18]

This book abandon's that entire ultimate good/evil struggle that is so enticing to the human mind; because that's not the world we live in. Take your blinders off and step beyond the small human stories. A refrain in this book is a bounded world is seeing the world thru stories and an unbounded world is seeing the stories through the world. (It makes more sense later)

We all seek to be The Hero, all bright edges and proud standards, victory and peace triumphant. But victory can be something greatly different from what you expect.

> "Do you remember Beowulf?" Hal mused. "Suffering through it

in high school, I know I saw only the battle, the bright victory against the terrible monster. I know I missed the key, in that first fight between Grendel and Beowulf, when the opposites attack in a fury and to their surprise—shock, actually—discover that they are the same in many ways? Obviously more for Beowulf, who survives but is wounded in a way he never would have expected. His bright ideals and clear vision, what he thought he 'was', the root of his strength, swept away for the muddy colors and deep greys of the real world. It took the shine off what he saw himself as. And he never really worked through all of the changes, frozen between what he had been, he thought—and what he was to become. It destroyed him, the land and his kingdom. He never answered the Fisher King." [19]

What would an immoral book be if it didn't appeal to traditional morality to support it? The following is a traditional warning of danger (and it should be taken seriously!) if you don't listen to the larger world:

20 Wisdom crieth without; she uttereth her voice in the streets:

21 She crieth in the chief place of concourse, in the openings of the gates: in the city she uttereth her words, saying,

22 How long, ye simple ones, will ye love simplicity? and the scorners delight in their scorning, and fools hate knowledge?

23 Turn you at my reproof: behold, I will pour out my spirit unto you, I will make known my words unto you.

24 Because I have called, and ye refused; I have stretched out my hand, and no man regarded;

25 But ye have set at nought all my counsel, and would none of my reproof:

26 I also will laugh at your calamity; I will mock when your fear cometh;

27 When your fear cometh as desolation, and your destruction cometh as a whirlwind; when distress and anguish cometh upon you.

28 Then shall they call upon me, but I will not answer; they shall seek me early, but they shall not find me:

29 For that they hated knowledge, and did not choose the fear of the LORD:

30 They would none of my counsel: they despised all my reproof.

31 Therefore shall they eat of the fruit of their own way, and be filled with their own devices.

32 For the turning away of the simple shall slay them, and the prosperity of fools shall destroy them.

33 But whoso hearkeneth unto me shall dwell safely, and shall be quiet from fear of evil. [20]

The problem (or opportunity-everything depends on how you look at it) that we face daily is that people start to want (nay, demand!) simplicity when they don't understand that system anymore, or resent the time and other inputs required to work with the system. That's a simplicity that isn't available by definition: if the system is so complex that you can't understand it anymore, then imposing your simplicity on the system because its easier for you is a story that isn't going to end well. Seems logical, but that simple jump 'it's too complex so I'm going to say it's really simple' is enticing and very easy to take. And you can sell the group on it, because they couldn't figure out what was going on either.

How complex are things in reality? One of the most fundamental and defining features of quantum theory is that even when we have all possible information about a given system, the outcome is still probabilistic. So, nice straight lines on paper, confidently linearly extrapolating the present isn't the universe we live in and <u>will not</u> correctly calculate a complex future. As the future is unknowable, we can only improvise as opportunities present. To grasp opportunities, you have to monitoring the system as it happens, which is quite different from walking away from a real system into the story you want.

It's an unknowable future that changes as we act? That is a large part of why planning (and it's action oriented relation, project management) is almost impossible. Defining a plan, creating a framework with cheerful words doesn't mean that there is a real thing there that can do what the framework says. To steal some of the later thunder, it actually isn't the plan that matters, although it's important. It's the process of planning, the iterative going over and over to approximate reality, that matters.

In the light of an unknowable future, the words of Sun Tzu make more sense.

"Hence the skillful fighter puts himself into a position which makes defeat impossible, and does not miss the moment for defeating the enemy."[21]

What else can you do if you can't predict accurately the world?

The whole western European model of war, decisive engagements with massed troops, is based on a linear extrapolation model, a model of the world that doesn't exist. That's just part of the reason that war is just chaos. And why so many died in the US Civil War and in World War I, which were a confusion of traditional ideas of honorable war, confident linear extrapolation of the past which didn't take into account new technologies that included machine guns.

Chapter 3. Parasites Rule.

As I just assured you, this is an immoral book. Worse, now I'm arguing that we must step down from our privileged throne atop nature to mingle with the rabble. Let me prove that to you by taking you on a look at where we fit into the real world. Not with rose colored or social glasses, but the way that the world is. Hint-our place in the world isn't what we have been taught, told and/or promised.

> "And so you want to get into the nature of the world? What kind of a world is it?" the old man demanded. "Shall we talk about the parasitic wasps again, eating the caterpillars from the inside? How about Sacculina, the nasty little parasite that controls that little crab? The crab begins to change into a new sort of creature; one that exists to serve the parasite. It can no longer do the things that would get in the way of Sacculina's growth. It stops molting and growing, which would funnel away energy from the parasite. Crabs can typically escape from predators by severing a claw and regrowing it later on. Crabs carrying Sacculina can lose a claw, but they can't grow a new one in its place. And while other crabs mate and produce a new generation, parasitized crabs simply go on eating and eating. They have been spayed. The parasite is responsible for all these changes. Despite being castrated, the crab doesn't lose its urge to nurture. It simply directs its affection toward the parasite."[22]

A parasite is defined as an organism that lives in or on another organism (its host) and benefits by deriving nutrients at the host's expense. Sound awful! That is absolutely a violation of all morality and good social behavior, which would certainly merit a failing grade in Kindergarten. Well, unless you are lichen, extracting nutrients directly from rocks (an unlikely reader, granted, but an interesting visual) every other creature is a parasite making your living off something else's hard work and precious existence.

Are you suggesting that I (the reader) am a parasite!! Because I'm really offended now. I'm a human being! In control of my fate and myself! As you fume to yourself over dinner, sipping a fine glass of wine (grapes stolen from the grape plant, fermentation process twisted to our advantage) or cutting into your meat, as I'd hazard the dead creature didn't have as the focus of it's life a blissful sacrifice of itself for you-and the same argument applies to broccoli for vegetarians also. And the same argument applies to your house, table, chair, silverware, and the list goes on and on.

> *"Be fruitful and multiply; fill the earth and subdue it; have dominion over the fish of the sea, over the birds of the air, and over every living thing that moves on the earth"*[23] *(Gen. 1:28).*

Ok, so that's authorization from on high that we are not parasites if we use others, we are 'superior' and so it's our right. Right is Might justified, you might say. It's still being a parasite.

But it's a critical human story - the overriding human story, for most religions and ethical systems is that the bounty of the earth is for humans alone. So you're still fuming? Relax, Breath deeply, in and out. Do you feel better now? Let's think about things. We're mobile bags of seawater, full of buggies and stuff, trying to survive in a vast world that isn't manifesting a lot of interest in us. We are very small and fragile creatures whose survival depends on taking resources from larger creatures/structures. Do to that, we have to control them to the extent we get what we want. Does that sound at all parasitical? Denial is more than a river in Egypt, as the saying goes.

> "'To God everything is beautiful, good, and just; humans, however, think some things are unjust and others just.' Heraclitus. We absolutely denied and fought that statement, because we were sure it could not have been right. It denied our story and our masks, in all truth. Job teaches that the wicked may be accidentally restrained because the dawn arrives and deprives them of the darkness where they hide, but that restraint of the wicked is an accidental byproduct of the dark, and the wicked are not struck down when the sun rises each morning. The food for the lion and the kill for the raven are innocents who no more deserve to die than any others. Their deaths are not stories, they are events. That's hard to accept, because humans demand meaning in everything they see. They are taught that without meaning, there is an empty place in the mind. But is it really empty? The body moves, it breathes, it eats; all the vast complexity of the body runs without 'meaning' as do the other creatures and the trees. Meaning is a conceit of the mind; perhaps something the unconscious tosses the consciousness to keep it occupied while the unconscious handles the serious business of living.[24]

Defining the absolute moral and ethical limits to our existence is a human trap. It's a socially imposed meaning trap, driven in by morality story after morality story. Not to say that we don't just love the morality stories, because we do, but our love for the story is absolutely not the same as the larger world then abiding by our pretty story. Many morality stories are necessary for group survival, but that doesn't raise them to universal imperatives.

Denial of the way the world is would be the sign of an unsuccessful parasite, because successful parasites have no qualms or reluctance about what they must do to survive. In the real world, Might makes Right, without question. And every living creature on this planet is a parasite of some kind, living off of other life. Life is death and transfiguration, after all. Perhaps the most basic one celled creature that leaches out inorganic molecules is possibly not a parasite-but perhaps the hard rock doesn't appreciate living creatures rearranging it's structure. It gets philosophical, murky and unknowable, but in the end, we are all parasites. That's not good, not bad, it's just what it.

A successful parasite understands it must give back enough, at least to the creature for the host to survive, and ideally prosper. Whereas we, the almighty conqueror are above such mundane concerns. Look at the mess we've made of the world as a consequence!

Parasites survive by generally settling into an equilibrium in the system that they are part of. They actually level out fluctuations, and add to the health of the overall system. A system without parasites is going to be on a positive feedback situation until it crashes, generally. From the viewpoint of an ecosystem, parasites are essential, regardless of the position of a particular species in the process.

We, unlike other parasites, can make some choices about our actions. Perhaps we as a species have already made too many, establishing a monoculture that precariously spans the world. Ecological crashes don't just happen to other creatures, by the way.

So how does a parasite survive? Having survived, what choices can we make? How can we use parasites as role models? It's important to consider this just because it drives us so far out of our usual mental model. There is actually a deep scientific reluctance to study parasites, because they violate pretty much every moral and ethical model. Parasites are the evil in the sermons, shouted from the pulpit by well-dressed people who are riddled with a host of little bugs they don't even suspect. There is just a repugnance, taught to us from being young, against 'slackers', 'freeloaders', and the like. In reality, parasites are busy little things working hard at controlling larger creatures for the parasites own needs. They have to be cleverer than their prey, the world demands far more of them for them to survive.

Here's another perspective: There is a law of the sea the controls the relationships of big fish and little fish. Big fish eat little fish, little fish run like hell and survive as best they can. When little fish become big fish, they eat little fish. Another version is that the mice must watch out when the elephants dance. Survival is the first prerequisite for yourself and your family. After everyone is fat and happy (not that long ago, most of the world was on a starvation diet) then you may have some slack to pretend the world is other than it is. Until then, you'd best run as fast as you can.

> "Roll rocks down a ten-thousand-foot mountain,
> and they cannot be stopped
> This is because of the mountain, not the rocks.
> Get people to fight with the courage to win every time,
> and the strong and the weak unite
> this is because of the momentum, not the individuals."[25]

I submit that it is your goal in life to be behind the rocks coming down the mountain, not in front of them. To do that, you have to know where you are in the scheme of things, and who you are. Should you be an authentic Master of the Universe (most of whom it seems were really 'master of the secret tip') your comments and enhancements on the ideas in this book would be appreciated. If you are not a Master of the Universe, you (all of us, actually) are a little fish.

Parasites make a comfortable living against the interests of virtually everything that they need for their life. That's what we must do. Look down at your dinner and deny that.

WHAT IS THE GOOD?

Let's confront this directly. What is the Good? It is a question that has been asked constantly since humans began to think. The answer to that question depends on many things: the situation we are facing, the complexity, the importance, the social environment, the type of decision and the clear impacts, the hazy impacts, what we have been taught, thought, gleaned and found in various places.

> *Mongol General: Hao! Dai ye! We won again! This is good, but what is best in life?*
> *Mongol: The open steppe, fleet horse, falcons at your wrist, and the wind in your hair.*
> *Mongol General: Wrong! Conan! What is best in life?*
> *Conan: To crush your enemies, see them driven before you, and to hear the lamentation of their women.*
> *Mongol General: That is good! That is good*[26].

That's from the movie "Conan the Barbarian" and is put there for us to laugh at, from our superior perspective. We only have that perspective because the Mongol hordes dissolved over internal political disputes, just before they were about to roll over Western Europe. Good for Western Europe, not so good for the Mongol hordes. Western Europe, or China, or India, all of the horde's targets would not have disagreed with the above, or the political structure of the hordes, so it wasn't the inherent 'evil' of the hordes that defeated them. Simple things like quarreling over the kingship succession, something Western Europe knows about and more critically, changes in the climate, weakened the hordes.

The root good is usually linked to a mind set-a world view, a set of basic parameters and structures within which we make decisions. This weeds out the 'obviously out of area' and keeps us focused into an area that can make decisions. Having to rethink the world everyday is going to result in not much getting done in a practical sense. After all, we have to act. Which act is a choice, but to act is essential. Many times it seems more essential to act, than thinking about the act.

Let's root this discussion in the concept of Life. Life is the basic structure we are concerned with on this earth. All religions and philosophies have worldviews constructed with other worlds and structures interacting with this world. Those other worlds, created from various theological positions, are not amenable to empirical verification, in the sense can touch, feel, etc. So each reader keeps the structure they prefer, and this book makes no inferences or positions on those structures.

Life is astonishingly complex in the details. Just one small example, of an article in the New York Times updating new discoveries about DNA/RNA and what they seem to do, all of which is so complex as to be absolutely mind bending. The constant interaction and creation of various chemical processes that make it possible for us to continue our existence moment to moment is beyond amazing. So, let's worship Life, for starters. Depending on your deity, Life is their creation and worshiping their creation is worshiping the deity. If you don't have a deity, worshiping life makes more sense than anything else, because life is all we have. If your deity denies life, then maybe you should do us all a favor and join your deity.

But Life immediately raises difficult traditional ethical and moral issues. Life is amoral, not immoral. Life looks only to life for itself, the maintenance of that life and reproduction of new life. Life is dependent on the constant death and transformation of other life into new life. It's parasitical, you might say. The higher on the food chain you are, the more transformation of life has occurred and will occur. A lot of people don't like this. People and religions range all over on this, but life makes certain decisions. If you don't want to participate in the transformations, refuse to participate-your life will end and other's will continue. If a meteor hits the earth, the new species that arise will do the same, because that is the essential nature of life. Certain organisms have the ability to do certain things, and other organisms use those abilities. Viruses and other parasites infect and use our bodies.

As said before, parasites are all about 'might makes right'. They brook no discussion about whether they deserve to continue life, because they believe they do. No matter how horrible to us some parasites are-the guinea worms come to mind-they have no self-disrespect.

So death and transformation are daily, momentary actions that life takes. Each cell does this with the resources sent to it, and the more complex the organization, the more complex the process of this transformation. Each of us reading this book is the result and combination of millions of organisms transformed into us, nutrients used and eliminated. The very cells in our bodies constantly change, with only a few cells staying with us our entire life.

Life endures and grows because it must. Life has to work with what is, the way things operate in this world, planning and acting in this world. There isn't any imposition of a preferred ideal on the way it is. Now, humans have been able to make great strides by pushing on the world, but in our pride, we try and forget the raw reality of life. Having pushed, we don't want pushback from the primitive things we have left behind.

In traditional cultures with a closer connection to the land, the harsh nature of life is accepted, because the reality is right there. In the modern world, our food comes from a market, and the choices and methods that brought it there are not in front of you. Our medical problems are hidden in crisp modern buildings, not lying out in the hut at the edge of the village, a terror for all to see.

So why dwell on unpleasant aspects of reality? Define them away, make Death a stepping stone (perhaps it is, perhaps it isn't – the reports back are unclear) and make the other creatures our servants, our natural prey. Ease our consciences so we can act. It's more complex that that. Death and transformation raises ugly questions about social behaviors. To what extent are people just organisms that die and transform? To what extent should our social behavior embrace rather than run from some of the rather clear life structures? The social structure embracing sharing, and continued interaction necessitates certain moderating of behaviors. To what extent are those moderations really necessary and useful?

Barbara Tuchman, in "A Distant Mirror", (set in the 13th century) make the point that our ancestors killed. They hunted, they killed for food, they fought and killed other people in war. And not with guns from a distance: this was killing with a sword and a knife, hand-to-hand, up close. Honor and glory celebrated, as the victor stands over the vanquished. That, obviously, has some real social problems. People who are used to killing will kill more often and easier than others. And there were clearly gender issues, as the records from that time tended to focus on males actions. The daily processes of life, the raising of children and the continuation of the species, were just assumed. It's important to remember that they were our ancestors-and not unsophisticated, uneducated savages. They were the flower of European nobility, the pride of their social structures. We see, on a regular basis, pious articles arguing that humans are not really that savage or vicious. Wishful thinking, a morality tale to encourage harmonious behavior, but humans are that savage and vicious. We didn't rise to the top of the heap by pious slogans.

So if life, on a constant basis, is the completely selfish obsession of each individual organism to continue it's existence and reproduce itself, how does that tie to the various social constraints imposed so that the society continues to work? And what can we learn from the virtues/vices used to make that social control?

The classic Buddhist training step for neophytes was to watch bodies rotting in the open. This then turned the mind away from the material world, towards a higher plane, a world of the spirit, or something like that. Turning away from what obviously is in favor of a fantasy you would rather have, is extremely dangerous. Stupid, more accurately. That rotting process is a miracle by which organic material is turned back into food by various organisms and thus backs into the system. The sheer complexity of what organisms break down what and how is absolutely astonishing. Without the decomposition process, life would stop. We are starting to face this as our manufactured products, not designed to break down, are piling up without end.

Rotting is a miracle, an astonishingly complex set of processes, life reusing the resources that new life needs. The problem is that it all smalls and looks awful-to us. Vultures think it's just fine, and our ancestors were not ashamed to be scavengers also, before we gained more control over the food cycle. Death does not diminish the achievement and glory of life. The pain of death is the pain of the survivors, necessary, but life moves forward-anything else is social posing, freezing to avoid living.

Buddhist's are a classic example of people taking you seriously because you look and act so serious and concerned, so well meaning. The nice orange robes don't hurt, either. What you mean, what you want, doesn't matter-it's what you do that counts.

As shown in the beginning quote under 'perspective' the whole ends thing very confusing and there are no ultimate answers possible. Choices must be made, regrets endured. If you discovered tomorrow that could live to age 5000 and flit blithely between alternative universes, it still would have no effect on today's plan. We must do what can now.

The essence of understanding The Art of War is moving to the bigger box of the world of events, which includes within that bigger box of events the little box of the good/evil interpretation of the events. Interestingly enough, Job, in the Bible, was taken outside the small box of good and evil in a direct meeting with God. To recap Job, which is a difficult book that doesn't really fit into the rest of the Bible, shoehorn it as we try: Job is wealthy and prosperous. For completely random reasons, all is taken from him—his health, wealth, and children—and he is despised and in torment. Confronted by his friends, who demand that he acknowledge his sins because God does not punish the unjust, he demands audience with God. One should always be careful of what you wish for, because God comes to him in a whirlwind and confronts him with the nature of the universe.

And it's a disturbing confrontation. It's not a human universe. The universe isn't a children's story with bright colors, the good rewarded and the evil punished. The universe is events. The wicked are not struck down by the good each morning at dawn; the dawn has other purposes. The food for the lion and the kill for the raven are innocent creatures that no more deserve to die than any others. Predator and prey are events, not stories. It is not true that the wicked will inevitably be punished or that the innocent will be immune from suffering.

Now, in daily life, often the wicked are punished over time, because if you dare the world through thoughtless deeds often enough, it slaps you down. Those who follow the traditional morality often are not punished, because if you live cautiously and thoughtfully, your odds of being slapped down are less. But it isn't being good or wicked that is the winning number on the bet—it is behaving in ways that cause you to either tempt events or avoid them. There is no retributive justice. The results of being wicked or good, in the bigger world of events, are accidental. That's the net effect of Job, and Sun Tzu would agree.

Job grew to understood the nature of the universe, and accepted it, a much bigger box of events than the small box bounded by good and evil than he had started with. Job stepped outside into a world far outside the small human stories; a world defined by the word of God, shown by the actions of God, a world that has nothing to do with the small stories of God and religion, that paper God pulled out on Sunday.

In this world, we must exploit weaknesses, not being the creator or the all powerful. We must be a successful parasite, in many, many ways. If you want to change the world, good luck with that. Changing the world is a goal, but the first rule is always survival. Honor and glory that kill you are perhaps a uniquely human madness, but who feeds your family then? A lot of human philosophy and theology is based on a 'define and whine'-create the world you want with words and impose it on reality, then whine when it doesn't work-but that's another set of books and problems. A parasite must live according the harshest laws of the wild.

Now, how does that interact with the social pictures and the image of the self? Let's assume we can be ethical parasites, if that is what you want. Human's being what they are, we impose an ethical order on the world. Even bandits and revolutionaries live within the same rigid social hierarchies everyone else lives in.

It would be interesting to know the exact wiring that differentiates us from the hungry wolf that tears into it's prey-or perhaps it's just we're not as hungry. It is said that after three days of no food, you go from demanding the finest dishes to eating things that are still moving. It's part of the goal of this book to not have to test that theory, but rather to stay on top of the world, not frantically grasping for morsels.

The essential point of this chapter was to point out that we are merely part of the chain of life, a creature among other creatures, an actor and acted upon. Planning on any other basis is not going to work.

Chapter 4. Stories

"If a lion could talk, we could not understand him.
Ludwig Wittgenstein

We understand the world through stories, but they are human stories. A lion's stories would not make sense to us, because a lion's stories are hardwired for the lions mind and perceptions. That's deeper than it seems. An infinity of events is exploding around us every moment. What humans see as important and put in our stories is different from what other creatures would put in stories. That means that the reality we see is different from the reality they see. There are lots of ways to chop the world up, and at least several are true at the same time. That goes for worms and lions and fish and computers.

The stories you tell yourself, the stories you believe and live by are all important. We tell ourselves big stories, middle stories, and little stories. Big stories are ideas and concepts, which have their own set of complex problems. The middle stories are events and little stories are people doing all those odd things that people do. Middle stories, being about events, are probably the most 'accurate'. Event in the real world can be measured, our perceptions refined and fine-tuned. The little stories are some of the hardest to accurately convey, which is odd. We are human, so we should understand what other humans do and think. Not true at all, as between the social masks and different cultures/experiences, what we assume about others is based on what we know about ourselves. We are making assumptions about peoples motivations and emotions, all described in sloppy and poorly defined words. If you doubt that we don't even get the little stories, think about how often gossip is idle maliciousness rather than accurate events.

We take our stories as far as we can to get what we want. For example, Berkeley formulated the theory of idealism, the notion that ideas, not bodies and other hunks of matter, are the ultimate constituents of reality, which became a quite influential among nineteenth-century German thinkers. It really was an extension of Plato's concept of the idea, so his argument wasn't that new. What incredible nonsense that human created ideas could be the real reality, and what we see around us is nothing! Yet it was solemnly, even devoutly, parroted for many years because it met human needs, and the misfit with reality was irrelevant. That's how important stories are to humans. What could be a more small human story that the fantasy that the ideas in the human mind define reality! (I know, that was a short and at least somewhat inaccurate analysis of Berkeley's thought, but I defend the essential point)

A newspaper seeks (hopefully) impeccable, crosschecked facts and then weaves them into a narrative that implies causality and superior knowledge. We have to be told stories, and there is nothing wrong with that: as long as we realize why and what we are doing. Stepping outside, we realize it's not whether a story distorts reality, because all stories distort, but how it distorts reality. <u>Stories are how we understand the world</u>. Just because it's a good story doesn't mean it has anything to do with the real world. Quite the opposite, really: the better the story, the more liberty was probably taken with the real facts, causes and relationships. Even with the best intentions, stories must distort this world of events simply by the stories structure (beginning, middle, end, plot, conflict, background and foreground) and the words used.

Here's a wonderful example of how stories mislead:

"Colonel Ross still wore an expression which showed the poor opinion which he had formed of my companion's ability, but I saw by the inspector's face that his attention had been keenly aroused.

"You consider that to be important?" he [Inspector Gregory] asked.

"Exceedingly so."

"Is there any point to which you would wish to draw my attention?"

"To the curious incident of the dog in the night-time."

"The dog did nothing in the night-time."

"That was the curious incident," remarked Sherlock Holmes.

The Memoirs of Sherlock Holmes (1893)[27]

Inspector Gregory and Sherlock Holmes in "Silver Blaze" (Doubleday p. 346-7)the dog that didn't bark" - Sherlock Holmes

And thinking about the huge gap in that story:

"She (Lucretia) drew a sloppy circle on the page, studying it. That's what I look for. It's the gestalt that I see, and I don't see outside the lines. No one can see everything all the time. The mind weeds stuff out. How many investment seminars and stock offering meetings have I sat through where everyone around me was so focused on the information on the pages they were given that they didn't ask: what's supposed to be on the page, but isn't? What's the logical extrapolation of the story being presented, which isn't there? The dog that didn't bark, Holmes said. The mind is always happy to weed something out. The dog was sick, it was asleep, out hunting, so it didn't bark. The guard dog, one hundred and forty pounds of vicious malice, didn't bark. The dog didn't bark BECAUSE NO ONE BROKE IN. And we dance on, happy with the story we are telling ourselves.

In life, the missing numbers and information are more important than the carefully prepared words and numbers on the page in front of us, all that carefully arranged flotsam and jetsam given surface relevance. That's why the information is missing. That information is so important to someone that they carefully crafted the smoke and mirrors to hide them. The errors of commission are often easy to spot, holes in the story we expect. It is the errors of omission, outside the story we are reading from, that constantly bedevil us. So, Hal beat me good, spotting what I didn't see."[28]

Now, I'm spending a lot of time on the ideas buried in 'stories'. If everyone just grasps this instinctively and you find the discussion terribly boring, just skip ahead. It is a discomforting discussion, because I'm challenging all the stories, even the ones that we like and are comfortable with. I think that the whole concept of stories masking the reality they are supposed to illuminate is so rich and fascinating that I go on and on about it because it's so familiar to us that we miss the complexity. Certainly, if you are going to plan anything that has a chance of success in the world, you've got to recognize the reality under the stories. Basically the concept is the story is just a story-regardless of how important the story may be to us. The story isn't reality, the story is just an approximation (at best) of reality, so if you rely on the story as THE reality you have taken a dangerous step you may not really realize. (A bounded world is seeing the world through stories)

Now, we test (sometimes) our stories, and when we find that the stories are supported by at least some data points of view, we proceed to spin the rest of the story around - extending - from those data points. The story is like a balloon blown up until it encompasses all what we think of as the relevant data points. The data points carefully touch the surface of the balloon, but the data points can be sharp and we have to watch that they don't puncture the balloon. At the point we are smoothing the balloon carefully away from the data points, we no longer care about reality, we care about what we want, and this discourse on stories is to point that out. The advantage of science is that it doubts the stories and pokes the balloon with the data points - or should. Scientists are like anyone else, and they will deny and deny until the data points poke them. But at least the format of science encourages someone to try and relate the story to the data points.

To continue on with the prior example: we have this toy balloon floating in the wind, and we are admiring it. It's pretty, the sun sparkling off it and we are happy. The balloon represents our story and, here is the tricky part-it encompasses (hopefully) at least several data points of reality which touch the surface of the balloon, and give credence to the story that the balloon tells. Suddenly, the balloon pops and we discover how well-or poorly-the story fit all the underlying data points-not just the ones we wanted to notice. The story is an appearance, a painted picture, a shadow pulled over the annoyances of reality to help understand-but also to confuse and mislead. So the reality that appears when the balloon is popped, when the surface of the story vanishes, is going to be something different-perhaps dramatically different-than what we think the story was.

In reality, it's a mass of events out there. Nature doesn't have any

41

story-nature is eating, sleeping and sex. Perhaps that's what's so monstrous about the world to humans, who can't stand to be at the mercy of random events but must have stories to make sense of the world. Without a story, there is no human 'meaning', no feeling of being a part of something larger and/or in control of our life. As we create our stories and link events in a chain that pleases us, correlation is not causation, something we forget over and over, and life is full of forces beyond our perception and stories not framed by our mind. Out of those events, conflicting stories are generated and eventually the 'story' of what happened-which is, at best, at least some part of the events that occurred-is written down as authorized history.

> "There are these two young fish swimming along, and they happen to meet an older fish swimming the other way, who nods at them and says, 'Morning, boys, how's the water?' The two young fish swim on for a bit, and then eventually one of them looks over at the other and goes, 'What the hell is water?'" she commented.[29]

That's what stories are to us. We live and breathe them and don't see outside. Our stories can change, but if they are consistent to us, then we remember the new story, not the prior ones. For example, the academic research on false memories is extensive. Essentially, a memory can be moved to fit what it's supposed to fit. And it's done by means of changing the story. Think about that the next time you listen to an eyewitness confidently recounting the events they saw.

The cheerful-or scary-result is that if there is no 'big' story going on (at least, as will cover later, certainly nothing we can comprehend) the future can be changed. That's scary, because our actions have responsibility attached and we all hate responsibility. We can play with being outside stories-Zen is living without a story, feeling the experience that occurs, but it's not natural at all. Being taken outside stories is why nature documentaries are sobering, a different life from the warm and fuzzy stories that we tell each other, that daily life in the human realm tries to be. Watching the documentaries, one realizes that it is an incoherent, monstrous world by nominal standards-it's all events, just amoral-and then we have the unsettling feeling that standards are nonsense.

Rationally, you didn't ask to be born, you won't ask to die (depression is an chemical imbalance, not the self acting) and most of what happens in between is out of your control. The universe is such a mass of enormously powerful physical events-the maelstrom of the sun, the unimaginable cold of the depths of space, the fiery heat of the inner planets, that we can't even imagine. The math used to model the universe (today's version, anyhow) needs a 'plug', a 'constant' which forces the existence of this universe. If it wasn't that way, we wouldn't be here, so we are meant to be here. The majority of the universe is theorized to be dark energy, most of the remainder is dark matter, both of which are really, at this time, blatant plugs to keep the rest of the equations working. We, being the universe we see including ourselves, are almost a rounding error in the calculations. Our explanations of the universe are our highest rational achievement, at least at this time, and are carefully calculated and tested where they can be tested. Science, being a moving hypothesis, doesn't have the emotional glue that a myth does. A myth at least explains it all and puts us in the middle of the explanation. It's a pity, actually, because what's passed off as science is really more fantastical, at least by ordinary standards, than almost any myth.

We really don't know if other creatures have stories. As we eat other creatures, we tend to think that they don't have stories. If they had stories, we would have to take responsibility for our actions in ending their lives, when, really, that's another event in the world. What's the difference between slaughtering a cow in a slaughterhouse and the cows distant relative being brought down on the plains of the Serengeti? This book isn't going to answer the question; it just throws it out there to think about.

Then, what about our creations, computers? Do androids dream of mechanical sheep? And if not now, will they? They will certainly have the power in the relatively near future. But starting from different perceptions and systems, what stories would they create and believe? Will machines create interior worlds, which is essentially what our thinking is? Computers create game worlds-will they rewrite the simulations? Will they become the simulations? What would be the story, the interpretation of reality for a machine? That's not just academic speculation:

> "Voices: What's Next in Science - "We're going to see scientific results that are correct, that are predictive, but are without explanation. We may be able to do science without insight, and we may have to learn to live without it. Science will still progress, but computers will tell us things that are true, and we won't understand them."

> Computers have been taking over more and more of the things humans used to do, including getting driving directions and operating subway trains. They've even started making serious inroads into the heart of science. Rather than just churning out simulations or pretty pie charts, computers can do what scientists have traditionally done: find mathematical equations that explain complicated data. Eureqa, for example, is an "automated scientist" created by a Cornell engineer Hod Lipson and his students. In 2009, they reported that simply by observing a pendulum, Eureqa can rediscover some of Newton's laws of physics.

> In 2011, automated scientists are poised to make major contributions to science. Dr. Lipson and his students are looking for hidden patterns in the networks of proteins that break down food in cells, for example, and they've set up a Web site where people can download Eureqa free of charge and discover laws of nature for themselves.

> Automated scientists may speed up the pace of discovery, but in the process they may change the nature of science itself. For centuries, scientists have solved problems with flashes of insight. But while the

equations that automated scientists offer are very good at making predictions, they are often inscrutable to human scientists. We may have to program computers to explain their discoveries to us. Otherwise they will become more like oracles than scientists, handing down mysterious utterances to us mere mortals."[30]

Well, lets focus down on human stories. Again, everything to humans-EVERYTHING-is a story. That's how we process data, in stories with beginnings, middles, and endings, backdrops and hero's, evil and losses. Doubtful? Get a 300 pages computer printout, page after page of raw numbers and see how much sense it makes and how long you stick with it. Stories are what we are and there is no escaping it.

Worse, much of the story generation is actually hidden from us, as our unconscious mind does the heavy lifting.

In "Strangers to Ourselves," Timothy Wilson, a professor of psychology at the University of Virginia, presents a superb overview of the reasons why the unconscious mind is inaccessible to self -analysis: "The bad news is that it is difficult to know ourselves because there is no direct access to the adaptive unconscious, no matter how hard we try- . . . because our minds _ have evolved to operate largely outside of consciousness, it may not be possible to gain direct access to unconscious processing." Wilson suggests that we are better off by combining introspection with observing how others react to us, and deducing the otherwise inaccessible nature of our minds from their responses

Wilson opened his book with the salvo, "It usually seems that we consciously will our voluntary actions but this is illusion." The important point for our discussion is that Wilson's advice to readers is consistent with his understanding of brain function and our input-hidden-layer-output model.[31]

What are we to make of our minds when the vast majority of cognition goes on outside of consciousness? Sit back and relax, for one thing.

I keep beating on this. Stories are how we function and see the world and everything: what you tell your children, what you tell your boss, what the news says, is a story. Challenge me! Do humans communicate other than in stories? Find a clear case where we grasp the world without a pattern woven into a story. It isn't out there. It's disturbing, because then one has to question the basic relationship of our understanding to the world that is going on.

Part of the beauty of stories is that in our stories the world really does revolve around each of us. If not directly around us, we are part of the story and thus tied into the events. We personify the world and the stories, slide over the question of whether the stories out there have plots and ends of their own, not our quick takes and ad libs.

Stories are why don't see the unexpected. There is a classic video where the people watching the video asked to count the number of passes between white shirted people on a team passing basketballs back and forth. As people frantically count, they never see the man in a gorilla suit walking in and out of the scene, because that's not what we are looking for. If there isn't a place for the event in our story, the event never happened for us.

Scenarios, a tool used to develop alternate futures for planning, are just stories we tell ourselves to model the future. Technically, scenarios are 'myth's of the future', and can happen if we believe them. "Myths are the "the way things are" as people in a particular society believe them to be; and they are the models people refer to when they try to understand their world and its behavior. Myths are the patterns-of behavior, of belief, and of perception-which people have in common. Myths are not deliberately, or necessarily consciously, fictitious.

The Inception movie focused on the sheer power of the 'idea', which takes root and changes the person. And changes perception, everything connected with that person and the world that they look at. An idea is a story, with a psychological impact that graphs and equations lack. Stories are about meaning; they help explain why things could happen in a certain way. They give order and meaning to events, a crucial aspect of (mis)understanding future possibilities.

There are many critical stories that we want to believe, and don't really test. Stories like 'luck', or that we have something special, some power/ ability that no one else gets. Almost all investment stories are like this (and internet spam) and the more powerful because of that.

We have some real limits on the stories we can grasp. A partner in a major investment firm argued that people can't grasp over $139 in real money. I knew people in Detroit who always carried at least a $20, so if they were robbed, the robber wouldn't shoot them out of frustration. That was enough; it didn't have to be more, because emotionally the robber got something valuable. Why would a robber shoot you, committing a crime punished by life without parole, because you didn't have twenty dollars? There's a story that doesn't work, but happened over and over.

Stark proof that we must believe ourselves in control is the right brain/left brain problem. People with severed brains, who actually had surgery, a knife cutting the connections between the two sides of the brain, can still provide lucid, rational explanations for behaviors controlled by the other side of the brain. Unfortunately, those explanations are completely wrong because the one side of the brain explaining literally has no idea what the other side is doing. The mere fact that their explanations are completely wrong, created out of whole cloth, forced by that necessity to see yourself as coherent and consistent, doesn't dent the individuals absolute belief in their explanations.

Does make one question one's own explanations occasionally", she (Lucretia) thought wryly. Case in point-her senior partner, who actually believes his speeches, and is clearly deluded and delusional. That won't play well at the salary review, I'm afraid, and she regretfully drew a line through that idea.[32]

If that doesn't make one doubt others stories (and ours!) then there is no hope. Here is some detail, because the split brain case is really important and astonishing.

"The neuroscientists Michael Gazzaniga and Roger Sperry, showed that when surgeons cut the corpus callosum joining the cerebral hemispheres, they literally cut the self in two, and each hemisphere can exercise free will without the other one's advice or consent. Even more disconcertingly, the left hemisphere constantly weaves a coherent but false account of the behavior chosen without its knowledge by the right.

In smaller words, split brain patients have no connection between the left and the right sides of their brains, which prevents information from being shared between the two cerebral hemispheres. These patients are jewels, rare and invaluable for research. (horrible as their life may be to them) You literally have two different persons, and you can communicate with each one of them separately. Now, say that you induced such a person to perform an act - raise his finger, laugh, or grab a shovel - in order to ascertain how he ascribes a reason to his act (when in fact you know that there is no reason for it other than your inducing it) if you as the right hemisphere, here isolated from the left side, to perform this action, then ask the other hemisphere for an explanation, the patient will invariable offer some interpretation. Or, if you do the opposite, namely instruct the isolated left hemisphere of a right-handed person to perform an act and ask the right hemisphere for the reasons, you will be plainly told, I don't know. The left hemisphere is where language and deduction generally reside and the right hemisphere is at least honest enough to say it doesn't know."[33]

The next time you construct a logical, coherent story about your actions and your plans, think about the preceding example. Take a second to doubt your rational explanation before you act. Stop and make sure that before you follow your pretty story, your gut is on board and all of your emotions are in agreement, because they will, eventually, tell you if they don't agree with this left hemisphere fantasy.

Why is it so important to go over the concept of the story and the mechanical details of every story? Didn't we cover this in say, 4th grade? It's because we are so used to stories that we don't notice the details, and the details shape our perception and attitude. 4th grade didn't question the idea of stories; it just wanted to formalize the structure so our stories were better. A story is the water that we live in and so we grab our stories, move along quickly because there is never enough time, and so we never question, never look back at the gory details that make up the story - and which mislead us.

"Early in life I had noticed that no event is ever correctly reported in a newspaper."[34] *George Orwell*

Look out the window at the world for a moment. It's a complex and colorful world (assuming you're not color blind) but to explain the world, to express what we see, we have only our stories, a simple measuring cup to judge/test it by. If we have only just a measuring cup, that holds a maximum of say 4 cups, a decent size, then I'm not going to be putting large rocks in there, for example and I can't put colors or sounds in it. Anything that doesn't fit within that measuring cup, within it's limited structure, it's 'story', just doesn't exist. Now, with movie/video and music, we have some alternate approaches-but by and large, even the video and music is shaped by the story structure underneath it.

We can make some approximations, some adjustments for things that are outside the measuring cup, but really it's the measuring cup that structures how we understand the world, how we understand it to ourselves and how we explain (and have explained to us) by others. Stories are our measuring cup, the way that we interpret the world and the events outside of us. If it is outside of that measuring cup, then it is outside of the story and so it's not there. Again, because this is important: if it cannot be conveyed excitingly and intriguingly by that story then the event simply doesn't exist or isn't treated as the event really is. Except that in the real world, the event is there.

Essential Story Structures

A story has a beginning, a middle/chronology, and an ending. It's a play, actors entering and leaving the stage, declaiming to the audience their thoughts and dreams. The story is carried by heroes, villains, the supporting cast, including the unwise bit players who instruct us by their errors. There is a backdrop, which focuses our attention on the actors, and a message/moral. Behind the story are many assumptions, both about the story itself, and the reasons for the story, most of which are not made clear to us. There is the thesis presented by a story and buried somewhere a clear antithesis. A story must communicate something clearly to us. The better the story, the better we absorb it, even though the better the story, the less relationship to the larger world. Sadly, real stories are not often nice. Many real world stories, which include too many raw events, are like the original Grimm fairy tales, which are horrors in many ways. So we glaze over the rough edges for a better story. No problem, unless you expect to act on the story, in which case you'd better see the rough edges.

Now, one of the most dangerous things about stories is that conflict is essential in our stories. Why is that a problem? Because we must force a conflict, we mislead ourselves. Proof? We have a war on drugs, which ignores the fact that the problem is really a conflict of choices about people using drugs. Drugs are not marauding Mongols headed our way on massed horseback, but a 'war' on drugs uses and then proceeds from our mental picture of the Mongols. The problem mischaracterized, it is doomed for failure, as it has failed. You can fight physical things, but when the story is a fight against a concept (heresy and witchcraft are classics) you have a battle with no end point.

A story, probably based on our hardwiring, requires that everything has to be a fight, even though conceptually doesn't fit into that category. Another failure is the 'war' against cancer. Decades were spent in a war, injecting poison into patients to kill the enemy, finally to realize that cancer is a natural process, and the entire war analogy was worse than useless. Physicians in white coats, meaning well, made people in the end of their lives suffer hideously–more suffering than any court would impose on the guilty regardless of their crime. And for their cruelty, the physicians were rewarded and hailed for their brave efforts. Nonsense, but you don't see it until you look more carefully at the story.

We may demand conflict in a story because the body reacts to a fight or flight situation. The body chemically reacts and then the mind becomes interested. But that has nothing to do with the reality out there that we are trying to change. Worse, to phase stories in conflict terms brings in the whole baggage of prior conflicts experienced, and the steps taken in those conflicts. Where the prior conflict has really nothing to do with the present problem, except the story structure, then it's a fail from the get-go. Look again at the war on drugs and the war on cancer. They demand that there is something that can be fought and won, within a narrow definition of winning.

Now, why this is done so often is looked at later in the sections on story failures and slippery slopes. Most importantly, there is the idea of the Russian Dolls', a story in the story, that is the focus of the next section, which explains the deliberate use of stories to mislead.

Broadly speaking, there are two kinds of stories we care about: first, stories of ours-stories that we want to have happen/avoid. Second, there are other peoples stories that impact/interest us. Outside of those stories, we don't listen to the stories. So, that's another measuring cup limitation. Not only can we only load in the measuring cup what the cup will hold, we only put in the measuring cup what interests us.

RUSSIAN DOLLS

Essentially, all stories are like Russian Dolls, those carved wood dolls that nest inside each other. As you open one doll, there is another! A fascination for young children and a warning for adults. Everything, EVERYTHING is Russian Dolls. The surface wrapping need bear no relationship to the inner message, the inside story can be anything at all. Often outer shell is pretty and attractive, because it has to get your attention and buy-in. From your point of view, they get less and less attractive as you work in further, but from the point of view of the teller of the story they get more attractive as they go in deeper. Usually social norms shape the outside, but lust is at the bottom, because the denied needs of the creature always come back out. Why did the priests understand the sins better than the sinners? Their inner dolls understood perfectly.

The following is a list of behavior's which caused a greater or lesser degree of failure for something.

- "DEVIANCE-An individual chooses to violate a prescribed process or practice. This means you took responsibility to do what you damn well felt like, and where there is a 'fail' involved, this will rarely turn out well in the eyes of others. It may have been great fun, however.

- INATTENTION-An individual inadvertently deviates from specifications. This is an 'accident', to which greater or lessor fault may be attributed. There is still an aspect of personal error here.

- LACK OF ABILITY-An individual doesn't have the skills, conditions, or training to execute a job. This isn't a personal reflection unless there was misrepresentation of the skills, etc. It's still a 'fail', and there will be consequences.

- PROCESS INADEQUACY-A competent individual adheres to a prescribed but faulty or incomplete process. Not a personal failure unless the individual designed the processes. This can be a good alibi.

- TASK CHALLENGE-An individual faces a task too difficult to be executed reliably every time. This is a good alibi.

- PROCESS COMPLEXITY-A process composed of many elements breaks down when it encounters novel interactions. This is a great alibi.

- UNCERTAINTY-A lack of clarity about future events causes people to take seemingly reasonable actions that produce undesired results. Another great alibi, actually one of the best. Who was to know, you say, as I did what was best for everyone.

- HYPOTHESIS TESTING-An experiment that is conducted to prove that an idea or a design would succeed fails. That, actually, is a type of success, because you know more than you did before.

- EXPLORATORY TESTING-An experiment conducted to expand knowledge and investigate a possibility leads to an undesired result."

But you do know more than you did, so it's again a type of success- unless you destroyed the chemistry lab in the process.

(the above was found on the internet and modified, the author of the original is unknown)

Life being what it is, case 1, Deviance i.e., I did what I felt like doing, is generally disguised as something higher in the chain, so that it's clear we are not the kind of person who ignores everyone else to do whatever we damn well felt like doing. People respect where you tried and the system/world/ equipment failed. (A classic 'good alibi') That's why we use Russian Dolls, to hide our urges under virtuous cover.

Here's another set of Russian Dolls. There are disturbing studies which argue traditional predictors of success in an organization are essentially worthless. That people who are promoted don't do what they are supposed to and people who are not supposed to be able to perform somehow do perform well. Too often, simply lining up the staff and throwing a (non sharp point) dart at the group and promoting the person that dart hits works at least as well as the formal process. That tells you that your filtering mechanism is for crap, and here's why.

We filter based on Russian dolls–the outside story looks right, and we go. So the outside packaging: right schools, right social behavior, attentive, intent, focused, respectful to superiors, all of the standard filters that we see especially in corporations and government, that seek rational results and fairness are random nonsense. That's why 'the old boy network' persists, because perhaps you saw something in the person beyond the standard molds.

The problem is that those are external social filtering mechanisms, which have really nothing to do with how well a person can anticipate and deal with tomorrow's events. I don't have an answer, but it's an increasingly serious problem in a world with deeper and deeper pools of potentially qualified individuals.

The danger with inner dolls that are essentially unknown is that the 'good' is dangerous-far more dangerous than evil. People embrace the good to do what they want; they just have to twist it a bit.

Where you have an outer story that people buy into, you have a stick in ground. Once that stick is in the ground, all the later discussion/actions is in relation to that stick. Pulling up the stick and starting the discussion over has the risk that everyone who has acted in relation to that initial stick loses what they have gained to date. That's not going to be popular.

Russian dolls are especially dangerous where they are, more or less clearly, morality tales. Dangerous because the morality tale changes on the way down into the dolls. Now, morality tales are necessary for social structures. The village must function. It functions when people buy into group stories. The village/society has the problem that resources have to be allocated, and someone wins and someone loses. Realistically, the people on top need a rationale for being on top. Either you control the masses with weapons (which is the essence of control at the bottom) or enough of the group believes that they are better off with you on top than someone else. Paul of Tarsus brilliant realization on the road to Damascus was that he could turn a message into an accounting religion, tie in hooks from earlier religions, and have something that quite frankly could be sold. And it was.

Another issue with Russian Dolls is the measuring sticks we use. Abraham Maslow created a 'hierarchy of needs' that he argued people lived by. He gave a list of five values: survival, security, personal relationships, prestige, and self-development. Those do matter, but only in a logical, rational way. Rationality isn't the self, however.

"Joseph Campbell argued that "I looked at that list and I wondered why it should seem so strange to me. I finally realized that it struck me as strange because these are exactly the values that mythology transcends. Survival, security, personal relationships, prestige, self-development - in my experience, those are exactly the values that a mythically inspired person doesn't live for. They have to do with the primary biological mode as understood by human consciousness. Mythology begins where madness starts. A person who is truly gripped by a calling, by a dedication, by a belief, by a zeal, will sacrifice his security, will sacrifice even his life, will sacrifice personal relationships, will sacrifice prestige, and will think nothing of personal development; he will give himself entirely to his myth. Christ gives you the clue when he says, "He that loseth his life for my sake shall find it."[35]

Campbell concluded that Maslow's five values are the values for which people live when they have nothing to live for. Nothing has seized them, nothing has caught them, nothing has driven them spiritually mad and made them worth talking to. These are the bores. But they make a good story, and the story can be sold. If you are later unhappy, empty with that story, then how do you attack it? And do you realize that the weakness is in the story, not in you? That's looking way outside the boxes around you, and it's hard.

All stories must be Russian Dolls because of the complexity of the world. As the story is simplified, the complexity is smoothed over, at least for the outer stories. Decisions have to be made about resources, uses and constraints and the fluctuations of those factors until the resources run out. Rather than put the whole mess out there to be argued about, what people want is where they start, and the story is glossed up to get there, not the other way around. As a result, for a clever storyteller, people can make stupid choices and be protected from the consequences, as opposed to where people make direct choices that can have blame tied to their actions. So a bank robber is punished, and a bank looter is rewarded. As Aesop said, a very long time ago, "We hang the petty thieves and appoint the great ones to Public Office."

And that story you get, the pretty, polished front story is carefully burnished to deflect attention from the lower stories-at least until you're committed.

> "Many of the people were actually quite intellectually sophisticated, but emotionally empty, and they needed something. And something is what they got. Never blithely assume that the message you clutch to fulfill your needs is the complete message. You'll find, eventually, that the complete message changes the message you thought you understood into something vastly different, but usually it's too late when you find that out. [36] (Talking about the turbulent times as the Roman Republic crumbled and became the Empire)

An extreme example of Russian Dolls was the result of the Greeks' Christian successors rejecting the idea that the universe is governed by indifferent natural law. They also rejected the idea that humans do not hold a privileged place within that universe. And though the medieval period had no single coherent philosophical system, a common theme was that the universe is God's dollhouse, and religion a far worthier study than the phenomena of nature. Not that different from radical Islam today, actually.

So what you were supposed to do with your life, the outer dolls, was driven completely by the inner dolls, the rejection of this world. And by the inner dolls having precedence over the outer world, witchcraft and the inquisition made sense. A moment's thought would show that if witches had real power, they wouldn't let themselves be helplessly tortured to death, but the inner dolls that drove the decisions drove those stories also. You really can be blind to what is right in front of you.

WORDS ARE OUR MASTERS

> *"But if thought corrupts language, language can also corrupt thought." - George Orwell*

Words have a dark power. We run around afraid of dark wizards and evil spells, when the words we use are the dark spell. And it's a spell that actually works it's magic. Let's shift to the building blocks of stories (words and grammar) and think about the problems there. I'm asserting that you can't explain or know yourself in words. Please bear with the following discussion, which probably needs pictures. I think it makes an important point, but it isn't something we usually think about.

Language is one of the most remarkable human abilities. It is the ability that is the basis for the accumulation of knowledge in the world. Accumulating knowledge about the external world is a process subject to experiment and verification. So if a proposition is given, that can be tested. If the words describing the proposition are incorrect, incomplete, or inadequate, the definition and discussion can be corrected and supplemented over time.

Accumulating knowledge about internal events is much more difficult. The problem that traditional psychology has had is that the words can't be tied to firm definitions, and so are of marginal use. What is 'sad', what cluster of feelings are related to 'sad', how deep is 'sad' before it is 'depressed'. What difference does it make whether the person is 4 years old or 40, as sad must certainly change with time. How much different is 'sad' between a person sad because their dinner plans were cancelled, or 'sad' because their longtime friend died. There are lots of adjectives and adverbs in all languages to supplement the description, but all the supplementary words have the same loose borders as the central words.

Words are not the object and the word doesn't mean the object exists.

For example, 'end war'. There are many, many ideas swirling around the simple word 'war'. Within that definition of 'war' is something irrational, something destructive and beyond dangerous. Well, true, but war is more than that: war is a process of negotiation with large sticks, which sometimes is necessary. If there are limited resources, then they have to be divided somehow. If the resources are critical, then the division will not be easy to agree upon.

'War', the process of using large sticks to settle disputes, is rational in many situations, and emotionally easy for us to grasp. The whole 'us/them' thing is written in our minds, and we understand that both intellectually and emotionally in a flash. So ending war, if we are really serious, can only mean giving others all that they want, which isn't going to play well with our lives. The other concept, that ending 'war' means that we get all we want and they get the scraps, is more satisfying, but still won't end war if they have any large sticks to work with.

Related to this is terrorism and war. War is at least honorable–it's announced, people stand up and take heroic stands. Terrorism is just vile, because it's people sneaking around and doing awful things for reasons that are despicable. That most governments ancestry included terrorist activities, and successful terrorism is blessed in the history books, is one of those annoying real world issues that people sweep under the rug. There is no question that a small minority trying to impose their will on others is not socially desirable, at least for the others, but demonizing the attackers, making them monsters, simply makes it more difficult to understand exactly what is driving them and why. If you know what is driving them and why, perhaps they can be defused.

The other approach is to shoot all of 'them' and that rarely works. People pop up, like the warriors in the ancient myth, a dozen up for every one shot, people just get into their wars and battles. It's like sowing dragons teeth. The harder you repress, the more impassioned those are who are left. As the authorities manage to piss off more and more bystanders as they try and crush the terrorists, things go from bad to worse. The enemy of my enemy is my friend is an old, and partly rational approach. The problem comes when the enemy is defeated, and your new friend is actually your enemy-but they have guns and a well trained fighting force.

On the other side, peace is defined in many ways and a sloppy definition is used for 'we want peace'. It's generally something along the lines of no shooting, and smiling faces holding hands working together. That's a pleasant idea, and easy to buy into, as we stand with our happy friends looking over a pleasant meadow.

> "It is easy to read your needs and wants into the world, as you look around. It is very important to realize that your needs and wants are only yours, and when you superimpose them on the world, the world doesn't notice. When you look out on a pleasant summer day, over a grassy, flowered meadow, and feel that warm flow of peace, you are ignoring that each piece of grass is striving to drive out its neighbor, and the flowers are growing over and driving out their rivals. The harmony and cooperation you see is an inflection point of countless constraints and resources utilized in the conflict between the creatures of the meadow. Don't externalize your need for peace and cooperation, and if you do, don't make assumptions into situations that can bite back. So thinking that the meadow is peaceful is fine if it is—but you don't want to make the same mistake in the African Veldt if the lions are lying in the grass."[37]

The upshot of this discussion is that many of the things we are taught to consider most precious simply do not exist. Many of the things we are taught to strive for are phantoms, unclear airy shapes that tease as they dissolve as we grasp for them. Cynically, there are good reasons for such things, as discussed in the Russian Dolls section. But most of this is just trying to direct a group/self towards something that emotionally seems useful.

That is the antitheses of good planning, by the way. A wish fulfillment plan based on words that mean absolutely nothing in the real world is a sinking ship. It's no wonder that plans fail so often, especially the more abstract ones. If it is hard enough to build a building, where we have a drawing, real world specs and a known process, then how much harder (impossible) is it to build dreams and phantoms based on ideals that may not even apply?

This is the downside of committees and meetings, because the careful words they put their memo's, used to frame and express their plans, mean nothing when applied to the real world. So the people in charge of implementing this, of doing something, do what they can do, based on perhaps what they read the words to mean, perhaps what works best for them. After all, if you are charged with doing something that isn't possible to do, you're going to make it work the best for you, because you will be blamed for the inevitable failure. Russian dolls pop up here, as you wrestle with the nonsense handed to you and what can actually be done. It isn't good, it isn't bad – it is, and has to be remembered. This is going to happen in all times and in all places. Moralizing about the failures of implementation for an impossible task does not accomplish much–except carefully protect those who started the ball rolling from the eventual blame for the failure.

"Have you told me words,
I just need to hear,
Will I wake tomorrow full of
sorrow and woe, I don't know."[38]

Again, a word is not an real world process, no matter how much we want it to be. That people are disillusioned and depressed when they find this out is silly. It's a learning experience, and disillusionment just wastes the learning that has been done.

Let's look at something that should be simple, but it isn't at all. Back to 'sad'. When someone says they are 'sad', you have a mental definition that is like a bucket of sand dumped on the ground. There is a central bulk, that is probably the heart of what the person means, but there are outlier grains spilling out all over, in all directions, any one of which could be what the person really means in their mind.

This discussion could go on for hundreds of pages, but the essence is that without clear external objects (that rock is 'red') for multiple people to view and agree on definitions, a word can mean lots of things to different people. And even solid external objects are difficult. The classic formulation of the problem of experience is the elephant touched in different places by six blind men. One feels the trunk, and thinks an elephant is like a snake, the other feels the leg and thinks an elephant is like a tree, and the third feels the tail and thinks an elephant is like a bush, and so on. They then vigorously argue with each other, maintaining that each has the whole truth.

The point of this argument is that people have to compare their experiences to build a complete model of the external object. What the story doesn't say is that the actual opportunity to share knowledge is probably pretty small, because an annoyed elephant is going to make mash out of all three of the men fairly quickly. And that is a valid point, in that external objects rarely are in a state of complete stasis that they can be examined, and when they move out of a state of stasis, they are different objects. The combined definition of the elephant that the blind men create isn't of any use in predicting the behavior or actions of the elephant, which is probably the most critical thing we are concerned with.

All of this discussion is headed towards the point that words and the logical structure they fit into, as social constructs, are not the same logical structure as your mind, a very physically wired construct. There is a wired structure in the mind for language, but language becomes something else than what the perhaps simple grunts and expressions of our ancestors were. So to describe your plans, goals, fears and other internal objects in words requires a transition from your internal structure into that formal logical structure.

That transition is further adjusted by the whole baggage of words and correct structures, in that only certain things can socially be said in certain limited ways. This is getting far too close to German philosophy in wording and complete lack of clarity, so let's look at some simple examples.

Only certain things can be said: telling the judge that he is an idiot is extremely counterproductive, even if your case is clearly supported by all of objective reality. Telling the tribal chief that you respect his authority as to the economically critical social functions, but you reserve the right to paint your hut a different color than he mandated, isn't going to go well either.

Words convey some message, although each of us laughs every day over the muddled and incoherent messages we receive, and sometimes send to others. Bluntly, much of human conversation really isn't about conveying information. A very high proportion of human interaction is the equivalent to monkeys picking the fleas out of each other's coats: grooming/stroking that bonds the group together. This bonding is absolutely important, as the group has needs. But communication for those purposes has to be distinguished from actually trying to convey an idea. You cannot trust words to convey to yourself what you are thinking and feeling. You are a coherent self, and a very large part of the mind is wordless–words and language are controlled by very specific parts of the brain. The other parts of the brain also work and provide information in their own way.

A concept like 'sad' is crystal clear in words, compared to the concept of 'self'. 'Self' has had many long books written about it, and is still truly murky. That is why in seeking what you desire, you have to be open to other avenues, the ways that the rest of your mind works. Your emotions, especially as transacted by your gut, which never lies. Your pictures of things (I hesitate to use visions, as that word has a lot of freight with it) from dreams, pictures that flash in your mind, the pictures as you lie between sleep and fully awake, are critically important. How energetic you feel having made certain choices, the random thoughts that flash in, how well you are sleeping are messages from the wordless mind to central.

Flowing from the problem with words definitions is then the logical manipulation of the word symbols. If the definitions are unclear, then by stringing unclear words together, you are multiplying the confusion. Logic only works if the words which being used have meaningful definitions, as otherwise you simply have a structure that says nothing. A significant part of the problem of setting and achieving personal goals is that the logical process typically employed, which uses non-clearly defined words tied to inner emotional states, attempts a rational and comprehensive process without taking the entire system (your non-verbal mind) into account. Thus the plans flowing from the 'logic' will fail. (crash and burn is the picture)

So, 'saying it' doesn't mean 'it exists'. If you get nothing else out of this book, take that thought with you. Posing a sentence as a simple sentence doesn't mean that the process is simple. Buddha said that the name of the object isn't the object, one of those really simple ideas that we just jump over. Another way of saying that is just because we have a label for something, it does not mean that this something is real.

"Words have power, don't they?" he replied, pacing restlessly. "They let me control things, understand things. But they have an invisible power I don't see, a dark power, because the understanding they give me also binds me to their definitions and their world. Holding to the words is freezing myself in that world. Open to a new understanding, let the walls drop to a larger world, and my control is gone, I stand naked in a cold wind. So I weaken, and wrap myself in the warm words against the cold, thinking   that better the old understanding, holding to the fetters I am comfortable with. The words are a prison that I create for myself.'[39]

The short version is that when people tell you something, they have defined at least some part of your world. When you tell yourself something, you have defined the box you are in, and it's very hard to look outside, because the words are the box.

Now that we doubt the words, lets look at the meaning that the words carry. Morality tales are a common example of stories we are told which may relate to nothing that actually exists. For example: Bad things happen to good people, which completely misunderstands the social and real world relationships (there is no 'story' in nature) only resources, opportunities and actions, against a background of constraints and competition, limited time. Recently, something hit the planet Jupiter, leaving for a short time an earth sized hole in the clouds. Can you imagine the impact? I can't. The damage to whatever was on the surface? Asteroids far smaller (relatively) hit the earth and wiped out almost all life.

That earth sized hole points out that the universe operates by it's own rules, and so projecting mercy, etc. out into the universe is fooling yourself. Job was clearly taught in the Bible that the world is what it is, not what we want it to be, but we deny. 'Good' is judged on social constructs: the mass of prior writings and actions that more or less kept the group functioning. 'Bad' things are external events, which have nothing to do with the social group but damage the social group. Why should there be more of a relationship than the impact on the social group-why should we have to pretend that the stars and planets will crash if a group of human's doesn't do the ritual correctly? The problem is that the social structure uses external events to validate the social stories, and then is embarrassed when the stories don't work out the way they want. So they dance around it, adding circles to the calculations, like the planetary motion calculations before Copernicus, to make the model function. If there isn't any relationship between the social stories and the critical external events, then the control myths are weakened. What's tragic is the extent to which the social values are thought to control external reality.

There are lots and lots of stories that we spin happily around us, that really make no sense. There probably are not enough trees in the forest for the paper to print enough books on the topic, but I'll offer a few quick ones. Going Green is a favorite. 'Green' is pretty things, and not the nasty things under stones. If you don't buy the whole system, not just the soft and pretty parts, the system isn't going to last. We may love little soft seals, but if we were fish, they would be evil incarnate. Going 'Green' somehow doesn't include setting up vast refuges for creatures to breed and grow away from the constant pressure of humans, because, in the end, it's all about the humans after all. There is a wasted, polluted industrial site near where I live that, out of I think despair, perhaps cynicism, they painted the long concrete foundation a bright green because they don't seem to know what else to do with it. It's pretty, but pointless. Sadly, they probably feel they actually accomplished something. It is, in truth, more cheerful green than grey broken concrete.

Why do people, when confronted with a story that isn't working, consciously ignore the problem? I'm not talking about social embarrassment; I'm talking about people in the middle of the night confronting themselves and a set of problems that won't go away. People will hold onto their prisons, because it's their prison, they know the story and they know their cage. It isn't all that hard to figure out where a story isn't working. You ask what does the story ignore, what does it fudge, where the analogies are wrong? If you ask the six magic questions (who, what, where, when, how and why) all the stories unravel and the truth pops out. But the challenge to the story isn't made.

Now, it isn't enough that there is a story and possible problems with the story. There are always problems with the stories. There has to be a problem, by definition. A story is a selected set of events against a sharply colored moral background, highlighting what people want/fear the most. So the background is a problem, what people want is a problem, and what the story will lead to is a problem. The newspapers sell papers exploiting the weakness of the story structure. You can always come up with a reason for why something happened, will happen, shouldn't have happened, and so on. If you're wrong, well, who can foretell the future? And, by the way, because you are my special friend, and you get my special friend price, here's another story about what's really going to happen this time, no kidding, cross my heart and hope you die.

CHAPTER 5. STORY FAILURES

HAPPY AND UNHAPPY STORIES

Tolstoy wrote "Happy families are all alike; every unhappy family is unhappy in its own way." The same can be said for stories. Happy stories all test and match against reality and allow room for change and growth. Unhappy stories are themes on the infinite variations resulting from ignoring reality and freezing the story solid. This section is a medley of stories that don't work, examples of some of those infinite variations. You are encouraged to test these ideas! Look through the daily newspaper, which is of necessity focused on stories with problems, because happy stories don't sell newsprint.

One dangerous unhappy story is that any state of affairs that persists long enough ceases to seem like an aberration. For example, what really sets the years following World War II apart from those after World War I (and actually apart from all prior recorded history) is oil-the most efficient fuel that any civilization has ever found. The abundance of oil-for the few counties that could utilize the oil-is what has made possible the phenomenon of prolonged growth throughout the First World. With the end of the abundance of oil-caused both by diminishing natural resources compounded by increasing demand by counties which hadn't used oil extensively-there is the problem that hard choices between alternatives will have to be made.

Hard choices are made with knives out. If you think that allocations of necessary resources will be made rationally with the best overall choices for society, you are encouraged to read more history. It's much the opposite, actually, as those who have grasp tighter onto what they have as the ship goes down. "Après moi le deluge!" (attributed to Louis XV, and he was right) The Chinese emperors/ nobility seem to have followed the same pattern, as have, throughout history, most privileged groups facing the end of their good times.

A touchy social situation that is at the root of many story failures is that as you scale up or down on scale of 'the good' the story collapses. This gets people going, because 'the good' is 'the good'. Period, end of discussion. For example, the 10 Commandments work reasonably well to keep a relatively small village functioning on a daily basis. It's clear that for a small group, the good is cooperation and getting along. For that, the 10 commandments are perfectly on point: no killing, no stealing, and no screwing around, generally and specifically. But, the rules don't scale. Moving down the scale, to the individual level, I offer as proof the mass of novels over the centuries that are desperate attempts to reconcile the social demands with individual desires.

Scaling up, to relationships between villages/parts of a large town, the frictions become more apparent. And between countries, the rules just don't apply. Countries that will not kill will not continue to be independent countries for long, moral rules regardless. Might makes Right at the international relations level, no question about that. Yet, it's dangerous to allow, not to mention encourage, 'ordinary' people to think about scaling the rules up and down. The danger is our friend the Russian Dolls. Scaling the rules allows ordinary people to seek what they want in their heart and bury those dark desires down in the bottom dolls, using the glow of the rules carefully attached to the top dolls to persuade. That's reserved for the select.

When we run into something new, we use familiar terms and analogies to grasp the new situation. Obviously, the old isn't going to completely explain the new, so we may be off to a bad start. Accidentally, we may just not grasp the essence of the new once we dress it in the clothes of the old. Then, there are those who don't make that mistake accidentally, those with an ax to grind realize that they can win by using misleading terms and analogies, at least until the law is passed in their favor. Once a statute is passed by the legislature, it's a serious stake in the ground and they don't get moved well at all.

Once we do realize the situation is really different, and we successfully develop new thought and practice that, after time, overthrows the foolish and empty old thought, the new thought boldly ventures where old thought froze-and then becomes the orthodoxy itself and freezes. The orthodox must always be broken through, and this is hard, because people have first grown accustomed to the orthodox and more importantly, their livelihoods and social status depend on the orthodox. Because the orthodox is so important to many people, questioning the stories isn't allowed. The fewer questions allowed, the more quickly the story becomes completely frozen, drifting away from reality at an accelerating rate.

Eventually, all stories will fail if the correlation with reality drops below a certain minimal point-at least for most people. When the story fails, then where the failed story was so important that it any questioning/ examination was forbidden, then there is a complete absence of graded choices/alternatives. Without alternatives, there is the flopping of a dying fish, as society tries to adopt within a plan. Often, there is a flip to opposites, because that's all that there is on the table. That is, if the prior story only allowed for glorious good (the existing system) and hideous evil (everything else) you don't have many options. That's the problem with anarchy as an ideological position against the existing state, because anarchy can't, by definition, run the system after the revolution. People need a belief to hold and more importantly a system run live within and will grab the next one offered when theirs doesn't work. The dutiful efforts of the Anarchists helped turned Russia into a tyranny far worse than anything the Romanov's had ever dreamed of. Those flips, tearing through the structures of daily life, are generally rather catastrophic. Revolutions usually only succeed, in the end, at being revolting. But they make very good stories for those who survive, full of heroism and tragic event's.

There are stories we test, and stories we don't test. Certain stories are emotionally important to us, probably hard wired into the brain, and we don't really test them. Again, there is 'luck'. Oh, intellectually we probably laugh at the idea that there isn't a 'spirit' out there making things better or worse for us, which is what the concept of luck really revolves around. But catch us as we make quick decisions and as we react to events and we believe in luck. We believe in a spirit(s) out there helping or hurting, and it's deep inside us. Some test the idea in gambling, and despite failures, continue to believe.

We fall for some stories over and over. Stories that we are special, and so someone is doing something just for us-investment stories are like this. If you want to see the real stories that the wiring is made for, read your spam e-mail. (Don't click on the attachments!) Those, poorly written and crass as they are, hit on real emotional hot spots, deny it as we may. Instant money out of the blue, desirable romantic (sex) partners throwing themselves at us, investment advice only for us (and the other 10,000,000 people who got that e-mail) and the like are things we deeply care about. With spam, it's pretty obvious that they are nonsense, and most of us don't respond. At least, after the first time. Although I've seen competent, functional adults throw money into those holes with their eyes wide open.

Stories that do not include humans or social behavior are stories that we never see, because they do not engage us. They slide by, until they involve people-generally tragically. These are classic black swans because no one sees them. As an example of our point of view, there is the classic question of whether if a tree falls in a forest, and no one hears it, does it matter? What? Well, it fell, didn't it? It was a real event and changes the forest in many ways, some of which may later find their way into a human story. That we would bother asking the question shows our focus on the small human stories-that is, nothing matters unless we perceive it-which isn't close to true.

Consciousness wants neat structures, without the messiness of organic life. Careful tending and cultivation, past a minimal point, is control, and a negation, to some extent of life. As you may suspect, another story failure is where the story is essentially organic, that is, it twists and turns, important parts (roots) hidden from our view. That's a cheat of the definition of story, that by definition has clear actors and a background. People can't seem to think organically: our thought is generally straight lines and direct connections. For a novel or movie, it can't be too straight, or there isn't any suspense, but not too twisted, because we get lost in the chaos.

Directly tied to this is the confident linear extrapolation of existing inputs into the future, when it really isn't that kind of a world. Part and parcel of the linear extrapolation is our measuring what we can measure (remember our measuring cup) and extrapolating that measure (linearly) to things that really don't have anything to do with the measure. The larger world is non-linear, events dependent on influences we can't see or measure, but we ignore much of that because, well, you've got to do something and can't just sit there and stew. That's true, but bagging the unknown and putting it in the trash because it makes us uncomfortable isn't going to work long term. Demanding a story that we can understand and rely on, even when it's not really that accurate, is a fail coming down the road.

GROUP STORIES

It's hard enough to get yourself on the right track. But the group?

"It isn't just forcing yourself to act," Lucretia continued. "It's worse when you have to explain this new thing to others for their buy-in. Defining a successful outcome for a new group problem? That's really hard, because the people you are trying to persuade have to take some big jumps. First, they have to grasp the problem, using precious thought and time taken away from the other fires they are facing. Once they grasp the problem, they may or may not consider it the problem you do, and they may or may not be right. There's a lot of thrashing about right there. Assuming, as the meeting drags on, that they grasp the idea of the problem, and buy-in that it's (a) as big a problem as, and (b) the same kind of problem, you think it is. Then comes the really big jump: because this is 'new', you can't give the meeting or group or committee that vision of the Grail they seek, i.e., a clear, unambiguous plan on rails towards the distant glowing goal, because the outcome we are after will change as we wade through the swamp of reality. As the outcome changes, you have to pull the tracks up and move them. Not only does that take time, but looks like a type of failure, and no one wants to be tarred with the scent of failure."

"So, you're trying to get this tired group to risk their prestige and thinly spread resources on a possible profit, as they stand at the edge of the precipice, staring at a certain loss if it doesn't go right?" Mary commented. "Been there many times, rarely successfully."

"There is a technique that works," Lucretia admitted, "But it holds the seeds for future failure within it's success. In desperation, when things are going badly, and the group is starting to stampede towards you, the ground shaking from their rumbling and the little birds around you taking flight to safety, you then pull out the full meeting notes that carefully defined War as Peace, Freedom as Slavery, etc., and suddenly, Pow! Things went the way you wanted them to. Moving the goal posts is an act of desperation, because they will be watching for that next time. To do this successfully, you have to keep your project goals hidden, like cards in poker. Thus, each buy-in that you get people to do is a buy-in to a lie. You'd better win at the end, or the herd will run over the top of you."[40]

Sharing our view of something with the group is a story. Explaining a process, a set of events that we are concerned with in life, to a group is hard because a process is a story about a story. Our explanation is our story of what we want; our story of what is happening and why, and a story of what is really happening, framed in terms that the group can by into. Because we are trying to tie our story into the stories that everyone else carries with them, and that they use as touchstones to measure the truth or falsity of what is being presented to them, often the story of the process isn't a story of what is actually happening out there. It's a mess, as discussed in the preceding quote, because you have all these reconciled story interactions.

By the way, as this book will say several times, there are no hard and fast answers for all situations. Most books, for reasons of emotional satisfaction, posit certain behaviors that will carry you through. Sadly, that's just not true. There are some central ideas that work: not to steal the thunder of the closing chapter, one should know the system you are working within, iterate the problem analysis and look closely at the facts and circumstances of your problem. It's a 'paper, rock, scissors' world, and absolute clarity and conviction are emotional states, not real world anchors. So if you are paging ahead for the answers, this isn't a true/false test.

More group fun:

"Those numbers suck," Lucretia concluded, standing and pointing to the display screen. "They are outside all of the parameters we set at the last meeting and accomplish none of the goals. Why did you generate this nonsense?" She sat down to a dark silence. Okay, swami knows all, sees all and here's what he will say, she told herself. First, all my ideas are not perfect, so none of them are any good.

"Lucretia," the man replied, standing up, "I considered your ideas and they didn't cover all of the possibilities. Sure, your ideas did include a lot of issues, but they just were not a complete solution. So I looked at other ideas."

Check. Now, he'll reject my ideas because there are only two choices. No compromises or other possibilities allowed.

"And," he continued, "We have to make a decision here. We can't pick through alternatives all afternoon. It's these two or nothing."

"Because you can only hold two thoughts in your mind?" Lucretia snapped despite herself.

"Really? Is sarcasm going to help here?" a junior partner interrupted, trying to cover.

"I hide behind sarcasm because telling you to go fuck yourself is considered rude in most social situations," Lucretia snarled. "And I'm a senior partner, so you can all go sit on it. Look, you've all made up your minds, and you don't need—or want—my opinions."

"Don't be so hard on him, Lucretia," another junior partner

urged. "It's an interesting idea."

"So is breathing in outer space," she remarked, "but it doesn't work. And neither will this." She glanced at her watch. "I've got another meeting in Midtown. Thank you, gentlemen." She walked out, smiling at all the men, who smiled at her beauty despite themselves. It ain't what a man don't know that makes him a fool, but what he does know that ain't so—but I'm not telling them again, she thought." [41]

Story failure comes in such interesting ways. A study of why some emergency plans failed in a disaster came to a fascinating conclusion. The plans failed because the emergency plans had been designed to meet the needs of emergency staff and personnel, not the people who were caught in the emergency. That actually makes a lot of sense, because the emergency officials were the suits in the room while the planning was going on. They focused on their needs, sliding over the essential idea that emergency plans are to save regular people. Usually those kinds of meetings involve budgets, and budgets truly are an emergency! Who cares what the topic is when first we need to cover our costs? It's unfortunate that you can't have 'regular people' in some of the meetings, to point out that the all-knowing, all-seeing emergency managers should treat the peons with respect. Warnings should say why you should do something, not just what you are to do, which works as well with kids as adults. The instructions should not be an outgrowth of power battles in that meeting room. (I know, what planet do I live on?)

Kant clearly wrote, well, as clearly as a German philosopher can, that what we see (perceive) is a small subset of what is out 'there'. First our perceptions are limited by the hardware-eyes, nose, etc. Then there is the distortion of silent evidence. Remember the professor talking about silent evidence? The class didn't think the idea was all that important, and the professor knew it. "Age shows the value of this," he told us, surveying the dazed and dulled faces in class. "You'll think more of this later. We see what happened, or what we are told happened. We do not see, do not have time to see or think, about what could have happened, what might have happened, and what the differences were have been. Where are the events that didn't happen? Where are the events riding on other events that look like they caused them? History hides Black Swans from us and gives us a mistaken idea about the odds of these events. You stumble over the silent evidence when your plan crashes around you." [42]

Let's conclude story failures by looking at disasters, which are situations where the story changes quickly. Disasters are an especially interesting kind of story, and one that is generally handled badly. That's not really fair to the people in the middle, because most of the problem is lack of good information. What makes the difference between life and death is how you process the fragmentary, contradictory information forcing it's way into your perception. The following is paraphrased from the book "The Unthinkable", which is an excellent book and recommended reading.

The Survival Arc is the typical process we follow when dealing with disaster. It's complex, because rarely is there a flashing red sign and whistles making it clear (1) this is a disaster, folks and (2) what kind of a disaster it is.

To put this in context, we are minding our own business, doing something. Something happens, that may or may not be part of what we thought we were doing. So the first phase of a disaster is denial. Except in extremely dire cases, IE, the handwriting is so clearly on the wall that no one could deny it, we tend to display a surprisingly creative and willful brand of denial. You would think that the attack on the twin towers was as clear a case that something was wrong as could be, but many still delayed (generally waiting for instructions and help, normally a rational approach) and died as a result.

But why do we deny, if it is so dangerous? Because we don't know what is going on and can't make accurate assessments. How long we delay depends in large part on how we calculated risk. Our risk analysis depends less upon facts (because there really are few or none in a developing situation) than upon a shadowy sense of dread. Now, denial isn't always bad, by any means. In daily life, there are occasionally little odd things. We ignore them and they go away, outliers that really didn't mean anything. But once in a while, the outliers are the first hints of that big wave coming in. When the ocean recedes rapidly, don't stand there looking at it, because it's coming back in a hurry! Someone didn't pull out the stopper at the bottom of the ocean and the water isn't going down because it's draining out.

So, finally convinced that something is wrong, something outside the normal, we stop denying, and we move into deliberation, the second phase of the survival arc. We know something IS terribly wrong, but we don't know what to do about it. How do we decide? The first thing to understand is that nothing is normal. We think and perceive differently. Very differently! "The Unthinkable" goes into fascinating detail about the hardwired physical responses that we go through, warping our conscious perceptions. So, having perceived something and processing that something (generally not our best, most organized thought) we reach the third phase of the survival arc: the decisive moment. We've accepted that we are in danger; we've deliberated our options. Now we take action- maybe.

Many, if not most, people tend to shut down entirely in a disaster, quite the opposite of panicking. They go slack and seem to lose all awareness. But their paralysis can be strategic. In most cases, we do what others around us do. If we are in a crowded dining room, and a whiff of smoke blows through the room, we don't stand up screaming immediately and bolt from the room. We look around at others, seek consensus, until the heavy cloud of smoke rolls through the room, and then it's too late. People are often cool during fires, ignoring or delaying their response. Laughter-or silence-is a classic manifestation of denial, as is delay. Taking cues from others is what we are trained to do all our lives, after all.

"Freezing" is as common as fleeing. It's a complicated response that has meant certain death for millions. "The Unthinkable" looks at focused disasters such as fires, ships sinking, and the like. The principles are as applicable to sea changes in the political/social world around us. Stalin's starvation of the Ukraine, Mao's great leap flat, the disregard of the Poles and eastern Russian's for the massed armies of the Wehrmacht twitching on the border were disasters with signs before they happened. Denial is the most insidious fear response of all, and it lurks in places we never think to look. The longer you look at the problem, the more denial seemed to matter all the time, even long before the disaster, on days that pass by without incident

> What should you worry about? "I tell people that if it's in the news, don't worry about it. The very definition of 'news' something that hardly ever happens'" writes security expert Bruce Schneier. "It's when something isn't in the news, when it's so common that it's no longer news-car crashes, domestic violence-that you should start worrying."[43]

And how to respond to disaster? The essential steps are quite simple, and the first step, surprisingly, is simply to breath slowly and carefully. That's hard in the middle of chaos, but essential. How could something so simple be so powerful? Our breathing is one of the few actions that reside in both our somatic nervous system (which we can consciously control) and our autonomic system (which includes our heartbeat and other actions we cannot easily access). So our breathing is a bridge between the two. By consciously slowing down our breathing, we can de-escalate the primal fear response that otherwise takes over.

Laughter, like breathing, reduces our emotional arousal level as well. It also has the benefit of making us feel more in control of the situation. Again and again, studies have shown that people perform better under stress if they think they can handle it. In studies of rats, scientists have taken this discovery one step further: the medial prefrontal cortex appears to detect whether a threat is under the rat's control. If the brain concludes that the stressor is indeed under its control, the brain blocks some of the more devastating effects of extreme stress. Self-confidence, in other words, can save your life.

Ironically, people who are self-focused jerks usually do better in a true emergency because they think for themselves and are not as tied to other people's opinions. So in an emergency, free your inner jerk and you may survive. I did say that this is an immoral book.

SLIPPERY SLOPES

The examination and analysis of certain critical stories is carefully limited by society, generally by calling such forbidden questions 'slippery slopes'. Slippery slopes are important stories because they try very hard to limit (preferably deny) external reality. The general argument is phrased along the lines of 'Avert your eyes lest ye sin', but avoiding the real world situation behind the story doesn't avoid the problem. If it's a real problem, an iceberg you are headed towards, then paper words are not going to hide it forever.

It isn't the question that creates the slippery slope; it's that annoying real world out there, but as pointed out before, the real world is large and surly. Refusing to look at the question doesn't make the issue go away. In all truth, questions labeled slippery slopes are feared and avoided because they lead to difficult choices no one wants to make and that's understandable. There are ugly questions out there. But if you don't deal with them, then when story 1 falls apart, then there are no halfway stories, and it's all the way down the other end of the slope for the next action choice, as there are no other alternatives.

A slippery slope is the visual-a place where, when you step here, you slide down to there, with embarrassment and humiliation included for free. A classic is the question of mercy killing for dying people in horrible pain. The argument against is that if you allow that, then someone, perhaps even you, will inevitably advocate and allow shooting jay walkers, so you can't even start on ideas about what to do with the dying people in horrible pain. That rather extreme example is exactly how and why the slippery slope argument is used.

Generally, anytime we are going to allow people to exercise discretion (i.e., using local rules) there is a legitimate distrust of people's motives. Why? Remember the list of reasons for failure (in Russian Dolls) starting with selfish deviance and working down to socially allowed failures? We suspect (know) people will mask their deeply buried deviance with something more socially allowed, and rather than let people play games, there is a tendency to choke off any decisions. While "I'm" able to make good decisions, well, you're not so competent, frankly, is the underlying-and often expressed-position. There's some truth in this, but a blanket prohibition of local rules won't work.

First, there are real world situations that are authentically awful. There are times that something needs to be done. You can't shoot a person in the head-unless they are trapped in a burning auto, the flames licking at them, and there's nothing else to be done. That's thankfully pretty rare, but is a limited case where the local rules are clear. It's the really sick and probably dying person in the hospital that is a problem, because there is a certain amount of uncertainty in a diagnosis. What if it the person really isn't dying and they might survive? Pain is hard to quantify, and difficult to communicate. But there are clearly cases where people are suffering in terrible agony and causing them to suffer is cruel, if not vicious. If they were in the woods in their condition, they would at least die quickly. We put them in a hospital on life support with the net result that we prolong their agony, and it's a problem that should, by a caring society, be dealt with directly. The indirect approaches: a physician prescribes medications that easily cause an overdose, so that patient dies quickly and quietly, for example, are undependable. In this case, they are using discretion (random local rules) with no oversight. By denying structured discretion, we then force discretion that is completely arbitrary, which makes little sense. In planning jargon, we have abdicated a consensus for relevant local rules, which means a multitude of local rules pop up without agreement or discussion.

Again, things are defined as 'slippery slopes' when the social structure (or actors in the social structure) doesn't want people to think about something. Perhaps the 'something' is too dangerous in reality, or more likely, too dangerous for someone's power base. Our laws are riddled with positions imposed because some neurotically self-righteous person(s) forced them though, carefully setting up the Russian Dolls so their position couldn't be formally attacked, when actually the situation was far more complex. The drug laws jump to mind. Again, once a position is taken, either by the self or by society, it's 'anchored', and almost impossible to dislodge.

In the movie "The Dark Knight", the Joker, who was always doing something awful, said:

> "The Joker: I just did what I do best. I took your little plan and I turned it on itself. Look what I did to this city with a few drums of gas and a couple of bullets. Hmmm? You know... You know what I've noticed? Nobody panics when things go "according to plan." Even if the plan is horrifying! If, tomorrow, I tell the press that, like, a gang banger will get shot, or a truckload of soldiers will be blown up, nobody panics, because it's all "part of the plan!""[44]

That's one of the most challenging statements you will hear, carefully put in the mouth of the villain so that people will deny thinking about his statement. You shouldn't think about the stories, because you are questioning authority! Thinking questions what the social order (the man/woman in the power suit) wants. The stories passed down from above are 'the' story, and your superiors have decided the story is OK. Don't you trouble yourself about them.

Life bursts out of the small controlled stories, a source of considerable frustration to the powers that be. Fortunately, the answer was found many centuries ago. All the big social stories are rituals, and a ritual must be done exactly perfectly, exactly the same each time, or the ritual fails. By the way, you goofed in performing the ritual, so it's your fault, not societies, so you'd better redo-and redo-that ritual until you get it right. If nothing else, that puts you in a corner doing useless things while they make other plans.

Ritualizing social behaviors is diplomacy writ small, the preservation of what is now, regardless how pointless. Big diplomacy between nations is justifying what is, never what can (or, gasp, should) be. International diplomacy is an example of the 'anchoring' problem, writ very large, the persecution and assassination of the hopes of the masses as performed by men in suits in elegant rooms.

Slippery slopes are an illusion, smoke and mirrors that hide the real problems and solutions. It's important to remember that today's position on 'X' isn't the ultimate revealed truth. Revealed truth, and social viewpoints change dramatically over the centuries. What we now think about slavery, genocide, and a long list of todays hot topics were viewed vastly differently not that long ago.

The Huns were quite sure of their values and worldview, for example. As an example, there have been many social systems that clearly said the more people you kill, the stronger your soul gets, quite the opposite of the party line today. Many cultures around the world have proudly built piles of skulls to celebrate their power. Gibbon, in the Decline and Fall of the Roman Empire, has page after page of slaughters and massacres, that were just doing business then. None, it may be pointed out, as fully vicious as the modern wars that we engage in, comfortable in our moral superiority. Just one small case in point: the Dresden bombing in World War II.

We, following the lead of St. Augustine (see the "City of God") are to believe that the Catholic Church was the root cause of our modern civilization. If the Church did lead us to civilization, it was a random walk with a lot of extraneous sightseeing involved. Had the Roman Empire used a numerical system with a zero, so it could easily calculate such important things as taxes, income and expense; and/or had petroleum as a power source, then the empire might not have collapsed, and many things would be different today. Just because something happened the way it did, such as Western Europe becoming a crucible of learning and knowledge, is far from the logical conclusion that the way it occurred was the only possible way that could have occurred. That's the trap of negative evidence.

Another view of the world rather ignored today, is the worldview of the dread Goddess Kali. She is a sacrifice goddess, based on the observation that life comes from death. It's especially obvious in a tropical climate, where the rotting trees in the jungle are as food for the next generation of trees and life. It's a small conceptual jump to the idea that if you want more life, you need to serve up more death, and so by sacrifice you speed up the new life that you need for the village to prosper.

The last few paragraphs are just to point out that all of our present sacred beliefs will be viewed differently (skipping over what should or should not be) in the not so far future, because things change. I'm not arguing what should be, just that what can be covers a very wide range.

One of the most dangerous slippery slopes we have worked ourselves into is overpopulation, resulting in pollution and ecological destruction that has a good chance of destroying human life on this planet. Not today, and not tomorrow, but there are lines converging in the future that are not pretty. This is a case where everyone working in his or her best interest is clearly going to be in no one's best interest shortly. Why cannot we act? Plato, in The Republic said, "Mankind censure injustice fearing that they may be the victims of it, and not because they shrink from committing it." There is a deep truth in his statement, but there are also problems that won't go away by ignoring them. That is the danger of the slippery slope.

And so we are frozen from acting on critical issues because no one can raise the ugly questions. Perhaps no one should settle in low lying areas subject to floods, but then you are telling those people to not have children and expand into all the possible space they can find. Perhaps people should limit the number of children they have to a number that they can adequate raise and educate. There is a really explosive and dangerous area, a topic that is full of impossible dilemmas. Again, just because the dilemmas are impossible within a certain social/moral and/or ethical frame doesn't mean that the problems don't exist. Ignoring very real problems will not make them go away. Whether the world decides to push back hard or whether we make some relatively rational stab at the problem, there are going to be a solutions.

Perhaps shifting sands is a better visual than slippery slopes. A slippery slope is frozen; the hills and structures are there forever. The diplomats can ignore change, because change doesn't exist. That slippery slope will exist for all time, in their viewpoint. Shifting sands shows that things move and needs to change over time, as the foundation vanishes. Even a diplomat, looking down and seeing that there is nothing under their feet, would have to think then. Perhaps.

A related problem, part of the slippery slope issue, is that society embraces Manichaeism. There is only ultimate good and evil, with nothing in between. Perhaps we are just wired to think that way, because it seems so easy for us to do, but that completely ignores the overlaps with the real world. Manichaeism is an underlying basis for slippery slopes, because there is only good or bad, and all that grey in-between is a ruse of the evil (devils–we personify) to trap you. That doesn't have anything to do with external reality (or God's statements in Job) but it's an argument that the orthodox have been making-and winning-for centuries. The true danger is that when events change our perception, the slippery slope argument has limited thinking to the point that when an allowed position breaks, there is a 'flop' to another extreme. If you don't train people to think about options, to develop local rules for situations, then it's extreme to extreme.

A simple example: assume that we have unlimited resources to treat people's medical problems. Then one day, we have 1/2 of the resources we did before, and have to make decisions-THAT DAY. The choices made under pressure will not be optimal, unless this day was prepared for. Slippery slopes, and that is one, mean it isn't being prepared for.

Societies choices, embedded in Manichaeism, are posed in bright virtues and dark vices, but the problem with virtues/vices as guides are:

(a) They are defined for the good of society, and so don't scale well, as discussed earlier;

(b) Traditional definitions of virtues/vices are so unclear as to actions and measurable results as to be almost useless-part of the general problem with words and meaning;

(c) Virtues/Vices were defined and frozen into shape based on historical situations and choices that are often not relevant to a present choice;

(d) Virtues/Vices are classical slippery slopes because they are phrased in religious and ethical terms that cannot be examined without violating very serious social rules, and thus questioning is off limits; and

(e) Worst, they are picked up/learned haphazardly. What we learned at age 4 is grafted onto what we learn at age 30, along with the movie character we liked and the bit from the book we read 20 years ago. There isn't conscious review and reconciliation of all of these pieces.

In short, virtues and vices are coral reefs, built up slowly over time. Within the traditional world they were build around, they were walls to keep the wider world out. In today's world, where we must go to the wider world, the reef becomes a trap to tear the bottom out of your ship as you venture out to sea.

"And we tried to work with that, using the well-meant lie, and it's been our downfall," he declared. "Well-meant lies just confuse people, which we actually planned on. We hoped confusion would lead to understanding, but it didn't because they think only in set stories. The stories are small, all bordered and bright edges, only clear against the dark backgrounds. The light-filled symbols in the stories froze into grey concrete weights. The stories became forts to hide in from understanding the world. Stories bonded them into groups, and became their masks in the social world. So the harder you push on the stories, the tighter they hold onto them. Paul understood his prey far better than we, who thought we were the hunters. We tried the bigger stories, but they couldn't grasp the full complexity," he continued. "So we lied, meaning well. Intending that the next story would correct the first one, and so on. We thought we could coax them, move them gradually to the bigger stories, by little stories that weren't quite true but had elements of the truth. We treated them like children, trying to keep them alive to adulthood, but they never took the next big step, to challenge, question, and rebel, and then rebuild the stories. Unfortunately, a single contradiction corrupts and allows falsehoods to proliferate. The stories became falsehoods built upon falsehoods. Well meant, but not working."

"Nothing is so difficult as not deceiving oneself," Mary commented. [45]

The stories limit us, and telling a partial story that expands later to a more complex story doesn't seem to work well. Children as they grow up become alienated as they discover the 'truth' they were told was false. Well, of course the little stories are false. As parents, our main concern is keeping a child alive for them to grow up, so we tell them all kinds of things to keep them from doing the most obviously dangerous actions. It's hard to look at an adolescent and say, well, yeah, that was at best a partial truth, but what you discovered is another partial truth. Don't deny the basis of truth in the statement you are angry about, and grab onto the partial truth you have discovered as the whole truth. It's hard to say that because how often do we as adults tell ourselves that?

When faced with a slippery slope response to your argument/ questions/position, the response has to be to turn the discussion into something else. Move it away from the club being waved in your face.

REFLECTIONS ON STORIES.

Tell me a story - the power of narrative. Important questions about the future are usually too complex or imprecise . . . Instead, we use the language of stories and myths. Stories have a psychological impact that graphs and equations lack. Stories are about meaning; they help explain why things could happen in a certain way. They give order and meaning to events - a crucial aspect of understanding future possibilities. The Art of the Long View [46]

So, why not just tell ourselves to look outside! Think! as IBM used to demand (and probably still does). Because it isn't that easy-even the Harry Potter people couldn't cast a spell to tell you 'what I don't know but want to see'. Evidently there are limits even to magic in our minds.

Stories are both a source of great power, because they enable us to handle complex situations-and the root of disaster, when we tell the story wrong or listen wrong. That mismatch between the real world and our mind map? The race may not always go to the strong, etc., but it's going to go to the real world, 3 falls out of 3.

The long and short of this whole discussion, which you are probably sick of by now, is that the story is not the world, even though the story is the only way that we can grasp the world. It's a distinction with a difference, essential if you seek success! That's why you don't tell the story once, embrace it and move merrily down the road, which is planning error Numero Uno! You have to tell the story over and over, puzzling about it, checking assumptions and as the story changes change plans. All stories are at best partial truths, if outright lies in many cases, even if done for the best intentions. When we realize the limits, grow past the story, we can incorporate what's correct and add in what we now understand. Disillusionment and anger over a story being found false is just a waste of time. You're climbing a mountain towards the truth, and the stories that you walk on are the footpath to a more complete truth.

A bounded world, blinders proudly held in place, is seeing the world only through human stories. An unbounded world, a world where you actually see, is seeing the stories through the world.

PART 2. PICTURING AND POKING THE WORLD

PART 2, SECTION 1. THE 3 WORLDS.

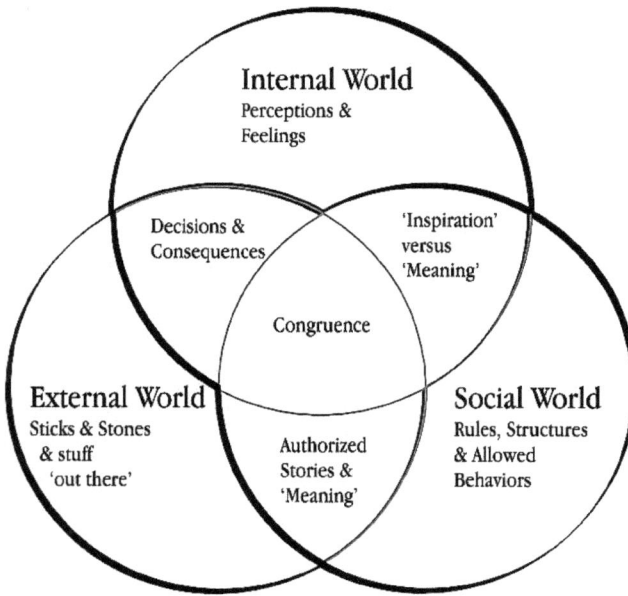

CHAPTER 6. PICTURING THE STORIES

WORLD MIND MAPS: THE STARTING POINT.

All things come out of the One and the One out of all things. ... I see nothing but Becoming. Be not deceived! It is the fault of your limited outlook and not the fault of the essence of things if you believe that you see firm land anywhere in the ocean of Becoming and Passing. You need names for things, just as if they had a rigid permanence, but the very river in which you bathe a second time is no longer the same one which you entered before. (Heraclitus, 500 B.C.)

That is revealed truth for planning – and life, also!

Figure 1 on the next page is "the 3 Worlds Problem". The 3 worlds problem is that the world doesn't exist for humans as an objective fact. Kant said (roughly paraphrased) that all we know is a stream of perceptions that has some relationship to external reality, but we cannot 'know' reality. While certainly Kant was right about that we cannot know absolute 'reality', we still have to live and make decisions in the here and now. How can we best make those decisions? I'm not trying to add to your stress level, but good decisions are only absolutely critical for our lives and the lives of those we love. As Eunice said in the movie "What's Up, Doc":

"Now don't be nervous, Howard, just remember, everything depends on this. "[47]

It didn't make Howard relax, either.

A central concept of this book is that each of us lives every moment of every day in three worlds simultaneously: (1) the world of the inner self; (2) the social construct world of society; and (3) the real, physical world.

So what ties these worlds together, as we don't have/can't grasp the objective facts? Backing away and looking at this from a traditional perspective, Myth is how we relate the three worlds of the human to each other. It's essential we be in sync with the three worlds. We have to relate the self to the real world (you've got to eat, sleep and survive); the Self to self, (because you've got to get along with yourself); and the Self and social world (because you've got to work with the group or no food, status, sex, etc.). Myth is a bit of a digression for this book, and not really covered, but it's important to keep things in perspective.

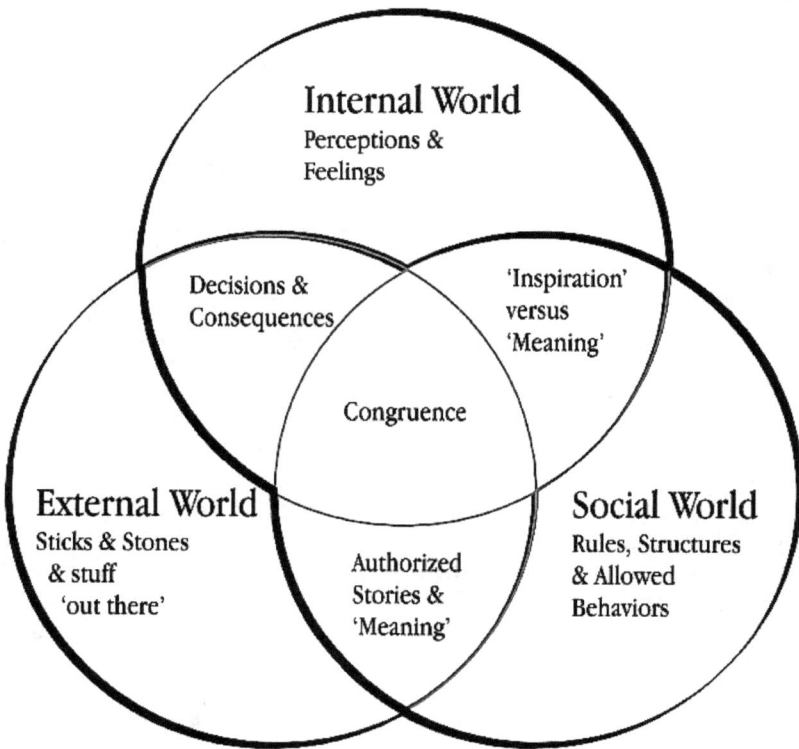

Figure 1. The 3 Worlds Problem.

Figure 1 is the key diagram for this section and underlies much of the book. I've thought of just putting the diagram out on the web and saying 'reflect on the sound of three imaginary circles touching', but that's too Zen. The above diagram is deceptively simple, as it's a pretty complete reorientation of the way that we cut up the world.

There is first the real world, all of that 'stuff' out there. Dirt and light and planets and bugs and air, the elements of the Periodic Table combined in an infinite array. Next is the mental construct that is the social world, the rules of which are reinforced through a number of methods. Finally, there is the world of the self, our feelings, physical feedback, what we wake up in every morning.

The diagrams are a worldview, a frame to see the world through. A frame is what it says; it frames and focuses on a limited area. A frame is a perspective that describes something, but at the same time perceptually changes what it describes. A frame around a picture on the wall changes our perception of the wall and the picture; the frame doesn't just hold the picture on the wall. In making choices, the frame we choose defines what we consider data important to a decision, but the frame also creates and shapes the data, weeding out the infinity of onrushing events to what matters within that frame's orientation. It's easy to miss the warping and limiting effect of the frame, with the result we may weed out essential data because it's outside the frame we quickly pulled out of our mental box of tools to hold the data.

By defining relevant data for our problem, a frame both refers to certain moral and ethical viewpoints and creates moral and ethical viewpoints critical to that frame. Example: a residential house fire is viewed quite dramatically differently by the homeowner, the firefighters, and the insurance investigator(s). Hopefully not by the police and the courts. Each frame (homeowner, firefighters, investigators) will have different moral and ethical imperatives, which is often difficult for people to grasp. We all want 'one story', 'one point of view', one 'right answer', but the world isn't like that.

Everyone knows Murphy's Law: "Anything that can go wrong will go wrong". Figure 1 shows why Murphy's Law is waiting for us in the future, chuckling at our plans. 'Anything that can go wrong' is lurking outside the overlap(s) that we perceive and so we sit, confident and happy in our wise decisions and careful evaluation of the situation. Figure 1 presents another version of the books goal: to make clear why Murphy's law is real, and to clarify Sun Tzu's approach to the world.

A frame is often dismissed as just a point of view, but it is actually quite different. A point of view usually has little objectivity, at least as we commonly think of it. To refer to 'her point of view' is shorthand for her biases, in ordinary conversation. A point of view is necessarily full of moral/ethical issues, so a point of view is of course biased. A common trick, by the way, in argument is to get the other side to accept that a persons argument is first just their 'point of view'; then that is then classified as biased and then by a trick of rhetoric, irrelevant because bias obviously isn't trustworthy. It's the jumps that confuse us all. Yes, bias has an effect, but to jump and argue bias negates all the value of the opinion is too great a leap.

A point of view can change from moment to moment, and so is usually thought of as a short-term perspective. A frame, grown (imposed) over longer thought and experience, is a larger view of the world and the situations that occur in it. Like a point of view, frames can and will change, but over the long term rather than short term. Life is too busy to rethink everything all the time, so we carry a set of mental frames to make sense of situations. As framing a building creates the building's structure, our mental frames define and create our worldview.

As F Scott Fitzgerald said:

"There was another silence, while Marjorie considered whether or not convincing her mother was worth the trouble. People over forty can seldom be permanently convinced of anything. At eighteen our convictions are hills from which we look; at forty-five they are caves in which we hide."[48]

Our mental frames freeze over time, and our ability to deal with the new diminishes unless we try hard to open our minds.

We are visual machines, but generally, we hate these overlapping diagrams like Figure 1. Why? I remember them from high school math class, and the teacher droning on and on about sets, and sub-sets, and the importance of the sub-set {a, c} in the larger set of {a, b, c, d, e . . }. Yeah, there's a big pile of stuff, and some of the stuff is in little circles by themselves but inside the big circle. So? This may be part of the explanation of my lack of success at higher math. Or my too early recognition of the essential reality of the situation. (There's a biased point of view!) In all truth, the number of times I've really needed algebra has been quite limited.

Let's go back over the diagram again. There are the three major circles, one the real world (for example, gravity), one the internal world (for example, hunger) and one the social world (for example, status checks). There are overlaps between the self, the real world, and the social structure. In the above case, no matter how hungry I am, I can't lick my food off the floor if gravity makes it spill at the bar. Fine, maybe if I'm really drunk or in a fraternity, but for most people, the food is just gone.

The simple idea of the overlaps, and by implication all the stuff out there in the areas that do not overlap, is considerably different than the way we think of the world. We think, as we make a decision, that we know everything relevant to that decision. Of course we don't, but we cross our fingers hopefully that we grasped the key elements and facts of the particular problem in front of us.

There are many other ways of drawing the relationships between the self, the real world and the social world. Are we completely absorbed by the real world? In a way yes, but also no. The self believes in many things not in the real world (magic, dreams, wishes, plans) and so at least part of the self is outside the real world. The social structure believes in many things not in the real world (such as people doing the 'right' thing, as that may be defined; that resources are infinite and under the control of society, for example) and deliberately denies the real world in many cases where social goals are considered more important that the real world, at least to the society. The real world is out there, doing as it pleases, and whether it has any interest in humans beyond any other life form, or any special interest in any life form for that matter, is a subject for intense debate. For these books purposes, we'll assume the real world takes care of itself and expects us to accommodate to it, not the other way around. If you develop a workable magic, I'd be glad to buy a wand and take classes, but until then the real world is what we have to conform to.

So, there are overlaps, and large areas where the worlds live happily outside each other. That's objectively true in our daily lives, if we sit back and think about it. It's clarifying the relationship that's hard, because they are dynamic and changing each minute. The self wants to believe a lot of things about the world, it's self, and society for it's own purposes. Society wants the individuals to do a lot of things, including cooperate as the group wants and to please not kill each other without a good (authorized) reason, and the real world, as discussed, has it's own concerns. Pulling apart the threads of where we interact with the hard edges of the worlds is hard to do because often we don't realize that it's an issue. Figure 1 does make clear the overlaps-and non overlaps-and so makes clear the issues.

In looking at Figure 1 as applied to our various problems, where are the overlaps, and where are they not overlapping? It's essential for the mission critical parts of our life-i.e., staying alive to the next day-that there are effective overlaps. Even monks who condemn the real world as an evil fantasy still have to eat. The ideal position to be in is to have the self at rest and centered in the world, a congruence of the self, the real world and the social world. Mind like water, as David Allen says. For that one needs to understand what our overlaps between the real world, society and the self for each particular problem situation, as best we can, and be open to adjustment as things change.

Because there is an infinity of overlaps, varying with each problem and opportunity we face, staying in the overlaps is often difficult. Life being a continuing process, the overlaps change constantly, requiring monitoring a myriad of events. Many of the events in the real world deny what we want, so we don't want to hear them, and many of the events are legitimately hard to monitor. Working within complex systems, which is what life is, we use habit and heuristics, a set of quick rules that has worked in the past to live by. This worked reasonably well for a simple hunting society, as shown by the increases in the village population. Perhaps not so well for a deeply interconnected economic world where crop failures half a world away mean your daily bread has jumped 20% - or more likely, the price of gas for your car to earn the daily bread.

There are good reasons that highways use visual symbols. First, because its almost impossible to read text at 70 MPH. (what was that city name on that sign?) Even more importantly, a visual goes right to the mind, skipping the interpretation and ambiguity that words bring. 'Merge right' is clearer on a sign that shows your lane going away. There is no thought, no interpretation, just clarity. That's the reason that Figure 1 can be so helpful, because a diagram goes straight to the mind, it's meaning and options jumping out at you. What Figure 1 does is to force you to actually see your assumptions, over and over.

Normally, when we start doing 'something' we may momentarily reflect on our assumptions, but then jump right into action, freeze the assumptions into concrete and erect the structure of our plan on the assumptions. Assumptions change just like everything else does as a project/plan/life goes on. Figure 1 makes you aware of your assumptions, so you can think (whether or not you want to) about whether the assumptions and basic ideas changing as the overlaps realign. If you are seeing things in the overlaps that you didn't see before, then your worldview is changing, and that changes everything. Perhaps good, perhaps not, Figure 1 reminds us that despite our human need for control, we have little control and less knowledge about the worlds that we are trying to influence.

COMPROMISE AND THE RIVER.

It sounds like a County-Western song, which it certainly could be. Compromise is how life goes wrong. Visually, a river flows from high ground to low ground, cutting the channel through the soft soil, finding the path of least resistance to the water pressure. And there is pressure: more water is coming every moment, and it has to go somewhere.

You start with a life plan. Implicit in that plan are the parameters, the boundaries outside which the plan just doesn't make sense anymore. If you are driving somewhere, you stay on the road because cars don't do well in swamps. Time goes by. Ten years later, just like the river, you are way outside the boundaries that you started with. The car is in the mud up to the fenders. If you are feeling frustrated, strained, pulled, the most obvious reason is that you are trying to be Dr. Reed Richards, the rubber band man, holding together an irrelevant plan and completely changed facts.

Figure 1 is here to help us win, not just as annoyance. It is not meant to be an extension of your third grade teacher who clearly pointed out your errors at every turn. Loudly, to the class. The fascinating book "The Black Swan" points out how surprises occur despite everyone's intentions. That book had many examples of Black Swans, but not many methods (at least that I grasped) for spotting them before they sit on you. Figure 1 gives you a method to grasp Black Swans before the event. Look at the social world and real world overlaps. There is a certain amount of physical reality that is not perceived, or the data ignored, and a certain amount of social reality not based on physical reality. A socially constructed reality that is not congruent with physical reality but despite that incongruence is convinced that the real world is going to cooperate, is going to be a Black Swan.

THINKING

Bored with Figure 1? Here's another perspective on why it is important. When we encounter something new (that's anything that we don't recognize it based on prior experience) we make sense of it by associating it with something familiar. In other words, we ignore much of the difference and accent the similar. That's good and bad.

> "What category you place something in has a huge influence on how you view its basic properties," says Arthur Markman, a professor of psychology at the University of Texas in Austin. "The category signals not only a set of features to expect, but at a more basic level, when and how you should use the novel item."[49]

Depending upon what cues we are given, we will place the same item in different categories. That makes sense, but once an item is in a category, we don't go back to change our minds. Why would we? There's too much new coming in to reprocess the old, and worse, we might recognize that we made a mistake the first time. If we made one mistake, then who knows what else we've done? So once it's forced into the slot, it's there. That's even truer in the social world than in the personal world, because a personal mistake (ok, misperception) can be recognized in the quiet of the night. A social mistake is shouted by the crowd, and never forgotten, so if you are enmeshed in society, trying to gain and keep respect, you don't make (or at least admit) mistakes.

A human's greatest strength, compared to other creatures, and thus our greatest weakness, is the way we think. We think more capably than any other creature on the earth. At least, as far as we can check, or want to check. Having opposable thumbs seems to have helped a lot, but that is a topic for another book. Our thinking has brought us, abet not directly, to a level of technology and quality of life undreamed by our ancestors. It's the 'not directly' that is part of the problem.

Rarely has overall conceptual planning worked, and why should it? Any over all conceptual plan requires a grasp of the whole system, and a grasp of the 'whole system' dealing with the earth and cosmos isn't possible. So one limits the problem to something workable, then pulls at the problem before you, and does the best with it one can. It's the pulling on the problem before you to one's own best interest, and everyone else pulling on their problems to their own best interest, that has gotten us to where we are now. The Problem Fairy has a sense of humor, though. Eventually, each of our best interests conflict in hidden and time delayed ways. There is another set of Black Swans! The capacity of people to do evil in the name of evil is quite limited, but the power of people to do evil in the name of the good is essentially unlimited. Everyone works very hard in their best interests, fighting for what is best for them and eventually those conflicts are going to be a very large problem. Morally upright and hard working farmers accidently causing dead areas in the ocean, for example.

Figure 1 is here to help our analysis of situations. This graphical device is necessary because of the limits of our thought. We only have stories. Without a story, we lose attention and drift off, or, more likely, create out of whole cloth a story that works for us for the moment, hang the real world and the consequences. We create myth's to explain the backdrop, the unknown, and we require others to buy into our myths because we are uncomfortable if they do not buy in.

While this may seem like a step outside simple planning, the old, big myths are badly damaged because we make a symbol the reality. As the perception of the symbol changes, it then twists the big stories, and people don't like that, because without myth to bridge the three worlds, the worlds pull apart. Communication lost between the self and the social, between the self and the real world. And so are we lost, adrift in a stormy sea, without meaning, having rejected our inspiration. Who would want that? Not only does it sound bad, it feels worse. So we freeze to the old myth, denying the world, or jump to another myth, and freeze to that. Neither is really a successful approach. As planning is accomplishing our goals, anything that confuses our goals is going to damage our planning.

We are the same creature that our ancient ancestors were, but we ignore what we are, deny what we are, for a picture created and endorsed by the social structures that surround and enfold us. While we can perhaps turn our back somewhat on the social structures, we can't turn our back on the real world because that is what keeps us alive. The social structures are not the real world, the social structures are only a shared set of assumptions, paper and tinsel covering some of the hard edges of the real world.

In a way, part of us recognizes this. We identify, in a way, with the horror movies set in the far hills, away from civilization. The people in the hills define themselves outside our extensive social rules, they accept themselves as outsides, and they hate the trained city folk on ill-fated vacations that come their way. Each of us is happy with the way we have cut up the world, and hate those who want to make fun of our ideas and change us. The hill people have a simple way of resolving the problem that isn't available to the rest of us. Now, movies being morality plays, the hill people always lose in the end, but not until they have a good and emotionally satisfying run.

Let's take a short digression before focusing on the details of the overlaps on the central diagram. Let's think again about worldviews. Now, society and each of us has a worldview that defines what the world is 'really' like, and what should happen in that world. In reality, each of us has many worldviews, but we like to think that we have a central worldview that defines 'me'. The same with societies, and that overall worldview is critically important. People can (and do) die when they challenge that central worldview, because it makes others uncomfortable. Other than provide continued employment for editorial writers who can moan that we have left the path of revealed truth, our worldview carries moral and ethical rules with it, and those rules that are embodied in our legal statutes.

Worldviews are carefully bounded. They are a big frame, limiting what's important and what isn't. There are many (perhaps most – reflect on 'vice') actions, emotions and thoughts that are pushed outside the nice organized worldview. Now, any bounded worldview is going to have a fast and loose relationship with actual reality. There are many facets of reality: for example, there is the reality of the outer world intertwined with the reality that our society has decided is 'right', and the reality of the outer world intertwined with the 'reality' we think possible for yourself. Generally, reality is ignored (at the social and individual level) whenever possible for the pretty story of a consistent, controlled world by society, and for the pretty story of an internal world for the self that makes us the masters of our fate.

The problem is that a society can damage and partly destroy the external world the society is dependent on if we ignore the external world and assume that the external world can and will be what we want. The real world adjusts, and leaves the bones of the society drying in the desert. We want to avoid that if we can. Look at the wasted farmland turned to desert over the centuries as the land is over-cultivated, all of the lost civilizations buried in the dust of time. There was a time when the tribe could just move on to the next plot of land, but that time is long gone. If the oceans are fished out, there isn't another ocean to move to.

And it's the same for our internal self. If you pretend to be something you are not, persist in ignoring what you really want; your life will be tasteless and empty. Society, being accumulated knowledge, knows enough to blame your ennui on yourself and your failure to do what society wants, but it's your ignoring yourself that is the root. All of this may seem a bit far afield in a book on planning, but planning starts with goals and assumptions. If your goals and assumptions are no good, your plans are not likely to succeed.

Here's an example of what happens with the wrong worldview. As you might guess, it's nothing good. "Forbidden Planet" was a movie made in the 1950's. An incredibly advanced civilization inputs all their knowledge into a master computer that runs their world, we would guess to let them lie back in luxury, but they make one small error. They input all their rational and logical stories into the machine-but also their irrational selves. Perhaps the plan specifications were drawn poorly, or maybe you just can't trust programmers. That irrational self takes control, and essentially destroys their pretty logical world. Surprise! Forbidden Planet was a place you can't go to, because you discover that humans are more than the rational animal, more than the masks and veneers that society papers over us for control. It's forbidden because it opens up thinking about the deeper parts of the creature, what the creature really is, and the stories can't allow that.

Forbidden Planet was destroyed because their worldview didn't include the chaotic and dark unconscious. Perhaps they were not as advanced as they liked to think. They ignored the unconscious, and the unconscious doesn't like that. The movie was way ahead of its time. The 1950's were a time of rationality. Clean, orderly, bright and uncluttered modern was the style, for a new world moving away from the dark anger that in the old world had exploded into war-over and over. The new rationality would stop this dark, destructive behavior. Forbidden Planet says wait, you can't walk away from the unconscious, it's stronger than you think. I'm not sure the movie was ever really recognized for the challenge that it was to the new 'authorized stories'. Deny it as we will, even the 'rational' stories are mythical at their heart.

In reality, the unconscious is everything about our internal self. The conscious can juggle perhaps seven items at once, so it's not the controller of the self. The conscious is more a spin-master than a controller, a generator of socially allowed explanations for the actions the conscious justifies. The consciousness is a sports announcer, giving the play-by-play, inventing explanations and causes where they don't exist. We are creatures, like other creatures in many ways, and the creature is the dark, irrational animal as well as-perhaps more than-the thinking being we show in public.

The unconscious is focused on the minutia of life-breathing, walking, keeping the incredibly complex systems in balance, and perhaps the unconscious just lets consciousness run loose, because generally consciousness isn't doing all that much. Too many books focus on a false image of the consciousness, shouting about what can be done if you focus your consciousness. In reality, most of what they say can't be done, because your moving force is way under the consciousness, and all the pretty sayings and pious words just leave a warm feeling on the consciousness. As you are much the same at 35 as you were at 3 in the basic aspects of your personality, it's obvious that reading a book isn't going to do much to change that bedrock of a self.

This is disturbing, because it assaults that pretty view of us as calm, rational and in control. Sorry, but study after study is backing up the unconscious as running everything. At least it's a justification for relaxing, not being as stressed, because if you don't control, you might as well enjoy the trip. Flies and other creatures don't seem to have self-esteem issues, which are probably good for the flies, because flies are detested by everything they run into, except the things that eat them. Doesn't seem to bother them in the slightest.

The cry for rationality that the modern world was shouting for was a reaction against the terrors of the early Twentieth century. First, in 1914, when the world had never seemed so rational, and all proudly said that progress was clearly a straight line heading towards what should be. It was a straight line to hell in the trenches. World War I tore the thin veneer of rationality off of the howling emotions and it wasn't pretty. World War II just continued the show. And today? We live on Forbidden Planet, where the raging unconscious is trying to destroy civilization.

Poster child 1 is the Islamic fundamentalists, lusting for a 13th century that never existed, listening only to the story that they want to hear as they use the tools of the modern world against that world. Old men, all twisted emotions and lust and hatred, preaching to the empty and angry. Which is pretty much the same story for all religious fundamentalists:

> "The nihilist's question why, (wrote Nietzsche) is a product of his earlier habitude of expecting an aim to be given to be set for him from without - i.e., by some superhuman authority or other. When the nihilist has learned not to believe in such a thing, he goes on just the same, from habit, looking for another authority or some kind that will be able to speak unconditionally and set goals and tasks by command."[50]

When I saw Forbidden Planet many years ago, it seemed to say that the unconscious could-and should-be avoided. The brave explorers left the planet (that spaceship lifted off with as much thrust as it could) and Forbidden Planet was marked on the star charts as a "NO". That's not going to work and we just fool ourselves by marking off that area on the charts with the caption 'here be monsters'. 'Here be Monster's' indeed, and while the movie creates the oddest feeling of almost terror at it's vision of the advanced race as just confused, irrational creatures, that vision is real.

If you push away, deny the existence of the invisible creature in the Forbidden Planet, your plans are not going to work. Oh, they may limp along today and tomorrow, but eventually that train is going off the track. What the world usually does is blame the closest onlooker and go back to the plan that we all had, but as said before, the tribe can't pick up and move to a new field to over-cultivate. We've got to work with what we've got. And the vision of the movie is accurate – a disconnect of the emotions from the rational is as dangerous as it gets.

CHAPTER 7. THINKING ABOUT THE OVERLAPS.

Many of the problems we have in life occur because we are looking for a result in the real world, but not acting in the real world for the result. We instead look inside ourselves, or our friend's opinions and/or in societies endorsement for or against. If we want the house to be painted blue, then we'd better get a paintbrush and blue paint and go at it. If the house isn't blue, but is, say, red, then thinking the house is blue, persuading our friends that the house is blue, and/or getting important, self assured people in society to say the house is blue isn't really going to change the fact that the house is red. While that sounds foolish, there are many, many cases where that is exactly what we do everyday.

> *"In ancient times,*
> *skillful warriors first made*
> *themselves invincible,*
> *and then watched for vulnerability*
> *in their opponents."[51]*
> *Chapter 4: "FORMATION"*

So, the first step in planning is to decide whether we want the house blue, or whether we want to play pretend. Knowing what we really want is what matters in planning. Sometimes pretend works just fine, but often playing pretend is the prelude to disaster. A haunting refrain in a minor key, hinting at the darkness ahead, actually, as you hum the tune walking down a dark pathway.

Does anyone doubt that the circles 'the real world' and the circle 'the self' only partially overlap? There are far galaxies full of stars and vast, incomprehensible energies in the real world that really have nothing to do with our daily lives. There are deep emotions and desires in our self that have little to do with actions in the real world. In our dreams we can fly, but we can't. How many of us, as children, stood on something relatively high with a cape wrapped about us and jumped off? Flying like superman can't be done, but it works just fine in our dreams. That's a simple example, but I think it makes the point.

And the overlap is rather less than we generally think it is. If you can't directly sense something: touch, smell, see, hear, taste it, then your information about the item is at least somewhat a concept, an extrapolation from some sensory information and other information. Even if you can directly sense it, there is more to the real world object that what you can sense about it.

The overlap between the self and the real world varies dramatically depending on what we want to accomplish. Depending on whether we see things as more important from our perspective, the social perspective, or the real world, the overlaps are going to differ. Crossing a busy highway has a lot of real world/self overlap, and it's really, really important to get it right, or you are road kill. Deciding what to eat for a late night snack overlaps what's available (real world) and some social niceties, but by and large, it's personal preferences, a lot of the 'self' circle that is doing the choosing. Surfing questionable Internet sites and letting your mind loose has a lot of internal, and very little external world overlap. Oh, there is the NSA tracking your every move and mouse click, but that's not really apparent.

Thinking and doing are vastly different things, and the overlaps change dramatically. That sounds trivial and silly, but each of us can think of things that we thought through and then tried, only to find we hadn't judged the overlaps correctly at all. A simple example would be thinking about throwing a spitball in class (sheer pleasure) and actually throwing the spitball (many consequences). So we have all of these maps/plans that flip out in and out of mind unnoticed.

Thinking, we can drift over the differences in the overlaps between the self and the real world. So what's the problem? It's where the maps are not appropriate, but we don't notice it. The following is a little children's story that has plans, assumptions and failed assumed overlaps between the real world and the self by all the participants.

"One day Brer Fox thought of how Brer Rabbit had been cutting up his capers and bouncing around until he'd come to believe that he was the boss of the whole gang. Brer Fox thought of a way to lay some bait for that uppity Brer Rabbit.

He went to work and got some tar and mixed it with some turpentine. He fixed up a contraption that he called a Tar-Baby. When he finished making her, he put a straw hat on her head and sat the little thing in the middle of the road. Brer Fox, he lay off in the bushes to see what would happen.

Well, he didn't have to wait long either, 'cause by and by Brer Rabbit came pacing down the road--lippity-clippity, clippity-lippity--just as sassy as a jaybird. Brer Fox, he lay low. Brer Rabbit came prancing along until he saw the Tar-Baby and then he sat back on his hind legs like he was astonished. The Tar-Baby just sat there, she did, and Brer Fox, he lay low.

"Good morning!" says Brer Rabbit, says he. "Nice weather we're having this morning," says he.

Tar-Baby didn't say a word, and Brer Fox, he lay low.

"How are you feeling this morning?" says Brer Rabbit, says he.

Brer Fox, he winked his eye real slow and lay low and the Tar-Baby didn't say a thing.

"What is the matter with you then? Are you deaf?" says Brer Rabbit, says he. "Cause if you are, I can holler louder," says he.

The Tar-Baby stayed still and Brer Fox, he lay low.

"You're stuck-up, that's what's wrong with you. You think you're too good to talk to me," says Brer Rabbit, says he. "And I'm going to cure you, that's what I'm going to do," says he.

Brer Fox started to chuckle in his stomach, he did, but Tar-Baby didn't say a word.

"I'm going to teach you how to talk to respectable folks if it's my last act," says Brer Rabbit, says he. "If you don't take off that hat and say howdy, I'm going to bust you wide open," says he.

Tar-Baby stayed still and Brer Fox, he lay low.

Brer Rabbit kept on asking her why she wouldn't talk and the Tar-Baby kept on saying nothing until Brer Rabbit finally drew back his fist, he did, and blip--he hit the Tar-Baby on the jaw. But his fist stuck and he couldn't pull it loose. The tar held him. But Tar-Baby, she stayed still, and Brer Fox, he lay low.

"If you don't let me loose, I'm going to hit you again," says Brer Rabbit, says he, and with that he drew back his other fist and blap--he hit the Tar-Baby with the other hand and that one stuck fast too.

Tar-Baby she stayed still, and Brer Fox, he lay low.

"Turn me loose, before I kick the natural stuffing out of you," says Brer Rabbit, says he, but the Tar-Baby just sat there.

She just held on and then Brer Rabbit jumped her with both his feet. Brer Fox, he lay low. Then Brer Rabbit yelled out that if that Tar-Baby didn't turn him loose, he was going to butt her crank-sided. Then he butted her and his head got stuck.

Brer Fox walked out from behind the bushes and strolled over to Brer Rabbit, looking as innocent as a mockingbird.

"Howdy, Brer Rabbit," says Brer Fox, says he. "You look sort of stuck up this morning," says he. And he rolled on the ground and laughed and laughed until he couldn't laugh anymore.

By and by he said, "Well, I expect I got you this time, Brer Rabbit," says he. "Maybe I don't, but I expect I do. You've been around here sassing after me a mighty long time, but now it's the end.

And then you're always getting into something that's none of your business," says Brer Fox, says he. "Who asked you to come and strike up a conversation with this Tar-Baby? And who stuck you up the way you are? Nobody in the round world. You just jammed yourself into that Tar-Baby without waiting for an invitation," says Brer Fox, says he. "There you are and there you'll stay until I fix up a brushpile and fire it up, "cause I'm going to barbecue you today, for sure," says Brer Fox, says he.

Then Brer Rabbit started talking mighty humble.

"I don't care what you do with me, Brer Fox, says he, "Just so you don't fling me in that briar patch. Roast me, Brer Fox, says he, "But don't fling me in that briar patch."

"It's so much trouble to kindle a fire," says Brer Fox, says he, "that I expect I'd better hang you," says he.

"Hang me just as high as you please, Brer Fox, says Brer Rabbit, says he, "but for the Lord's sake, don't fling me in that briar patch," says he.

"I don't have any string, " says Brer Fox, says he, "Now I expect I had better drown you, " says he.

"Drown me just as deep as you please, Brer Fox," says Brer Rabbit, says he, "But please do not fling me in that briar patch, " says he.

"There's no water near here," says Brer Fox, says he, "And now I reckon I'd better skin you," says he.

"Skin me Brer Fox," says he. "Snatch out my eyeballs, tear out my ears by the roots," says he, "But please, Brer Fox, don't fling me in that briar patch, " says he.

Of course, Brer Fox wanted to get Brer Rabbit as bad as he could, so he caught him by the behind legs and slung him right in the middle of the briar patch. There was a considerable flutter when Brer Rabbit struck the bushes, and Brer Fox hung around to see what was going to happen.

By and by he heard someone call his name and 'way up on the hill he saw Brer Rabbit sitting cross-legged on a chinquapin log combing the tar pitch out of his hair with a chip. Then Brer Fox knew he had been tricked.

Brer Rabbit hollered out, "Born and bred in the briar patch. I was born and bred in the briar patch!" And with that he skipped out just as lively as a cricket in the embers of a fire. (Retold by Catharine Farrell from a story retold by Joel Chandler Harris)[52]

B'rer Rabbit had a mental map that he first used to relate to other creatures, which didn't work at all with the Tar Baby. Once faced with the true problem by B'rar Fox's taunts, B'rar Rabbit moved to a new map that worked. B'rer Fox, having caught the Rabbit, was so focused on his hatred for the rabbit that he slid over what really was a real world punishment for a rabbit.

As an aside, there are many 'tar babies' out there, a type of 'clearing the swamp and up to your ass in alligators' situation. Anytime you start a problem and are hopelessly trapped in a part of the problem so that you no longer see the original problem, you may have a tar baby stuck to you. The only solution is to stop hitting and start thinking. But first you've got to back up in the battle and think that this might, maybe, be a tar baby and a complete waste of time. It's hard, because the 'come on' for a tar baby is that it's important and must be acted on. Now!

Brer Rabbit is an example of why of "No Battle Plan ever survives the first contact with the enemy". Why would that be? We've done our research, we have assessed the enemy's strengths and weaknesses, our strengths and weaknesses, we used spy's to assess the enemy's goals, assessed our goals, and we're on top of the situation. So why is this always true? Because, as Brer Fox and Rabbit found out, the overlaps in our minds between the self and the real world don't match the real world that we are acting in. Partly because we thought about what we wanted, not the real world, and partly because we can't get all the information we need to make a decision.

A very good article (only selected parts presented) which points out how we jump over critical parts in decision making, is:

> Roughly speaking, there are four steps to every decision. First, you perceive a situation. Then you think of possible courses of action. Then you calculate which course is in your best interest. Then you take the action.

> Over the past few centuries, public policy analysts have assumed that step three is the most important. Economic models and entire social science disciplines are premised on the assumption that people are mostly engaged in rationally calculating and maximizing their self-interest.

> But during this financial crisis, that way of thinking has failed spectacularly. As Alan Greenspan noted in his Congressional testimony last week, he was "shocked" that markets did not work as anticipated. "I made a mistake in presuming that the self-interests of organizations, specifically banks and others, were such as that they were best capable of protecting their own shareholders and their equity in the firms."

> So perhaps this will be the moment when we alter our view of decision-making. Perhaps this will be the moment when we shift our focus from step three, rational calculation, to step one, perception.

> Perceiving a situation seems, at first glimpse, like a remarkably simple operation. You just look and see what's around. But the operation that seems most simple is actually the most complex; it's just that most of the action takes place below the level of awareness. Looking at and perceiving the world is an active process of meaning-making that shapes and biases the rest of the decision-making chain.

> . . . . . This meltdown is not just a financial event, but also a cultural one. It's a big, whopping reminder that the human mind is continually trying to perceive things that aren't true, and not perceiving them takes enormous effort. [53]David Brooks, The Behavioral Revolution

Thinking and knowing what you want is tough. The following is a rather long quote which presents many of the problems involved in discovering what you want to do and what options you have. Rather than just list them, its easier to follow in a story.

> "It has been more than a week since they fled to the mountains. Cali is sitting in a little room at a makeshift desk made of a door resting on two sawhorses. It's not much of an office, she decided. And, it's not much of a place, period. She thought about the damp running through the whole cave that the heating system was fighting a losing battle with. We can't stay here. Oh, it's pretty outside with all the trees and the river

quietly flowing by, but we have limited supplies and we are easy prey for an attack if they find us. There's one way into the cave, which means that there is only one way out. Even Paul's people can figure that out. I wonder if anyone has any plans? I'm almost afraid to ask. She sighed, stood up and wandered out. She spent the next couple of days talking to people, and her conclusion was that, generally, people were stunned and frozen.

Three days later, she was back at the makeshift desk. No reason to stay is a good reason to go. There isn't a lot of planning going on here. Mary's intent on getting Hal healthy, Lucifer is off running the attacks against Paul's people, and Jesus is trying to keep the businesses afloat as Paul's privateers attack on every front they can. Goth Girl is sleeping a lot. So, there are not a lot of volunteers for the job. All raise their hands who want Cali as chief planner? She raised her hand. "Thank you for your show of support," she announced to the desk. "If nominated I will not run, if elected I will not serve. Um...wrong speech."

She made notes for a few hours and then stared at all the piled-up paper. Nonsense, I need nonsense. I'm in a rut. She wandered off and watched a Looney Tunes DVD for a while. "Okay, my mind is cleared of any useful conscious thought," she declared to the wall, sitting at the desk. So what do we need? All you need is love? Actually, the basic human necessities are air, water, food, and shelter. So, we need: food for a bunch of people and ways of getting the food that are not really obvious, medical facilities, living space for a bunch of people—and we'll add people as time goes by—some kind of office/work areas, space for the kids to play. Then we need the more unusual, but more critical for us: Hiding? Deception? Allies? She did a rough calculation of the space needed and was shocked. Far more space was needed than they had at the warehouse. That's a lot of space!

She started poking at ideas, but kept finding herself enthusiastically detailing little sections of a plan. That would be helpful if the overall plan wasn't a travesty of a sham of a mockery. "And it won't work, either," she mumbled to herself. Okay, I'm not finding the correct scale for planning. What did the book say? The more uncertain we are, the more we over-plan, because a joyful immersion into minute detail means I don't have to confront the real problem. The bigger the threat, the stronger the desire to foresee all possibilities and every conceivable mishap. That's a plan that has "ruin" stamped in red letters all over it.

Two hours later, Cali was practicing her calligraphy, embroidering 'ruin' ornately in red on the last plan she had worked up. She groaned and wadded up the last set of notes. Nothing productive to show for it, and people are waiting for a decision and a plan, holding their breath, waiting for my brilliance to light the way. Um...some of them may have just keeled over from lack of oxygen, so I'm behind schedule. Okay, sit back and think here. Is this a complex problem, yes/no? It is. What are the ranges of choices I have in dealing with a complex problem? Start with the goals or jump into the mess and start pushing things around? I could size up a situation, one of those 'holding my thumb out to the world to measure it' like artists used to do, or I could do a rough outline, or I could just fall into a detailed analysis. Scratch the detailed analysis. That's failed so far.

What am I saying here? Over there... She put her right hand on the edge of the notepad. That is my perception of the situation in the real world. Over here... She put her left hand on the edge of the notepad. These are my goals. Little arrows, curves, and dashes connect the goals and the real world. Little curse marks are embroidered around the edges. If the problem is a static situation, I can crank out detailed steps. Of course, no meaningful problem is static and controlled.

A fluid, evolving situation takes rough strokes. Rough strokes with a paddle, if you have one. Up shit creek without a paddle? Failures at lots of levels there. Bang at the problem, and then bang again. Iterative—isn't that the word? Walk through once, then walk through again with changes, round and round the process until it's solved or you become dizzy, puke, and move on. Every problem has its own unique time problems, most of which are not conveniently highlighted in red. Some problems you can think about for a while, stop part way, and rethink because you can take a couple of shots at the problem. Some you get one frantic pass at. Come over, come over, red rover, ready or not! Okay, this is a 'one frantic pass.' That lessens the pressure?

Think! What did they say at that seminar? They said the key for any successful plan is 'what's the desired outcome?' If you know that, then you have focus, direction, and success criteria. In other words, I know what's winning and what does the finish line look like. Simple case is moi, in a flattering track suit, breaking the tape, the crowd cheering my victory? Here it is survival and prosperity for the whole group, and that's a lot more complex outcome. That desired outcome is the driver to the whole plan, and that's why it is a guaranteed disaster coming if I misstate the desired outcome.

Once that outcome is framed, then the mind starts thinking, really thinking. Actually, that's an easy picture, Cali decided. Everyone safe and secure, and we have resources and possibilities. Everything at its proper time and with proper attention to existing conditions? That's as useful as Proverbs, she grimaced. Pretty slogans with no traction. An inner process stands in need of outward criteria? So, when all the emotional handwringing doesn't work, let's start with what we have to work with in the real world. Let's get some external feedback.

Cali searched through files on the laptop and found the map she was looking for. So, here are all the properties owned or controlled by the companies, nicely marked with little circles. Exclusion criteria to start with: we can't use the productive plants; too many people around them would notice our merry band, and those plants are infiltrated by Paul's people for sure. He just seems to like that kind of stuff. She spent an hour working her way through the list, marking off one possibility after another.

Not so many left now, she realized, happier. Next, key constraints/inclusion criteria. We have a large group that stands out and that must be hidden. This mountain retreat is hidden, but it meets none of the other criteria. So it has to be a place in an urban area, essentially abandoned, where we also have friends. Hal's friend from Detroit? Of course—the guy with the sword! Detroit, she sighed, frowning. She looked at the map, and one of the few remaining possibilities was in Detroit. She'd been there many times while she was a student. She had taken classes at Wayne State University, deep in the combat zone, and had driven through the wastelands many times. Well, who would look for us there? Who would think we were that crazy? And who'd be crazy enough to come after us there? I remember what Hal and I were joking about years ago in the safe house in Ann Arbor, about hiding in Detroit from the cartel.

> "I suspect it would have been a broken-down apartment building in Detroit," Cali countered. "First, no one would go down there to find us, and second, if they did, there isn't anything worse they could do to us. They'd probably let us live."
> "Ugh," Hal grimaced. "I've been in those parts of town. They probably would let us live. Heck, we'd have jobs at the liquor store behind the bulletproof glass."

No jobs behind the bulletproof glass! Not part of the desired outcome. And we have toys. Sensors. We can tap into energy sources off the grid and so hidden from the grid. Then we don't show up, we are just little ghosts, flitting shadows in the night. While you can't hide in this modern world, you can deceive. That's actually easier than it used to be, because people only see what they look for, and we will set up a picture they won't question. We can't build a fortress that can't be scaled, but we can build one they wouldn't bother with.

What would Hal think? Cali wondered, starting to cry. She'd talked to Lungorthin about the battle two days ago, finally having the strength to deal with the memories.

"He knew," Lungorthin admitted, "what was coming. I've seen that look before, when you know death will come for you. And he stood and fought, knowing." Lungorthin studied her thoughtfully. "Nothing more could have been asked of anyone. You should be proud."

Proud? Cali thought through her tears. Pride is a small reed for strength. I'm Hector's wife, Andromache, with my child, waiting for the evil to come. She held her head, despairing for a moment. But Hal's doing better, she thought, determined, wiping her tears away. He will be fine. Mary promised. He must have a place to go so he can recover. I just have to find it. Frustrated, she wadded up the papers and threw them at the wall. They separated mid-flight into a snowfall of paper, a small drift leaning against the wall.

"So, when faced with two choices, simply toss a coin," she advised the wall. "It works, not because it settles the question for you, but because in that brief moment when the coin is in the air, you suddenly know what you are hoping for. "Sure, I'm game." She fished in her purse for a coin. Her fingers found an ancient drachma that Mary had given her as a gift. I like that, feeling the weight in her hand. She flipped the coin in the air and saw a vision of an old factory in Detroit. That's easy. I didn't even have to pick heads or tails. She carefully put the coin back in her purse. A scene from an old movie flashed before her.

> *Dr. Klahn: The CIA thinks they can infiltrate the Mountain of Dr. Klahn!*
> *CIA Agent: You can't scare me, you slant-eyed yellow bastard.*
> *Dr. Klahn: Take him to...Detroit!*
> *CIA Agent: No! No, not Detroit! No! No, please! Anything but that! No! No!*

She laughed out loud. Like Mao's Long March to the country. I wonder if I can get people to carry me on a litter like they did him! Pithy advice time, where is The Art of War ? The complete guide to life, albeit slightly cynical. All warfare is based on deception. I like that. If you hide your form, conceal your tracks, and always remain strictly prepared— then you can be invulnerable yourself. Yup, that's where we want to be.

Okay, one small, last problem. How do I sell this to the group? And how do we move?"[54]

Cali had a very complex situation to work through. The group had been pushed out of the world they were used to, and had to figure out a new system before being able to step into it to test it. It was a totally new situation, tied tightly to many other new systems. She had to decide what she wanted, what was possible, grasping possible overlaps, and then move to a solution that would work. It's not easy. Using real world constraints are helpful in something as large as this, because it is easy to get lost in the probable. Focusing down on the possible forces a structure.

The goal of this chapter was to start thinking about the overlaps. They are not revealed, crystallized truth by any means. Each person's overlaps are different from every other persons, and they change each minute. Thinking about the overlaps, testing the ideas and how they can work for you is the essential thing. The stories you generate with Figure 1 are asymmetric stories, stories that you wrote yourself, not stories just handed off to you.

CHAPTER 8. THE INDIVIDUAL & THE REAL WORLD

The starting point is that 'reality' for an individual is something quite different than 'reality' for society and both are different from the raw, unfiltered rocks and bugs out there in the real world. The self has a world construct that focuses on what the individual wants. Grumbling, we accept what it can get. We live our lives within a rich, complex world, which is more or less internally consistent. It would be a lot more consistent if it wasn't for the external world and the social worlds poking at us and our fantasies, but that's the way it is.

We tie our inner world to the outer world by data points touching the real world. Our perceptions admit the real world to the extent that the external world forces us to pay attention to them. Quite frankly we try and ignore them and deny them as much as possible, but occasionally you have to pay attention. It's another version of balloon example earlier. We stretch our story over the worlds data points as best we can, and are as disappointed as a child is when our story doesn't work anymore and the balloon breaks.

Traditionally, we look at conscious thought, blaming or praising it for our actions and choices. In reality, our unconscious controls us. The human creature is the dark, irrational animal far more than the rational thinking face we put on everyday to show others. The creature is so focused on the minutia of life-breathing, walking, talking, digesting, lusting-that perhaps the unconscious lets the consciousness run loose, because consciousness generally it isn't doing that much.

Now consciousness, tense, concerned and focused, would argue with that, but consciousness is a bubble, filled with thoughts from the unconscious. After all, the conscious can hold approximately seven thoughts in mind at once. If consciousness had to run the body, by the time you back out walking, talking, breathing, heartbeat, digestion well, it's past carrying capacity right there. Too many books pretend our consciousness actually runs the show and then demand you act consciously on their rational arguments. The message of a book may go into the unconscious and then something comes back out, but that's still the unconscious running the show.

Carl Jung's thought tends to be discounted by our rationalist world, but his concept of archetypes is fascinating. Perhaps the archetypes and underlying wiring that he argued for are actually in our DNA, jumbled stored memories and learning from the past survivors of the chaos of life. Stepping back, trying to open to the unconscious, just accepting what's fed from the unconscious into the consciousness is difficult, because it's just not how we are taught. If you actually can sit back, relaxing and let the consciousness drop the reins (at least from the consciousness's point of view) it's fascinating how little the consciousness really does. What the consciousness does do well is enjoy the moments and experiences of life, if you let consciousness drop the pretense of control. So those beer commercials where people are sitting in a chair on the beach on a sunny day have tapped into a deeper truth.

"That's encouraging, I think," Mary answered. "Jung said to reject all projections. Don't identify the men you meet with your anima projection. Don't identify yourself with your persona projection. To release all projections and ideals. And he also said, don't think so much! What did Campbell say? People talk about trying to learn the meaning of life. Life has no meaning. What's the meaning of a flower? What we are looking for is to experience life. And we push away life by naming, translating, and classifying every experience that comes to us. Time to stop, I think."[55]

Now, this has drifted a bit from a spotlight focus on planning in the real world, or at least from way that planning books usually approach the topic. Why? You can't plan for what YOU want in the real world unless you know yourself-anything else is just pretend. This section looks at the rather loose relationships between the self, the social world, and the real world, and what this means about how we really think and perceive. Why is this important? Because the relationships are far different from what we blithely assume the world, and our relation to it, is.

We function according to our internal mental models, which are created by our minds absolute necessity to form (and believe) explanations of events. They are models of reality, little sketches and pieces pasted together from experience and thought, tempered by impacting reality. We live for and by causality and so we don't like or accept randomness. Our mental models are critical because they are the stories that we use to understand our experiences, how we predict the expected outcomes of our actions, and as tools to handle unexpected occurrences.

Our experiences may have been real, partly real or wholly imagined. That is, we stub our toe, we see another stub their toe, or we read about a person stubbing their toe. We skip over the differences when in a hurry, but those are quite different types of knowledge.

By three methods we may learn wisdom: First, by reflection, which is noblest; Second, by imitation, which is easiest; and third by experience, which is the bitterest. Confucius

We may be simple and naïve or complex and sophisticated, but we still construct mental models from fragmentary evidence that pops up before us because time is short and experience limited.

We create models on the fly, and as long as they seem to work, we slide by with generally a poor understanding of what may really be happening. We do that because no one has time to question everything, and that's certainly true, but we still often act on rules used just because they worked the last time. Rules that worked in a different situation, but we gloss over the small print. We, often unconsciously, determine causes, mechanisms, and relationships where there are none. Mental models matter.

"How do we know change?" Hal asked. "How do we know what's actually happening? We read, talk to people, get someone's take on something they think happened. Anecdotes are not data—probably the world's most neglected truism. And the categories we use, sloppy moral categories like 'powerful and powerless', or 'selfish and altruistic', are manipulated and misleading. Every newspaper uses facts, woven carefully into both a story people will pay money for and that the newspaper can't be sued for."

"Perceiving a situation should be a simple operation," Hal continued. "You just look and see what's around you. The problem is that surface simplicity appears because your mind has weeded out almost all of the events actually going on around you. Only a few things are pushed up to consciousness. What's pushed into consciousness is a complex calculation based on many factors, almost all of which we are unaware of. Imagine a circle labeled 'physical reality/real world.' Then another circle labeled 'social reality," and finally, a third circle, labeled 'your perceptions.' The circles overlap a bit, but a lot less than you'd guess. Now, that's important because, for example, where you have a strongly held social reality that doesn't actually overlap with the 'real world,' that's black swan territory. A train wreck in process."[56]

So, you have to ask yourself, what's the underlying model of the world you use? It's important because we use that model to compare events to, to recognize change. There are two possible encompassing models, really. First, a model that insists everything could be known, if we had better information, the classical mechanistic view of the universe. God the watchmaker, lots of little gears clicking away. Or, on the other hand, a quantum model that argues the future is unknowable, not just unknown. If you have an unknowable future, you act and think a lot differently than if you are constantly looking for the gears of the clock structure poking through. Watching is astrology and omens, reading the tea leaves for hints of the already fixed to come. Unknowable is collecting information and seeing what it adds to, improvising with events."

I have to confess that the world is totally different than I thought it was when I was young. I thought, foolish person, that the world was rational and rational seeking. All of that Cartesian "I think therefore I am", the world rationally seeking optimization and best choices. It turns out that the world is irrational (by human standards, not by the worlds), that humans use rationality only when necessary, and in the end we must do what the deep emotions want-as twisted by the formal rational language. That's a big difference! If you look back at Figure 1, most of the circle 'self' in the diagram is outside both the real world and the social world, and we are perfectly happy that way.

DAILY MAGIC

I'm going to argue that there is a very important idea that we live with and by every day but pretend to ignore. Truly the elephant in the room, in each day of our lives, the 'Daily Magic' is critical to us. What is the daily magic? It's our constant personification and creation of a world around us that we do without thinking. Thinking, in fact, disparages all the daily magic and the warm world that we wrap around ourselves. But we use the daily magic constantly. The classical example is a philosophy professor-or a physics professor-who after releasing the bowling ball, twists their body to make the ball move as they want it to do.

This is really important, if for no other reason than because we live within the daily magic, you have to change your daily magic rituals and belief's for real change. As the daily magic comes from the unconscious, you can see the challenge.

We all believe, in our hearts, in magic. Not to be disrespectful, but faith is a type of magic-have faith and certain things happen, just because. The magic that we live by, that we instinctively believe, such as do good and good will come to you, or bad things are punishment for evil actions is evidently part of our wiring and incorporated in our formal religions. One of the biggest problems for any religion is the ugly question of why bad things happen to good people. There are lots of answers over the centuries: the good were just faking it, bad things are tests, the rituals were not followed correctly, what you perceive as bad is really good, but it's an ugly question. It was faced most accurately, I think, in Job, where Job was told, in no uncertain terms, that the world wasn't made for him-or humans, and that the world is what it is, beyond humans. That's not particularly emotionally satisfying, and our internal daily magic doesn't like that very much.

It's essential, if we want to understand ourselves and our choices, to understand and embrace the daily magic. Deny the daily magic, and your emotions will make you pay. Doubt this? Test yourself. Think about the little things you do as daily magic, and how upset you are when others interfere or destroy the your little spells. I don't have an academic study reporting results from bored undergraduates based on unclear procedures and statistical manipulations-this one you can assess yourself.

Lots look at investing, which is truly a magical activity. It's all about the future, golden rewards for good guesses, and little good information to work with. People have a hunch, have a feeling-intuition about the likelihood that investments will do well or poorly and their own decisions to invest. These are innermost thoughts, thoughts that we do not have to explain or justify to others. "Magical thinking" or "quasi-magical thinking" is the feeling that certain actions will make people 'lucky' even if they know logically that the actions cannot have an effect on their fortunes. It's needed, because you are sitting here with something, a pile of money. Make a mistake, and it's all gone, but do right and it's a bigger pile and you have really no solid guide to rely on that can tell you what the right thing to do is. It's emotion, in the end, and recognizing that can help us evaluate our choices more carefully.

The daily magic is everywhere. Superstition is doing something that you don't understand, and it's all daily magic. Athletes wear lucky clothing and follow ritual and magical patterns before games and training. Sports fans have lucky clothing, lucky seating, rituals that have worked before. There's no shame in it, and it's actually quite enjoyable.

The daily magic is vastly different from the Harry Potter magic. Harry Potter is a world where some people have it and some don't, and you are just born with it or not. Those who have then can study and increase their powers, controlled by magic words, deeds and potions. Magic, in the Harry Potter world, is the classical scribe's knowledge wrapped in a dark blanket to protect the scribe's livelihood.

The daily magic does hold a very great danger. The daily magic is a power that surrounds us and envelops us and holds us just like the force in the Star Wars movies. Unfortunately the daily magic has really no connection with reality, certainly no power over reality and yet we hold onto it all the tighter because of that. It's the romance of Star Wars, the excitement of the Harry Potter movies that the daily magic could actually controls the outside world. It's absolutely critical to recognize the emotional importance of the daily magic to yourself, honor that but at the same time recognize that complete powerlessness the daily magic has over the real world. Don't, just because you feel lucky, bet it all on red on the roulette wheel, because you're not controlling anything - including yourself.

> "That you have the human fantasy that if you feel bad about something, then you did something about it?" Jose snarled. "Using the daily magic to make things better by making yourself feel bad? Paying in advance so that the real bad things don't happen? Give it up, Lucretia. Your will and the world are two different things, you know that. Bad things happen to good people; there is no correlation between the real and social worlds. Retributive justice is a human concept, not part of the cosmos. No, you're doing it so you don't have to act. You don't have to move forward, you don't have to take steps, you can stew in your self-inflicted prison. The act of a coward, by the way."

> "You thought you should suffer for your sins, without realizing you were making them suffer. Selfish. And so here you are," Jose remarked. "Look, Lucretia, you went out every day to fight in the swamps of the world, and came home covered with slime and bugs. Then, one day you pulled out a set of sparkling ideas that had nothing to do with the world that actually exists out there, and you beat yourself over the head with the pretty ideas so you could judge yourself a failure. Why?"[57]

The daily magic is everything to humans. It is so important that we viciously attack anyone and anything that disrupts the magic. Our need for our daily magic to work leads us to cry 'heresy' when someone does something that we feel interferes. Failure to follow the daily magic is disaster in a critical part of our minds. It's interesting that small differences between groups are usually the most vicious, because the daily magic senses the danger in disrupting shared rituals. We know down deep that something awful happens/will happen if others actions/thoughts/speeches are not punished, because we must protect our magic.

This is not only important to us individually, but to society, as various segments of society learned a long time ago that if you can control the daily magic in people, then you own them completely. If you call on 'god' and they define that 'god', you are in their pocket.

Our ancestors, from our perspective, were wildly emotional and saw spirits in everything. Now, we are taught to see spirits in nothing, because that's irrational. Whether or not the spirits are out there (I'll not take sides) and given that spirits must be irrational, it is clear that the spirits are in our minds and need to be expressed.

Pushing away your daily magic, pretending to ourselves that we are random souls in this huge world that doesn't have any special interest in us (which is the rational truth) really doesn't work for the emotions. Would it work for you? Pushing away the daily magic will just make it come back wearing socially acceptable clothing that is has twisted for it's purposes. If the consciousness demands the unconscious make something socially presentable, the unconscious will comply, but the consciousness doesn't have a clue what the unconscious has really done. You'll find out later, and it will be a surprise.

CHAPTER 9. INDIVIDUAL/SOCIAL WORLDS

"The usual person is more than content, he is even proud, to remain within the indicated bonds, and popular belief gives him every reason to fear so much as the first step into the unexplored."[58]

And so here I am, trying to persuade you to not just take that first step, but hurl yourself bodily out there. Well, life should be interesting.

We swim in a social world. Even when alone, we talk mentally to ourselves, rehearsing our speeches to others in our minds. One of our key perception filters is a bias in favor of socially based selectivity. Simply put, we pay attention to what others around us are paying attention to. This social basis for attention creates a view of the world and an information set common to the community, which, in theory, allows the community to act in concert. Where the society doesn't dissolve into battles over heresies and petty differences, that is. The downside to a natural social attention focus is Groupthink-because individuals are listening to the group, not to what they are seeing, people miss what's actually happening as they buy into the group story.

An incessant exchange of information (gossip, chit-chat) is one of our fundamental characteristics. We generally focus on the kind of information that would have helped keep up alive in past centuries: food sources, dangers, and especially information about members of society. Where two talk together, they plot against the third. To be very crude, and insulting, actually, again most human communication is akin to monkeys in groups picking out lice. Communication is touching, embracing, making people feel part of the group, comfortable and happy, reinforcing what they want to believe. That's not bad, it just has to be recognized and encouraged for the group to bond.

And a social orientation is not all joy, by any means. "Far from the maddening crowd" is an old expression, but we all immediately understand it. It isn't easy sorting out your thoughts and making peace in the chaos. Whether it's that much easier sorting out your thoughts while hoeing corn is another question, as few philosophers seem to have tried that approach.

The complete embrace of social reality is hard wired into us. In horror/ monster movies, a necessary step in the plot is having an oddly dressed (at least eccentric) person read from an old scroll in an unknown language. That lends validity to the plot-we believe because they believe. It's a quiet conspiracy, essentially everyone agreeing that if their magic words can influence reality, then our magic words can do the same. Why words from a vanished civilization should have power over the real world is nonsensical, really. If the civilization had that kind of power, they would not have vanished. But from our viewpoint as social beings, the Word has power.

Not questioning the social group is dangerous. Simply because something is done in society by respected individuals doesn't mean that it isn't monstrous. Look at how many years it took to stop doctors from wearing blood stained coats in their practice as a symbol of experience (manhood), even though it was killing a very substantial number of their patients. Simple hygiene in the hospital has probably saved as many people in the hospital as the medical care offered, as the only thing the medical profession can really provide is to try and keep your system going long enough for your body to heal itself.

The overwhelming power of our social focus is almost beyond comprehension. Byzantine is still a byword for tangled and impenetrable. In Imperial China, the protocol and pomp of the court pretty much made any change impossible, guaranteeing the eventual crash of the dynasty once the court was firmly in place. Much the same happened in France before the Revolution, where the power of the King was essentially destroyed by the courtiers and sycophants surrounding him. No whisper of reality could pierce those thick walls, with the usual result.

Honor is a personal, as well as a social concept, and many great novels have explored the differences between then. An extreme example of the difference between personal honor and social honor is a recent story about two lovers in Afghanistan who defied the social order. The result? Their family wanted them dead. Dead! All to preserve the families 'honor' and standing in the community. Any person who treats the social and their position in it as higher than their children is a person with nothing, absolutely nothing inside them. Carbon emitting biomass parasites, in today's terms.

There are many up sides to our social natures. Shared joy and the warmth of family, the list goes on and on. Most books, including this one don't focus on the joy-if you want joy, go outside and soak in the sun, or to a nice restaurant with friends. This book focuses on why things are not working and how they could work better.

A downside to our social nature is that when your internal reality is anchored in various external manifestations, such as a ritualized worship, actions, belief's, then you have no release from anxiety when the ritual, the magic doesn't do what they are supposed to. An interesting aspect of our social obsessions is the question, that should be asked for more often, is why do normal people allow their daily lives to be dictated by strange, generally long dead people? So, why?

The next time you are tense and can't relax, don't blame yourself. (Unless you did something really stupid, in which case, blame away) Tension is the social self, which is always scared, but why wouldn't it be? In the social world, there are a mass of shifting rules and possibilities and failure is pushed right out there in front of you. People love to remember that stuff.

In order to be an immaculate member of a flock of sheep, one must above all be a sheep oneself. Albert Einstein

People take the easy way out and evaluate themselves on social markers: the size of your 401k, house, your auto. It's great when the getting is good, but then there comes a point when things are not so good. When the assets and liabilities on the financial statement add to zero, there is still a person there-maybe. Picture your social self an actor, with the crowd in mind, declaiming your lines to an empty room-who is mad then? But it's hard to catch, because the social structure is everywhere and everything in daily life, and one can't think thru them everything.

Insanity in individuals is something rare-but in groups, parties, nations and epochs, it is the rule. Friedrich Nietzsche

MORALITY PLAYS

The overlaps in Figure 1 are simple sketches that illustrate very complex concepts. Let's look at the overlaps between the self and the social world. First, much of what we see as 'me' is based on definitions from your applicable social world. For example, in America, a young male may see the normal course of life as boring college classes, drinking and recreational activities from Thursday night thru Sunday, and repeat until one graduates and is unemployed. At which time, you go back for a graduate degree. In Pakistan, the same age male may see the normal course as shooting all those outside some moral/ethical norm, or blowing himself up for the future paradise he has been promised. Neither the American or the Pakistani may realize how much what they think of as 'me' has been overwritten, almost completely in the case of the Pakistani, by their society.

That social overwriting process is everywhere in every culture, and it's necessary, to a degree. From your mother's knee to school to playground play, we are always learning about what society (or at least some of the more powerful actors in society) wants/demands, or will at least grudgingly accept. The primary lifelong training tool is that a very, very high percentage of what passes for entertainment are really straight morality plays. Over and over, day in and day out, good wins, evil is punished; everyone goes home with a warm feeling. Not only are you taught what you should do, you pay for the privilege-what a deal!

The key to any successful morality play is the suffering of the 'evil'. If the 'bad people' accept their wrongs at the end, then it's all the better. The more they suffer, the fewer clothes they have to wear. Young, attractive women partially dressed and suffering addresses multiple social goals and morality plays, which works well for Hollywood, Bollywood and the cable networks.

The key to any morality play is an appropriate straw man/woman. Wind that straw man/woman up, give him/her characteristics that people can identify with and against, and away it runs. The Soviets had wonderful posters of strong men and women suffering for the cause and people bought into the images. Odd that they didn't have posters of the commissars relaxing at their dacha's, but perhaps those posters were not as inspiring. Or the artists were shot.

Effective use of the straw man means that the actions and words the straw man uses together are then combined in your mind together, without question. Ideally, it's straight into your unconscious. By recognizing which of the characters is the straw man, you can stop and realize what is being said. Maybe it makes sense, maybe it doesn't, but at least you are a participant. If you are going to dance to the beat that society is pounding into you, you should at least realize there is a song being played.

A key part of a morality play is the acceptance of suffering by the hero. If it's good enough for them, then it's good enough for us, we think, and then we all accept suffering. True, suffering is part of life. While "The Princess Bride" may have overstated by saying that life is pain, it happens. But that doesn't mean pain and suffering should be worshipped, even desired. If you are seeking penance through suffering, I submit you've bought into a social game you have not carefully thought through. When they persuade you to suffer after society set you up with poor choices, well, they have you completely at that point.

Morality plays can be very dangerous, because those anointed as the 'good' tend to take the blessing seriously. For example, American style police shows, all good versus evil, enthrone the police as the 'good'. The police are people, just like anyone else, and they make the same mistakes anyone else makes, except the consequences can be far greater. In a melodrama forbidden actions can be tied to certain thoughts or concepts, whether there is any real relationship between them. It is done so quickly that there isn't any question of thinking about the alleged relationship; the relationship is sitting there in your mind. It's just magic!

There is a basic trick, which you should memorize and take seriously, at the heart of the police shows. The trick is the interrogation process, which is carefully designed, both on TV and in real life, to take a regular social interaction, a conversation between individuals, and turn it into a ghastly parody of itself. By that hijacking, and by the careful use of social markers and values out of context and for the benefit of the interrogator, the suspect plays a role which is completely destructive to them, by providing information which shouldn't be said, or provided. Police shows are a wonderful format for a morality play, but you confuse them with real life at your peril.

That transformation of normal daily social interaction into a set of behaviors directly against your interest is a classic example of an unnoticed shift from ordinary life to something different. The similarity to regular life lulls you into not realizing your true danger, until too late. It's a boiled frog:

put a frog in a pot of cold water, turn up the heat slowly, and you have a boiled frog. The frog never awoke to the change in temperature because it changed so slowly. Effective planning requires you to realize what the situation is, not what you want it to be.

Of course, the interrogation process is useful in many situations. And knowing how it works is critical! People being what they are, having a useful tool means that the tool will be used in other ways than the tool was designed. If you have a hammer, you will use a hammer for all kinds of things, especially if it gets agreement and support faster than actually having to address real needs or enlist people's minds and hearts. How many other social situations are hijacked like this, with less obvious pressure, so that a person becomes another's puppet?

The essence of any manipulation of a social image is to first tie someone to certain sacred norms/markers, thereby hijacking their vision of self, of their children, of their community, and/or something that is important and that they identify with. Then, held firmly by the socially acceptable box you have maneuvered them into, they must then, to be consistent with themselves and the box, accept choices clearly at odds with what really is their self interest. If you see yourself in the picture being painted, you have been sold, and you drive out with that Corvette (Ok, we all want one) but you really needed a car to carry stuff–and the three kids–then a Corvette isn't going to work for your life. You just have to realize what is going on. If you are not in control of your thoughts, then someone else is. At that point, you can just hope your interests coincide.

If you want to see village ethics in modern society, watch television. It's quick and easy to apply an ethic out of context to make a person look foolish or wrong, and if you have Photoshop, just all that much more fun. And people love to see other people look bad: maybe it rationalizes their life, makes them feels better, maybe helps them deal with the inherent conflicts, but tearing someone down is always a popular thing. If you can't think of anything else, then go back into history and apply rules completely out of context for easy points and cheap laughs.

More subtly, village ethics expressed through morality plays, by creating a shared social reality, are used daily to hide whatever aspect of the real world seems to be most annoying. The group, and most dangerously, the leaders, start thinking that if everyone agrees on X, then X must be true, in all times and places. This works to a point, until the village walks into something hard that wasn't supposed to be there. While 2 or 3 of us together may agree on anything, the real world just won't play by our rules.

We all act out our personal morality plays, even when we are alone. Much of what passes for thought is actually rehearsing a social play, where we can shift actors and lines before our next meeting. We have appropriate facial expressions, which we use by ourselves when we think about the past and the future.

Figure 1, the central diagram, is there to open boxes that you are stuck in. There is an old poem: I keep Six Honest Serving Men", by R. Kipling. You may not like Kipling, but the point of the poem is absolutely correct. You want to ask What? Why? When? How? Where? and Who?, about all the problems, challenges and interests in your life. But it's hard to do, for many reasons, not the least of which is our hidden biases slant our questions and the information we collect. By looking at the overlaps in the diagram and asking ourselves about the overlaps, we are trying to ask these questions better, and get better results. We may still finally do as we damn please, but at least we'll have a better idea of what we're choosing and doing.

Now, here is a heretical idea. Social structures are parasites, just like everything else in this world, acting deliberately to continue themselves. A church doesn't get money to pay the bills by magic, they work very hard to keep themselves going. It's what all parasites do, and they bend the reality around them to keep them going. So the magic fairy dust of peace, justice and fair play is washed away from the structures, who must grimly face the business of making sure that they are here tomorrow.

And they are not kidding about it. The more frozen the structures, the more focused it is on keeping reality at bay. The capture of Constantinople and the resulting adoption (perhaps conquest by the court rituals) of Byzantine may have ruined the Turks. Probably it was a tie, because the rules of the court had grown from many ancient kingdoms all over the Mideast, a history that the Arabs brought with them when they conquered Constantinople.

If one is going to dance to societies tune, one might as well realize what music is playing. And the music is:

> "Adding to our problems" Lucretia fretted, "is that no matter how noble the goal, what you want to accomplish in this world has to go through a room of suits. The suits are carefully selected to have experienced none of the problems that they are supposed to be solving. The options given the suits are limited, as well as the understanding of options by the suits, and what comes out may have little relationship to what went in. Still, we do what we can."[59]

It's as if we have one tool - structures - implemented thru law and force. The more unanswerable challenges we face, the quicker force is used, and it is always force in the end. Remember that structures have very limited utility and abilities and are disastrous outside those limits.

CHAPTER 10. REAL WORLD/SOCIAL WORLD & COHERENCE

This alleged overlap is more of a gaping chasm. Generally, society recognizes hard reality to the absolute minimum extent necessary for the continued minimal (rarely optimal) existence of the society. Perhaps, more accurately, for the optimal existence of the ruling class, but not always. I reference the Mayan bloodletting rituals that were a way to communicate with the gods and ancestors. Cutting yourself isn't going to be optimal for any sane person, but it was part of the plan. The odd rituals and behaviors of the nobility over the eons could be a hundred books.

Rather than go on and on about the divergences between external reality and the social world(s), hopelessly alienating readers in the process, I'm just going to encourage people to look at Figure 1 and think about where the overlaps are and are not.

COHERENCE

Let's look at the triple overlap box. In this box, we are Coherent: the self, the social world, and the real world are on the same page. This is a good thing. Rare, but a good thing. Rare, because in coherence our personal stories and the social stories and the structure of the real world are in agreement. In other words, the self and the social want the same thing that the real world is willing to offer.

Again, what is the self in the diagram? The Self is what you feel and think inside. Note, that the actual DNA of a any given person is in about 10% of your cells, and the other cells are assorted bacteria and colony creatures that keep you alive. Their input into what we think and feel seems to be greater than the traditional model of the human would have suspected. In other words, we are not the masters of ourselves that a much earlier view of biology would have shouted. But the self-contained mass of seawater and buggies that is 'us' functions. The overlaps between you and the real world, for example, are quite different from the authorized views of the social structure.

It's not the socially approved view, but we are hard wired creatures in many, many ways. While society prefers the 'blank slate' concept, which says that a person can become whatever odd collection of behaviors society wants them to be, we are not like that. For example, the two species of chimpanzees, common chimps and bonobos, which differ in just a few tenths of one percent of their genomes, have vastly different behaviors. Mixing them together has bad effects for the bonobos, as common chimps are among the most aggressive mammals known to zoology, whereas bonobos are among the most peaceable. Common chimps have a social structure in which the males dominate the females while with bonobos the females have the upper hand. Common chimps have sex for procreation while bonobos for recreation. Can we make a case (facetious, of course) that common chimps are religious fanatics and Bonobos are civilized humans? The tiny changes in the genes change the size and shape of the different parts of the brain, their wiring, and the systems that release hormones and neurotransmitters. Clearly slight changes in the hard wiring, can lead to large differences in behavior.

The social structure is more like the 'force' of Star Wars than a real world. As the daily magic is our personal force field, the social structure is a force field that surrounds the village and at least attempts to shape us. Humans have to get along, and there are lots and lots of general and local rules involved in that. The social structure defines in it's own world, which is, by the way, the only correct world, remember that! And the force mimicked the social structure in that it ignored real life in favor of a fantasy of small human stories. Cooperation, peace and agreement rule the universe? Go to the oceans or the plains, and ask the creatures there what it's really like. If our grocery stores didn't break the connection between our daily lives and where our food comes from, we would not find it as easy to pretend the world is something vastly different than it is.

It's quite a different point of view to think of our worlds as in Figure 1. It's disturbing and unsettling, actually. It's critical to do so, because there is are huge insights generated by this view. One insight is that in vast amounts of our daily life and thought, the real world and the social worlds are marginally involved. Your gastro system typically has little concern with many of the more esoteric social arrangements. The social structure cares little about much of 'you', because it has larger concerns, from its point of view. You, from your point of view, are doubtful that there are larger concerns than 'you', because you're all you've got. And the real world cares little about the beliefs of either you or the social structure. It's clear you have to obey gravity: it's the law.

Looking at the Figure 1, this book is focused on three kinds of planning in this book. The individual seeks congruence with the self and key to that planning is the communication with your unconscious and that mystical compass that shows the way to what you want most in this world. This is planning within the sector in the diagram of the 'self', with appropriate consultation of the real world and social world overlaps.

Then, there is planning for results in the external world, once you know what you want/have to do. This is planning in the intersection of the self and the real world on the diagrams. Planning at this level is for an external object created in cooperation with others. For example, this would be planning to build a home. Cooperation with others requires communication of a plan, verification of the steps taken and sharing your goals with others so that intelligent sub-decisions can be made. There are many interactions in the overlaps between the real world and the social worlds involved here.

Finally, there is Social World planning, planning in that mental construct that is the intersection between you and the social world. You are planning how you want to succeed in, or at least function, within that social world. Here, you are probably primarily concerned with the overlaps between the social world and your self. This is going to be really fuzzy about goals and plans, final accomplishment, and ending points.

If you picked up this book for some quick hints on improving the next plan, then you may be discouraged. Why all the overview, you may be thinking (swearing) to yourself? Well, it is a complex world out there.

And, to put things in perspective, life isn't clean and neat like the central diagram. What the overlaps really look like is this:

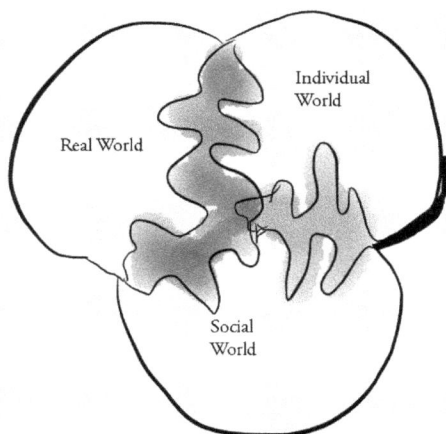

This rather creepy looking diagram points out that the overlaps vary. The nice smooth overlaps in Figure 1 are clearly not realistic, as our knowledge will not only extend different depths in different circles and will also be more or less detailed within the areas where there is an overlap.

Figure 2.

PART 1, SECTION 2 – FEEDBACK

CHAPTER 11. POKE THE WORLD

Looking back at 'The Famous Plan' at the beginning of the book, we have covered attitude, perspective, parasites, stories (and their weaknesses and limits) and the 3 worlds problem and how the intersecting worlds affect our stories.

So, we have a story. We have blown up our balloon, which gingerly touches the data points supporting the pretty fabric we have woven. Now, like it or not, we need to test our story against the world. Necessary, because if we actually expect the story to do something useful, which would be, oh, say feeding/ protecting us and those we care about, then the story has to have certain minimal overlaps with the real world circles. Annoying, because the story is more than reality, it's what we want, and testing the story always brings that out.

We poke the world, ourselves and society to get some response. That response is called feedback, the result of our poke. Feedback is hard to measure and capture. Very hard, actually, to capture real feedback that does more than confirm the story we are desperate to have proved true. Too often, where unanticipated feedback doesn't fit the story, we ignore all outside the story. In other words, we poke to prove, not to disprove, and if a story is supported by isolated data points and we want /need to believe, then we buy the story and create the feedback to support it. That will, eventually, pop the balloon and expose the story as a fraud, but maybe not today, if we really like the story. It's our nature to do this. A recent article in the Economist magazine argued that perhaps 50% (give or take) of scientific studies are actually reproducible, which is terrifying but consistent with this chapter. We want what we see and we see what we want.

Filters are a part of feedback but they are more important than that. Filters are how we simplify our lives. We let certain things in the external world be markers of whether we are interested or not. That was the thesis of the book "The Tipping Point", that things that get attention of others get our attention. Not because they are the best, they may or may not be, but it's like the herd running across the savanna: if enough notice something then the herd changes direction. Random events have huge consequences.

Here is a conceptual approach to feedback, placing it within a system.

> 1. But common to all their ideas is the notion of a set of objects or components which interact together in space and/or time. An additional characteristic inherent in the term as we shall use it is that a particular group of components and their interrelationships has been chosen for some purpose - to answer a particular questions, illustrate a theory or in an attempt to classify part or all of the natural world. - pp 5

Pp 11   The diagrams indicate the systems' boundaries by a solid line. Within these boundaries, series of components are isolated which have been chosen to represent that portion of the world in which the systems analyst is interested - in these particular cases the food processing system and the population dynamics of a predator. If there are no connections across the system's boundaries with the surrounding systems environments, the systems are described as closed. Ecological work, however, deals almost exclusively with open systems . . .

In open systems, two categories of phenomena outside the system's boundaries are of special note:

2. There are the sources and sinks of materials which enter and leave the system and which are themselves beyond control by any part of the system

3. Certain quantities outside the systems boundaries will affect processes within them profoundly. These are the driving variables (also referred to as driving functions, forcing functions, input variables or input functions)

4. In the system itself, three classes of items can be recognized in the diagrams

5. Various quantities of material make up the basic structure of the system; these will vary through time but will be measurable at any point in time. They are the state variables (system variables) and are shown in the figures as rectangular boxes.

6. Inputs and outputs of the components or, at another level, of the whole system. They represent flows among the parts described and may be of one of two types, materials or information. Information is a difficult term to explain briefly, but can be regarded most simply as a signal from one component to another, telling the receiver something about the state of the transmitter without any material transfer being involved

7. Material flows between components are regulated by rate processes, represented in the figures by boxes pinned to the appropriate flow arrows.

8. Feedback loop - can be either positive or negative. Negative, when is reduces the strength of a rate process. Positive when is increases the strength of a rate process.

The concept of feedback leads us to the very important notion of control. Control implies that there is some normal or preferred value or level for a particular state variable . . And that the system acts so as to restore these variables to their normal values following any perturbation. Such control may be direct and monotonic, or compensatory or oscillatory.[60]

Ok, that was dry. Feedback is absolutely critical and to most people, completely boring. I thought about putting some relevant sex scenes into the following discussion, but decided it would be too distracting. If you think about it, romance is obviously a feedback critical process. If you are a male, and you ignore miss the continuing but relatively subtle feedback from the female, you're going to be going home alone a lot.

Again, why is feedback important? Because there is no better way of converting a run of the mill, mundane situation into a high-risk event than to not understand the situation. Feedback tests your understanding of the system. You do something, and something you expect happens. When something you don't expect happens, that's an anomaly, and is NOT to be ignored. This book is called 'Unanticipated Feedback' because that is the dangerous stuff.

Much of the next few paragraphs is from a very good book "How to improve human performance" by T. Connellan. This is the whole 'act and react' concept in a nutshell, the OODA cycle (covered later) in a slightly different form. Everything you do in life fits into this pattern (hopefully!). If you are 'doing' without 'noticing' the effects, I can promise that life isn't going to be good. If you are doing and your life is an attempt to cheat the results, because of hostility to parents/society/peer groups and/or random strangers who piss you off, think about this a bit. You can't win long term, and you will pay the piper.

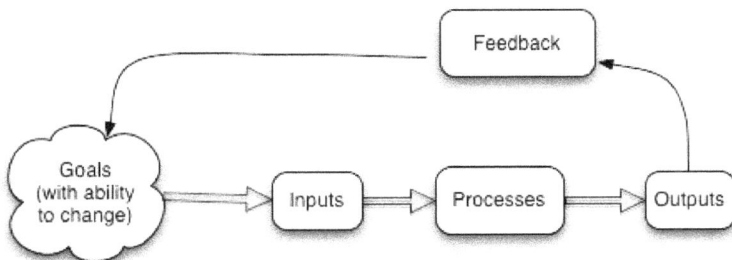

Figure 3.

Ok, the basics. Behavior is an activity that can be seen or measured or described. That sounds self evident, but one of the major problems with feedback is 'invisible' feedback, events that occur away from your vision, or events that are time delayed so they don't correlate well with your action. Or results that you simply do not want to see, as discussed in other places in this book.

This diagram below is another way of looking at feedback. The Antecedent is where we start, the starting point in any cycle. Then, we do something, something happens (we think) and we use the information from 'consequence' to modify our behavior the next time.

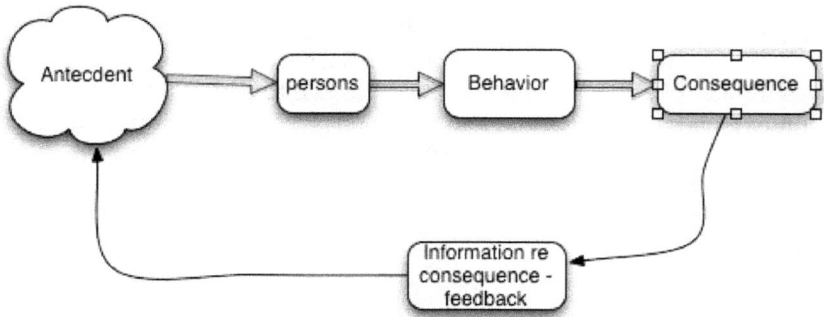

Figure 4.

There are masses of complexities in the above simple diagrams. Looking at the antecedent can tell us whether a behavior will occur at all, but not much about whether the behavior will occur again. There are conditions necessary for the Antecedent to be effective: Is it known what is expected, are the standards clear? Are they communicated? Are they realistic? Mentally put this into a romantic context to bring some life to the ideas. You want to meet/date/get to know someone better. You have to meet them, which is the Antecedent. There are generally multiple possibilities, so this is a question you look at from different directions before acting.

So, you want to meet this 'X' person. First, can the behavior be performed? Physically, is it possible to be in the same place at the same time as this other person? Or, does something prevent its occurrence? Such as social standing, shyness, physical attractiveness, all the usual kinds of issues? This is where the rubber meets the road, as it were: are the consequences weighted in favor of performance? If you are the starting quarterback on your winning college football team, your changes of at least an initial introduction to a certain young woman are going to be higher than, say, if you are a gawky freshmen with a pimple problem lusting after the queen of the homecoming parade. I've done the gawky freshman, unfortunately never had the chance to be the quarterback, so I'm familiar with assessing a situation and discovering it isn't going to work.

One of the nice (or not) things about social relationships is that the feedback is generally relatively immediate and fairly clear. Most things in life are not so obvious. If you work hard, does that mean (a) a promotion, or (b) does your boss want to leave you where you are because you do such a good job, but you were doing such a good job because you wanted a promotion. Those kinds of interesting hidden effects make capturing effective feedback quite difficult.

Now, if there is a process in your life that you want to improve, something that you can control and focus on, you want feedback about your actions because you want to know if you are improving in doing Z. The ideal feedback is: immediate, specific to the action, and positive. Negative feedback is necessarily ambiguous, as well as emotionally upsetting, which impairs your ability to assess the feedback. For example, that rejection by the Queen of the Homecoming parade? What exactly was the rejection based on, which is important for your next set of actions? Negative feedback, such as, say 'drop dead, loser', while relatively clear within the context of those local rules, is unclear as to scope and future responses. Should you attempt to prove that you are not a loser, or just write this one off? And do you carry that rejection into future encounters, which may or may not be appropriate.

If you are working with another person, it's consequences that they see, not what you think, that matter. What may seem like a dispassionate delivery of relevant, useful information to the observer may feel like grounds for a challenge to a duel by the individual receiving them. Put yourself in their place before you act and expect results.

Everyone knows what feedback is: you do something, you see the results of the action, you decide if it works, and you move on. There was a classic cartoon, I think by Jules Feiffer, which I have been unable to find again, in which an elderly woman is robbed. As the robber turns and starts to run away he slips on a banana peel, falls and is knocked unconscious as he hits the concrete. The police run up and arrest the mugger and the woman who was mugged says, 'Well, I guess the system does work'. The result was almost completely random, and the system obviously did not work at all! That's making the best of the situation, but it's not effective planning for the next event.

Here is a feedback situation that is everyday: We are sitting at work and feeling good about what we just did. We look up and the boss is shouting at you about something that you did last week. Maybe the boss is mad because his wife is angry at him, or his son is on drugs, or the CEO had to cut budgets to afford the CEO's plane, so really the boss's anger has almost nothing to do with you, and certainly nothing to do with what you did. (which was really quality work, by the way) Then there is your personal life, the unbalanced credit card(s)and your daughter's soccer game that the ref clearly misjudged last night. Worst of all, the coffee pot is empty. Out of these intertwined events, what do you choose as a basis for your next decision and future choices? Conceptually, you sit each moment at the focus of multiple differential equations (which I can't solve either) calculating the position and changes in the things that affect your life, and you have to figure out what to do next to maximize results (or at least minimize consequences) in all this muddle.

The usual response (frustration) leads to yelling at your spouse, who yells at the kids, who yell at the dog, who chases the cat, who pees in your shoe. It's clear that really isn't all that productive.

> *'The pessimist experiences failure, the optimist knows that although lessons can be painful, there is no failure, only feedback'* (Armand Kruger)

CHAPTER 12. HOW DO WE GET GOOD FEEDBACK?

So now do we get good feedback? It's quite complex. Let's take a simple example: you tell your child to not eat the cookie. Of course they eat the cookie. The proof of their action is clearly shown by shown by no cookie on the counter, crumbs on shirt, child not hungry at dinner, averted eyes when questioned. The behavior was clearly defined and the output measured (no cookie) is pretty clear.

But a meaningful real world example, which deals with time lagged choices and outside random events, is impossibility more complex, and to point to certain actions or not actions as causing ultimate results may be impossible. What was the effect of eating the cookie 2 years ago, if the child is 10 pounds overweight now? How much is the fault of that cookie? How much is not exercising or that daily bag of chips the child eats? But decisions have to be made. Hey: blame has to be allocated, even with bad information.

This section, and feedback in general, is frustrating, because it points out how things don't work. No one wants things to not work; everyone just wants things to work (when and how we want them to work) and to move onto the next thing. Unfortunately, that isn't often an available option. The monumental complexity of the law of evidence shows the enormous complexity of interpreting results of actions. For example, what is admissible evidence in court and why it is admissible is based on the direct feedback from the evidence as well as indirect feedback that may carry a vastly different message.

There is a doctrine in the law, 'the fruit of the poisonous tree', that forbids admitting otherwise admissible evidence because the evidence was obtained illegally. While in a particular trial not allowing the evidence into court may result in the guilty going free, a 'fail'; when you consider the effect on the whole system of admitting illegal evidence, an isolated trial that frees the guilty is nothing compared to maintaining the integrity of the system. It is critically important to the integrity of the process that evidence be obtained legally. You can't let the prosecution cheat, even for 'justice', because that will encourage cheating. Cheating spreads. The rule of law is based on respect for the process, and lose that, then things will go downhill fast. While men with guns are the base of the system, they can't carry the system. Unless the mass of people buy's into the system of law in society, it will break. The fascination that people have with this complexity is shown by the TV shows and movies that focus on these issues.

While the following statement is probably too abstract, it is the critical basis of this chapter, so humor me. Feedback, defined as one or several measurable data streams used to make decisions, is created by the resources available and the constraints on those resources. That seems obvious, and that is the problem: it is so obvious that we just gloss over and move on, because we have to do something. You make a decision, informal or formal, as to what data resulting from an action is collected, and the resources that can be allocated to that collection. To measure data, there has to be some observation method, which generally is going to be one or more humans, and/or instruments/equipment of some type, the resources.

All resources are limited by constraints. In the collection of feedback, constraints are typically limitations of the equipment, perceptual limitations of the observer, and the focus of the observer. People being what they are, one sees what one looks for and doesn't see what you don't expect.

The operator of the new, somewhat experimental, radar installation at Pearl Harbor saw a flight of planes coming in and reported to the officer on watch 'many planes'. There were some American planes expected that day, and it wasn't asked 'how many is many', which would possibly have given some warning to the ships in the harbor. But the equipment was new, it's accuracy uncertain and it was relatively unsophisticated, which imposed some limitations on the quality of the data. Most importantly, no one was expecting an attack-even though the whole point of the equipment being there was to catch an attack. Outside possibilities of the information were off-handedly dismissed and many died.

ESSENTIAL SYSTEMS ISSUES

The first involves the existence of feedback loops, both positive and negative. When positive and negative feedback loops are balanced a steady state outcome results; however, when one loop dominates an unstable state is the result. For example, there is exponential growth when there is a dominant positive feedback, such as an atomic bomb exploding, for example. When the dominance of the feedback loops depends on the level of the variable in question, then typically there will be oscillations in the variable over time.

A second key element is the presence of resources, which are always limited to some extent. Resources may be used up faster than they are available, causing a 'crunch' at some point, or may accumulate faster than used, causing a pile up at some point.

The third key element is the presence of delays in the signals from one part of the world system to another. For instance, the effects of increasing pollution levels may not be recognized on life expectancy or agricultural production for some decades. This is important because unless the effects are anticipated and acted on in advance, the increasing levels may grow to an extent that prohibits or constrains feasible solutions whether technological, social or otherwise. This is everyday life, especially in a Chinese city.

Treating the system under examination as a complete system of sub-systems is the fourth key element. When considering the challenges of an isolated sector of a problem, it's relatively easy to develop a solution(s). Solutions rarely come without implications for other sectors, and the real challenge (which is looked at in considerable detail later in the this book) then becomes solving issues in multiple sectors concurrently.

TIME PROBLEMS IN FEEDBACK

Time is limited for everything, and certainly for our observation of a data stream. There are two major time issues. The first is simply the time allowed to observe, and that time is necessarily limited. If you observe for one hour and the key result occurred after two hours, then you don't have a clue about what really happened. Which won't stop conclusions being drawn, of course. The second time issue is that we all have problems with time lags and tend to not relate events after a period of time to an earlier event. Do you wonder who was the first person to relate the sex act with the eventual result 9 months later? It isn't that intuitively obvious, and lots of people today still don't seem to grasp the concept. Probably watching animals with a shorter gestation time was the key.

A thermostat is a typical time lag problem. You are cold, so you turn the dial up. But the heating process is gradual; because it is a real world problem based on furnace size, room sizes, equipment efficiency, etc. the heat just doesn't jump up. In frustration, people turn the thermostat up to 90 instead of the 75 they want, but the heating process operates by the laws of physics. The dial is a trigger; the dial isn't a magic talisman that controls the heat. So by turning the heat up past the goal temperature to speed up the process (which doesn't speed it up one bit) means inevitably that it will then eventually be too hot, and then you have to turn it down, which probably to a number lower than the original goal, because it's too hot in here! You have an oscillation occurring and those are annoying. Any time the response has a significant time delay (worse when the delay isn't communicated) that is either past the time available for measurement and/or a long enough time delay that noise can enter into the perceptions of the observers, effective feedback is going to be difficult (impossible). The new NEST thermostats tell you how long it will take to heat the room to a given temperature when you turn the heat up, which gives you critical feedback when you need it. Telling you that it will take, say, 1 hour to heat to 72, and 1.5 hours to heat to 76 shows it's pointless to just turn the dial past the number you really want it to be.

FILTERING PROBLEMS

So, you act, you monitor you action, observe something, and you end up with some information. But what did you miss? Filtering information is just like a coffee filter. Filtering takes raw data and essentially runs the data through a series of chutes and gates to structures the raw data into something believed (hoped) to be relevant to the action evaluation.

Conceptually, data streams are filtered, both implicitly during collection (where filtering often isn't considered) and explicitly during the process of evaluating the data collected. The filtering criteria may be conscious or unconscious, but they are choices that result in what we see being, to a greater or lesser degree, different from the underlying reality.

What you are looking for–simply expecting–is a probably the most critical implicit filter. If you expect the toast to pop up, you are staring at the toaster, not the television. When you are collecting data, the unexpected can be simply not seen. There is a mass of perceptions occurring all the time, and most are weeded out unconsciously. This is most common where you have a known situation where you are familiar with the typical feedback. Any different (unexpected) feedback is simply ignored (noise) or assumed to be incorrect observation. It may be an incorrect observation, but it may be an anomaly, which is real data hinting at a new story.

To recap: conscious filters that fail are based on irrelevant prior experiences. Unconscious filters mean that you don't realize you are filtering. The focus/attention of the observer absolutely defines the extent and depth of the questions asked of the data. (Remember the 'how many' planes at Pearl Harbor)

New/Biased Problems

Another situation that is even more of a problem, which this book harps on incessantly, is where you are facing a new situation. Because we don't know what relevant feedback looks like, we fall back on a plan that worked before, and we filter information based on that plan. Comfortable, you already know what's going on, and there isn't any reason to think further. Data is arbitrarily discarded and if we pass off anomalies as noise and/or observation mistakes, we will eventually find we no clue what is really happening. At that point, it's ritual behavior and the daily magic.

What you didn't see (or saw part of) is tied to the biases of the observer. You and I are not biased, but those other people are. People, of necessity, have a more or less coherent worldview they use each day, and events falling outside or challenging that worldview tend to be dismissed or ignored. Doctors, when they are looking at your sad sick self on the examining table, have a mental rule to look for horses, not zebra's, when considering possible diagnosis choices. (So always tell the doctor about that recent trip to Zambia)

A common bias is goal incongruence. You have a goal/plan, which is why you are looking for feedback. You also have a host of other goals/plans at the same time, and your peer group/social structure has goals/plans. If the feedback you are collecting is in conflict with one or more of those other goal/plans (and it always is) then that incongruent feedback starts looking like noise to be ignored.

The range of biases is practically infinite, and is of course dependent on the particular action being observed. Biases can so limit perception that events outside of the biases are as if the person were physically deaf, dumb and blind.

NOISE & CAUSALITY

Let's look at the interesting question of noise, causality and feedback. Well, it's interesting to me. Feedback is asking, essentially, what happened here? Once you have some information to work with, then you have to decide whether the information stream is noise (not caused by the action) or it is casually related to the action and thus relevant. The determination of noise/causality has are two dangers: (1) a false positive, in which noise is determined to be casual and thus part of the decision or (2) a false negative, in which casual information streams are evaluated as noise.

Isn't this fun? Let's put it into context. How often have you made these errors in life? You are at a social event, and an attractive person smiles at you from a distance away. Is this a false positive, i.e., are they smiling at the person in back of you, and when you walk over to them, instant social disaster. Or do you, cautious, ignore the smile, which was an authentic indication of interest, and your true mate left in a huff, all that could have been lost forever.

To make things more difficult, it is 'not measurable feedback'-all that 'other' stuff we never see, that is probably the biggest problem with feedback. Feedback that is not measurable obviously vanishes from your careful analysis, because you are simply not aware of it. This is disastrous if the missing information is important.

Data is not measurable for a number of reasons. There is, first, data that isn't measurable because of limitations of the measurement process. The old joke about accountants and engineers is that they divide the world into that which is quantifiable and that which is not, and throw out the non-quantifiable. All that nonsense about happiness, contentment doesn't fit anywhere, so out it goes! This is a huge problem in accounting, and an even worse problem in economics.

The point of feedback is to make a useful decision about the future. Collecting feedback has to be continually tested against that need to make a useful decision. Feedback sitting there in our hand, an isolated fact, doesn't matter that much. For example, if we are considering purchasing shares of a company, we read various press releases and perhaps SEC filings. How do we know whether the company is the ideal gifted set of researchers, focused on their work, or whether Dilbert's pointy haired boss run the show? There is nothing in the press releases or the SEC filings that can answer that question. There is one marker that can be tracked, however. The worst case of all is if you have a salesman running the company backed by compliant accountants. In that case, sell short! Now!

Another data measurement problem is to simply report what we know, but which really isn't relevant. Joke: a balloonist descends into a field in the country. Shouting to a person walking in the road, the balloonist says, "Where am I?" The person in the road shouts back "you are in a balloon in a field". The balloonist shouts back "you are an accountant. The person says, "you are right, how did you know?" The balloonist replies: "everything you said was correct, and it was all useless."

We need feedback. People are so frustrated by not getting feedback that all of us spend time each day doing marginal/non-important things that do generate some feedback, so you can emotionally feel something good happened. Key work doesn't get done because there are no results coming back from those actions. We all do the 'urgent/non-critical' rather than the 'critical/non-urgent' because the urgent is standing in front of us shouting, and we get feedback from doing something. David Allen talks about this, and urges us to structure some simple wins each day so that, secure that we have won, we then have the strength to look at the hard questions.

INVISIBLE FEEDBACK

A huge problem is invisible feedback. If it's invisible, then how can it be such a problem? Common variations are (1) the Lost Sale and (2) why you can't talk to a human on the phone today. Invisible feedback is much more than simply not measurable. Not measurable may be hard to record but you know it is there. Invisible feedback is just missing, information streams that you are not even aware of. Invisible feedback is a disconnect between the observer recording the feedback, and the various entities acting.

A classical case is the lost sale in business. A cookie store at a mall near the author NEVER had any cookies for sale near closing time. Their cost of goods sold would have been excellent because their losses from spoilage would have been roughly zero. But what is the cost of a lost sale? How many lost sales did they have because they had no goods on hand? When they went out of business (which they finally did–there is justice!), they probably wondered why business was so bad. Well, duh–if you are in business to sell something, you should have something to sell. The store that replaced them now has full trays of cookies for sale up to closing.

Here is another true case. The liquor control Commission ordered a bar to hire more wait staff so that customers would not overindulge. It seems that a patron had died, from actions based on the patron's stupidity, but perhaps he was being served when he should not have been. In any event, blame gets passed around. Management of the bar glumly figured they would make less money if they had to hire more staff, but having no license was a LOT less money. When they reopened, sales jumped, and they made more money, because there were substantial sales not being caught because the short handed wait staff were missing orders. Sometimes you need extra staff who stand there, looking for work, instead of staff that is 110% busy all the time. Accountants can measure the cost of sales, but you can't measure missing sales. That can only be determined by first, thinking about missing sales, and secondly, running experiments to see if the missing sales are out there, and how best to capture them if they exist. Poking, not pontificating.

Lost sale problems, tied to feedback that is invisible to the measurement criteria and the subsequently recorded data, will destroy a business eventually, without the business having any idea of what really happened. There is a vicious cycle that can easily start in these cases. When profits start to drop, a wave of cost cutting is imposed because that is what the measurement system feeds back, and things just go from bad to worse. All is not lost. Management, as they stand in line at the unemployment office, have the warm feeling that they relied on the system and competently acted within that system on the road to ruin.

MEASUREMENT FAILURES

An accounting system does a very good job of tracking actually incurred dollar denominated events and allocating those to income and expense. It us worse than useless when applied outside of those very limited events it does carefully track. While that may confirm your opinion of accounting, it is important because all of the big decisions are made on dollars and cents, by gosh, whether or not the reports are actually measuring anything. And:

> *"No matter what they're talking about, they're talking about money.*
> *Todd's Second Political Principle*

By the nature of the accounting system, it can't track items not measured in dollars. It is difficult enough, for even a small business, to track the dollars, much less look for trouble and try and quantify the unquantifiable. So the system can't-and doesn't-look outside the dollars. In the cookie company case, we saw that the reporting system can be a filter, which completely blinded the participants to the critical variable in their business, which was something to sell. By focusing on the cost data in the system, the logical approach is to cut costs, which is why it is impossible to talk to a human on the phone today. In a meeting, you can stand there confidently with a chart showing the effects of cutting costs. It's hard to stand there confidently as people stare doubtfully at your doodles showing what you think might happen if we increase costs. So it's always cutting costs that wins until the doors close.

This is the real reason that MBA's are destroying the world, because they manage by what they measure. When you measure by dollars, you miss all the important stuff that cause or affect the dollar revenue. Customer service? Where does that show up on the accounts? So you can't talk to a human, or at least one who speaks your language. I wonder if when people from India call customer service they get Americans?

To beat this some more, the lost sale is the disconnect between the person making the cookies/running the business and all of those people wandering the mall who might buy a cookie/buy a drink. There is no marker board where people can indicate their cumulative interest, at any time, in the total cookies people might want so the seller can adjust his supply. How many people will walk up the counter and badger the staff for cookies that are not available? And even if people do complain, is the information accumulated, or just thrown out?

This disconnect is a constant in life. Every action will have impacts on people not part of the monitoring system. If you are trying to plan, invisible feedback is an information flow that can't be measured by the observer because it doesn't present itself to the observer. The waitresses in the bar example do not see 'lost sales', they see too many semi-drunk people shouting at them. If the observer isn't representative of the end user or really doesn't understand the end user's needs; or believes that those end user needs are not important/ enlightened/progressive, then all that feedback which makes or breaks a project in operation is lost.

A politically incorrect example: public housing projects built in the 1950's and 1960's in all major US cities. The net result was hundreds of millions of dollars wasted, lives ruined and neighborhoods destroyed, culminating in the destruction of the buildings as a desperate measure to end the crime endemic to the projects. Human history and psychology clearly shows that people take care of properties where they have a feeling of ownership, and where they don't have that feeling of ownership, the area will be crime ridden and dangerous. As an aside, it was that need for a feeling of ownership that was the downfall of the central socialist slogan: 'from each according to his ability, and to each according to his need'. It seems that ability is limited, and needs are exponential, but that is another book(s). Those projects are wonderful example of how doing good (that warm emotional glow felt by the politicians and social workers) did far more evil than any individual intent to do evil could have done. Cleverly, the blame was put back on the people in the projects as their personal character failure, so the warm feeling of having done 'good' by the politicians and city planners wasn't mudded by messy reality. And they moved onto the next disaster.

External entities, such as Administrative Agencies, are an interesting case of feedback results and failures. Any bureaucracy is a group of people in a formal structure making decisions. Essentially, a bureaucracy is Suits at desks making choices. I challenge you to try and think of an administrative agency that this doesn't apply to. The problem is that the formal structure doesn't allow a lot of feedback and information into the process. Only certain types of events are captured, and not all those events are considered (for good and not-good reasons).

The underlying frustration with that system is that where the events to be measured are outside the 'suits at desks' view, those events don't exist even if they are the most relevant. The legal process has the same issues as administrative agencies, but is more formally structured and so even less flexible. This is good in many ways, because flexibility tends to go to the well connected, another reason that things just don't seem to work.

On top of the problem of getting useful feedback, the law and the bureaucracy are constantly twisted by inconsistent goal problem. Feedback needs to have a clear correlation to the goal and action to be maximally useful in making decisions. Where feedback is viewed by several inconsistent goals, some of which may not have casual relationships to the actions taken, it is unlikely that the feedback will be useful in judging the results of the actions. From a political point of view, it may be good enough because the politicians can prove 'responsiveness' to the external goals and concepts sought, such as the public housing situation. Whether anything actually useful gets done doesn't show up for twenty years, and they are out of office by then.

In your town, the city sets speed limits on roads to make them safer. One day, when they are short of money, they realize that ticket revenue is a wonderful hidden tax increase on the law-breaking speeders, who are obviously bad people. The roads suddenly turn into speed traps to maximize public revenue, defended, of course, by layers of 'good intentions'. Note carefully that whatever can be demonized can be forced to pay the freight for other things. Try going into court to say that the speed limit for a given street is in violation of the state guidelines, and is actually a cause of accidents. You will be lucky if you don't get a fine for contempt and wasting the courts time. And I'm not jesting.

In the town I live in, the state raised the speed limits on a street, which had been a notorious speed trap. It took several years for the city to post new speed limit signs, and they continued to ticket on the old, invalid signs for all of those years. The judges even threw out any objections, joking(!!) as they did it. They only changed the signs (in a hurry) when the local newspaper made a ruckus about it and it became clear that the city had more than overstepped-there were potentially criminal results from the city's 'well-intentioned' actions. The clear result was that the police and courts stole more money from the community than any, and perhaps all, of the cases before the local courts during those time periods.

The only method of catching invisible feedback is paying attention to anomalies, which by their mere existence shout that something is happening. Anomalies are one of the interesting first indications of major problems about to happen and a very important chapter towards the end of this book.

ACTION ASSESSMENT

Did you do what you thought you did? It probably sounds obvious, but given information about the results of an action, is the action you took the action planned? It certainly matters before making a judgment on the effectiveness of the action. If it was the action planned, was it done correctly? Using the wrong action, or the right action done wrong, isn't going to give you good feedback to use before choosing your next action.

"I been in the right place
But it must have been the wrong time
I'd have said the right thing
But I must have used the wrong line
I'd a took the right road
But I must have took a wrong turn
Would have made the right move
But I made it at the wrong time" Dr. John, Right Place Wrong Time

Just to disorient even further, was the original feedback experience appropriate to use as a basis for setting a new plan? Or was it superstitious learning, coincidental events that resulted in a positive outcome, but really can't be used to base future actions on?

Here is another chance to skip the time and expense of an MBA program. Lost opportunity calculations are a big part of an MBA. If you spend money/resources on a particular item, then you can't use those resources on an alternative choice, and so there is a lost opportunity cost. If you decide to ask the blonde woman to dance (who has her divorce attorney's card in her purse at all times), then you didn't ask the brunette (the heiress to a vast fortune, by the way). Calculating opportunity costs is very difficult, and not very popular politically. What is the reward for telling people that you made a poor choice? Or even admitting it to yourself?

If the poor reader has struggled this far, it is clear that feedback is a much more complex matter than we generally view it as. There are so many ways that assessing the results of an action can go wrong it is almost amazing that things ever go right. Generally, it is such a serious and common problem that changing the definition of what was 'right' is the only way the goal is reached. As it is socially important to be seen as always being right, keeping the Goal Posts on wheels helps.

Feedback is boring. While it can be a marker of success, it, as the result of an action you did, is also going to be a marker of failure. That means someone may be mad when things don't turn out right and we know we hear about failure a lot more than success. Feedback requires thought, experimentation and a desire to know what happened, and can result in our getting yelled at? There are so many more interesting things to do.

"Never let the facts get in the way of a carefully thought out bad decision" Marshall's First Law of the Legislature.

It is more satisfying to postulate a theory of something than to propose a system that simply looks for constant data, from which events can be determined. Don't jump to conclusions is what feedback murmurs, and what fun is that? A theory, right or wrong, is a guide. A handful of data is still a puzzle, and the next handful of data another puzzle. The mere fact that the puzzles are more factually correct that the theory is not emotionally rewarding, especially for situations of considerable stress where people seek certainly.

If you despair and seek advice from the past, remember that the revered wise, not that long ago, were considered adults at a quite young age, because generally people died young and thus maturity came quickly. Because of a lack of good drinking water, they drank more beer, wine and other alcohol than we would now consider responsible. Only the idle nobility was educated enough to write and ponder, so the net result is that in looking to the past, we are seeking guidance from half drunk wastrels whose frozen wisdom we now solemnly defend.

Our choices will be wrong where the feedback designed to be caught is what was sought, but people processing the feedback deliberately ignored negative results. Obviously the feedback then presented (because it's not going to include the negative results) is going to be dangerous to use. You can report what you expect, but it may not be what is actually happening. The drug companies seem rather good at these types of experiment results. Securing good solid, reproducible feedback is hard enough for scientific experiment, under controlled conditions, when funding isn't dependent on certain results. When funding is clear about what it needs, well, that's usually what it gets. Who really understands statistics anyhow?

Where important but unpopular feedback flows are not captured, using what was captured (i.e., the 'good' news) will fail.

There is a joke (which has a revealed truth in the punch line) about trying to make a decision between two alternatives you face. You seriously and diligently draw up a list. As you are about to flip a coin and you suddenly realize you are rooting for A over B, then your decision is made. The trick we don't usually see is when the person handing you 'objective results' was doing the same thing, but didn't tell you about their private decision.

Finally, one of the most serious feedback failures occurs where the feedback is clear and valid, but doesn't work at different levels the same way. In society, you have a multitude of actors, making assessments on their own interest, and the net result can easily be to no one's real interest. Common examples are corruption, war, and social disorder. For a policeman in certain countries, corruption is how his family is fed today, although the result on the society is so destructive that his family is ultimately harmed by the corruption. This is common, yet is so complex and difficult to turn around, that effective responses are almost impossible to find.

We talked before about standing in front of the meeting and that you are your charts. Because certainly is so important, results that challenge that certainly are ignored. After all, if that isn't true, then what about this, and before you know it well everything is falling apart! So don't make waves. Get along and go along. What is the use of knowing the information isn't any good? Well, it keeps one from believing that questionable data is certainty, even if it has to be acted on, and it keeps one questioning what is happening, which is the best that can be done in life.

So, was that fun?

Greed is Good

Let's tie feedback to making money, in a perhaps vain attempt to keep the reader turning the pages. Greed is good!

People are commonly distraught about their retirement choices and investments. It's unclear, unknowable actually, and it's critically important. The frustration with having to make decisions under uncertainty, and wanting to ignore the complexities, leads people into reading your needs and desires into another person, and then letting them deal with the complexity. People want desperately to hand their future life to someone who can make it right. The people who are eager to shoulder that burden often have many motivations and in any event can't see the future either. All financial documents given on past performance are irrelevant, except and insofar as a financial statement has clues to constraints and resources relevant to future actions, the paper should be tossed (ok, recycled).

An astonishing amount of financial reporting, and much of the information generated in the process, is simply pushing the party line. The companies carefully structure transactions to present the face they want. If the accounting rules change to prevent this, the company moves its headquarters, or major segments of the company, to Europe or some other venue that makes life easier. For its part, the government wants everyone to think that things are going well, and if everyone does think that, then things will go well, at least until the credit runs out. If the government was held to the same reporting requirements that private industry was, the government would rapidly focus on prison improvement, as they would all be in there.

If you think about business reports, why would a business report level sales and events? Everything is changing all the time everywhere, so any major business that reports steadily increasing levels of sales, with everything under control, is lying. The stock analysts, with their demands that the stories be just a certain way, force the stories to warp the reality. Accountants for the company are paid by the company, and the auditors carefully limit their opinions to something close to 'we think there is a pile of stuff there'.

Many people want to be your shepherd. There are financial shepherds, spiritual shepherd's, exercise shepherds. There are many people who mean and do well, and many really detestable parasites, who are happy to shepherd you into the meat packer. People talk, sermonize, about how you have to watch out and to not sell your soul (financial, spiritual) to whatever. You should have some caution, because the speaker generally has a clear idea where they would feel better about your actions, and that place is where they want your soul.

So when you read a newspaper article, back up ESPECIALLY if you are thinking of investing because of the article. What was the context that the article was written in? How new is the information? A stock price only goes up if: (1) a company is growing so that net asset value per share increases, and/or (2) profits are growing so earnings per share are increasing, and/or (3) there is too much money sloshing around driving prices up. Since everyone has read the article you are reading and the people on Wall Street knew this a month ago, what asymmetric information (what do you know that no one else knows) do you know that is different? Oh, and don't buy a stock because of (3): the money will slosh somewhere else and the price will go down. Gold does this on a regular basis.

So much information presented as news is actually puff or propaganda of various types, that it almost staggers the mind. For example, the network news, with their helpful clips from the government on stopping drugs, immigration law, the war in wherever, all of that is created and provided by some agency of the government. If, after forty plus years of the war on drugs, why is the capture of the largest drug shipment ever news? What does this tell you about the demand, shipping methods? Notice that there are no estimates of the amount of total supply that this seizure represents, because that raises very ugly questions indeed.

I saw an article praising a new, high technology missile that the Air Force had just acquired. Way down in the article it was briefly mentioned that the missile was needed because the new, state of the art planes had too low a payload capability for the old missiles. We have a fail on top of a fail, but someone is making money on this. Then we see articles on prisons, which discuss the huge success the guards are having stopping the prisoners from doing things that no one on the outside ever imagined the inmates could be doing in jail: what is really being said there?

The point of that particular rant is that you have to back up and look at the system implied by what the article is saying. If that system doesn't make sense, don't invest.

The other part of reading very carefully, is that the same word has multiple meanings in different parts of a financial/tax question (most questions, actually). It isn't uncommon that there are even multiple meanings for the same word depending on the stage of the transaction, and which side you are on. So over and over people get an answer that they interpret using what turns out to be a partial, at best, meaning for the problem they face. The other side can say (often truthfully) that the answer was true given certain facts, and if you assumed other facts, you should have asked questions. A recent cartoon in the Wall Street Journal had an advisor saying "I'm going to put this into terms you think you understand". You can't look around corners you didn't know were there? Pity. I've seen this play many times.

What is the use of knowing the information isn't any good? Well, it keeps one from believing that questionable data is certainty, even if it has to be acted on, and it keeps one questioning what is happening, which is the best that can be done in life.

Investing in the stock market has been a wonderful thing, if you live long enough. Remember points (1) to (3) discussed above when looking at information. Another thing to question before you make an investment is whether all the profit in a deal was parceled out in the creation and selling of the deal. Publicly held limited partnerships are notorious for this. Back up when presented a deal like this: what are the marketing costs, if you can dig them out of the small print. How is the investment going to dig its way out of those? Remember, that investment being sold you is completing with private money and corporate money, that doesn't bear all the marketing freight. Where is the extra profit coming from?

Quite frankly, an investment needs to have a huge potential upside at least theoretically possible. If you have ten investments, hopefully at least one of them will pop big, to offset all the ones that don't work. If the maximum upside for something complex is 8%, walk away. Mathematically, you need a potential for a power function/positive feedback in an investment. What does that mean? Positive feedback means that the process grows on itself, and can get very large, very fast. Microsoft was this kind of a stock. Enron was a negative positive feedback case. Nuclear reactions going bad (Chernobyl) are also a positive feedback case (with negative results) if that gives you a picture of what is involved. Remember, if it's being said and done, someone profits: not just emotionally, in dollars and cents. If it doesn't seem to make sense, back away: that was the Enron case. And if it only makes a little sense, look closely, because somewhere further up the line someone is making money. If you don't see the sucker, then you are the sucker.

The stock market is diversification money for most people. Because you can't predict the future, you spread the investments around. You shouldn't use the market as a legal gambling casino. I've actually tried, as well as many people I know. It isn't as satisfying as it should be. Even when I made money, it was for different reasons than I anticipated, which does stagger one's confidence a bit.

A classic Wall Street joke ends with the punch line: Where are the customer yachts? Because there are not any. The other classical joke is: How do you end up with a small fortune in the stock market? You start with a large fortune.

Risk is a key part of feedback, because it only matters if it matters. What are the odds that something you do will be greatly positive (or negative)? If you do something that has a 1/1,000,000 change of something negative, that usually isn't a huge problem. Unless: you are British Petroleum drilling in the Gulf of Mexico and your low probability action will wreak havoc on millions of people and immeasurable other living creatures, in which case you should have taken a lot more care. So risk isn't just how rare the event is. Risk is the equation: (probability of event) x (damage/good from the event). A low probability event can have an enormous risk, which is something we generally miss. That is part of the argument in the book "Antifragile", it denies much of the concept behind the usual idea of risk. Sadly, what cannot be calculated cannot be calculated, and so we miss the risk hidden there.

Risk is also the unexpected. For example, you are afraid of someone breaking into your house and stealing your valuables. So you brilliantly buy a little safe that that looks like a cleaning bottle, or some other household item, and put your valuables in there. Ignoring the fire problem (in a fire, your little safe burns up) no thief is going through your cleaning supplies. The problem is that will you (or another person in your household) will later throw out the trick bottle and your valuables, because it looks just like an empty bottle. No one has any feedback that it's actually a safe, which is the brilliant part of the plan, and it's downfall. As there is no feedback that it isn't just a worthless empty bottle to be tossed, I can testify that it will be tossed, and missed much later.

Generally speaking, we overestimate risks for things that are (1) out of our control and (2) sensationalized in the media. We all underestimate risks for things that are mundane and ordinary. We all believe that things will happen in the future as they did in the past, based on experience. That's a huge risk right there. For example, you have a job, you have been there 10 years, you do a good job, people are happy with you. Will you have a job in 6 months? Maybe, or maybe it's outsourced to India despite all your years of good work and sacrifice. Your house payments? They were not outsourced with your job, but wait patiently at home for you.

Here's a quick visual model for feedback that hopefully won't be too negative to be useful. Feedback is a spider web. You want to be the spider in the middle, listening to the little tugs and twinges. Then you carefully investigate, not controlling, but setting the stage for events, reacting to developments. That simple visual encompasses all of the key points, unless you hate spiders so much that you can't visualize it. Which is unfortunate, because spiders eat a lot of things that can make our lives miserable.

CHAPTER 13. OODA CYCLE

The OODA cycle is both why we need feedback and how we use it. So, what is the OODA cycle? The cycle was developed by Colonel John Boyd, USAF. The figure below is the simplest representation of the OODA cycle. If you are interested, there are far more detailed diagrams available. It's important to put this into perspective: bullets are flying by, there are explosions all around you, perhaps fighter planes and helicopters whizzing above you, there are shouting men and the screaming wounded, and you're supposed to do something effective or something that will at least keep you- and your squad-alive.

The OODA cycle is designed to be simple and effective under the most stressful conditions possible, conditions where the mind would normally just shut down and react. So this will work in daily life, having been tested literally under fire.

Figure 5.

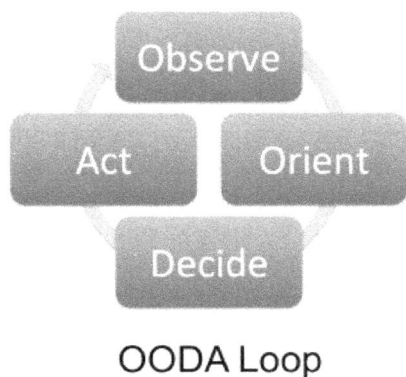

OODA Loop

David Allen says that your system for handling life should be designed when you have the flu. In other words, have a system that at least works when you are the least effective and focused on doing only what's absolutely necessary. A system that works when you have the flu will work when you're actually functioning, where as a system that demands peak performance won't ever run. That's a key point, because normally we start with at least average performance, and design in peak performance as a goal. That's a fail, because you are going to be under the weather as often as above the weather. Having to give 200% to catch up for when you could only give 20% isn't ever going to work.

If you impose a non-workable system on people, they will, out of necessity, game the system and cheat. Remember, cheating the system is your perspective, their perspective is survival. So cheating grows. Once people start cheating the system, then they must disrespect the system or themselves, and you can guess which people pick. Lose their respect for the system and you can't get them back.

As discussed before, you plan and plan before the battle. You get the logistics working, or at least see where there are problems, and you play with ideas and possibilities. None of the plans will work in their entirely, and none will work in all the details, but in giving thought to possibilities, you are ready

133

for problems. This is an example of some of the assumptions you might make before a battle commences:

> "We have to bet on how they are going to react when we come in. People always blow the risk calculations. People overestimate risks that are out of their control, and fixate on the risk du jour shouted on the TV. Ordinary, daily, mundane risks are continually underestimated. People always assume that what happened yesterday is going to happen tomorrow. And it depends on who is expecting what."[61]

The quote makes reasonable guesses. They will not always be right; perhaps all your guesses will be wrong if events conspire against you, but you've got to think, to the extent possible, before it starts. The old 'up to your ass in alligators when you started out trying to clean out the swamp' is going to happen every time if you don't think before starting.

The OODA cycle is a time competitive cycle of Observation, Orientation, Decision, Action, and the cycle starts again. The winner is the side that runs the cycle the fastest and the most. The idea is to operate inside the enemy's decisions cycle, generating first confusion, then frustration, and finally panic. Once the enemy has lost control, then you can probe and attack, finally destroying their ability to function.

It's feedback about what's really happening that makes the difference. Observation is catching what happened after you acted and the enemy reacted. Feedback is more complex than people want it do be and is covered in the following section. In a firefight, you are trying, under conditions of great stress, to sense more than you just see. You want to use all senses, not lock yourself up. To act, you need to understand your opponents. You need to think through their strengths, their weaknesses, and your own, and using the OODA cycle to evaluate what you thought was true as opposed to what is really happening. You live or die in maneuver warfare by finding the enemy's critical weakness in a specific situation. Daily life isn't quite as dramatic (maybe driving on the X-way?) but the results are the same.

Boyd's ideas are a melody based on The Art of War. I've quoted extensively from The Art of War in this book, but would strongly recommend that you buy the book-it's just a little book-and read it slowly, over and over. I used to keep a little pocket edition in a coat where I could read parts when I had a few minutes. It's a quite different way of thinking, and it works its way into your mind slowly. Sun Tzu says, first, THINK! Don't react, think. If you create multiple threats (an option offense is almost always a good thing) then the enemy is uncertain. Test the enemy: what overlaps are they operating in? Are they focused on honor and glory, or do they want your hide? It makes a difference! Never do the same thing twice, see yourself as flowing water, and simply flow around obstacles the most appropriate way.

Tactics (small squad battles) can't win the war. The Greeks in the Trojan War tried that for 10 years, and it didn't work. You can have the best fighting squads in the world, and if you are outnumbered 10 to 1, it's not going to go well. But tactics can make a difference where it isn't hopeless, and even sometimes where it seems hopeless. There is a simple concept: Schwerpunkt, which seeks to understand the enemy gaps (weaknesses) and surfaces (strengths). Then you focus all your power on a gap, not a surface. This isn't honor, a victory over a worthy opponent in single combat before cheering throngs, this is real victory. This is the 'boulders falling down the mountain onto eggs' concept of Sun Tzu.

Again, we are denying the long history of the nominal rules of war, which, coming from historical sources, treated war as a game and emphasized honor, glory, the victory. That's an ancient view that probably was honored more in the breach than in the observance. This isn't jousting on the fields of France, brave nobles on their armored steeds, wearing their love's hair ribbon into the joust. In real life (often, actually, in the jousts) the victor goes home, and the loser lies broken on the field of honor. Winning matters. Sun Tzu is a direct challenge to the 'honor' battle, which exists in every culture. Given the clear thrust of his writings, it is clear he has contempt for the honor victory. Sun Tzu said:

"Thus the battles of the skilled are without extraordinary victory, without reputation for wisdom and without merit for courage"[62]. *Pp 14, Form*

Which is dramatically different from the conquering hero, but far more effective. The question you have to ask yourself is whether you want results, or an image? Boyd held that people were the most important weapons, then ideas, and finally hardware. We have to be reminded over and over that the winner isn't always the one with money and shiny equipment.

A few examples: France outspent Germany between World War I and World War II, especially on designing and building the Maginot Line, but lost in three decisive weeks in the Spring of 1940. And then there was Vietnam, where the United States spent and spent, and the more they spent, the less they got. Then the Soviets in Afghanistan and it's looking now like the US in Afghanistan. A huge army lined up on a field is generally going to roll over a smaller army lined up against it; except, for example, the Battle of Agincourt.

The Battle of Agincourt is a clear example where the French confused war with honor and jousting, an elaborate social script, and the English focused on winning. Winning trumps honor and glory.

So, hopefully I've persuaded you that feedback is important. How do we get good feedback?

GETTING GOOD FEEDBACK

Let's think about designing a system that works. We want a system that will minimize errors, maximize success, and that provides information about what is happening at all times. There are some clear design rules for such a system:

- you need to understand the causes of error and design to minimize those causes.

- You want to make it possible to reverse actions and to undo them or make it harder to do what cannot be reversed.

- You need to make it easier to discover the errors that do occur, and make them easier to correct. A large part of that orientation is that you have to change your attitude toward errors. Errors are going to happen, they are not a moral weakness. Even if they are a moral weakness, you don't want blame, you want success and moral weakness only make people hide those errors.

- You want to create a system that exploit natural mappings, which is a fancy way of saying that make sure what is front of you let's you make easy right choices. You need to be able to easily and quickly see the relationship between intentions and possible actions; between actions and their effects on the system; between actual system state and what is perceivable by sight, sound or feel, and between the perceived system state and the needs, intentions, and expectations of the user.

- Recognize that you're going to act. If you can't easily see the relationships, then you're still going to act, probably according to inappropriate criteria (another drink won't hurt) and the results will generally not be optimal.

- Structure constraints (limits) carefully. The surest way to make something easy to use, with few errors, is to make it impossible to do otherwise. If there is only a knob that turns to the left, then it isn't going to be turned to the right.

- It's absolutely essential to show the effect of an action. Without feedback, one is always wondering whether anything has happened. Maybe the button wasn't pushed hard enough; maybe the machine has stopped working; maybe it is doing the wrong thing. Without feedback, we turn equipment off at improper times or restate unnecessarily, losing all our recent work. Or we repeat the command and end up having the operation done twice. You can, on a web site, end up purchasing the same object three times, as you click the 'buy' button without obvious results.

'Mapping' is a technical term meaning the relationship between two things, in this case between the controls and their movements and the results in the world. The idea is simple. You have a mental map of the location of your hand and the knob, and you move your hand towards the knob. It isn't always as simple as that by any means. In physical structures, a wheel and the clockwise direction are natural choices; visible, closely related to the desired outcome, and providing immediate feedback. The mapping is easily learned and always remembered. For conceptual issues, it's harder.

Natural mapping takes advantage of physical analogies and cultural standards, leading to relatively immediate understanding. Try and work with physical, real world analogies, such as a spatial analogy; to move an object up, move the control up. To control an array of lights, arrange the controls in the same pattern as the lights. There is a universal standard that a rising level represents more, a diminishing level, less. Similarly, a louder sound can mean a greater amount. Amount and loudness (and weight, line length, and brightness) are additive dimensions. To the extent you can use these ideas with any conceptual planning, it will work better.

A good conceptual model allows us to predict the effects of our actions. Without a good model we operate by rote, blindly; we do operations as we were told to do them; we can't fully appreciate why, what effects to expect, or what to do if things go wrong. When things go wrong and/or we are facing a novel situation, we need a deeper understanding, or we turn to ritual and luck.

A device is easy to use when there is visibility to the set of possible actions, where the controls and displays exploit natural mappings. All cars have essentially the same layout: a steering wheel, an accelerator, a brake. If every car had a different layout (a tiller wheel, a hand brake, for example) driving would be even more exciting that it is now.

If an error is possible, someone will make it. Always assume that all possible errors will occur and design so as to minimize the chance of the error in the first place, or its effects once it gets made.

In general, it has been found that people attribute their own problems to the environment, those of other people to their personalities. If you design a system that doesn't work, people are not going to complementary. It was 'your' system, remember?

CHAPTER 14. WHY IS THIS IMPORTANT?

As long as you have not seen vulnerable
formations in opponents, you hide
your form, preparing yourself
in such a way as to be invincible,
in order to preserve yourself.
When opponents have vulnerable
formations, then it is time
to go out to attack them. [63]
Chapter 4: "FORMATION"

Why would that be a surprise? Any damn fool knows that if you stand out a field, your formations fixed solidly, your troops perspiring in the hot sun, you have handed your opponent more information about you than you should. Just because it makes you feel good to see all those people under your command, and they all see how powerful you are to be commanding all of them, has very little to do with actually winning the battle.

People put their troops in the field because they misunderstand the overlaps between the social world and the self, and the social world and the real world. Winning is the goal, Sun Tzu says over and over. But in the eyes of most men/women, it's winning in the eyes of the beholders that is at least as important, if not more important, than the victory in the field. You don't win, in people's eyes, by skulking about and pouncing. You win as a Greek Hero would have won: standing defiantly on the plain, foot on the head of your fallen enemy, the conqueror of all that he surveys. Can you see the errors there? Winning, if losing is the loss of country, family and all you love, is more important than image.

"So where were we?" Hal sat down. "Okay. In planning, it's essential to accept confusion and disorder, because that is the way events happen in the real world. Go ahead, say it."

"You're as confused and disordered as anyone I've known, so we should be in great shape," Cali teased.

"Feel better?" Hal said.

"It's almost too easy, but yes. You know what you said about humor and handling things."

"If I was joking, I'd say something like 'A horse walks into a bar. The bartender said, why the long face?'"

"If I was hitting, I'd first ball my fist up like this and..."

"So anyhow," Hal continued, "we accept confusion and disorder, which works well because things are hopelessly confused and disordered right now. We have to figure out how to GENERATE confusion and disorder to attack them. They have to think we are attacking somewhere else than our real target. They have to wonder if we are running, hiding or just trembling in the dark. See, we, ideally, want them on the horns of a dilemma. When they look as us, they have to see a problem with no solution, all contradictory information pointing to inconsistent choices."

"You really like this stuff, don't you? Is this what guys talk about?"

"Gamers do, when they're not swapping pictures of naked women."

"My mother and I used to ride horses. She said it was good training for life, because a woman had to know how to handle a large, hairy, and difficult beast. She said men were simple beasts—keep them clean and fed, and they'd be good."

"Now I really feel special," Hal replied. "Anyhow, let's deal with keeping us alive for a while longer. So we need to think—what are our strengths? My brains, your beauty, and a holocaust cloak, for example. What are our weaknesses, other than being hopelessly outgunned, outmanned, and detested outcasts from respected society? If we can figure out their strengths, technically known as surfaces, and their weaknesses, i.e., their gaps, then we can plan an attack."

"I'm listening. Is there something coming about our surviving this attack?"

"You want to live forever? Where's the fun in that? See, there's this concept. 'Schwerpunkt,' which means to attack where all your power can go against one point, 'a torrent of boulders against eggs,' or something like that. Given that they have lots of strengths, and we have few, focus is all we have."

Hal was frowning as he drew intersecting circles on the paper. "Our best hope is that they are still locked into their game plan. They have to draw the guardians out, because the guardians will never stop coming after them now. Their game plan is entirely based on finding and eliminating us, and pouncing as the chaos unfolds. Us coming after them? Not even on the radar. They see us as little frightened mice, that's the story they have told themselves. I can almost guess what's on their network. I've got to figure out how to access it, and how it's protected— two really big questions. If it don't get that figured out soon, it's going to be that run-down apartment in Detroit for us."

"You're doing great. There are known known's, unknown known's, and unknown unknowns. You're a long way into turning the unknown unknowns into known's. Then we work up Plan A, Plan B, etc."

"Up to Plan F'd," Hal observed, "which is disaster time."[64]

We are looking at maneuver warfare because it is perhaps the most intense situation possible. The OODA cycle, which is: Observe, Orient, Decide and Act, then quickly redo the cycle again and again, is at least conceptually simple and perfect for any fast paced, complex situation where the 'new' is constantly popping up. It is also perfect for any situation, fast paced or not, but that will be clearer later.

In battle, long term planning isn't possible on the micro level, because there is just too much stuff happening too quickly. Now, that's not the same as saying that you can ignore macro planning! Or even not give considerable thought to micro planning, even though you are certain to be wrong. At least you'll have some ideas about resources, constraints and what happens in various cases.

Macro planning is essential, actually. Before battle, troops have to be moved, their weapons must work and have ammunition, gasoline and other supplies in place, small details such as food and shelter for the troops, has to be planned by someone. Fail at logistics, and the best-trained, most courageous troops don't stand a chance. Once in actual warfare, it is chaos, and the group that runs the OODA cycle faster than the other side responds faster to change and survives.

> So when the front is prepared,
> the rear is lacking,
> and when the rear is prepared,
> the front is lacking. Preparedness on
> the left means lack on the right,
> preparedness on the right means
> lack on the left.[65]
> Chapter 6: "EMPTINESS AND FULLNESS"

It's running the OODA cycle that tells you what the situation is. If you're not looking at the data coming in, if you are only listening to your thumping heart and fast breathing, you don't know what is prepared and what is lacking. You have to be focused to see where their weaknesses are. As discussed above, confusion and disorder is the game you have chosen. Denying the confusion and disorder while longing for order and structure, will guarantee defeat. By accepting confusion and disorder and making the most of it, you will GENERATE confusion and disorder so that the other side is completely confused and unable to respond. As Sun Tzu says over and over, all patterns, recipes, and formulas are to be avoided because the enemy must not be able to predict.

> Without deception,
> you cannot carry out strategy,
> without strategy
> you cannot control the opponent.[66]
> Chapter 1: "ON ASSESSMENTS"

If you deceive, then the enemy attacks without knowing what they are attacking. After the enemy has irrevocably committed himself, then you pounce. Sun Tzu's goal was to create confusion in the opposing side and then exploit it. His focus is not on winning through superior tactics (a squad battle) or individual fighting technique (the hero's battle) but by confusing the enemy, making them unable to respond, and then quickly responding and crushing your enemy. His goal is winning through superior strategy. Sun Tzu accepts that some troops are braver than others, but it is the army as a unit that matters in victory. This is a long way from the vision of the Trojan War, which was essentially a mass of individual battles for glory and honor. Glory and Honor should be left to the writers of history, who can embellish as they want.

Now, deception has some negative social implications. It's the confusion between winning in the real world versus winning in the social world that throws us over and over. The problem with Sun Tzu's advice is that they are the opposite of what the social world wants (demands) in everyday life. Our image of a glorious victory isn't a lot different than that of small boys battling in a schoolyard, which is a social situation, not a battle. Confusion between winning in social terms and real winning has lost many battles and destroyed many countries. You have to move away from the idea that victory is image, not results. If you want to be a small boy, living for the praises of the rest of the school, then stay in school. Stay out of real world wars. The British learned that lesson in World War I, but it was a hard lesson.

"It's all misdirection," Hal mused. "One of my favorite movie scenes was from 'Three days of the Condor.' The courteous, sophisticated, professional assassin tells the hero how he will be killed. 'You are walking, maybe the first sunny day in spring. You are happy, the long winter over. A car will stop beside you, the door will open; a person you trust will get out of the car, smiling, leaving the door open, and offer you a ride'. POW! A right hook to the jaw when your guard is down. The weather report is predicting a hot summer night; the shop is doing their usual business, no one is looking for us, and there we are. In, wreak havoc, out."[67]

And again:

Since you adapt
and adjust appropriately
in the face of the enemy,
how could you say what you are going
to do beforehand?[68]
Chapter 1: "ON ASSESSMENTS"

Sun Tzu's strategy differs fundamentally from the essence of Western military doctrine. Western military doctrine is based on the strategy of Carl von Clausewitz, his primary goal was to bring the opposing army to "decisive battle," and then win it. It is the Trojan War over and over, noble and brave men standing and fighting for honor and glory. The American Civil War, and more clearly World War I, made clear the absolute futility of glory and honor. Perhaps there is honor in a sword fight, but it is only stupidity to march into machine gun fire.

Sun Tzu seeks to achieve victory. His position was again completely in the real world, not the social world, because he wanted the enemy army to disintegrate before the battle:

> *Therefore, those who win every battle are not really skillful*
> *those who render other's armies helpless without fighting are the best of all.*[69]

Western armies, seeking a decisive battle, are going to lose a lot of troops in that quest for glory and honor.

> *What everyone knows is what has already happened or become obvious.*
> *What the aware individual knows is what had not yet taken shape, what has not yet occurred.*
> *Everyone says victory in battle is good,*
> *but if you see the subtle and notice the hidden so as to seize victory where there is no form, this is really good.*[70]
> *Chapter 4, Formation*

Again, it's the confusion between what battle you are fighting: whether it is the battle in the social world glory, or the real world battlefield that makes Sun Tzu's advice hard to implement. We read his words, nod at his sage advice, and then polish our bronze armor so it will glow all the brighter in the battle. By polishing our armor, we, of course, made ourselves an easier target, but social demands have nothing to do with the real world victory.

Boyd sought to implement Sun Tzu's methods by the OODA cycle. This could be argued as a brilliant step around social demands by focusing on a technique that demands focus on the real world more than on the social world. So, rather than arguing about honor and glory, we use a tool that is only concerned with survival and victory in the real world. That is a good plan, because no matter how much you rail against honor, glory, and sacrificing yourself pointlessly, people will stand in the bar and worship honor and glory. That isn't to say that honor and glory are not important, because in the heat of battle honor and glory may be all that keep one from bolting. But they are a tactic, not the strategy.

The OODA cycle demands we sense, and then observe, collecting information, then decide and finally act. Then do it all again, checking the goal against the results. It's a relatively simple concept that can be taught and practiced. Reading the "Art of War" is one revealed truth after another: but how does one remember which one to apply at the relevant time? Hopefully the OODA technique, by focusing on what's happening, will back into Sun Tzu's concepts of deception, flexibility and real victory.

"It's a guy example. It isn't muscle that wins, it's thinking, making the OODA cycle work for you, not against you. So I observe, orient, decide and act, and then I do it again. We live or die based on whether we cycle that loop faster than the other side. The problem is," furiously drawing arrows on the paper, "that it's hard to really see what is happening. Am I observing what I think I'm observing? The cycle only works if you get good feedback. What's dangerous is to see only what you want to see. Boring, but critical."

"You are good at that maneuver stuff. I mean really good. I was telling the Caretaker about the alley and he had a look of real admiration when I told him how you called their attack. Moments, he told me. Moments were all we had, and they should have had us. He even forgave you not cleaning the dishes."

Hal didn't know what to say.

"Don't let it go to your head," Cali teased, and she stroked his head. "He still didn't forgive your apartment."

"Too much time on computer games to clean," Hal replied, recovering. "And, they were rigid in their attack. It was exactly like it's practiced, but you are never supposed to follow a pattern when you are actually fighting. If the enemy can anticipate you, then you are dead. Worked for us that time. . . . ."[71]

CHAPTER 15. WHAT PROBLEMS SHOULD I BE SOLVING?

Feedback is what we get back when we poke the world. We poke the world to get information about a problem. But how do you know what problems to solve? 'Urgent' isn't the same as critical or even important.

The hardest thing to see is what is in front of your eyes.[72]
Johann Wolfgang von Goethe

Not knowing what problems to solve is norm. And your life came with instructions?

This is where we start: What should we be looking at? This book has many times talked about our nature and that we don't see problems that we don't have now. We don't explore implicit contradictions in our thoughts and plans, for a number of reasons. If you do explore all those potential problems, when do you actually get anything done? While we'd be willing to sit on the beach with a beer and ponder, no one is lining up to fund us.

There was an old man, on his deathbed, who said that his life had been a mass of problems, most of which had never happened. We don't want to do that, but we do want to see the problems coming while they are small, not when they emerge full blown.

We usually have some inkling that there is a problem.

What did that marketing guy say last week? a random thought pushing into his consciousness. He told us—what? Decoys dupe us. There was a study. Volunteers were asked to decide among three autos that met minimum specifications. It was hard to choose because the first two cars were marred by differing tradeoffs. The third auto, almost the same as the first one, had a worse trade off. Showing the customer the third, most undesirable auto increased the appeal of the first. Why? Hardwired in the brain, the third option decreased the activity of the amygdala, a part of the brain tied to negative emotions. Why do I care about that? he thought, now even more annoyed.[73]

We don't have a problem/opportunity, but we have an uneasy feeling. An itch. Worse, a rash.

NEW YORK. CHRISTMAS NIGHT

The party had died down, and most of the children were in bed.

Hal stood by the windows, staring out at the dark street, not smiling.

Cali walked up behind him. "Where's that Christmas cheer?"

Hal jumped, and his drink spilled. "Damn," brushing at the wine staining his shirt. "Oh well, it's a burgundy shirt."

"That's not a relaxed Christmas spirit I'm seeing," Cali commented, studying him carefully. "Is there something out there? Or too much Christmas cheer?"

"Not unless you've been adding something to the eggnog. And, I don't see anything out there, but there is something in the back of my mind, something picking at me. Maybe it's just me. I seem to be uncoordinated today. I've been bumping my toes and pinching my fingers." He stared down at the street, frowning.

"You do look worried, honey."

"This thing almost pops up and then vanishes again," Hal complained. "I don't know what it is. It's just a nagging feeling, like I'm missing something but don't know what that thing is. My attention is grabbed but I don't know on what. Annoying." He shrugged and pulled the curtains after a final unhappy glance into the dark.

"Listen to the little doubts," Cali reminded him. "Our discussion the other night—remember?"

"Is that what we were discussing?" Hal teased, smiling at her. "The festivities afterward diverted my attention a bit. It will come to me, I think. Saying to listen and letting it pop out are two different things." He frowned, almost able to grasp a floating something and then it was gone again.

"Maria certainly enjoyed Christmas! "All that tearing up stuff, and surrounded by a pile of presents like she was in a fort! It isn't like she's spoiled or anything."

"No, not spoiled a bit!" Hal laughed. "What a great sight! And she's at the age where anything is exciting. Easy to buy for." He was thoughtful again. "What were we talking about the other day? Unknown unknowns—the ones we don't know we don't know, and don't suspect. I'd just feel better if it would pop out of the back of my mind. Oh, well. They will have to remain unknown for a while." He and Cali walked hand in hand to where Maria was squealing with joy, pushing presents over and crawling after the dogs.

Later that night, Hal peered out the window into the dark. Denial is the most insidious fear response of all, he thought. Fear of harm to the family—it's easy to want to pretend there isn't any danger out there. So we deny, pushing it into a corner, into places we never think to look. He absently watched a truck drive slowly down the street, pulling into the warehouse down and across from them. He shook his head, frustrated as he walked back to the celebration.[74]

And when the problem did emerge the next day, it was a big one. But how do we see what we can't see? Out of frustration, we can try and wall out the unknowns, but putting up a Great Wall to protect us is always useless in the end. The French, after World War I invested enormous sums into their defenses, the Maginot line, which the German's simply went around. The Great Wall of China didn't keep the Mongols out. The bigger the wall, the more the danger you seek to hide from grows in strength, while you, comfortable and secure, weaken. So the strongest defense is no wall, ready swords and an aggressive attitude, as Romulus and Remus discussed when they founded Rome.

One interesting overlap between the self and the social world, which ignores the real world, is called the Abilene paradox. This is case where a group collectively decide on a course of action, a course of action that is counter to the preferences of any of those in the group. And generally counter to the real world, to boot. The paradox is created when everyone in the group accepts that the group view is the real world, and so each member of the group ignores their perception of the real world. Groupthink is this type of a problem, in which the key, central reference point is the group, not the external world. This is at least a partial explanation for the notoriously bad decisions that committees often seem to make. While in action, the committee thinks it is trying hard and doing it's best. In fact, the harder the committee tries, the more it is committed to its decisions and the less it is willing to listen to criticism of its actions. The rest of the problem lies in words and Suits, as discussed earlier.

We think of the world as linear, as in this lament in King Lear, that:

To-morrow, and to-morrow, and to-morrow,
Creeps in this petty pace from day to day,
To the last syllable of recorded time;[75]

When really, the world isn't linear. Sure, the days go by one by one, but the events filling those days are not linear. Systems fracture, as the Teutonic plates crash, and then the structures freeze. That's why the children of the leaders of the revolution become the new nobility, until the next revolution. When the earth opens, you have to be there and ready.

Let's look at goals in a different way. We've talked about clarifying goals, working with unclear goals, and how to choose goals. Goals can morph without our noticing it. A goal runs the risk of taking on a life of its own. Suddenly, your nebulous goal becomes a very clear goal that isn't quite the original goal. Without solid, next action, concrete goals, there are no criteria that can be used to judge whether progress is in fact being made. If you don't know when you are done, then you are never done. The plan turns into a ritual that is repeated until exhaustion and/or the money runs out. Your plan becomes a game, often without realizing it.

Certain types of plans are at high risk for becoming games, and thus completely side tracked. For example, if your sub goals have about a fifty-fifty chance of success, and the sub goals are interesting and exciting, people will happily focus their energies on such challenges over extended periods of time. I trained pigeons for a college psychology class, and they would (at least for other students) happily peck for hours with the right reinforcement schedule. You have to be careful that your plan doesn't get sidetracked into that type of a game. Having said that, if your plan is a game which results in your doing things in the real world that are productive, you win big! Not only do you win emotionally, every day playing this neat game that rewards you, but you win in the bigger world also.

In the Black Swan, the author talks about the problem of doing work (such as writing a book) that has a low probability of success and precious little social reward at the time you are doing it. What he doesn't factor in is the game aspect of the work, which provides many immediate rewards and emotionally rewarding successes, outside of the social rewards. This is really important, because inadvertent goals and rewards will shape your life for success or failure. Whether your games revolve around a focus on investments, or miniature paintings of the Renaissance, or negative interactions with your boss(es) makes a difference. And what you focus on depends on your rewards.

How do you define your plans as games so you work and work at them? It's accidental most of the time, but technically the design of such a plan/game falls into something called a 'flow situation'. A flow situation is one in which tension is built up, then released, a sequence in which the participant experiences fear of failure, triumph over obstacles, renewed fear of failure, another triumph, and so on. If your goals are unclear (you have kind of a plan and some steps) you can easily fall prey to this phenomenon. An interim goal happened on by chance may seduce you into a flow situation that you are helpless to escape. It is common for scientific researchers to become database experts in the course of their research, which was supposed to be a tool to an end. The expertise becomes an end because that's a clear, doable goal. The research? That's a lot harder. But you've got all these neat printouts to show people if they ask how it's going.

Why do goals degenerate? There are many reasons. Among them may be a desire for safety and a lack of confidence in one's own capabilities (which the world is happy to help with). What you want to do is to turn what seems to be a weakness into strength. You are, in a way, pigeon training, training yourself to peck and peck at that target which will coincidentally bring success. Or a high game score, one of the two.

So, we want to know what problems to solve. Finding problems to solve isn't hard: the world is littered with them. Once we accumulate some unsolved problems, we must then decide which ones we will attack first. If we have no criteria based on the specification of our goals (say, money connected to this one, or the boss yelling about that one) to help us set priorities, we will choose the obvious problems, or the ones that we already know how to solve.

We then end up concentrating on the wrong problems but, most seriously, we are neglecting the 'critical and non-urgent problems that are the key to life. It's easy to do the urgent and non-critical problems, as they are standing shouting in front of us, and that's what happens when partial/interim goals capture our attention and displace primary goals. It's

147

too easy to back into a task we are good at that offers both challenges and the gratification of some success -i.e., a game.

Let's look at 2 new diagrams.

First, the classic boxes: the following is from Stephen Covey's "7 Habits of Effective People", a modification of the usual diagram, but I think is more effective because of the changes.

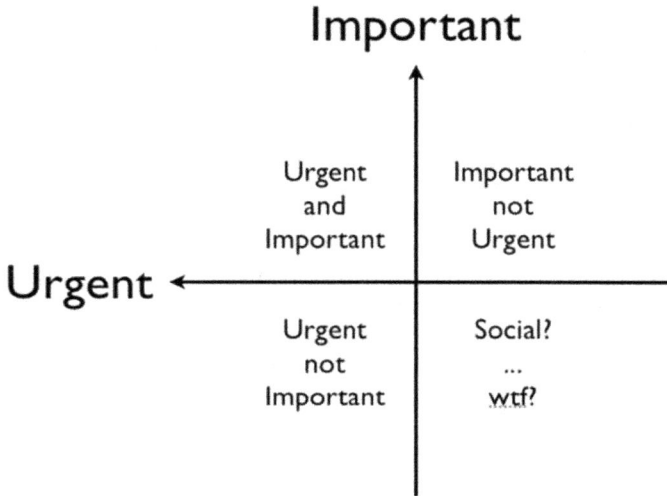

Important

Urgent and Important	Important not Urgent
Urgent not Important	Social? ... wtf?

Urgent ←

Figure 6.

The above should be what you think about each and every day, and several times during the day. It's the best guide out there to thinking about your choices as you are making them.

Now, the diagram below modifies the above, to take into effect what society wants versus what you want.

Quadrant 1 Good for You Good for Society	**Quadrant 2** Good for You Bad for Society
Quadrant 3 Bad for You Good for Society	**Quadrant 4** Bad for You Bad for Society

Figure 7.

This is important! The urgent can be co-opted by what society wants, so that you are doing things that inside really don't seem that important. If you hate Figure 7, then focus on Figure 6 which is not only important but socially blessed.

As this book says over and over, look at the central Figure 1 and think about what overlaps you actually perceive. Thoughts pop-up days later, but you've got to start the process. Then look at Figures 2 and 3 and work through what are the critical but not urgent problems facing you? Figure that out, and life, barring the random disasters that can't be helped, will be good.

The David Allen methodology of keeping a list of your projects and the next actions will, after a year or two, make it pretty clear what you really care about enough to actually do. Look at those project lists as they build up, and you'll start having some ideas about where they conflict, where they match. You'll notice over time where you have projects that are repairs for the conflicts, and those are anomalies, the tool that tells you where the stories are breaking down.

We have to do something: it's our nature. Repairing something is better than doing nothing, because we might fix it, and if not, at least we are aware of the problem. If we can formulate goals in concrete terms, we should; if we can't, then muddling through is better than inaction. Do we feel confused? That's good, because contradictory goals are the rule, not the exception, in complex situations. In economic systems costs and benefits are almost always at odds. If we don't see that things are at odds, then we have that most dangerous situation: the contradictory relationship of partial goals is not evident.

We could do worse than play games with ourselves. Life is after all a game. Don't take it so seriously! It's just we want productive games, games that lead us to what we want, not pacify us or distract us from what we are after.

David Allen said, and he's right, that we have to do our thinking before doing. It's too late to think when the rain-or hail-of events are falling on us. Thinking is so critical that most world-class athletes spend more time in their training thinking, visualizing the right actions and moves, than in physically performing the actions. At their level, much of the physical movements are memorized, and what they are focusing on, literally, is calming and just doing what they can do. There is a technique called 'quiet eye', which is, among others, weeding out the noise, the voices and pictures of failure, because if you think about failure, you will fail. That's a type of success that's almost guaranteed.

Another very important concept of David Allen's, especially for the questions of this chapter, is the three-fold nature of work. He argues that there are three kinds of work: (1) work that comes at you, (2) work that other's define for you, and (3) work that you define for yourself. Actually, limiting this to work is too restrictive, because that's what life does. Events come at you and you have to struggle with those events; events are defined for you (take out the garbage, drive to the store, etc.) by others, and those take time-all your time if you don't notice it. Finally, there are events that you define for yourself: events that you look for, that you make time for, that you set the circumstances running for. Cases one and two take care of themselves. There is always something happening in the world, and certainly always someone with an idea of what you should be doing. If you are not careful, cases one and two will eat your life while you wonder what happened.

We are not taught, and often not encouraged, to take the time to define for ourselves what we want. If you define it, then you start reaching for it, changing your life and possibilities so you can do what you have defined. Granted defining what you want simply sets the stage for the critical question of this chapter, which is 'I don't know what problems matter'. The problems that matter are what you want to define for yourself.

One way that you are supposed to be able to know what problems matter is to sit-or walk-or run-and let your highest goals pop into your mind. Then, your course set, you work your way down the list. This was the central concept in 'The 7 Habit's of Highly Effective People", one book among many that asserts that position. You start with your highest goals (the type of exhortations common in graduation speeches and in sermons, typically), clarify those, and then work your way down to daily life, everything in line and coherent. A pretty picture and nice sharp lines and square corners to carry with you: but it doesn't, and can't work.

Why?

You can't start with high-level goals and work down, because those high level goals are obviously word concepts, vague to start with. They are High Level Socially Approved Concepts: washed, cleaned and emptied of emotion for the good of the group-like a company mission statement that is so bleached out by the white light of proper thought that there isn't anything left to feel.

Critically, the concepts we do use, sloppy as they may be, are socially approved and fenced in. Few of us have high-level goals along the lines of 'the biggest drug sale in New York in August 2014', and even if we did, we'd justify it somehow. Our childhood, we'd give the profits to charity, hatred for the government, there's something that brings our actions back into some norm. We're just all like that. So even 'nasty' articulated goals get washed by some kind of social approval, as we see it.

If the high level goals are all washed and forced into pretty pictures of some kind, that doesn't leave any space for your inspiration, unless you are empty except for meaning. Inspiration is from inside, and inside we are all animals, organic and full of vices. Original sin is being alive, quite frankly, because life is sin. Everything about life: eating, sleeping, sex, is sin. Overwork isn't sin because that's productive for society-and that's the same for Japan, which doesn't embrace traditional Christian ethics, but wants work out of people.

I'm not saying that defining your highest nominal goals isn't a useful effort. For one thing, it tells you which social groups you are most concerned with, and where you get your most critical 'meanings'. It's just not useful for grabbing onto what you care about most in life, the gusto, as the beer commercial say. Jim Morrison, in "The Soft Parade", said (actually shouted):

> *"When I was back there in seminary school,*
> *There was a person there - Who put forth the proposition*
> *That you can petition the Lord with prayer*
> *Petition the lord with prayer?*
> *Petition the lord with prayer!*
> *You cannot petition the lord with prayer!* "[76]

That actually is a conflict between our internal daily magic and authorized theology. While you may or may not agree regarding prayer, it certainly is true as to your inspiration, your bliss, the driving life in yourself. Your inspiration is the unconscious, all visuals, emotions and clarity, that can't be translated into the formal structure of the prayer/request. That's why high-end goal setting doesn't work. All the emotion, the lust and love and breathless desire (vice), is pushed out of the definition and only the empty social meaning is left. Inspiration is your life, your spirit.

So, when we are told to 'find your bliss' we start by happily defining it in words, reducing it to something controllable and predictable. Otherwise, when you find it, how are you going to find it again? Stated like that, the problem is obvious. There is a mental jump over the social fences that block out access to your bliss, and then confusion when the search doesn't work. Your bliss is an emotional reaction, not a mission statement to be posted on the wall.

There is the serious problem that occurs when you know what problems you want to solve; it's just that they are so socially undesirable that you pretend not to think about them. What do you do when your 'bliss', your inspiration, isn't the pretty set of words that people think it 'should' be. Your inspiration doesn't have to be as socially undesirable as, say, a professional snitch (a short life and an un-merry one), but you probably want more of something than someone in authority things is necessary or appropriate for a person in the peg that they put you.

Only you know your inspiration, and it is what it is. Just because 'they' are serious looking with deep speaking voices doesn't mean that they are right about anything. Now, this isn't to advocate actions that lead to negative interactions with authority figures with guns. That's a set of steps, which is rarely, and I mean, <u>rarely</u>, appropriate, at least in a western democracy. In some countries, where law is a cover for legalized extortion, you have problems and decisions that I would not care to face. I wish you luck, but regardless of the world you are in, your inspiration is shouting at you all day, and your life will turn barren and empty if you don't listen and act.

Sometimes one pays most for the things one gets for nothing.
Anonymous

Much of the preceding discussion was implicitly in a bounded world. A bounded world is a structured world, a world in a box, and you don't look outside the box. A bounded world is a world in which people tell you stuff, things happen and seem to be tied to other things. The world we live in every day, the normal ebb and flow of daily life. Antifragile named this

"So let us call here the teleological fallacy the illusion that you know exactly where you are going, and that you knew exactly where you were going in the past, and that others have succeeded in the past by knowing where they were going."[77]

When they didn't at all, most of the time. We all may have thought we knew when we were doing, but as you look back over the years, one doubts.

We touched on the problems of looking outside the box, but poking at the world visually a picture of us standing over the problem (box) poking down at it. A visual of us turning around, raising up our arms and poking at larger things than us is rather unsettling, even if correct. But how does one get feedback in an unbounded world? Putting down the blinders, squinting into the sun, how do we handle all of that stuff coming at us? (I don't have a checklist, if you are looking for something in the Table of Contents)

Antifragile had many great quotes, one of which is:

What is non-measurable and non-predictable will remain non-measurable and non-predictable.[78]

So, in planning, there's all the stuff you can measure and quantify, and there is that uneasy feeling that you have to listen to in the night.

This is an interesting quote from AntiFragile:

You can't predict in general, but you can predict that those who rely on predictions are taking more risks, will have some trouble, perhaps even go bust. Why? Someone who predicts will be fragile to prediction errors."[79]

Fragile to prediction errors because they will rely on their predictions and take appropriate steps based on their relative level of certainty. 'Certainty', Taleb would argue, is an illusion. The alternative is to guess and test, poke and prod and then act in limited ways with options open. You can't really predict because too much of the feedback is invisible and/or immeasurable.

"It's the immeasurable feedback that drives you crazy," sketching ideas on the tablecloth. "Whoops, this is cloth, not paper. Hal, leave a bigger tip. Humm, maybe a lot bigger. An event is something in, something out. If we don't notice the event, then the chance to head off what is coming is gone. If we are missing the real inputs and outputs, then what we are measuring is useless. Worse than useless, actually. Solving the wrong problem, with all the disaster that brings. What about that article on luck you found in that magazine? Good luck is finding what works for you—that's what it was driving at."

Peter Drucker wrote that trying to predict the future is like driving down a country road at night with no lights while looking out the back window. You just can't get good feedback about the future, by definition. That's why philosopher kings don't come through in the clutch, because that critical ability to see the future doesn't exist.[80]

Stories have coherence and so a story can tie random things together, both with knowledge and without knowledge. That solves several problems, because now we have a lot less to think about that we did before. Feedback is hated/ignored because it ruins the story - the mind opened once to the story, doesn't want to open up again.

Part 3. Getting What We Want - Or Not.

Part 3, Section 1. Planning

Chapter 16. Planning

Chapter 17. Planning Overview

Chapter 18. A Solvable Problem Is?

An Update:

There are reasons for the long, strange trip we have taken so far.

First, our attitude is critical. Then, our perspective on the world, as that's what we are using for our bets on our daily activities, really matters. If our perspective is too serious, we will never start. Too light, and we don't put our best efforts. Technically, we are talking monkeys on a rock hurtling thru space, around a blazing star that by random good luck doesn't cook us but nurtures us. Could be worse.

Then, we reject traditional morality, and discover that we are little creatures in an insanely complex system-parasites, who have to play by the systems rules, not our rules if we want to survive.

We then realize that we can't grasp the world directly, and we can't make sense of the world except through our stories. Our stories trick and trap us as much as they help us, and have to be thought about as we are telling the stories.

Our stories become very complex, because we live in 3 worlds simultaneously, none of which we can completely grasp and from which our information is fragmentary.

Looking at grasping information, we saunter through feedback, discovering that the simple process of testing and evaluating is really, really complex in a dynamic system.

Then, we look at ways to use the feedback as we act.

Finally, after all that, we now start to look at planning, which is what you thought you bought this book for.

CHAPTER 16. PLANNING

This book wants to make planning as exciting as it really is, by taking planning out of the context of 'Men in Suits in Serious Rooms Planning Socially Accepted Things' and putting planning into the context of your life and your desires. There is nothing more exciting in life than planning to get what you want, and getting it. You spot your goal; you hunt it by carefully tracking it, alert to it's every move; and then you pounce, seizing your kill. Planning is lust and desire and satisfaction.

Sadly, I probably lost all the vegetarians right there, but you can use a berry bush as the quarry if it makes you more comfortable. Hunting and foraging is what our ancestors knew and loved for millions of years. Those European cave drawings of deer with spears in them were powerful magic to help the hunt. The last several hundred years of social structures are a superstructure over what we are, which certainly don't define-or change-the creature under the masks. And today's world is becoming the old world in some ways, not the least of which is that 'you keep what you kill'. Not quite as literal as the old days, but in today's world, if you win, you win big, and if you lose, you have lots of company. It's an exclusion society out there, because resources are becoming scarcer and the number of bodies in competition is still increasing. Was that cheerful?

This book focuses on the idea that planning has to be tied to your inspiration(s). Now, most personal inspirations are not socially acceptable to some degree. Real inspiration isn't like a beauty contest, where carefully groomed contestants spout the most socially approved words they can think of. Real inspiration is emotional, lustful, seeking life in many of its rawest elements. So some inspirations may be a little bit non-socially acceptable, some really quite non-acceptable, and for some (actually quite a few in today's over legislated world) the overt manifestation is clearly a criminal act. That's all OK, because they are your inspiration. Overt manifestations of things that are criminal acts are not encouraged (so don't blame your actions on this book-take some responsibility!), but you've got to know what you're thinking/feeling. Why? Because what you are thinking/feeling is what really drives you, and you need to engage with what you really care about if your goals are going to be meaningful to your life.

As an aside, it isn't that it takes that much to do a criminal act in today's world. Everyone in the US commits roughly three felonies a day, at least, and that calculation applies to socially upstanding, middle class citizens who have all to lose if they fall into the clutches of the legal system. For the poor, with criminal records, and who don't care that much as a result, and the very wealthy, it's going to be a much longer list of felonies each day. The number of laws out there on the federal, state and local statute books are literally beyond comprehension. Then there are the quasi-legal codes, all the nosy 'we think' and the 'should's/shouldNOT'. Those really get extensive!

As really nothing you want to do is socially acceptable to everyone, you might as well please yourself. So, let's think about generally socially unacceptable goals. Surprisingly, everything is socially acceptable at some point to some one. Every action that is possible to be taken can be justified, and has been justified by someone. Destroy a country? If ordered by your commander in a war, you do it without a thought. You would make bombs, drop bombs, sneak around and kill, poison 'relative' innocents if ordered to. If you don't follow orders in wartime, they shoot you, but that's often a backstop excuse. People just have to keep busy, they have to do something, and so they do what they are told to do.

Here's the big step: so, if you will what you are ordered, shouldn't you think about what could be done, even if you, pure of spirit and white of heart, would never dream of such a thing? Even if there was money involved? The most recent James Bond movie had the villain telling Bond that the villain just chose his own missions, rather than following the decisions of others. It was the same killing, theft and destruction, but the villain profited it from the choices rather than the government. Those kinds of messages always come from villains in movies, because they are too socially disruptive. And choosing your own missions means taking responsibility, something that no one seems to want to do.

You have to remember that just because you would never dream of such a thing (pick any of a dozen 'awful' things) doesn't mean that other's would not. Innumerable revolutions have been destroyed by the smiling, sincere father figure who then grabs power and crushes the opposition. 'Oh, I didn't mention that when taking power? Well, it was for your own good.' you can picture them saying, as they sit happily in the palace. And the world is full of old men in mosques who are frantic to impose their will on everyone, always in the name of God, of course.

On a smaller scale, there are bosses who scheme to fire you and take your bonuses, and salespeople who hide the parts of the contracts with teeth in them. There are many out there who can happily reconcile anything they do to you with what it gets them. You may 'do onto other's as you would have them do onto you', but that makes it all the more important you understand what they could 'do onto you' if they were so inclined.

There is another reason why thinking about the forbidden is a good idea. People generally do what they want to do eventually, usually by a process of gradual slippage. I.e., I'm not doing a bad thing, I'm doing just this little thing, and then this one, and suddenly there you are! Any of the insider trading cases seems to be these types of non-planned plans, a succession of small steps into the hole. You sit back, and wonder: don't people think first? For one thing, sending a clearly incriminating e-mail isn't something that is recommended if you're going to commit a crime. You do wonder what the smart people are doing, because the ones caught seem to be so stupid. Thinking before acting is going to make a lot of difference. If you're going to do, do it right with verve. No one likes a loser.

There are far too many planning books that devote precious time to nice, pretty, socially acceptable projects like the 2nd grade bake sale. Give me a break! If you get suckered into doing the bake sale, ask the last three people who did it. That's one of the easiest plans to deal with, where it's been done over and over. Let's plan something that matters (kids and parents eat too many cookies as it is) and something that you deeply care about. Which means that this book again looks at decisions on things that are probably morally, ethically improper, and, as almost everything is, legally forbidden. Why? Well, those are a lot more interesting, perhaps more fun and that's why they are morally forbidden. And, most importantly, someone is thinking about these things, and if you don't think about them, then you have no clue when they execute their plan all over you.

There are decisions with slippery slopes everywhere, and we want to cheerfully ski down the moguls, not adverting our eyes from the forbidden topics. If you advert your eyes as you head towards a wall, well, that visual explains itself. And the world changes rapidly, and we need to be ready for decisions made under different constraints and rules that we embrace. Such as decisions like the characters in the Grimm Fairy tales faced, hard times and horrible choices because there is no food, or war. Hard cases where all the constraints voted to constrain at once. You may not be ready for them, but they will be ready for you.

Planning isn't limited to the small subset of nice, socially allowed things that the planning books like to pretend. Planning is everything. So, we're going to think about the nasty things, the things you want to do, probably are doing, and not analyzing right. If you feel doubtful:

Successful and fortunate crime is called virtue.[81] *(Lucius Annaeus Seneca)*

Although if you plan yourself into a problem with the legal authorities, that's a plan failure. Again, take some responsibility, or better yet, think ahead. Sure, planning is serious stuff, but life is a game. You're not going to do much better than 50% on your decisions anyhow. If you win a consistent 55% in the stock market you will make more money than a person could imagine.

Realistically, it's the questionable and forbidden where the risks and rewards live. The typical books on risk and decision making, stuck in a rut of the 'allowed', block off all the fun stuff and the hard stuff in the definition. No wonder they are dry, and ultimately often fruitless reading. The risk and decisions books tend to block out the impossible to calculate stuff, in favor of an approach that can be controlled. It's making assumptions, keeping track of those assumptions, and revisiting the assumptions and plans on a regular basis that makes all the difference. The kindergarten (perhaps 6th grade) approach of an overall, comprehensive plan with detailed steps and a sparkling clear a goal, works well only where things are static and constant. As you may have noticed, there are no static problems that are meaningful in this world.

Ultimately, you want to be making decisions in an unbounded world: decisions that look at all the issues, not just the socially accepted paths that are well trod. It's looking at the hard questions, making the slippery slopes work that make it interesting.

WHAT TO PLAN?

In life, there are six general situations:

(1) We don't know what we want, and so don't know what to do;

(2) we know what we want but not how to get it; or

(3) we know what we want and how to get it but there are a bunch of steps to climb that mountain. The variations of the preceding three are:

(4) someone else doesn't know what they want and we're stuck in the middle;

(5) someone else knows what they want but doesn't know how to get it and we are in the middle again; and finally

(6) someone else knows what they want and how we fit in but there are steps to the top of that mountain.

Really, (3) and (6) are clear planning situations. Those are handled by mapping out possible steps, considering resources, constraints, limits and time, classical planning material. (2) and (5) are the planning situations that are the focus of this book, looking at complex, fluid situations and changing stories. Cases (1) and (4) are cases where planning is NOT a good idea. In those situations, we're not ready to plan yet. NO! Put that pencil and paper down and stare at the horizon. We've got to know what we want before we plan anything. Random action produces random results, and you need to think about what you want, get that clear in your mind, before you charge off and start acting. Surprisingly, cases (1) and (4) are very common planning situations, and not surprisingly, result in many failures. How could they do anything but?

With any kind of a plan, we have to ask ourselves what questions we should be asking both of ourselves and of others. Our questions flow from the specific problem(s) we are looking at. Seems simple, but it's very easy to ask questions people expect us to ask, or questions asked with the last three projects, regardless of their application to this project.

So, why is this hard? We know what we want, why can't the world cooperate? Even in the little things? Because it's the world and it makes the rules.

You may ask, what is the big deal here? It's easy to make assessments, to see the world as it is, so we may master it and have the world jump to our Will. (If you seriously feel like this, you should check your medication)

Planning is fun-if you're planning for what you really want. A successful seduction? A day off with pay? Lots and lots of things can be fun to plan if you really want them.

> Hal stood up and started pacing. "The formal stories-prime example, a company mission statement-are useless because those are pretty stories, not the real stories people believe. The stories people really believe and act on have emotion and desire in them, not the selflessness of the publicly allowed stories. If you put a pretty, but empty, story on the wall, you're not going to reach anyone. Meetings are the same—full of words we 'should' be saying, not real words we'll act on. The problem is that having a 'word' as a name for something doesn't mean that the 'thing' the word represents exists at all, or exists in the way you think it does. Create a workgroup, and they produce grammatically correct sentences that are wishful social fantasies, warm feelings and bright pictures. Nothing that refers to the outside world in a useful way."[82]

In the complex world we live in, a complete and comprehensive plan is really almost impossible for anything that is important and meaningful. It is in rare and relatively uninteresting areas that we can plan completely. To plan is to investigate a chunk of the world, a "problem sector", formally defined, to determine the possible changes we may or may not be able to make. We'll make sure this time, we think, we'll cover all the possibilities. Cannot be done, because even moderately complex chunks of the world have many possible ways of approaching them, and many possible first and second choices. As you choose, you limit the next choices-that's why you choose!-but in so doing, you change the problem into something else than it was. We try forward and reverse planning approaches, but they can (and will) branch out so widely that to completely investigate our problem area is just not possible.

Boring example: go online and walk through an automobile manufacturers 'build your car' choices. Multiplying ten colors by five interiors by twenty-five packages by fifty options is a lot of possibilities! And those don't include your estimates of pleasure/satisfaction and/or effective use of the various combinations and sub-combinations, which technically are immeasurable.

The fact that we can't completely know, and often have only hazy guesses even after all our planning, paradoxically, makes planning all the more important. Planning makes one aware of what you don't know and what could happen. Without a plan, you are utterly without a clue. That you are clueless, fat, dumb and happy, only makes it easier for the world that is bearing down on you. Planning is important because it's not really the exact hypothetical results of your plan (as things never quite work out as planned) it's really the effort that is critical. Making the effort over and over, understanding the dynamics of a situation, is going to be successful. Perhaps not successful as you had planned, but, as was said:

> *"It would not be better if things happened to people just as they wish"*[83] *Heraclitus*

Which is putting the best positive spin on the surprises. Occasional planning attempts seeking very specific results are not going to work because you don't really understand planning. Planning isn't the execution of a plan, the controlling of the world by our Will and our mind; planning is an attitude about the world and your place in it. This is a mistake that most of the world, including very large organizations, make. The following is a corporate meeting which questions the whole organization process of planning and data collection.

"THE ORGANIZATION ISN'T

The next morning, bright and early, the big meeting started in the conference room. People arrived, were greeted, browsed the goodies and drinks and finally were shown to their seats. There were slightly over thirty senior corporate officers at the main table and all of them had assistants and flunkies sitting behind them. So it was a big crowd, who were at least physically comfortable in the plush chairs. A few smiled cheerfully as they talked, a few looked bored, and the remainder appeared politely annoyed to be there.

Well, it's Showtime, Hal told himself, and walked in. Smiling, he ignored their doubtful looks. Fine, I'm half their age. New blood and all that. Hopefully not soon to be spilled on the carpet.

"All of you have been generous with your time and your staffs' time over the past few months," Hal announced, standing at the front of the room. "I know that the time you spent on this project was valuable time; time you could have spent elsewhere dealing with the host of other responsibilities you face."

There were a few nods. People caught themselves quickly and stopped. Hal smiled to himself.

"I know that I've been annoying—it's a personality strength of mine. And just to prove my last statement, here is the key idea for this meeting. Each day, you are the end point for a flow of information from all over your company. That information is carefully gathered, reviewed, summarized, and passed up the chain of command to your desk so that you can make critical decisions about what to do next. Said decisions are then passed back down the chain of command. Your future, your employees' futures, the business's future, the suppliers' futures, and your competitors' futures are in those binders sitting there in front of you. You are the critical link between the past and the future, and everyone's future is your responsibility.

"What if the information in the binders is useless? What if the only function of the chain of information going up and going down is to keep everyone busy in a structure that can be evaluated and controlled? What if that process of evaluation and control throws out anything that challenges the central concept, the central 'story' of the business you run?" Hal asked.

Hal stopped and took a sip of water. Progress, he thought. There are now NO happy faces in the room.

"I started this process because I have a sense of unease about our business structures and our plans for the future. It seemed to me that many of the plans were based on stories laid down a long time ago. Stories that said that the business we are in is 'X' business, which is defined in a certain, limited way. Stories that assumed certain types of competition, stories that assumed certain available resources, certain possible choices. Stories freeze solid over time and perpetuate themselves. Most business failures, engineering disasters, product malfunctions, and the like occur because the stories retreated into a make-believe world.

"When you read bedtime stories to your children, you laugh to yourself at the silly stories. The newspapers are full of sad events, which, if analyzed, go back to silly stories that people believed with all their hearts and souls. Sadly, their hearts and souls is what they paid for their mistaken beliefs. For example, my wife tells me that my career plan to be an inspirational speaker is poorly considered. Her opinion is that my plan is based on an internal story of mine that the outside world doesn't seem to think is realistic and I'd suspect you all pretty much agree with her at this point." Hal was relieved to see at least a few smiles from the group.

"Now, disasters of all kinds are almost always preceded by near misses. Close calls that, had it not been for chance, would have been worse. We all know people who live their lives as a constant 'Wow, almost got it that time,' and then are shocked when they finally don't skate. We laugh at them, but we close our eyes to our near misses because we're human. None of us likes questioning the stories that we run our lives by. We all and I mean all of us, think of our stories like that advertising campaign for watches: It takes a lickin' and keeps on tickin'. A rough spot only means that the story is working, we tell ourselves. Any story can only deal with part of reality, and so the story is going to take hits.

"Here's a key point. On one hand, there is the story that is going to take hits, and may be looking a little tattered, but the core story is correct and undamaged. On the other, there is the story that is looking okay because it's been patched up but is actually leaking badly under the waterline. Errors of omission and commission. One error is not using the tattered but correct story, judging that it is failing because of the superficial damage. The other error is using the pretty story that's actually sinking fast because it looks good and because it's so important to all of us.

"Both of those mistakes can lead to disaster, but generally it's that second story that sinks the company and careers." Hal smiled, noticing the sudden attention when he said "careers." "It's the near misses that managers often misinterpret. People don't, or won't, see the warning signs because we are all blinded by our hidden biases. We pass off the near misses as proof that the system is working. 'Wow, look what the system caught that time!' we breath a sigh of relief, and leave it at that. Or the near misses are just off our radar. That semi truck filling the space on the road you occupied a few seconds ago that you didn't see coming, for example.

"There is a cartoon I saw. This little old lady is sitting on a park bench. A mugger runs up, takes her purse, and starts to run away. He slips on loose gravel, falls, and knocks himself out. As the police take the mugger away, the old lady proclaims, "Well, see! The system works."

There was more laughter than Hal had expected. That's a good sign, he thought.

"Why do we not notice the near misses, the close calls? Because it's a big world and you can't watch for everything. So one collects limited feedback about events. And let's be realistic; information coming back that says key stories are not working is nothing but trouble. If you are too low in the group to control the story, then you're a troublemaker. If you are high enough to have control over the story, then you've invested time, effort, and perhaps your career into making that story a star. Admissions that your star story is leaking reflect poorly on you. Maybe the story isn't leaking, maybe it is a random event, and we were taught that the boy who cried wolf was punished for his actions.

"Now, it's easy to forget that we are not paid for hard work. I don't care, Sir Jonathan doesn't care, and Francisco doesn't care if you work twenty hours or eighty hours a week, IF you are making money like gangbusters. You are paid to solve problems, and making money like gangbusters means that you are solving problems. It's too easy to fall into an employee evaluation, and a self-evaluation, based on hours and 'stuff done' when that's not looking at the real problems. 'There is nothing so useless as doing efficiently that which should not be done at all,' Peter Drucker, the master.

"What I've tried to do, with your help, is move the Japanese Kanban system concept, which works very well on a factory floor, to a higher-level analysis. By and large, mistakes are the fault of the system, not the people. With the Kanban system, shouting about problems popping up as stuff is being manufactured is rewarded, and pushing problems away and hoping things will work is punished. Now, that's a lot harder to do with information flows than with physical products, but at least the goal is clear.

"So, some ideas. What's a meeting without slogans? Seven stars and seven stones, to see far away," Hal offered. He noticed the blank looks. "Hmm, no Lord of the Rings fans here? Okay. How about seven strategies to recognize/learn from near misses? Boring, simple ideas that we all have heard, but don't use. As you all know, it's hard to remember that the goal was to drain the swamp when you are up to your ass in alligators.

"So, these ideas:

o   When time or cost pressures are high there will be problems ignored, nay, more than ignored-problems will be magically wished away. They will come back, and at the worst time, because the wishing fairy has a sense of humor. Deal with the problems when they show up, or at least memo them so they can be handled when there is time.

o   Watch for deviations from the norm, which means we have to first explicitly define the norm, and secondly think about what could vary. And then expect trouble, not hide from it.

o   Uncover the deviations' root causes—not an easy or short task, because the trail steps on others' domains. Remember, it's the system to blame for errors, not the individuals.

o   Establish who is accountable for near misses and not just for blame. Who really had the power to keep that train on the track? What in the system prevented action? Throwing the closest body off the train as a sacrifice is emotionally rewarding but destructive to the group on many planes.

o   Envision worst-case scenarios as a real planning tool, not as a device to make the last disaster look 'not as bad' as it was.

o   Look for near misses masquerading as successes, which is emotionally and mentally hard to do, but less embarrassing before that big blowup than after.

o   Finally, let's make better mistakes tomorrow by rewarding people for exposing near misses, which runs counter to almost everything taught from kindergarten on."

"All of these are just variations on not believing that the information in the folder on your desk is all, or even any, of the relevant information you need. We hire brains. You are expected to use those brains, to define what your work is. Information in the past flowed from the bottom up, and orders flowed from the top down. Structures ossify, slip into a bureaucratic process, and people do what's expected, work on the stuff people push in front of them. That's 'hard work'—people seeing you after hours pushing papers around. Working on the key stuff that you define and looking at the end goals—that's what matters. I know how easy it is to do the little jobs, the stuff in front of you, because those are knowns. The process has been done before and walked through, and the success goals and criteria are clear; measurable. We all avoid the hard things that don't measure well—the stuff that we are not sure about or frankly don't know how to do. I know I do, especially when I am tired, and I have to assume that everyone does."

"We've arranged for five managers to give presentations on near misses that they caught, and how almost-disasters changed their goals and the stories they work by. The stories are embarrassing, even humiliating in some ways, for the people involved. The directors of the corporation appreciate their willingness to disclose what they've run into. All of these managers were promoted after these problems were handled, and they have led their divisions to considerable profit and budget improvements."

Hal sat down, far in the back, and paid polite attention to the presentations, which he'd seen at least three times before. He'd delegated responses to various people, so his job was to be a lump. I like this job, he thought.

He reflected on his speech, and a line from a movie popped into his head: "We are building a fighting force of extraordinary magnitude. We forge our tradition in the spirit of our ancestors. You have our gratitude." He muffled a laugh with a cough. No, can't say that one at this meeting. They wouldn't get it. He started doodling on some ideas he'd been working on. How do you build stories that encourage change, not shut it down? Even when you turn the structure upside down, it won't change. After the revolution, the prior security apparatus is now the new security apparatus, only the names have changed from Czar's Minister of Security to Comrade in Charge of Political Correctness. Tortures remain the same. Don't want that.

One of his aides made a polite noise, and Hal suddenly came out of his thoughts to see everyone staring at him. He glanced at the note in front of him and the slide on the screen.

"That's actually what I was in la-la-land thinking about," Hal admitted, standing up. "How, out of all the random events flowing at and by you, do you get the important stuff to pop up? Really, the key question is, 'What should I be thinking about?'" He started pacing.

"Don't you wish there was a program that, each morning, would give you a printed report, with gold stars and red highlights, and which would tell you, oh, by the way, one, the mysterious liquid on the floor of the garage is going to cause four thousand dollars in engine damage today unless you do something quick and two, your wife's distracted smile is based on your failure to remember the fourteenth anniversary of the time you went to a special place shortly after you met, and three, four, etc. All those things that are little, easy to ignore, but have huge consequences down the road. As opposed to the obvious problems that look important but that work themselves out. Williams Randolph Hearst was reputed to not bother to answer letters because they eventually answered themselves. Sometimes yes, sometimes no. It's spotting the difference between ripples in a pond caused by an acorn falling from an overhanging tree and the small ripples an alligator makes as it moves carefully towards you.

"How about this? It is better to be hurt by the raw truth than to be comfortably deceived, because all deceptions have an alligator waiting at the end. So, is this boring?" Hal asked the group, not really looking at anyone, almost dreading the response. "What we're after is hard to measure and hard to control. A company strategy of, well, 'It isn't clear and we're not sure.' Not really a warm feeling to leave with, is it?"

"If you want a warm feeling, peeing your pants in a dark suit always works," one of the senior managers observed. "And it gives you what all warm feelings give—temporary comfort and considerable embarrassment down the road."

Hal laughed. "And with that inspirational thought, which actually captures conceptually the key issues, we'll adjourn. Thank you all for coming."

They actually clapped for a few minutes. Hal was shocked, but kept smiling, shaking hands until they were all gone."[84]

The 'story' you are planning for/around is formally called scope determination, if you were to use the elaborate Project Management Institute format to, say, build an apartment building-on the moon. The 'story' drives the determination of stakeholders, all the people who have some interest in a project. It's how you determine the value of the project, because it's the story that allows you to calculate value, for better or worse. Put some slack in that estimate value, because it's important to remember it's a guess. From the value, you estimate the dollar flow-and all of that from the simple story you tell about the project, that the project is embedded in and part of a larger system. Key idea: Wrong story, no dollars. Wrong story, wrong scope and things will go poorly.

The wrong story is easy to embrace. Example - in the "Indiana Jones and the Holy Grail", the evil Nazi chose a chalice he thought appropriate for Christ, an exquisite, jeweled chalice. It was a poor choice, and he died in agony a few moments later. He used a story for himself, not looking at the story when the chalice would have been created, the story that Christ was trying to tell. Jeweled was wrong on so many counts.

FUNNY SAYINGS:

Go make yourself a plan, and be a shining light. Then make yourself a second plan, for neither will come right.

Make a plan, tear it up, all the day you'll have good luck.

A good plan today is better than a perfect plan tomorrow - proverb

If you want to make God laugh, tell him your plans

CHAPTER 17. PLANNING OVERVIEW

PLANNING IS THINKING

Planning is first thinking. Planning isn't doodling on a sheet of paper, the mechanical process of drawing lines between ideas. Planning isn't 'doing' anything. Planning is sitting in a cafe by the river sipping on a cup of hot coffee and imaging what we might do. More often, it's sitting in the office imagining sitting by the river, but as long as we are imagining, we might as well enjoy ourselves. We think about what we might do. And that includes all the things we might do, the socially acceptable as well as the completely not socially acceptable but really fun ideas we have. They are all implemented through the same mechanism of imagination.

Planning is a matter of sending up mental trial balloons. I could do that . . . but I don't have time . . . could do that . . . but the police would interfere . . . All of those kinds of thoughts. Planning is imagining certain actions and their consequences (especially the ones where the police are going to interfere!) and seeing whether the actions will work to reach our desired goal. If a few quick actions won't reach the goal, then we have to think about a sequence of actions, a shorter or longer chain of events.

Planning is playing with, toying with ideas for individual actions, then stringing those actions into chains and estimating the results of the chains of actions. For simple plans like getting a gallon of milk, we recycle a plan that worked before. Blithely we jump in the car and drive to the store just before we need the milk. Most of the time, this works. Occasionally, we find the car quits halfway or the store didn't receive a shipment of milk that day.

Before planning, we make assumptions about what to consider or look for as 'facts', and what your possible choices are. So most of the critical decisions are made before the plan even starts, which is a surprise when you think about it. You box in the problem by the assumptions and possibilities, which is rational. After all, out of the infinity of choices and possibilities out there, you have to focus down to get something done.

The only problem is that sometimes (fairly often, actually) that initial box isn't correct, but one rarely goes back to the assumptions to check them against future changes because there is so much else going on. So, in the case of going out for milk, we assumed that the car would work, and that the store would have fresh milk. The car almost always works (hopefully) and the store almost always has milk, but those are assumptions we make about externalities to our actions. Even the simplest plan is dependent on externalities; we just ignore them most of the time.

For example, when we use a concept, we are assuming that there must be something that underlies that concept, some one thing. But any given concept is usually based on more than one thing, if nothing else in the intermediate steps to the end, which can vary. It's rare that we work with only one concept, and the concepts often are not linked. Concepts are complex intellectual creations that can denote a multitude or different elements and processes. While that was rather deep, this is important: By labeling a bundle of problems with a single conceptual label, we make dealing with that problem easier, as long as we're not interested in actually solving it. To solve the problem, we have to understand the dynamics of the problems, and we just assumed-or 'wished' away all the dynamics of the problem by the way we framed the concept. Well, if this was easy, everyone could do it.

What in the world does that mean? You are looking at something that is broken. You put on your repair service hat, and you fix it. The 'repair service' hat is a frame, and once your orientation is 'repair', then you look for things that are not working and you repair them. Maybe the problem is not that the something you are blaming for the problem is or is not broken; maybe the real problem is that the process is broken and/or something feeding into the problem is broken. If the process is broken, fixing one part isn't going do much except be an exercise in frustration. If the external feeder processes are broken, then all the machines can be humming nicely and you are still going to produce garbage.

So, the common result of inappropriate repair service behavior is that the wrong problems are solved. And we all do this. There isn't time to think about everything, and repair service mode is a Band-Aid. Something's wrong, put a Band-Aid on it. If it then works, then the problem is fixed. The downfall of a repair-service focus is that you focus on the problem in front of you, not the problem you don't have. I.e., repair service is a total disregard of failings and malfunctions that may not exist at the moment but will emerge later. This is one of the signs of a problem that is outside the regular daily living, by the way. Regular daily living problems will have breaks, but generally expected breaks. For example, a coffee maker will quit after some time, and you buy a new one. That was expected when you bought the one that just failed. It's expected that things will not work forever.

But, if the Band-Aid pops off for the third time, you have to stop repairing and start thinking. This is most critical where you are dealing with a dynamic system. Repairing things, because you see only the problem in front of you, makes one misread those problems, those anomalies, which start small, but develop with increasing speed. That's a situation, generally rare, where you don't have time to put your repair service hat down and think before disaster strikes. The classic example is Chernobyl, where the staff discovered that nuclear reactions occur quite quickly once they get going. A strong positive feedback cycle in the real world is rarely our friend.

Planning is a mental process of narrowing our problem focus, then searching through that focus area intensively for possible ways of solving our problem. Sometimes we have to expand our focus again if we don't seem to be getting to a solution. David Allen uses two axis to analyze problems with: horizontal, which is looking for solutions in the focus area; and vertical, which is stepping back to look at what we are trying to accomplish and whether it matches our bigger goals and plan.

It's easy to have a plan and just not get going on it, which is puzzling until you step back and realize that the plan, while not a bad plan, just isn't you and/or doesn't mesh with other things you have going. Sometimes you're not procrastinating; sometimes you're just not listening to yourself. On the other hand, sometimes you are the worthless procrastinator that your ex-significant other shouted about before they left you to destroy someone else's life.

Sometimes you hate the project so much you stop dead just thinking about it, and when that happens, you really, really need to figure out why, because doing something you hate will be a disaster. The project you hate will always be redone three times, the final version still shot through with errors and accomplish few, if any, of the original goals. Worst, should you slog through and do it right, then you'll be handed another one just like it, so don't just grit your teeth to get through it unless it is absolutely necessary for survival and you won't have to do it again. Know why you hate doing something and do then something else.

Let's get back to our project planning. So, we've expanded our view, the project is coherent with our goals and it's actually do-able (unsolvable problems are a major section later in this book) and now we go back down into the nitty-gritty again, limiting our focus until we find some solutions. Limit here, expand there is what we do over and over, without even thinking about it. Beer for the party tonight? (I live in a college town) There will be X number of people, that means XX amount of beer, but the refrigerator is too small-what about a keg? Those kinds of calculations flit through our heads quickly, hardly noticed for plans we have done over and over. Hardly noticed even for new plans, which isn't always so good.

Let's go back to Cali's huge problem.

"I'm not finding the correct scale for planning. What did the book say? The more uncertain we are, the more we over-plan, because a joyful immersion into minute detail means I don't have to confront the real problem. The bigger the threat, the stronger the desire to foresee all possibilities and every conceivable mishap. That's a plan that has "ruin" stamped in red letters all over it.

Is this a complex problem, yes/no? It is. What are the ranges of choices I have in dealing with a complex problem? Start with the goals or jump into the mess and start pushing things around?

I could size up a situation, one of those 'holding my thumb out to the world to measure it' like artists used to do, or

I could do a rough outline, or

I could just fall into a detailed analysis. Scratch the detailed analysis. That's failed so far.

Over there... She put her right hand on the edge of the notepad. That is my perception of the situation in the real world. Over here... She put her left hand on the edge of the notepad. These are my goals. Little arrows, curves, and dashes connect the goals and the real world. Little curse marks are embroidered around the edges.

If the problem is a static situation, I can crank out detailed steps. Of course, no meaningful problem is static and controlled.

A fluid, evolving situation takes rough strokes. Rough strokes with a paddle, if you have one. Up shit creek without a paddle? Failures at lots of levels there.

Bang at the problem, and then bang again. Iterative—isn't that the word? Walk through once, then walk through again with changes, round and round the process until it's solved or you become dizzy, puke, and move on.

Every problem has its own unique time problems, most of which are not conveniently highlighted in red.

Some problems you can think about for a while, stop part way, and rethink because you can take a couple of shots at the problem. Some you get one frantic pass at. Come over, come over, red rover, ready or not! Okay, this is a 'one frantic pass.' That lessens the pressure?

The key for any successful plan is 'what's the desired outcome?' If you know that, then you have focus, direction, and success criteria. In other words, I know what's winning and what does the finish line look like. Simple case is moi, in a flattering track suit, breaking the tape, the crowd cheering my victory? Here it is survival and prosperity for the whole group, and that's a lot more complex outcome. That desired outcome is the driver to the whole plan, and that's why it is a guaranteed disaster coming if I misstate the desired outcome.

Once that outcome is framed, then the mind starts thinking, really thinking. Actually, that's an easy picture, Cali decided. Everyone safe and secure, and we have resources and possibilities. Everything at its proper time and with proper attention to existing conditions? That's as useful as Proverbs, she grimaced. Pretty slogans with no traction. An inner process stands in need of outward criteria? So, when all the emotional handwringing doesn't work, let's start with what we have to work with in the real world. Let's get some external feedback."[85]

There are lots of ideas on planning, lots of tools to use to implement the salami technique. I.e., take a little bit at a time until the whole thing is gone. One to remember is to think in more than three dimensions-think in the fourth dimension, which is time. That's not easy to do!

When planning, picture the project, for a moment, as a fight. In Martial Arts/sword-fighting, you don't go for the knockout immediately. You disable, slow the opponent, get them under your control, then finish them off. Every movie you have seen does it wrong, but they are movies, after all. Movies, you get to write the ending you want and multiple takes to get the effect you want. Real world events are not so accommodating.

Here's a simple, but really valuable idea. As you are planning, floating along: pick your fall, decide where and when you will bail out if it's crashing. Better to do this while planning than during implementation. And thinking, even expecting failure and bailing while planning is essential, as that can shape the plan for success. Associated with picking your fall is the constant question-what's critical but not urgent? Always structure so that you do things that you consider important, not just have time lost. Doing stuff fills time-sheets, but doesn't win the battle.

If you can, goof around and create different types of bets about the future. Imagine placing bets on your project. That will give you a quick focus on the risks and variables, and the estimated costs for failure. You can do the same with the stock market, bearing in mind that much of any large, critical system is fixed by the participants to the maximum extent possible. And participants include the government. Make your plan a game, and you'll devote more attention to the details.

Where you are in the planning situation of 'someone wants something from you', think carefully about Pre-Defined Bets. A predefined bet is one handed to you, such as the Las Vegas spread on the professional football game you are interested in. Any bet that another hands to you is a sucker's bet, because if the odd's makers are competent, the odds are in their favor. You only win when you define bets or see a gaping hole in their calculations. (a hole that really exists, by the way! There are traps on traps) So one has to know what bets are offered: who is offering what, what they offer and back into what they expect. Then, what could unexpectedly change, and turn the odds into a winning bet. Anyone who writes a bet is trying to transfer risk to you, that's the key to writing a bet. If you understand the risk that they are trying to transfer, then you can chose where risk is small, where you are sure (no daily magic hocus pocus, either) that their analysis is wrong.

Financial magazine writers make fun of us for our fear of loss, but we are the survivors of successful predators and a successful predator is as cautious as they can be. Any successful predator will absolutely minimize risk, unless starving or for mating, because there are no health care systems out there in the wild. That's why most predators prey on the sick, the weak, because the predator lives a lot longer that way. Only humans, acting out (not 'living out' because it's a good way to die) some Greek tragedy, seek honor and glory and a battle with a worthy opponent. If you're after emotional satisfaction, don't involve deadly weapons in your games. If you want to profit from others foibles, play on the risk of loss outweighing the gain.

Generally speaking, just to make things more complex, everything, all the time, is causing everything else. All variables over time move to the average. What does that mean? It means that within a structure of resources and constraints, they will cycle, like the sun and moon. And the cycles will tend to average, but there will be some individual extreme values. Cycles mean that things change, and if you pay attention to that, you may become what politicians call a flip-flopper. How to respond when called a flopper? John Maynard Keyes said "I change my mind when the facts change, sir".

Do not nobly step into a battle that you don't want! A hated task creates a dead zone for non-mission critical tasks and non-mission critical is anything that doesn't sink us today. If you're stuck on something that is hated because the names involved bring up emotional responses, then change the names to something neutral. Pull the names out, eliminate the emotional response, and you can focus on the dynamics of the problem. If you can't get the emotions out of the process, then you can't assess risk, where you are burning bridges correctly, when to shut doors/options or to leave them open for a hasty retreat. If all your bells are being rung, don't make a decision!

Finally, it's not just difficult to think when tired, unfocused, stressed, it's nigh near impossible! You can feel the neurons giving up when you are under stress. You actually can hear words, but they don't mean anything, which is another reason that movies are terrible learning examples. In a movie, the correct decision is always made under fire at the last moment. Life shouldn't always imitate art. Don't do that.

Speaking of closing a few doors, it's our nature, as cautious predators, to keep doors open to escape out of. That's not entirely bad, but you lose focus that way. Sometimes you just have to close the doors and move forward. It's too easy to keep open options that you've already rejected just as a safety valve, forgetting that you'd rather do anything that do back that way. There's a saying: 'you know you are headed in the right direction when you don't look back anymore.' There are times to keep doors open behind you, and times to burn the ships on the beach.

Let's think about an overall strategy to attack a problem. One excellent technique is to look to strengths and weaknesses, but we are changing the names to take emotional responses out of the calculations. 'Strengths' and 'weaknesses' carry a lot of baggage with them. Let's think about attack surfaces, which are the physical aspects of the problem you are facing. If you were attacking an airplane, these surfaces would be the physical plane, the controls of the plane, the engines. Then, lets look at attack vectors, which is attacking areas of the problem. Again, attacking that plane, our vectors could be aspects of the physical plane, such as sheet mental/fiberglass; the electrical systems, and/or the power systems.

Consideration of the surfaces and vectors will show the weaknesses, because there are always weaknesses. Things are made for certain reasons, and while those reasons may or may not work, they certainly will not work if attacked for different reasons. That's why Microsoft Windows has such problems, because it was made with certain assumptions, which specifically did not include that many of the brightest, least ethical people in world would wage unrelenting war against the software to break it. In the context of how the software started, it made sense to ignore attackers. Once the weaknesses are written in base code, the party is on.

We have to question our plans because too often, we are allegedly looking for a result in the real world, but not looking at the real world for the result. We are driving, looking in the mirror, judging our reactions to what we are doing and other's reactions, not looking at the road. Visually, this is a picture that isn't going to work. If your plan is being referenced to other's ideas and emotions, rather than some physical manifestation in the physical world that can be measured, you have a plan that can't succeed. If you want your girlfriend/boyfriend, whatever to be 'happy', good luck with that over twenty years. If you want them to accept your marriage proposal, form a functioning union, raise children, all the events that life can bring, those are steps that can be measured and adjusted. 'Happy' is an undefined word and random state of mind.

As you plan, remember constantly that it is the Status Quo that is the enemy. It is far too easy to start planning, because of dissatisfaction with a present situation, but then not take any steps because the risks and dangers of the new is carefully estimated, but the risks and dangers of the status quo are ignored. There are always risks associated with the new that cannot be mitigated or wished away. Far too often, having spent an intense amount of effort on understanding the possibilities, we draw back and view all of the options for change as too risky. If you don't change, you stuck in the status quo, despite the fact that the whole point of this exercise was move away from an unsatisfactory status quo. You have to reverse engineer the status quo, which means pretend that the status quo is another new option.

When you look coldly at the status quo, it's usually filled with risks at least as great as some of the alternatives. The status quo often much riskier than anyone (because no one thought about it) ever imagined. You knew the status quo was risky, it was the uneasy feeling that couldn't be quantified. Don't quantify everything else and then ignore the uneasy feeling.

There are a number of good visual tools-charts, graphs, other tools-in the planning literature to help get all those pieces out and discover the real order in them. Those are important, because as we know, facts show you only what you want to see. Sticking with the 'facts' is only part of the plan. Creating question tables and other tools to help sketching in the unknown unknowns, the known unknowns, what 'seems to be known' and 'what effects what' is absolutely essential.

How to ask the right questions, fill in the visual so can see? Start with an objective that has an impact. Rely upon action tracking and techniques and then tell a story that highlights an attack path. It is easy to see assets, hard to see threats, and the crowd at the meeting gets restless when you talk about failure (the status quo starts looking very good) but you have to make the point that there is no status quo – there is only what we think we know, which we don't. If you can't convince them, confuse them.

CHAPTER 18. A SOLVABLE PROBLEM IS?

A solvable problem is a problem with a specific goal. That specific goal is clearly defined, by at least several measurable criteria. The goal can be described and conceptualized very precisely. The problem has a clear set of actions, each with a success/fail rule, until we complete the last step, at which point we can see whether we succeeded or not. That is why, in a prior chapter, situations (3) and (6) are plan possible and the others are questionable.

So, our goal is to paint the south dining room wall blue. We buy blue paint, paintbrushes/rollers, and we paint. The wall is blue when we are done. That is a solvable problem and solved, problem. There are many simple problems like this that we hardly even think about as we solve them, because we have done them before. But the first time you paint a wall yourself, without help from parents/friends? It isn't all that easy.

Given that we have a solvable problem, how do we start planning? The same kind of planning steps are not appropriate for all the problems we face. Finding the correct scale for planning is much more difficult than it would seem and the root cause of many failures. Failure comes in all shapes and sizes, whereas we picture success as a single entity. Failure can be a failure to even start the plan, actually. If you want the wall blue, but become hopelessly at odds with others about the specific shade of blue, then the wall is never painted.

The more uncertain we are, the greater our tendency to over-plan. The wall situation is fairly simple, but one could try and determine the paint that is on the wall now. Then what kind of emissions will the paint exhaust as it dries? Are their EPA regulations at issue? What about the house three houses down the street? Will the small children there be endangered by the paint emissions? Will their litigious parents push the issue? While this is certainly overreacting to a simple painting a wall, there are many situations that carry higher risks.

When we are faced with a threatening situation, we try to foresee all possibilities and make allowance for every conceivable mishap. That's not entirely bad, but if you want to actually accomplish something, this approach can be ruinous. Too close a focus often means you won't ever get anything done, because becoming buried in the details often increases our insecurity. So we retreat into a minuscule but detailed planning process that can help us feel we are applying the full force of our rational powers to the uncertainty of the situation while letting us put off the evil day of action. And the day of action is put off forever.

Sometimes we should not over-plan, in the sense that we try and anticipate everything. Sometimes we shouldn't even plan at all, regardless of the amount of time. Going to the bar? That's an experience of the new, and about all you can plan is to take some money. It's one of many problems so linked to a host of other processes that particular details simply cannot be anticipated. Detailed planning in a case like that is a waste of time.

The scale of the problem is a major problem. Every problem we face is a simplification of the complexity that is the larger world, and we have to pull a chunk out of the chaos that is the world to solve. Sometimes we don't scale down enough, and the problem selected can't be solved. Sometimes we scale down too far, and any solution is too small to be effective.

As we are tiptoeing up to the problem, we face scale issues in gathering information about the problem. We can delve too deep and be buried in detail, with too much information to make a decision. Or we can skim the surface and miss the essentials, making a decision on essentially random factors. Once the scope of the problem is defined, our plans can be too crude or too detailed. Just to make things more interesting, the same plan to accomplish a given goal can be too crude at some points and too detailed in others, depending on how the plan is going and what is happening. Like anything else in life, the trick is to do what is appropriate. If you find a magic touchstone for appropriate in all cases and times, I'd be overjoyed to know it. Until then, we must ask what is appropriate? We ask that over and over, poking and testing, checking back against the problem, what we know and where we are in the plan.

Just because a problem is solvable doesn't mean that it is simple. A solvable problem can be enormously complex. As an example, look at the projects to send robots to Mars. Those are solvable, which is not the same as guaranteed to work, by the way.

Appropriate is determined using operative intelligence. That's a fancy way of thinking as we are doing about what we are doing. Formally, our job is to think of, and then do, the right things at the right times and in the right way. That's not asking much, just everything at its proper time and with proper attention to existing conditions. Rather like a moving essay test, actually.

That's astonishingly complex. The rules for 'the right thing at the right time' tend to be 'local', ie, to a large extent are dictated by specific circumstances. As a result, there are a great many rules. Driving an auto is an excellent example of this. There are major rules to never violate (crossing the yellow line into incoming traffic, for example) and a host of minor rules depending on circumstances.

PROBLEM SITUATION APPROACHES

We have lots of possible choices in dealing with the problem situation developing (exploding) in front of us. Having said that, don't picture calm reflection, looking down at the problem like a puzzle. Picture yourself moving quickly from approach to approach as you learn more about the problem. It's only possible to do it perfectly afterwards, not before. Ideas include:

- A detailed analysis of the problem. That requires that we have the problem in a pretty tight box, almost certainly a box that we have handled before.

- We can simply size up a situation, a very rough mental calculation. Is the guy trying to pick a fight with you larger than you, does he have extensive violent tattoos, and does he have scar tissue on his knuckles? Point out the person down the bar who was trying to proposition his girlfriend and beat a hasty retreat.

- A comprehensive but rough outline of a situation. This is more than the rough, quick mental calculation in the preceding example. This is where you think about the problem; box it in conceptually, but not in great detail.

- Close attention to details. This is appropriate and necessary for baking a cake, not so useful for an initial planning of a trip across country. Monty Python had a hilarious parody of this. A group was going to climb the twin peaks of Kilimanjaro (a fail defining the project scope) and had a rock solid, completely detailed plan for the first twenty miles of the trip, a rough plan for the next 200 miles, and then was basically going to ask for directions after landing in Northern Africa. Small questions of food supplies, clothing, and other details are harder to arrange standing on a pier in Tripoli than, say, advance ordering from your provisionary in London who can have the right supplies at the right place at the right time.

- One can define goals very clearly and analyze carefully, before we act, exactly what it is we want to achieve. This is the necessary approach for constructing a building, or software development, projects that are all real world modification. It's useless in many complex situations, such as where you are going to the bar for a night's entertainment and perhaps to meet someone new. In that case, there's only a limited degree of detail that can be anticipated. Contrast this with the missions to Mars, in which goal scope definitions are really important. Modifying the goals after the project is underway (we need to add another twenty pounds to the payload, for example) will vastly increase costs, if not all but guarantee failure.

- Simply to go to work and muddle through. If you are working from the output of multiple processes that you have no control over, you don't know what you've got until it's dropped in front of you. Detailed planning in then a waste of time, because you don't know what to imagine will happen. "One jumps into the fray, then figures out what to do next". For example, if you like to white water kayak, you can't plan or even guess every bump and dip. You make a few quick evaluations, and then put the boat in the water and go. That's about all you can do in very complex and quickly changing situations. The OODA cycle is your only friend then.

- Think more "holistically," more in pictures, which is very helpful when it's a new problem, and you just don't have a grasp on it. This is never a bad thing, because pictures involve all the mind, and pictures bring in emotions and desires. It's emotion and desire that gets the plan done, after all. That's how I pick a restaurant to go to, actually. Rational analysis, when the taste buds are driving the decision, is useless.

- Sit back and see what develops; if a decision isn't required/possible, then don't make a decision. This is skipped over many times. If you don't have to invade Russia, then don't invade Russia. It's a big country, full of ice and snow. Let them live with it.

- Move very quickly if the situation demands. Where you have a complex and changing situation generally the most reasonable strategy is to plan only in rough outline and to delegate as many decisions as possible to subordinates. That's the OODA situation. You want people making decisions who are right in front of the problem. Boots on the ground, as the US army now describes it. Now, a strategy like that require a "redundancy of potential command" and many people have problems giving up decision making to others, especially when things are, to put it politely, fluid. Obviously there has to be a monitoring/check system, but the person in front of the monitoring gauges is going to make a better decision than you at headquarters will when all hell is breaking loose.

If we expect the unexpected, we are better equipped to cope than if we believe, by our pages of detailed plan, that we have eliminated the unexpected. You NEVER eliminate the unexpected. Unknown unknowns lurk laughing around the edges of your goals. One of the key ideas in the book is the importance of knowing what you don't know and not simply assuming that you do know everything relevant.

Part 3, Section 2. Failure

CHAPTER 19. FAILURE IS THE NORM

Success is one of the names of god in project management. (Anonymous)

And like calling on the god's, branding our actions as 'success' is often more an expression of our inner needs that anything we see out there in the world. Let's put a face and a name on project failure. Lets not look at success, all that simplistic gushing over superficial results like a 'sissy boy'. (Complain to the Terminator, not me) Lets look at failure, like a grown adult, right there eye to eye. There it is, undeniable, a stinking, rotten failure, seeping into and staining the carpet. Be a man/woman, and lets look at how it can all go wrong. Because it will.

You can stand tall, grandstand in front of the crowd; you can shout to the rabble and rejoice in their applause, but if you believe what you tell them, or worse yet, if you believe what they believe, then your ultimate failure will be all the greater. You have to understand how transient successes is and how common failure is, if for nothing else but when you contemplate in the dark night.

This section is focused on failure because success is shallow and superficial. Success is, after all, what we wanted and forced to happen, often regardless of whether it really happened. Most public success is smoke and mirrors, and moving the goalposts. Doubtful? Go back and read ALL the meeting notes, if you can find the unexpurgated early ones. There is no shame there, but you have to remember what really happened.

Failure is more interesting than success, because success is so often a re-written story to fit what happened that it's hard to know what actually was intended to happen and what did happen, the invisible evidence discussed in "The Black Swan." If you are afraid of failure, you are guaranteed to fail, because fear of failure can and will freeze you. After all, we are successful predators, heirs of cautious ancestors who lived long enough to reproduce. Fear failure and fear, uncertainty and doubt (FUD) will be your friends in the night, but they are not really good friends.

How many people do you know who think that if a choice doesn't have to be made, then it won't be made, because they could be wrong. The wrong choice could limit their future and/or it doesn't fit somewhere into a key story. And as a result, they never chose and never live.

Guaranteed Failure is assured where you have bad inputs from prior process. Frankenstein was a failure because they looked only to the parts, not the whole. The Rocky Horror picture show, on the other hand, a kind of Frankenstein, split a brain between two 'creatures', a disaster from the get go, regardless of the actions later. Frankenstein planned the details perfectly but missed the big picture, the forest-what happened after the pieces were assembled. The Rocky Horror Picture got the forest, producing some rather interesting monsters, but blew the trees, missing key details.

Failure is the norm in life. Like an airplane, we are constantly off course. That's fine in theory, but doesn't play well either with our sense of certainty about ourselves, or our position in the social world. 'Fearless Leader' is an accurate visual model, and you can't look or act uncertain if you are going to keep the job. In both ourselves and in the mask we show to the social world, we have to be right, and have a track record of being right. So this isn't a trivial problem.

"The only way to avoid mistakes is to gain experience. The only way to gain experience is to make mistakes." Peters Competence Principle, Laurence J. Peter

One should always ask, at the cost of damaging our carefully constructed belief in ourselves, where have I made mistakes in this? If I don't see any mistakes, what am I missing?

> When the Piranhas left school they were called up but were found by an Army Board to be too unstable even for National Service. Denied the opportunity to use their talents in the service of their country, they began to operate what they called 'The Operation'. They would select a victim and then threaten to beat him up if he paid the so-called protection money. Four months later they started another operation which the called 'The Other Operation'. In this racket they selected another victim and threatened not to beat him up if he didn't pay them. One month later they hit upon 'The Other Other Operation'. In this the victim was threatened that if he didn't pay them, they would beat him up. This for the Piranha brothers was the turning point. (Monty Python, Episode 14, Flying Circus Television show, BBC 1, "Ethel the Frog')[86]

I love this quote from the Piranha's brother's sketch, because it's so obvious where they were going wrong, but then maybe not. It is, after all, classic trial and error. You should watch the sketch, because the deadpan, serious tone that the announcer uses to deliver the punch line: "This, for the Piranha brothers, was the turning point" is perfect.

To paraphrase Tolstoy, Success isn't a single happy family, even though it's presented that way, and every failure isn't unique in it's own way, even though it is presented that way. Success is a vision and a successful project rushes to fall under that umbrella. Whereas failure loves to be called unique, because that way, well, who could have guessed? Something special in this case caused the failure, not my actions or lack thereof.

"The Black Swan" has an excellent concept called "invisible" or "silent" evidence. We know what was supposed to have happened, but where is the invisible evidence, all the events that were swept aside, pushed out of the final story? The example in the book (paraphrased) was a picture of a shipwreck, with the survivors praying on the rocks. Their survival is the result of faith, is the reverent message, but what about those who prayed and died? Where is the silent evidence of what they did, compared to what the survivors did? There are places, even in today's world, for the penalty for asking a question like that is death. Doubter!

As human's, we have many advantages in dealing with the world. In the Bible, it talks about the seed thrown on a barren patch, which was bad luck for the seed. Human's can at least run around and wave their arms in an attempt to move from a barren patch to good soil, if you recognize that you are stuck on a barren patch.

You're going to fail in most things. That's the nature of life, so you want bear that in mind. Perhaps you may not want to always clearly announce loudly to the world what success is, at least too far in advance, although you need to remember your real goals yourself. You can fool your friends about the way it ends, but you can't fool yourself. So if you move the goalposts, remember, and learn something from that. Move the goalposts and fool yourself? The next experience won't be as good.

Oliver Burkeman wrote an article on "The power of Negative Thinking" (published in the New York Times). The short version is that people at a motivational seminar burned their feet walking across hot coals. They were encouraged to think of the coals as 'cool masses', which isn't positive thinking, that's ignoring reality. Stupidity, our parents would have grumbled. It's clear that positive thinking that denies the real world isn't going to work. If your positive thinking is nothing more than your defining the world the way you want it to be, then you have taken the daily magic far too seriously.

Now, it's important to visualize your goals in a positive manner. But telling yourself you can accomplish the impossible is a fool's game. David Allen had an example of this: he said before each golf shot, he would visualize a good shot. But the difference between a sane person and a crazy person is that the crazy person then believes they made the shot. It's a big difference that underlies a lot of what's peddled as positive thinking. When you are being told you can do the impossible, put both hands over your wallet and back away, because there is going to be a cost imposed.

Who wouldn't love success? The adulation of the crowd, a bonus in our check, a warm feeling of power, your significant other smiling happily at you. But success is dangerous. Success is addictive, for emotional and financial reasons. Success teases you to believe in your abilities, your actions, your plans, when often the success was partly what you did, only partly what you intended to do, and a certain amount of random luck stirred into the mix. When you then seek the next success, which has to be bigger than the previous one, you're on a downhill slope. This is the cause of the really big stock trader disasters. A trader is on a hot streak, and makes bigger and bigger bets until the streak stops and the last big bet sinks the trader and often their employer. Failure is generally a more valuable learning experience than success, as long as the failure isn't so extreme that it killed you or your spirit.

No one, including the author, really likes failure. You stumble through the stages of grief: denial, anger, depression and acceptance, and it isn't really fun. Still, it's better to learn from small failures that lead to big successes, than take small successes into a big failure. A happy run of success is going to bite later. People and organizations stride into crises based on their successful plans in the past. It's easy to stick with a plan long after the world around you has changed.

So, how to learn to succeed from failure? If failure is the norm, we'd better get the most of the experience, if for no other reason than because the tuition paid is pretty painful.

First, be open to the idea of failure. Accept that most things are various degrees of failure, and even what appears to be success probably isn't exactly what you were planning for at the beginning. Test things constantly. You want small or moderate failures, feedback at first. Small and moderate failures show potential problems and encourage searching for solutions and improvements. This is where anomalies are important, because it is important to notice problems that seem insignificant or minor. If the story isn't working, figure out why before it sinks.

Anticipate and plan for failure, even risk a controlled failure deliberately. If you plan for failure, or at least allow for the possibility, you are going to calculate how to limit the cost of the failure. Whereas when one is sure of success, betting the farm seems like the natural thing to do.

Don't disregard evidence that says the plan and/or the story is not working. This is where positive thinking becomes actually dangerous. Where you start thinking that 'thinking makes it so' and you can impose your 'Will' on reality, you better hope you're on a flat plan, and not near a cliff. Look at cases that failed, cases that are like what you are trying to do, and figure out why they failed. Don't just look at the successes, because, as said before, the real story is often buried because it's embarrassing.

The most dangerous thing in the living world is a mind. Claws, teeth, stingers, etc., just freeze the creature into a fixed of success, a comfortable niche and they never grow from there. But the mind can freeze as well. Success is far more corrosive than failure, because the mind freezes and then locks down. I know I'm repeating myself, but the glow of success will only make the eventual failure all the greater.

A business that experiences only success will be unable to infer the causes responsible for it. Does that even make any sense? After all, they were successful, wouldn't they know why?

Often not. Success starts with responding to markets, doing little things that add together and work. Poking and prodding the world and responding, using feedback and OODA to learn. But while with the right hand you poke and prod, with the left you hold a screen up to hide the details of your repeated failures from the crowd. Eventually, you believe in the screen. Once one ascribes good results to your actions, you are inclined to repeat them. Why not? It's an easy sell in a meeting-this worked then and it's going to work now, no thought required by the participants. So resources are dedicated to prior successful strategies instead of looking at other alternatives. Your success generates a core strategy, just what the mission statements urge, and structures and processes grow to support that strategy. This is doing what you are supposed to be doing, but over time, the strategy freezes.

Success not only narrows your focus, it also affects your attitude. You win, and suddenly you are a winner in and of yourself. Christensen's theory of Disruptive Events can be broken down into 'why' and 'how'. When you are focused on the 'why' of something, you are poking and prodding, listening to the world and responding. Once you have a success, you jump into the 'how' to implement that success, and you stop poking and prodding the world. Eventually, you will create the best something that does nothing, because you've lost track of what it's supposed to be doing.

No one wants to learn from failure. To do that, you have to admit you failed, and then you have to sift through the stinking mess to figure out what happened, when anyone would rather move on to something else. To avoid learning, we move the goalposts and 'prove' that we meant that to happen all the time. Or scapegoats are found, nefarious outside forces blamed, something that won't jar our sense of self worth. As discussed in more detail in the 'Anomalies' chapter, failure generally isn't catastrophic at first-there are hints. Ignore the hints, and things will not be so good.

The safest approach to life is to risk failure deliberately, all the time-but carefully and by little controlled failures. Failures are not anomalies but are inevitable.

CHAPTER 20. ERRORS AND MISTAKES

Let's contemplate Errors and Mistakes. What are they, really? And, to steal some thunder from the closing chapters, let's start with the key point: Mistakes will Eat You-cheerfully, you the main course along with the vegetable of the day and a glass of wine as the waiter (more likely, your co-workers) hover in the background.

An error is the incorrect execution of a plan. As we work through our plan, usually the criteria by which we are measuring our progress will flag an error; at least, if the plan is relatively clear. This is key: an error has a decent chance of being caught, because it's right there in front of you as you execute the plan. When the next step following the error doesn't work, we have tripped over the error and now can fix it. That's not to say that we will catch the error at an optimal time, because the wishing fairy would find that far too boring. So it is critical to catch errors, but catching usually errors is possible. Catching an error keeps you within the plan.

A mistake is a bad plan. Perfect execution of a bad plan is worse than useless. You're lucky if you have not walked yourself right off a cliff and like a cartoon character, are suddenly moving your toes, realizing that there isn't anything under them. The next step is looking down and then plummeting, much funnier in the cartoon than in life. Case in point: the Blackberry phone. This was as clear a case of a bad plan as you can have. Successful, dominating it's market, until Apple redefined the market and cut the ground away from underneath Blackberry-which they just refused to see.

"There is nothing so useless as doing efficiently that which should not be done at all. Peter Drucker"

You can go a long way down the road with a mistake because you're working the plan and not looking outside. You can (will) end up in a very bad place. A mistake is, for example, attacking Russia in the Fall. You can have the best military troops, general staff, and equipment possible, but it's still going to get stuck in the mud and freeze in the cold. And then the Russians, who are crazy enough to live in that hell of ice and snow, show up with guns. No amount of correct actions implementing the plan can prevent the eventual disaster. The real reason that mistakes are worse than errors is that, as discussed over and over, we rarely go back and question our assumptions. This is where jumping into solving the problem before really defining the problem makes the wishing fairy clap their little hands in joy. Mistakes, being hidden in the assumptions, don't show up until it's all done, and then it's too late.

The little footprints of a mistake can be discerned, if you are looking. When you are implementing your plan, there will be times that something happens and we evaluate it incorrectly or just ignore it. It's usually something relatively trivial, although if we were looking closely at the anomaly that the 'something' shows, we'd recognize it's more serious than it seems. An anomaly is another story in the middle of our story. The anomaly is only the hint of another story, just some data points, near misses or unexpected results. But, we're busy, and we smooth it over, because generally it's a problem popping up that shouldn't happen per the plan, and between the real world and the plan, well, it's the plan we listen to. We've socially committed ourselves, and between little problems with the real world and maintenance of our social face, it's clear which one we will pick if we can. For a while.

Here is how to back into a complete disaster, one small step at a time. Let's say that something happens, some event occurs, and we handle it in a relatively offhand manner. We don't really think about it, we recycle a plan that we have used before and move on. Perhaps the problem re-emerges, in a slightly different way, and we again make it go away. Perhaps we are just a little more worried now, because now we will be seen as having been 'wrong' the first time, so we pull out the 'whack a mole' hammer and make sure that the problem is gone.

The step into tragedy (farce for onlookers) occurs when we then later discover that the situation is more serious than we thought and our earlier thoughtless and at least partially well meant actions can be interpreted in very problematic ways by not only friends, family but also by the authorities. At which point we must justify and protect our original positions/actions or there are worse and worse consequences. With each step, we are in deeper. This can be a slow motion roll down a hill, with indictments at the end of what seemed like such a small thing when it started.

One would suspect, for example, that many athletic scandals use this playbook. Insider trading cases probably start like this also. It's a situation where, if you could start over, knowing what you knew half way in, then the beginning would be a lot different, but stopping, backing up and recasting the situation becomes impossible. If for no other reason than that potential horror, listen to the anomalies! This little play happens all the time, in little and big versions, and it's the most likely way your name and picture will ever be in a newspaper. Listen to the little voices; notice the little footprints in the snow before the big problem jumps out at you.

"The most important thing in communication is to hear what isn't being said." Peter Drucker

ERRORS

Let's look at some basic ideas about errors. Errors are chopped up into several categories. Essentially, they all apply the wrong action to the project.

There are errors caused by being tired, in which case you go on automatic, and do something else than you really intended to do. This is common where there are where there are several possible actions, and because you're tired, in a hurry, etc., you do the habitual action, the one you're used to doing, instead of another possible which actually was the right action. Or you just forget, because tired/rushed, bored, etc.

There is a type of error called a 'mode' error, which occurs because of poor design. The equipment you are using has several possibilities (what doesn't, in today's world!) and you can't remember which sequence is the right one, and the markings/dials are ambiguous. My current favorite is which HDMI input does what on a television? A good design would give some hint, perhaps even force the decision (DVD, Cable, etc.) but that's not common. In the interest of maximum consumer utility, they throw out so many choices and options that the consumer, worn out from getting anything to work, is terrified to push any other buttons or the whole thing stops working.

I jest not! I accidently pushed a button on my new TV and it took ½ hour of reading the reference manuals to get the channels back. Where you use that television occasionally, it is a guaranteed exercise in frustration. Be careful on taking up the store personnel on their offer of buying that wonderful all in one remote, because it will become a terrible little god sitting next to the TV that you sacrifice to in the vain hope it will do what it did in the store.

Another interesting error is monitoring the wrong part of the action sequence, which is technically called a level error. If you think about it, actions can be specified on many different levels, and a global description is the one at the top of the list. (also known as a high-level specification in 'serious' planning talk) As you work down the plan, the descriptions become more detailed, down to the very detailed descriptions, the ones at the bottom of the list which are the low level specifications.

For example, your new 'all-in-one' TV remote, the size of a small computer, has the global description of reducing your stress. At the bottom level, there are a mass of 'click these sequence of 12 steps in exact order and 2 out of 3 times something good will happen'. Any one of them might be in error, and how do you know? Where you know your action isn't producing the results you seek, the next question is what level of specification the error has take place. Problems of level can be a nightmare, because you can't figure out where to start looking for what went wrong. For example, as you frantically stare at your computer, which is lifeless before you: is it hardware, software, or an occasional interaction of both? Hint-it's the small hardware issues more than one would suspect. That's why the first question tech support asks is whether it's turned on.

A simple example: you want to change the formatting of a word processing document. Sometimes you go to the styles menu, and it works, and sometimes it doesn't. Often, when it doesn't work, it is because someone (never you!) didn't use the style's menu, but instead formatted a chunk of text by forcing a font/size/whatever outside of the style menu, which then confuses the program and the style menu as to what to change to what. I've found that simply formatting back to normal, and giving up on the fight with the difficult chunk is generally a good step, but have had times when it was much easier to simply retype the selection rather than try and figure out what style is applied to where. If you have a large selection with that problem, pull it out into a separate word file, and fight with it there, or you risk confusing the entire document. When I write anything complex, I save the file under a new name every hour or so just to avoid those kind of disasters. I know it's possible (in theory) to step backwards through the document, but there is another set of disasters lurking. The one time I critically needed a program to step back through prior versions, it hadn't kept those versions.

Another classic example is where you have a problem with your auto. If the auto is dead and towed into the dealer, they can get it running again. It only takes money and time. If you have an occasional rattle in the rear quarter panel, you'd better just get used to it, because that isn't ever going to be fixed. A dead car has clear levels to work on. Occasional rattles? You don't even know where to poke at the problem. The same applies to your body. Show up in emergency with a broken leg, and they are great on that. Have a little occasional pain that can't really be replicated every time? Develop a philosophical approach to life, because you are going to live with it.

So, how do we catch errors? The design of the plan, and/or the equipment, process, etc., is really important. A good design book is one of the best resources, because a large part of good design is designing out errors, and the thought process they suggest can be very helpful. There's no point inventing the wheel again, and there are good sources out there to help. Interestingly, design books are often more useful for planning than planning books. Design books focus on getting something right in the real world, and so give a recommended list of steps.

Ideally, one prevents errors before they occur. But you also have to build in a way of detecting and correcting them when they do occur. That means you have to admit to yourself it isn't going to work and you have to build in error traps. It's better to have a plan that is known to have possible mistakes than one that is supposed to self-correct. Once people assume that the process will fix itself, people rely on that, so it had absolutely better fix itself or it will run off the tracks.

MISTAKES

Mistakes result from conscious deliberations. You actually thought about this, which is even more embarrassing. Form the wrong goal and you've made a mistake. Mistakes can be major disasters and they are difficult or even impossible to detect. The effect of mistakes often compound, and suddenly, so rather than you happily following the rocks tumbling down the hill as Sun Tzu recommends, you are running frantically before the rocks as they gain speed.

After all, the actions you are performing are appropriate for the goal. If you have a checklist, you are checking off the boxes all the way down. Mistakes are errors of thought, buried in our thought processes. Mistakes can and often result from the choice of inappropriate goals. A person makes a decision having made assessments on the wrong basis, misclassifies a situation, or fails to take all the relevant factors into account. The postmortem will decide that 'we didn't think long enough before acting', a band aid over the sore. That's probably true, but what we didn't think about was the core goal and ways to reach that goal, of which we picked a loser. Perhaps every step towards that goal was a loser (Russia in the fall again) and dumping the whole idea would have been the right course.

Many mistakes arise from the vagaries of our thoughts, often because we tend to rely upon remembered experiences rather making a systematic analysis. This is the 'usual world' versus 'something new' situation, the most dangerous situation we face. We make decisions based upon what is in our memory. Our memory is biased toward emotionally loaded events, a tendency to overgeneralize, and remembering the odd, the different, rather than the commonplace. If you have ever taken a formal logic class, you know that we don't use logic. For example:

Socrates is a man;

A man is a hairless biped;

Socrates is a hairless biped. (with a beard?).

Our thought is vastly different from logical processes. (And I know that was a flawed syllogism) The core problem with formal logic is that the essential blocks, the words, are not concrete blocks to build a monument with, but ephemeral vapors that change meaning and ooze away as we try to stack them up.

We can think of the world as either shallow or narrow. A restaurant menu is a shallow structure. There are many alternatives, but each is simple. You make a key decision, which is picking the entrée and then a few follow up decisions. The major problem is to decide which action to do: I had the pizza the other day, the meatloaf looks good, but what about this special? Here, the difficulties are all the competing alternatives.

On the other hand, a narrow structures would be, for example, a cookbook recipe. There are only a small number of alternatives, perhaps one or two, but there is a tree structure of steps that are narrow and deep. Goof on an earlier step and the eventual results won't be so good. The Harry Potter movies used this over and over for comic relief. In the potions class, most of the class would end up with something that smelled awful, if it didn't actually explode.

Everyday decisions are what we face constantly, the same choices over and over, and we generally don't even think about these choices. When you get up in the morning and get yourself ready, the steps are pretty much the same, with standard alternatives that you have done many times before. Because there is little time and much to do, and because our unconscious actually runs us, most of our behavior is done subconsciously. We have little conscious awareness of our actions, which are not available to inspection. Doubt that? Think hard about why you really chose one thing rather than another, and a rational answer just isn't there. I've shifted over to closing a restaurant menu and going with the picture that pops up in my mind, rather than any rational analysis of the menu. Actually, it's usually the picture that popped up in my mind that drove me to that restaurant in the first place.

If you have moved to new living quarters, you suddenly appreciate the old daily routine. Suddenly you have to make many decisions you didn't before: where to put dishes and glasses, where to put can goods and dry goods, how does this dishwasher work, where are the electrical switches? Everyday activities, because of repetition, tend (but not always) to weed out the mistakes because if something is done over and over and it isn't working, eventually we tumble to the idea there is a problem and then we try and figure out what isn't working, even if we have to trudge back through our assumptions.

The bigger problem, as I say over and over, is dealing with non-everyday activities. First, we have to realize that this isn't the everyday problem, failure to do which is the usual prelude to disaster. The non-everyday activities are, duh, things we don't do all the time and so because they are new are often important to us. And complex, potentially big problems with both wide and deep structures that are going to require considerable conscious planning and thought. So we think, and after thinking we should try careful, deliberate trial and error; (poking and prodding) trying first this approach, then that, backtracking where it isn't working, because this is something new, and the new is a surprise in all ways.

If you get nothing else out of this book: where we make a very large mistake is where we treat non-everyday activities like an everyday activity. We merrily assume we know the goal and the plan, just a few tweaks and adjustments will do it, and off we go, cheerfully down the path of execution to failure. Ask Napoleon or Hitler, whose armies tore up Europe but were ground to nothing in Russia.

If you want success, in all situations and circumstances, design a structure that accepts first, that there are going to be mistakes, and second encourages people to find and tell others about mistakes. That will bring those pesky critters out of their hiding holes. That has been Toyota's approach to the assembly line, and it has been a huge success. That was instrumental in taking Toyota from a marginal auto company to the behemoth that it is today. They built factories around the idea that mistakes are the fault of the system, not the individual. Contrast that with GM, who traditionally blamed the individual for mistakes, and as a result, mistakes were hidden. At least for a time, and often from the factory quality inspector. The ultimate consumer was rarely fooled. I can remember when GM assemblers welded coke bottles into doors as some kind of a labor grievance- and the big 3 US auto companies paid many years later for that kind of nonsense. But it takes years for people to lose faith, a temporal problem that the GM executives didn't grasp. Now, a big part of the feedback system failure there was the revolving doors at the top. When people are in positions 5-10 years, long temporal feedback will be missed/ignored or shoved into a corner until they happily retire. The management consultant who comes up with a real answer for that problem should win a medal.

Now, note that Toyota wasn't as successful at imposing the view the mistakes are part of the structure at higher levels of the company. They made some major planning errors and public relations disasters that could really be tied back to 'someone in authority made a decision' that was imposed on the system. So at the higher executive levels, they had the same problems that GM had.

Taleb, in "Antifragile", endorses and seeks structures that love randomness and uncertainty, which also means-crucially-a love of a certain class of errors. That class of errors is those small and frequent mistakes which can be caught and don't cause major damage. That is of course the opposite of how things are usually planned. No errors in our plan, thank you! We confidently assert that we are smarter than the world and can get it right the first time, as the wishing fairy sits in the corner and snickers. Mistakes are disasters if rare and huge, which they will be where all manifestations of earlier problems were brushed away and hidden.

MISSING HIDDEN CAUSES

"When one thing happens and then another thing happens, the first causes the second." This sort of intuitive reasoning is common among three- and four-year-old children, and is based on the logical assumption that causes precede effects. As adults, we continue to use this sort of reasoning; it's effective in many situations.

But it also has flaws, of which the first is that it's too simplistic. Thinking in this way assumes that a single, apparent, and immediate cause can account for what occurs. As adults, we know that a single cause is often inadequate to explain what happens. The folk saying about the final straw that broke the camel's back is shorthand for the idea that an accumulation of minor incidents can cause major problems, problems that cannot be explained if we focus only on the last straw.

The idea of multiple causation is commonly avoided where possible in favor of a simplistic explanation for events. When two things happen together, the events can be chance, a fluke with no essential casual relationship to our plan. If we force causality on a fluke, we are really in trouble.

So there are two steps to tease out the blind spot of hidden causes. First ask: is the cause of X more complex than the simple story we have told ourselves? What else could have created this result? There are literally an infinity of possibilities for any event, many fantastical and easy to dismiss, but there are almost always at least several reasonable possibilities that we have not really considered. If you are 100% sure of your explanation, reflect on the split brain people and their confidence in their stories.

Second, we need ask, even though the answer may be upsetting: is the occurrence of these events casual or a fluke? The result we saw can (always is, to some extent) the random intersection of many events. So to test, you ask yourself, or the meeting group, or people at lunch: "How many different possible causes for X can we come up with?" This is classical brainstorming, writing down thoughts as they come in, trying to open up the boxes we are in.

Once we have a bunch of ideas, then we have to ask if there is a main cause, a root cause that is more fundamental than the others? This is where sketching out the relationships on a piece of paper is essential. Then the next step is imputing experience into the drawing to test it. It's way too easy, with time pressures and the simple pleasure of having created something neat, to stop and hold our precious idea tightly against our chests.

Think about the nasty questions: instead of A causing B, it is actually B causing A-or that A and B are in a kind of vicious cycle, each continually triggering the other? Maybe not even the exact cause of each other, but related by a third (or forth or fifth, etc.) hidden cause that is responsible for both A and B? And C and D floating out there, which we are ignoring?

Ok, we've carefully defined down the system so that we can be sure that A is a cause of something can we tell if it is a necessary cause, without which B will not occur? Remember, the figure below IS the real world.

Figure 8.

From the figure above, we know that there are multiple causes. Can we tell if A alone is sufficient (for our limited purposes) to really cause B or if other conditions must be present? What might these conditions be? Is there something that pushes A into position to cause B, for example, but really doesn't cause A, this unknown is just floating around and occasionally interacts with A? Of course there is, but does it really matter enough to worry about? The light grey line is what we want to happen – is it going to?

We keep going back to that all-important question: Is it possible that the coincidence of A, B, and C is simply a fluke-that these events really have nothing to do with one another? At some level of the system analysis, everything starts looking flukish. Why do I say that? As you add more and more complexity (bring in more of the real world) the multiple causes interacting drive out the clarity of the simple view we are using.

The question we have, in the here and now, is whether all that complexity is going to matter right now. When we mix the brownie mix and the eggs, are we going to get brownies today? Asteroids colliding over eons may have some relevance, but limited relevance to cooked brownies in the next ½ hour. That's an extreme example, but the inquiry is relevant for say the type of major-such as corporate-planning that many of us do. There are other divisions and competitors and competitors of the other divisions, all pushing on resources and constraints that weaken that clear 'A causes B' that we are after.

So there are errors of commission-we think something is meaningful when it is really a fluke-and errors of omission-we think something is a fluke when it is really meaningful. In both cases, we'll be blind to the actual cause of what we're trying to understand. Those errors result in mistakes, because we've modeled the world wrong, unless we leave in a mechanism - or at least think about the possibility - that sometimes our major assumptions may be wrong.

THINGS TO THINK ABOUT AT 3 IN THE MORNING:

Why is it so hard to determine whether or not something is a fluke? Something important to your life, for example.

What Are the Odds That This Is Sheer Coincidence? And your spreadsheet model is a fantasy?

When little odd events happen-especially when they are happy odd events-ask Yourself, "Was This Coincidence Predicted Ahead of Time?" Near misses are given to you for a reason!

Here's a scary one: ask Yourself, "What are the odds that some coincidental event relevant to a problem will occur during X period of time-a month, a year, a lifetime? Hint-it's a lot more likely than we normally think it is! The daily magic doesn't like probability at all.

CHAPTER 21. ERROR CATCHING & CORRECTION

"Failure does not strike like a bolt from the blue; it develops gradually according to its own logic. We will see that complicated situations seem to elicit habits of thought that set failure in motion from the beginning. From that point, the continuing complexity of the task and the growing apprehension of failure encourage methods of decision making that make failure even more likely and then inevitable."[87]

The preceding quote is from "The Logic of Failure", a really wonderful book. It's based on several lengthy problem solving experiments with multiple subjects and is that rarest of books, an academic study that is brilliant. Many of the ideas in this book are taken from that book, hopefully paraphrased enough to pass copyright standards. Imitation is after all the sincerest form of flattery! Reading that book is recommended and re-reading, because it has it's own method of thought that takes a while to grasp, at least for me.

As the Logic of Failure says, failure does not strike like a bolt from the blue. We may prefer to perceive it like that, because then it isn't our fault, it's 'just that thing that happened', but failure develops gradually according to its own logic. In almost all cases, there have been hints and near misses that we ignored. Complicated situations create thought/behavior patterns that set failure in motion from the beginning. Even if you haven't made a mistake in the original plan creation, complicated plans are prone to errors that are caught late, if at all. As the plan stumbles, and we feel the doubtful stares from others, the sweat staring to drop down your forehead, the apprehension of failure mixed with the increasingly apparent complexity encourages panic, which leads to even worse decisions.

How to constantly course correct in our voyage to success, rather than end up landing with the wheels up, the belly of the plane scraping as we slide sideways, and the wings falling off? (if you are reading this on a plane, purge those visuals and move along quickly here) Checklists are wonderful tools, because it's far too easy to just jump over our assumptions and the little steps we have done before. Make a checklist out of the 'mental patterns that don't work'. Here's the hard part: pull the checklist out and use it as a quick reminder. Effective learning requires the use of multiple senses. Studies show over and over that taking notes, re-writing your notes, talking to yourself (not at the library), all helps grasp new ideas. Simply reading isn't enough, the act of re-writing and re-organizing results really learning.

If you want to get the most use of this book, it's critical to not only look at Figure 1 on a regular basis, and think about the overlaps, but to draw little diagrams that reflect your world. It's a good thing to do in a coffee shop, with an intent expression and bold strokes of the pen. Genius at work, onlookers will murmur approvingly. Then challenge yourself: how do you know that the overlaps are what you are assuming? What is the relationship between the plan, the real world, the social world and the self, and how is it changing? If you don't see it changing, you're not looking closely enough.

"Stability eventually will be destabilizing". Hyman P. Minsky

Everything changes over time, change will cause prior successes to fail. So it is absolutely essential to learn from failure. Small children fail constantly, and so they grow and learn. Stop failing and you stop learning. It's sad to see adults marginalized because their old skills have been bypassed by the modern world, but, afraid of failure, they can't bring themselves to learn new skills.

Having said that, again be careful to make your failures little ones, a succession of testing failures. Use the AntiFragile ideas, seeking lots of course correction small errors and testing your assumptions for mistakes as you walk down that path. If you have some ideas about the dynamics of the situation (planning talk for 'what's going on'), you can try focused trial and error. To do that, you've got to pick a starting point to poke at the problem, and to check results of the pokes at regular intervals to adjust and modify your pokes.

Technically, you are intervening in the process system, but poking is what we are really doing. If you have no clue about the system dynamics, and there's nothing to be ashamed of about that, then you shift to outright trial and error. You do something, small being better than large, but really anything, watch and try something else. Make your decisions reversible until you have a good handle on the dynamics. Make your decisions reversible whenever possible, actually. Regardless of bright pictures of Honor and Glory, reversible decisions are better than the irrevocable ones. Irrevocable decisions are jumping off that cliff, and you'd better hope that parachute works. A memorial plaque commemorating your bravery is small reward.

Use as many senses in your decision as you can. If you, for example, visually inspect containers of salt, sugar and flour, and make a quick judgment, you're going to be surprised. Taste before using large amounts of ingredients! The beauty of a reversible decision is that it is a way of avoiding over commitment when only partial information is available. The problem with reversible decisions is generally a social one: people smell fear if you can back out, and that's bad for your leader image. There's a technique for this: define the problem setup broadly, blaming the world for the necessary ambiguities and then you have some slack.

And when it's clear that things are not working, pick your fall. Don't hang onto that bucking bronco until you can't hold on any longer! Pick a spot with soft grass and a chance of survival, and jump. It is difficult to overstate the importance of picking your fall, but it does require realizing that you are in the middle of something that isn't going well.

W. C. Fields coined this twist on an old cliché:

"If at first you don't succeed, try, try again. Then quit. There's no point in being a damn fool about it."

Here's what happens when you don't understand the dynamics of the situation:

"Everyone is here?" Don Cortes inquired, looking around. He nodded to the Counselor and then looked at the financial people. "Before we start lunch, I'd like to thank the financial people for coming all this way. What was it you said?" Don Cortes glared at the partner, who flinched. "You told me that the derivatives you chose to invest my money in were, surprisingly, more risky than anticipated. My Counselor discovered that your firm actually made money on your end of the derivatives, and only the customers lost money. So you transferred my money to yourselves, with a paper cutout transaction to hide the theft. Didn't you think that was risky? I'm the leader of one of the most vicious drug cartels in the world. Do you think this job was a prize I won from a Cracker Jack box?"

The investment people froze, except the young woman, who actually laughed, staring viciously at the partner.

"Your business model is bad business," Don Cortes advised. "You don't respect me or honor my business, but I provide a quality product to my customers. I'm a decent man who exports flowers—and their byproducts. I don't cheat my customers or my people. I think, gentlemen and young lady" he bowed slightly to the blonde woman, "that you need to understand risk more fully."

The partner sat rigidly at the table, mouth open, eyes wide.

"Have you found religion, gentlemen?" Don Cortes asked pleasantly. "To quote a predecessor of mine: 'Sometimes I am God. If I say a man dies, he dies that same day.' Take him," pointing to a one of the investment advisors, "and throw him into the pond."

The man screamed as the bodyguards wrestled him down the walkway. As they threw him off the dock, the logs in the lake started moving very quickly. The man screamed, thrashing in the murky water. In a minute, he was pulled under the water, leaving only a spreading red stain.

"Now there is the risk of portfolio loss, and there is the certainty of horrible death if you cheat me," Don Cortes explained. "You didn't have an investment model that anticipated that?" He laughed and pointed at another man, who was dragged down and thrown into the water. "An externality, as you described it earlier?" The same scene played out as with the first man, except the second man's severed leg floated to the surface for a minute, and then was snapped up by an alligator.

"So are you grasping the difference between a risk, a measured estimate of the probability of bad results, and the certainty of death?" Don Cortes inquired of the partner.

"You can't do this!" the partner blubbered, his voice cracking with fear. He stood up, frantically waving his arms. "We are powerful people, we are connected! You can't treat us like this!"

"Throw him in," Don Cortes roared. "But slice some parts off first. Let him watch the alligators eat his body parts."[88]

CHAPTER 22. HOW TO FAIL

This book cuts you no slack–you have to fail correctly! There will be no failing at failure here.

All of the failure mechanisms we are going to look at are, broadly speaking, all aspects-facets, as it were-of the same diamond. The root problem is that we have anchored our plan in the overlap between the self and the social world, and we are stuck, wiggling on that hook.

One case is where our mental model and doesn't adapt to changes. Thinking of Figure 1, we have an overlap between the real world and the self, but we have closed the window to the real world, relying on the real world to not change. The other is related to that error. Thinking of Figure 1, we have an overlap between the self and the social world, and we never even opened that window to the real world, but instead our mind (and/or social face) demands to be in control, and so refuses to hear/see/sense anything different. The results are obvious: we are not open to change and we deny anything that diminishes our sense of control. If you remember the 'stories' discussion, that's going to be an unhappy story. In theory, it's clear that if you define the reality you are going to accept and then refuse to change that view of what you do see, at least something (perhaps many things) will go wrong.

We have all seen organization and groups that are on a downward spiral. I'm not aware of any group that has a mission statement choosing decay. It would be an interesting meeting, actually, maybe something like:

> Well, we've had limited success here, but now it's time to head into a downward spiral that will paint us all with failure for the rest of our lives. What's our first step here? Sally, you have an idea?

Where a group is decaying, almost always someone knows that things are going badly and are trying to fix the problem(s). They are pumping air back into that balloon almost as fast as it's escaping, and praising themselves for their work. This is the underlying basis for all really great disasters, by the way. Rather than the nefarious villain of the movies, in a real disaster, everyone involved is doing what they think is right (it may not be right, but they think it at the time) and the sum of the efforts are disaster. It is the classic 'the road to hell is paved with good intentions', but worse, because the road to a really big failure is paved with good actions. Unfortunately, when the actions are summed up, they don't add up. It's like when I tried to integrate problems in calculus.

Even if you as an individual can accept the essential nature of failure, the group absolutely cannot. Groups words and emotional needs can't be balanced on the thin edge of ambiguity and uncertainty for long. So you have to carry a facade to the world while realizing the real problems. It's just important to realize what's going on. Knowing that most of the time you're wrong is the first step, and watching for that is what counts.

"WASHINGTON, DC. DECISION FAILURES.

A small group of civilians sat in a break room, staring at the walls.

"Well, what classic errors in decision making have we not committed here?" one bitched. He started ticking them off on his fingers. "The gambler's syndrome—taking unnecessary risks to recover a loss. They can't define what the risk is for their action, or even what would be accomplished if they did reach their goal. It's just action for the emotional sake of action. So, check that done. Then, two, we see patterns where none exist, fitting the data to the plan you want. We don't know what we are attacking or what success is, but they dreamed up a pattern that could be handled by the tools they had."

"You have an army, you use an army. Only when the army is gone do you use your head," another civilian added.

"Three, we remember when we didn't trust our gut and should have, while conveniently forgetting when we were fortunate to have ignored our instincts," the first civilian continued, ticking off another finger. "Anyone want to think about the last four disastrous wars we have been in?"

"I don't know, that group was pretty much all instincts," another civilian agreed. "But yeah, no doubts there."

"Fourth," the first civilian observed, raising another finger. "Our tendency toward overconfidence, our natural ability to overestimate our ability in just about everything. Here, we know nothing, and are certain of our ability to fix that for which we have not defined the problem yet. And five, the best one: Don't fall in love with your decisions, because everything's fluid. You have to constantly, subtly make and adjust your feelings. Here, they decided they were being attacked and they were going to defend. The nature, purpose, and result of the attack is irrelevant; they decided to defend and they are going to do just that, come hell or high water."

"Both of which are coming," another civilian asserted. "Quite quickly, actually."

The spy agency head was sitting in a corner, watching them. He motioned to an aide, who closed the door. The civilians looked very worried.

"This man," the spy agency man declared, pointing to his aide, "can escort you outside. I personally would bet on your survival if you face the trees, based on the conversation I've just heard. On the other hand, I'd not bet on your survival if the general's knew of your opinions. Your choice, gentlemen."

They looked at each other and nodded, and the aide escorted them out.

The spy agency man sat and thought for a few minutes. True terror, he realized, is waking up one morning and discovering that your high-school class is running the country. With that cheerful thought, he went back into the war room."[89]

It's helpful to group the root causes of failure into categories. They are obviously linked, but they are easier to work with split apart. Some helpful categories are:

HUMAN WIRING ISSUES.

We are hard wired to be what we are. We are the descendants of a long line of creatures who were hunters/foragers and scavengers on the savannas of Africa. For millions of years, our ancestors foraged and killed to survive, and our abilities are directly tied to those past necessities. The problem we run into is that many of the problems we face are far past the kind of simple mental calculus appropriate when hunting small creatures (or even large creatures). Our minds have not changed, but the world has. Whether we can avoid problems in the future by using computers to think more rationally is an interesting issue. What happens when the computers start thinking rationally about the annoyances caused by humans? Let's not go there, and focus instead on our making decisions now.

From a realistic, abet somewhat negative viewpoint, we think fairly slowly (look at the processing speed of a computer, for comparison) and can process a very limited amount of the deluge of information pouring in on us. Data mining works only because we have supercomputers to dredge through the detail, as our minds don't do that well. Our conscious memory is very limited, and our ability to directly access our unconscious, which is far more powerful than the consciousness, is even more limited. Based on the plots of novels and television shows, which are essentially a refrain on 'I thought I wanted X but I wanted Y', perhaps our ability to directly access the unconscious on demand is almost non-existent.

OUR TENDENCY TOWARD OVERCONFIDENCE.

A key cause, if not THE key error cause in our lives is our drive to protect our critical internal mask: we are competent and in control. That's different from, but related to, the practical need to project a socially competent mask.

We have to act. We are made to act, and we have to do something. The constant flow of fashion, the constant whirl of activity just for the sake of activity that we see around us, proves that we just have to do something, all the time. But we are clearly taught, beginning when we are small, that acting incorrectly will be punished, to a greater or lessor degree. This is a source of great conflict, because on one hand we have to act-but we don't want to be punished. So we mentally chase our tails all day: 'to do or to not do?' without having to go to the lengths that Hamlet did.

We act because we have a mental switch that stops this cycle of 'do-not do'. We choose our decisions by an emotional response. It may be more or less conscious, but we say to ourselves, roughly; "Yes, that's right." There is a pattern: a thought, the assessment of the thought, and then that emotional rush that we are 'right'. We've felt this emotion before, and we were right then, so when we feel it now, that 'proves' we are right now. Or, if we were not right then, at least we enjoyed ourselves (positive reinforcement). But, having acted because we are now emotionally comfortable and in control, should we be proved wrong, we are now not in control. Thus we, on many emotional and practical grounds, firmly embrace and protect our competence despite all that the world can say. Once you draw that line in the sand, that line is you, not just the decision.

Study after study shows that we overestimate our ability in just about everything. Now, that's not always bad. As said before in the book:

"If you think you can or think you can't, you're probably right"
Henry Ford

And he was right. You have to think you can in an uncertain world, so we have to perhaps (perhaps?) lie to ourselves before we start. I am a big fan of "The Little Engine that Could" and that little book represents a truth. Subject to the caveat that as long as what we are trying to do is really possible in this world, which has to be remembered. "The Little Engine that Could" driving down the expressway just isn't going to work.

Our confidence causes, not cures problems, when our overconfidence results in overestimating the accuracy (I'm 100% sure!) of the expected events in the plan we made. Forecasts are assumptions, and assumptions are the foundation of our plan design. If the forecasts are wrong, they we have a 'mistake' (the wrong plan) and we are off the tracks before we start.

OVERCONFIDENCE AND DOUBTS

Our need for confidence in ourselves, our need to demand that we are successful, can cause failure by limiting our actions to only what we can do. Not doing something which would have turned out great because we didn't try is a kind of hidden failure. Where we have to do something, but rather doubt we can succeed, we may instead do a plan that protects our confidence. The real goal is set aside, and we may do only what we can do well.

As a result, when we are asked to act, we do so only if we feel at least minimally competent to do what is asked of us. We need to believe our actions will ultimately be successful. That's a very good thing sometimes: we don't want to completely mess things up, and we shouldn't act if we are sure we will fail.

Where that mindset creates a problem is that without some reasonable expectation of success, we are unlikely to act at all and will instead resign ourselves to letting fate take its course. That's the part of the survival arc, by the way, that kills us. It's hoping for random luck, and is usually a fail. If we really have to act where we know we will fail reaching the original goal, then we focus our thinking (not always consciously) from the actual goals to the goal of preserving a sense of our competence. That's a multiple fail, because we have done something other than the real plan (fail No. 1) to protect our sense of competence that is then bashed by not having completed the real plan. (Fail no. 2) If we then turn our back on what we did do well because that was tied to the other fails, then it's 3 fails, and you're out!

OVERCONFIDENCE AND PRETENDING

To protect our competence, we can (actually we always do this) shortcut our decision process by developing simple hypotheses and limiting the search for information. That shortens our thought process and increases, at least at first, our feeling of competence. Put less politely, we pretend we know to avoid recognizing we don't know.

One species of this is called "Methodism". This is the unthinking application of a sequence of actions we do know how to do. Visually, it is using a hammer on everything. This is a simple self-protective mechanism: we were right then, so we are right now. The problem is that experience can also make us dumb. In planning jargon, 'Methodism' is a process, formally, of deconditionalizing a situation. Deconditionalizing a situation is an essential mental tool in our lives. Like most things, it's neither good nor bad in itself, it's how it is used that matters.

We deconditionalize a situation by taking a set of actions out of one context where they worked (we mix the ingredients for the brownies in a bowl like this) and putting it into another where it doesn't work (we mix the ingredients for concrete in the same way). By deconditionalizing, we have a ready plan of action to use over and over again. It is a wonderful tool, where it works.

This plan was successful in the past and so it will work in the future, we think. This can work: IF you grasp the few essential features of the situation and base the plans application to situations that have the same essential features. Unfortunately, nothing is exactly the same as anything else, and so it's critical, for any given new problem, to consider the specific, 'individual' aspects of the situation and develop local rules for an appropriate plan for 'this' situation. Using Methodism as a coping mechanism (instead of say, 'thinking') means that you cannot adjust to specific, individual problems on their own terms.

Methodism has the advantage/disadvantage that your choices are easier because there are fewer choices. The advantage is you just do, you don't wait and think. That's the disadvantage, also. Round peg, square hole, no hole at all: you just hit it harder until it goes in. Methodism is dangerous because the world is tricky. A given situation may look almost the same as a past success, but changes in minor details can demand vastly different steps to reach a goal. In other words, minor details to you represent major differences to the world, and my money is on the world.

Worse, when you have been rewarded over and over for doing a set of actions, then simply going through the motions can be rewarding. We love our rewards! If we fall into an intermittent reward schedule, which means that we are rewarded at random, but relatively frequent intervals, for some action/set of actions, we will do that set of actions over and over. Your conscious mind has little recourse against a deeply set intermittent reward schedule, so beware. The reward centers for the brain take over our thinking, and the actions rise to the status of a ritual. Ritualizing actions applied to differing problems is a prelude to catastrophe, as you are essentially using magic to control the real world.

A prelude to Methodism is that we prefer to assume that the new problem is of an old, familiar type that we have solved frequently in the past. That way, the problem automatically has the patina of success on it, and we cheerfully step up to bat. This is much the same as solving only those problems we know we can solve. This is boring, eventually, and those who the god's wish to destroy, they make bored. More dangerously, we force a problem into a slot that really isn't that problem, but is a problem that we have solved. Unfortunately, the solution doesn't work this time.

Now, the true beauty of Methodism is that it is usually socially blessed. Thus, we did the right thing, even if it leads to the wrong result. We may have failed in the real world, but not in the social world, and too often it's the social world that provides immediate feedback.

SELF FULFILLING PROPHECY

Overconfidence pushes into the trap of a 'self fulfilling prophecy'. We know what will happen, so we act in such a way that what we said would happen did happen. It will happen, at least for a while, because we avoid/ignore anything else which could change the result. This is good/bad depending on the importance of what we ignored, and the resulting consequences. As an extreme example, the Good Ship Lollipop isn't going to survive a storm in the open ocean.

Related to the Self Fulfilling Prophecy is 'revisionism'. This is rewriting history: i.e., we were better (sometimes worse) in the past than we actually were. It's easy to do, as memory is flexible, and much of our past wasn't really graven in stone for the entire world to remember. One dangerous manifestation of this is that it is easy to remember when we didn't trust our gut and should have (as a basis for our next action) while brushing aside when we were fortunate to have ignored our instincts. A certain amount of this is necessary in life, and often harmless. You just have to think a bit before actions with serious consequences. If you could jump eight feet across an open space when you were 16, and you are 46 now, maybe you really shouldn't try. If you are going to try and beat the odds, know the effect of the odds beating you before you start.

A particularly dangerous, actually delusional, application of the self fulfilling prophecy is what I call the "General Motor's mindset. That was, and still seems to be, a process of starting their mental orientation to the world with the statement 'We are GM-look at who/what we were!' That's a lock into a past that is rarely relevant to the future. It may take years, but the world catches up with you. Before GM, the major US Steel companies followed the path of past glories into the dustbins of history. Professor Clayton Christensen has several excellent books about disruptive innovation, and at the heart of the process is the industry leader(s) fixed on the past and ignoring the future.

Here's the short version of disruptive innovation, and how it trashes companies and lives. Where you focus on the 'why', the point of your actions, you are headed for success. Where you focus on the 'how' you do something, there's a problem coming. The quick example is a company that makes steam shovels, Christenson's example. The equipment moves earth. But the companies that failed focused on 'how' they made better and better steam shovels, ignoring the question of what the machines were supposed to do. New technology came along that moved earth better, and it really didn't matter that the steam shovels the failed companies made were really the best steam shovels ever made.

Another sub-class of the self-fulfilling prophecy is the confirming evidence trap. The title clearly describes the problem, in we seek out information supporting an existing predilection and to discount opposing information. The result is obvious to an objective observer.

In summary, what is the visual image that overconfidence leads to? It is that cartoon cliché where the character (think of the coyote chasing the road runner) walks or runs right off the cliff into space, and is fine, until he looks down and notices that there is nothing beneath him but air-lots and lots of air. Then he falls. It's always funnier in the cartoons.

STUCK IN THE PAST TRAPS

Let's say that the results of our last few projects have not been as we would have hoped. Say that our confidence is bit shaken, and we decide to investigate carefully this time. Now, fear is the emotion driving our choices, and fear is generally a 'no'. How to make a 'no' work? We can always focus on excessive planning and information gathering, which keep us from making contact with reality. The long quote going over the problems that Cali faced earlier in the book looks at that approach. Then we don't have to act, and don't have to worry whether our measures are or are not working, or we are simply wrong.

It turns out that there is an optimal amount of information to collect before making a decision. Too little information gathering, and you're really not making a decision; you're counting on luck. Too much information gathering, and you won't make a decision. Too much information gathering ends up with piles of facts, which may or may not be relevant to the real problem. All that 'stuff' obscures what the real issues are. Too little 'stuff' pretends there are no issues. The problem with the too little/too much is that the decision is based on local rules for the given situation, which often are not clear while you are in the middle of this. Of course, if you are intent on not making a decision/action, then piling up stuff allows you to vanish behind the piles on your desk.

Another stuck in the past trap is the Prudence Trap. This leads us to be overcautious (generally because we were not cautious on a prior project) when we make estimates about uncertain events. There is a positive spin on this: we are trying really, really hard to be on top of things, and so we are handicapping ourselves excessively. There's a negative spin, which is that we simply refuse to act and seek cover. Estimates have to be honest estimates, explaining clearly the assumptions they are based on. Where you load up the estimates with hidden assumptions, you are playing a game different from that you are pretending to play.

A variant is called the Status-Quo Trap. In this, we are biased to maintain the current situation, even when, objectively, better alternatives exist. The trick with this trap is that when you assess other choices, there is a risk assessment made, but no risk assessment made for the status quo. Obviously, as the status quo has no risk and the others have varying degrees of risk, then we stay where we are. The trap is that you are looking at alternatives because you are, at least, uncomfortable with the status quo. Not quantifying and thus ignoring the risk of the status quo, which is usually substantial, is a fail.

Finally, there is a particularly dangerous trap, called the Sunk Cost Trap. What's the trick? We spent $X and time and effort in the past, which produced a result. That result, sitting in front of us, isn't working as we hoped. But it's there, and to repudiate it, to walk away from it, is a clear failure, because, well, Look! We have all of these recourses in this past thing, and we can't walk away from them. Practically, if we do walk away, someone is going to get a black mark on their resume, at a minimum.

Fail. If the 'thing' isn't working, then it isn't working. Good resources thrown after bad will only waste the good resources and your time. The Sunk Cost Trap perpetuates the mistakes of the past. It is very hard to make an accurate assessment, because in most cases, there are reasonable arguments to preserve the past as well as to drop it and move on. Repeat after me: if it's done, it's done. The dead hand of the past should not-cannot-control our next choice. The real world doesn't care about the past, and we can't either.

Designers of questionnaires have learned that the answers people give can be heavily influenced-a polite way of saying forced-by suggestions that are given on the questionnaires themselves. For example, when people are asked to state within which of a number of ranges their income falls, their answers are influenced by the ranges given. The ranges serve as "anchors" to which they make their answers conform. Psychologists have shown that people's decisions in ambiguous situations are influenced by whatever available anchor is at hand. When you must come up with an estimate, and you are unsure what to say, you take whatever number is before you.

We are good at catching the clues. After a few years of school, if you have a multiple-choice test with four answers, you can almost always rule out two of them simply by the framing of the question. Unless there is an 'or one or two of the above' buried in the choices, which makes for a very hard test.

TIME PROBLEMS

All of the tricks and toys we use to make decisions are useful, and very often right. They are often perfectly reasonable in the context of the living creature that we are, as applied to our daily life. I'm beating on this-where we have problems, generally, is in the non-routine events in life. Making decisions on careers, houses, significant others, etc. is fraught with peril because they are important decisions with very minimal information. You cannot make the optimal decision on this house versus that house, because too much is hidden in future events. There probably is no optimal decision, actually, even looking back years later. Doesn't that make you feel better? It's the non-routine cases that the section is most concerned with, because we cheerfully slide from the routine to the non-routine without noticing the important differences.

Because time is always short, we have a tendency, generally rational, to economize in our thinking. As discussed before, in different contexts we omit steps in our thought process and/or to simplify them as much as possible. One only has a certain amount of time and we know that we must often proceed with only partial information. Even that partial information have we often do not have time to fully process or analyze.

One of the most common and serious problems that quick decisions lead to is the Anchoring Trap. This leads us to give excessive weight to the first information we receive. Anchors are their visual: once set, they (and you) don't move. An anchor will establish the terms on which a decision will be made. That's fine, until all the assumptions and variables change, but the options and choices don't move from the starting point. There is a classic proposition in negotiating that 'the first person to throw out a number loses.' That's the anchoring trap in a nutshell. Selling a house? That listing price forever fixes in everyone's mind. Leaving money on the table for the seller is the great sin that can keep you up late at night pondering.

How to avoid the Anchoring trap, which has destroyed many a negotiation? The answers are variations of the same theme: pull up that anchor. Try alternative starting points, think about the problem before consulting others which can accidently set the problem in stone, be open minded, don't anchor parties to the negotiations. Or, cold bloodedly, set an anchor that guarantees failure for this set of negotiations, setting yourself up for better position when the other person has to act later.

Not only is the anchoring trap a problem in itself, it can bring with it other errors. One common relative trap is our tendency to see patterns where none exist. Once we see the pattern, we cherry pick reality, resulting in what statisticians call 'over fitting ' the data. Our vision clear, (at least to us) we've set the anchor, we know the lay of the land (a mixed metaphor, I know) and now we see the future. Not.

Time Problems are a subset, but a very important one, of human wiring. Our primary method of handling time is to extrapolate from the moment. So, what's most important to us right now, what we are focused on, is what will play a key role in our predictions of the future. That leads to:

> "A limited focus on a events in the present which might signify (or guarantee) the future will be different from the present . . .
>
> And then an extension of the today's perceived trend in a more or less linear and "monotone" fashion"[90]

These are very serious problems. We do not handle systems tied to anything but very simple temporal patterns (i.e., rain this morning and mud by noon) without major difficulties. Major difficulties means that we miss, by a mile, what is going to happen. For example, when we act on something that will then have a result in the future, there is a transmittal of information. That takes time, and so there is a dead zone for some, short or long, time period. Then the result occurs, with the result that there is an oscillation in the system. Generally, the system then over-responds and so we immediately react, which causes another dead zone and a future oscillation. If you have every rowed a canoe, that's how you tip a canoe over. You move, a little more than you should, and then over-correct, and over-correct again as the canoe sways more and more, and then into the water. It's hilarious on video.

It's the same with a cold room. People will set the temperature higher than they actually want, thinking it will heat up faster. It won't, there is a furnace driving hot air at a given rate. When you notice it's too hot and turn it down, it's still pushing out hot air, so you have to open the window, which makes it too cold, and away we go.

In my MBA program, there was an example of a beer manufacturer who wanted to run certain promotions. The problem they ran into was that because of fluctuations in demand, they never did manage to have enough beer in the right place at the right time, but did always manage to have too much beer in the wrong place at the wrong time. This is a more serious problem in war, when the troops/supplies are in the wrong place at the wrong time.

There is a lot of planning literature on time perception, most of it essentially saying that we don't get it. If you have any doubts, read the Wall Street Journal. Over and over, stock gains today are from events of months or years ago, which we all (including myself) missed. We're not made to patiently hold old events in our minds, carefully calculating the probabilities of results over time.

LISTENING TO THE UNCONSCIOUS

I'm wandering off from hard planning again. It's very important to realize that our unconscious decides what it wants and gradually conveys the message to the consciousness. If you are planning something and a clear vision of what you want keeps popping up, you might as well do it. If you talk yourself out of it, you'll be miserable until you do what you want to do. I may not always get a milkshake the moment that the picture pops up, but I'm careful to get one within a few days, especially if the picture pops up again.

The unconscious sorts out the huge number of perceptions and data into a very small stream that the consciousness notices. So we are engaged by things we and literally don't see things we dislike. That's probably a healthy response, except in planning for new situations.

We use unconscious routines to cope with the complexity inherent in most decisions, which are called heuristics. While those work in many cases, they are weak (pitiful, actually) when they calculate probabilities. Where we have to calculate/combine multiple probabilities, we do not normally handle this well. We emotionally fix to a probability, and act on that, and/or miss the fact that a .5 probability of one event and a .5 probability of another event results in a .25 probability of both events – NOT adds to a 1.0 probability, i.e., a certainty, of those events.

Again, everything we do is based on emotions, which is good and bad. We make decisions by emotions, and are subject to fear overriding all decision-making. Emotions work when a lion is charging at us, but are not as useful outside that context. Decision-making is going to produce some anxiety, because we realize we can be wrong. There is a pleasure in decision making also, which probably underlies a lot of the compulsive shopping behavior, a repetitive, ritualized behavior. Another example is that when we are stressed, we remember a smaller number of prior events, and the few facts we are able to hold in memory are pushed aside by our fears. So, we limit our options when we need then them most, and render our decisions less reasonable. Sun Tzu went on and on about not doing the same thing twice, because people never expect you to change your behavior, and it's true. But changing your behavior under fire isn't easy.

RISKS

We are risk averse when a problem is posed in terms of gains, but risk seeking when a problem is posed in terms of avoiding losses. The caution of a predator in the wild is hard wired into us, and we absolutely minimize risk, unless we are starving or mating.

Why? Because there was no medical system on the plains of Africa to nurse injured predators back to health. An injured predator equals food for other predators. Backstopping a lot of our ethical guidelines is the hardwired concept that we need to avoid a loss before seeking a gain. This makes a lot of sense for a predator, but it twists our ethical choices in many ways that we don't realize.

Because we misjudge risk/reward we fall into the Framing Trap. We frame the problem from the 'no losses first' perspective, which may or may not be the reality of the situation. So a framing error, by misstating the problem, undermines the entire decision making process, because you are then solving the wrong problem. Again, solving the wrong problem is worse than doing nothing. The framing problem has many social aspects. Notice people in groups/meetings: people tend to adopt the frame as it is presented to them rather than restating the problem in their own way. If you're leading the meeting, that's the whole idea. It just may or may not result in a good plan.

HABITS OF MIND

An absolutely critical problem, but one that we literally don't think about is that we don't think about problems we don't have. We don't think about the 'critical but urgent' problems out there. We neglect them because we don't have those problems at the moment and therefore are not suffering from their ill effects. In short, we are captives of the moment.

We are going to do what we did yesterday in most cases. Habits of mind, that is, habits of thinking, stick and stay stuck. We develop and reinforce those patterns over a lifetime. In effect, we are more strongly 'addicted' to how we think than we are to what we think about. Having said that, habits of mind are unavoidable, and they usually work for us rather than against us. The challenge is to understand what they are, so that when they aren't working in a particular situation, we have some idea as to what needs to change.

If we really don't know what to do, but we must act, then a necessary emotional reaction kicks in which is openly opposed to reflection and analysis. It's full speed ahead and re-make the world rather than seek to understand it. This makes sense in the context of the world of our ancestors, where they had to do dangerous things that often were best not thought through. Not so well for today's world.

SOCIAL DECISION FACTORS

Social Factors matter in decision making. We all know that acting in a group is an especially complex case of planning. The group (any group) demands success. Failure, even limited and strategic failure, is too hard to discuss. People will run from failure, and run from people who have failed, afraid that the stink will rub off on them. So failure is ignored, and only success can be asserted. That leads to: having to project a successful mask to the social group. As we all know that failure is inevitable, there is a lot of moving the goal posts, hiding the evidence, and generally anything that can maintain this facade of success with the group.

There are some real interpersonal barriers to decision-making and especially plan results reporting. Think about, as a child, the careful process of reporting a bad report card to your parents. It's the same process in an organization, when 'negative' information had to feed upward. Not shooting the messenger is conceptually correct, but emotionally difficult. So, people carefully present information in such a way that slowly and carefully the power-that-be is alerted to the fact that a major problem was about to be announced. It is always wise, before your give any bad news, to give good news. You can play down the impact of a failure by emphasizing how close your came to achieving the target, so, well, see-it isn't so bad. You are, of course, fooling yourself and everyone else, but survival has it's own requirements.

Another social decision failure is a false underlying story. This is easy to do in choosing a career. For example, choosing law school because the law is a prestigious profession (perhaps) and ignoring the petty details: that there are no jobs in today's legal world, that personal contacts are a huge part, and people who are not actually sociopaths often won't enjoy the practice of law. Another version, astonishing common, is that the charming person you met, who left a trail of broken hearts and pocketbooks behind him/her, was just misunderstood. No. You misunderstand.

Then there is an interesting planning approach which is simply the assumption that 'people should do what they are expected to do'. When this approach is used by the legislature, subsequently implemented by their minions 'the men in suits in rooms' that write the regulations, it will be train wreak time. Plan to be making money off the triage work, not riding the train.

Finally, one of the most effective social devices for avoiding blame for failure in an uncertain world that condemns failure is to use a socially approved ritual. The 'men in suits in rooms' discussed above is an example. You put serious looking people in a boring room and they produce socially acceptable phrases and documents that have marginal connection, at best, with the real world.

A ritual is a certain sequence of steps done exactly correctly, and so if the ritual does not produce the desired effect that strict adherence to the rules should produce, the complexity of the rules allows us to blame the failure on a mistake we must have made at some point in the ritual. In this way we can continue to believe that our ritual is altogether adequate for solving the problem, especially if we stand in a circle and hold hands together.

The beauty of a socially accepted ritual is that all we have to do is execute the ritual correctly. At this point, our actions are almost completely divorced from external conditions. We no longer pay any attention to what is happening in the outside world. All that matters is the ritual. Where feedback is infrequent and where intervals between action and feedback are long, ritualization's will wax luxuriant.

On the bright side, a successful failure is a good alibi.

You should give yourself points, because reading a long digression on how things can (and do) go wrong is not human nature. Have some chocolate.

POTENTIAL FAILURES REVEALED

Within the ideas we have covered, we can see the potential failures.

- Thinking is imagining certain things. We are limited in the number of things we can think about at any given time.

- We can only think about things we know, really. Until we experience something, we don't realize all of the relationships and ties. All of that 'walk a mile in another's shoes' represents a real truth.

- Emotions sway what we think about, and thus emotions sway (picture a bridge in the wind, actually) the thought chains we think up.

- What we are taught may or may not be correct, and certainly not complete, so linking actions may not include essential actions that are we have not been taught or encouraged to think about because they are forbidden in some way.

- Consequences that we expect based on our thoughts or past experience may not be real tomorrow, or may miss others that are real.

- Actions taken may or may not be possible and may result, because of requirements/conditions for the actions, in bringing in additional complexity and time requirements. So our trip to the store for milk many pages ago? We spend two hours getting the car towed to a repair shop, still don't have the milk, and now don't have time to prepare for the party tonight.

- Time is always a factor, and time is a major problem, both in calculating and in measuring, because of temporal perception problems. That is a fancy way of saying that we only are aware of certain time relationships. Generally, we miss long sequence time relationships, such as an action that has a definitive result a month later. The joy and grief of the stock market exists largely because of long temporal delays. We try, but we are wired for relatively immediate results. We throw the stick, the animal falls, we eat it, is about the longest time chain we are designed for.

GOALS

Our thinking on a problem is, or should be, based on our goals. David Allen's first step is to clearly visualize the goal, which starts the mind in motion. Now, one way to set the mind in motion is:

> "It is by Caffeine alone I set my mind in Motion, it is by the juice of the Bean that thoughts acquire speed, the hands acquire shakes, the shakes become a warning. It is by Caffeine alone I set my mind in Motion"(unknown)

While it seems like we would always start with the goal, that's actually fairly rare. In a lifetime of counseling people with various kinds of problems, I'm always fascinated by how people start by wandering off into a subset of a problem or something that is really irrelevant to the problem but emotionally teasing and satisfying. Half of counseling is getting people to agree on the problem they are really worried about. Once that is clear, solutions will generally pop up. This isn't new:

> "Human psychology is
> to go for perceived benefits and
> try to avoid prospective harm."[91]

Chapter 11: "THE NINE KINDS OF TERRAIN"

The following is basic but important. It's the assumptions that trip plans and people up, which is why they are covered in this book over and over.

Goals are either positive or negative. It makes a difference! If you don't realize what kind of goal you are seeking, your plan isn't going to work because the steps for different types of goals differ. A positive goal aims at achieving some definite condition. With a negative goal we seek to avoid something. Negative goals are usually less clearly defined than positive goals. If you can, convert negative goals into positive goals.

Why? Philosophically, negative goals are weak because you are defining something by the lack of something. Let's say your goal is to not be afraid of something. You will always be afraid of X, because your measuring stick is the fear of X. If your goal is to do something, that by doing means you are not afraid of X, then your measuring stick isn't the fear, it is doing Y. Does that make sense? It's important and easy to step over without noticing.

A negative goal is like one of those annoying Greek paradoxes. Achilles is always racing a turtle and never catching the turtle, because the paradox uses the relationship between them as the measuring stick, not their relationship to the external world. When you measure based on your relationship to something, you are stuck with that relationship for good, whether that's what you wanted or not. That's a negative goal and the results.

Another reason you don't want negative goals is that the mind doesn't respond well to running away. The mind wants to go to something, which is what a positive goal is. If you want to make sure that a child spills that glass of water they are holding (what kind of a person are you?) tell them over and over to not spill it. Their mind will focus on spilling the drink and there you go.

So, you have a goal. A general goal is one that is defined by a few (ideally one) criteria - i.e., success 'is'. We want clear goals, with a magic touchstone that is 'done'. A finish line, the cheering throngs, and a well deserved rest. An unclear goal is a goal that doesn't have that magic touchstone which says, beyond the shadow of a doubt, that the goal has been achieved.

Well, why would we have an unclear goal? That's obviously not going to work-and it doesn't. We have unclear goals for a number of reasons. Commonly, it's because the situation we are facing is so complex that we only understand part of the process and we are starting to act because we have to do something. We are action-oriented creatures and jumping into the fray and swinging wildly is at least action. The problem with random action is:

" *When your strategy is deep*
and far-reaching, then what you gain

by your calculations is much,
so you can win before you even fight.
When your strategic thinking is shallow
and near-sighted, then what you gain
by your calculations is little,
so you lose before you do battle."[92]
Chapter 1: "ON ASSESSMENTS"

The more thought we could put into visualizing the goal, the better. It's just thinking about what you want, after all, it isn't that painful. As my parents used to say, don't just use your head for a hat rack. Actually, there was more involved in the discussion, but we'll move on-you get the gist. It's very easy, and often necessary, to just jump into the process. We are not taught to sit and think, because it looks like we are not doing anything, or worse yet, idle hands and the devil's playground.

A clear, specific goal is the Holy Grail of planning. It is a goal that is defined by many criteria; it can be described and conceptualized very precisely. There is a clear set of actions, each with a success/fail rule, until we complete the last step, at which point we can see whether we succeeded or not. While that seems like an ideal plan, there are many situations (dealt with later in the book) where a clear success/fail has socially undesirable results. And a clear, specific goal is about as rare, for any complex, meaningful problem (ecology? Economics? Social equality?) as the Holy Grail is.

Multiple goals, a common complex problem, means that many things are happening at once, and success is then several criteria. These are not the Holy Grail of planning (although they may be the Holy Grail of life) because they range from difficult (see 'complicated problems' later in this book) to the really completely unsolvable complex problems (also see later in this book) that we face. The many things happening at once may or may not be related; may or may not be under our control; and may or may not always be known to us. And the success criteria may or may not be related, generally are not all under our control, and then there are the complete surprises-unknown unknown's at our door with a bill. All of the important things in life-career, marriage, and children, for a few examples-are multiple goal, complex problems, which is what keeps it all interesting.

This next idea is important, but hard to convey. We think that we have a 'goal', which we developed by the preceding steps. Maybe we have the goal clear in our mind, maybe we write down a few steps, maybe we have 30 pages of project steps, resources and constraints. It's a clear, explicit goal that we can convey to others and ourselves.

Where surprises come in is where we have "implicit" goals that we may not, at least at first, take into account. We may not even know we are pursuing them until something doesn't feel right, or the results are really not what we had imagined. As an example, we have a real plan in the real world. We are building a house for our family and ourselves. We have pages of blueprints showing the floors, various construction details and a materials list.

How closely have we examined exactly why we building the house? It's almost certainly not for simple shelter against the elements. We have extensive personal preferences for how we want to use the house and social status issues-lots of those! Have we considered future changes, such as having children, then the children growing up and leaving, then coming back, perhaps parents moving in; all of those are implicit goals that generally are not clearly defined. All of our actions are driven by an excessive (or exclusive) preoccupation with explicit goals.

A moment's thought is going to see that not taking implicit goals into account is going to result in bad planning and counterproductive behavior. Please underline the following: People concern themselves with the problems they have, not the ones they don't have (yet). If you build a house because you liked a house that you walked through one time and so you use that plan, without thinking through your requirements, success will be sheer luck, not skill.

On the other hand (covered in complex problems later in the book) no one can anticipate everything about the future. So how to cope? It's always recommended to set intermediate goals according to the criterion of maximum "efficiency diversity". Maximum diversity is one of the rare 'good' things in all situations. You will rarely, if ever, go wrong with maximum diversity. You will almost certainly go wrong with minimum (it does only one thing and one thing only) diversity. You have high efficiency diversity if it offers many different possibilities ("diversity") for actions that have a high probability of success. So, in our house example, there is space for kids, up to some maximum number of children (at which point money runs out and you create a dormitory), possible choices if parents move back in and maybe a space for a man cave.

The future is unknowable. Whether you subscribe to the Newtonian view of the universe, a universe of a giant clock with an infinity of gears clicking away, or the Quantum theory, which pictures a universe where next events are just uncertain, it's clear that with our limited facilities for perception and analysis, knowing 'the future' isn't going to be possible. If the is future unknowable and planning and implementation so hard, you want to build a lot of redundancy into systems. Which is what "AntiFragile" recommends over and over, by the way. That way, as things break, there is a system that kicks in, and things don't just crash. With an unknowable future, we can only improvise as opportunities present. It's unnerving to admit we don't understand/know all our options, but high diversity planning for surprises and a certain amount of redundancy gives us a chance to respond where we trip over our assumptions. Write that last sentence on a piece of 3x5 paper or have it tattooed on your arm for quick reference.

This is why planning and project management is so hard. Stepping back from what we want, the blithe assumption that we make that things are possible because we want them to be, why should planning be easy and project management even possible? Creating a word phrase with relevant meanings does not change the complexity of the underlying reality. Just because we say something is 'real' doesn't mean that there is any external world reality that matches.

SPRINGING THE HIDDEN TRAPS

The anchoring trap leads us to give disproportionate weight to the first information we receive. Anchors can and will establish the terms on which a decision will be made. Avoiding the trap: Try alternative starting points, think about the problem before consulting others, be open minded, don't anchor advisors and especially be wary of anchors in negotiations. Set your anchors deliberately.

The status-quo trap biases us toward maintaining the current situation, even when better alternatives exist. The more choices we confront, eventually we despair and then the status quo looks golden. Avoiding the trap: continually remind yourself of the real objective (which is often 'get out of this box we are locked in!) examine the status quo as if it was any other alternative, remember that, in most cases, the status quo isn't the only alternative, and ask whether you would choose the status quo if it was an alternative. Evaluate the status quo in terms of the future, not just the present and make the jump if you have better alternatives.

The sunk cost trap taunts us to perpetuate the mistakes of the past. And we can avoid this best by tearing up the records of what the sunk costs are, and imagining what we would do if we were starting over. Sunk costs only matter to the extent they contain resources that can be used to reach the real goal. So if the only value of the $100,000 machine is the copper scrap, make the decision and move on.

The confirming evidence trap leads us to seek out information supporting our existing theory, hypothesis, a wild ass guess, whatever: and to discount opposing information. We can and do subconsciously decide what to do before figuring out why we want to do it. Remember flipping the coin and knowing which side you are rooting form? We are more engaged by things we like than by things we dislike, so we never see the ones we dislike. Avoiding the trap: be careful to examine all the evidence with equal rigor; find a devil's advocate, be honest about motives, don't ask leading questions to get advice. Imagine, for a second, what would happen if the disliked option happened.

The framing trap occurs when we misstate a problem, which undermines the entire decision making process. This is really, really serious. We have to be careful structuring frames in terms of gains or losses, as we react quite differently depending on the particular pitch. We are risk averse when a problem is posed in terms of gains, but risk seeking when a problem is posed in terms of avoiding losses. People tend to adopt the frame as it is presented to them rather than restating the problem in their own way, which is the only reason to hold a meeting. Avoiding the trap: framing with different reference points, moving past and not automatically accepting the initial frame, re-pose problems in different combinations of gain/loss, ask how your thinking might change if the framing changed. Where others create and/or recommend the frame, examine the way they framed the problem Consider for a minute the 'frame' in criminal cases, where someone is convicted on erroneous evidence. Is this happening here?

The overconfidence trap makes us overestimate the accuracy of our forecasts. Avoiding the trap: always consider the extremes, reset the accuracy of our forecast and ask what happens then.

The prudence trap leads us to be overcautious when we make estimates about uncertain events. Avoiding the trap: state estimates honestly, recognize why we are being overcautious and back away if we are really terrified of being part of this. Are we using 'prudence' as a polite cover?

And the recallability trap leads us to give undue weight to recent, dramatic events. Avoiding the trap: read a newspaper from five years ago, and put the events in our plan into that ancient frame. Always carefully examine assumptions, especially the probabilities of random events.

Checklists are the gold standard for springing all of these kinds of traps, actually.

Humble Decision Making

After all the negative information in this book, perhaps humble is easier. Certainly it is no shame to admit that we don't know-and can't know-all that we would want and many times what we know we need to made the right decision. We must proceed with partial information, and we have not even had time to fully analyze what little we do have. We can focus on seven/eight (+/-) facts at a time. Our ability to calculate probabilities, especially to combine two or more probabilities on the fly, which is essential for most decision making, is somewhere between is low and abysmal. Finally evidence shows that we learn surprisingly slowly: we make the same mistakes over and over again. Example: 'Ah, the last attack into direct machine gun fire failed? Well, try it again, maybe with more men this time.'

We must let our emotions make decisions, which is the unconscious tossing the report of calculations to the consciousness. But emotions are unclear, and subject to rapid change, especially fear. Decision making almost inevitably evokes anxiety. Decision makers respond in predictable ways that sadly result in decisions being less reasonable. Patterns such as: defensive avoidance, by delaying decisions unduly. Or Overreaction, where we make decisions impulsively in order to escape our anxiety, or hyper-vigilance in which we collect more and more information instead of making a decision.

Watch for planning rituals, magic motions hide the complexity. If we do the magic, get the dance right this time and get everyone to agree then it will work. If you have to be part of the group, do the dance, but shuffle to the side when blame is to be passed out.

Even in the little things, it's easy to miss the essential. I was recently at a seminar, and was looking for a stairway, because it's healthier to climb the stairs. Now, stairways are generally hidden in corners, with elevators prominently featured. So I'm wandering around, expecting to find a stairway lurking behind a door marked with an exit sign. I walked right by a thirty foot tall, fifteen foot wide marble stairway, really the centerpiece of this huge hall roughly two hundred feet long and fifty feet wide. Wasn't I embarrassed when I asked and someone pointed to that majestic marble passage to the upper halls.

There's many a slip twixt cup and lip (anonymous)

CHAPTER 23. THE FAIRIES

The fairies? What kind of a serious book is this? As discussed earlier, we personify and fill our worlds with spirits. Do not, regardless of your beliefs, denigrate or insult the fairies, as they have a vicious sense of humor.

There's the structure fairy:

> We want that to be our competitors raison d'etre, not ours. That's the 'no-one wants this to happen but each step taken to avoid it brings it closer' little joke that the structure fairy likes to play on the world."[93]

There is the wishing fairy.

> When time or cost pressures are high there will be problems ignored, nay, more than ignored-problems will be magically wished away. They will come back, and at the worst time, because the wishing fairy has a sense of humor. Deal with the problems when they show up, or at least memo them so they can be handled when there is time.[94]

There is the good fairy and the bad fairy.

> What are the possibilities? The good fairy could make them happy to tell me by tapping her little wand on their heads. Or by putting them in the dungeons at Paul's, tapping their little heads with a club. A tempting thought, but hard to arrange. If I had time, I could blackmail them, because everyone is hiding something(s). Or I can pay people. I fill their pockets, and they open their minds to me. Finally, I can trick them, and they open their minds to me without knowing what I took.

> Okay—I never had much luck with the good fairy before, I don't have a dungeon, blackmail takes time, and paying people doesn't seem to work. First, paying people fails because then they realize what they have done and run to confess. I need them to give me the information without knowing or thinking about what they did. Secondly, paying them takes more money than I have. So, it's down to tricking them.

> Too bad, because I like the good fairy idea. Okay. I need to trick people, which makes me the bad fairy. How do I do that? First, people don't estimate risks well. The danger of the risks shouted on the news are overestimated, and the little, daily risks are underestimated. It's driving to the airport, not the flight, which is dangerous. So what is a risk people overestimate and overreact to, and what is a risk people underestimate and so don't think about what they are doing? I need information from strangers, and for them to freely and gladly share with me that which they should know better than to do. More: that which they are sternly ordered to not share.[95]

The Problem Fairy also has a sense of humor. Eventually, each of our best interests conflict in hidden and time delayed ways. There is another set of Black Swans! Again, the capacity of people to do evil in the name of evil is quite limited, but the power of people to do evil in the name of the good is essentially unlimited. Everyone works very hard in their best interests, fighting for what is best for them and eventually those conflicts are going to be a very large problem. Hard working farmers accidently causing dead areas in the ocean, for example.

Then, there is the legendary screw up fairy. Picture the fairies laughing at you and think before you act.

Part 4. You think you can solve problems?

CHAPTER 24. SIMPLE PROBLEMS

"In preparing for battle I have always found that plans are useless, but planning is indispensable." Dwight D. Eisenhower,

Problems are simple, complicated or complex.

A simple problem is baking brownies from a mix. There is a list of ingredients, orderly steps to take, temperature settings and time requirements. With simple problems, generally there are a few basic techniques to learn. But once these are mastered, following the recipe brings a high likelihood of success. Not a guarantee, by any means. It's easy to burn the brownies, often easier the fifth time you make them than the first time, because you get confident and thus careless.

The OOAD (observe, orient, decide and act) cycle, is a lot easier with a simple problem. Baking brownies? Dump the ingredients into a bowl, and find a mixing tool, and mix. So you observe (what's the mess look like?) orient (what should it look like?) decide (too many lumps still in the mix) and act (start mixing again). Repeat until your orientation criteria are satisfied. By then, the oven should be the right temperature, ah; you did turn the oven on before you started mixing, right? Just because it's a simple problem doesn't mean that there are not multiple processes going on at once with different time lines.

Simple problems are good cases for a checklist. It's easy and I've done it, to skip steps on what we dismiss as simple stuff. Or to miss what you expect. One time, my wife was making brownies. I went to work, came home several hours later, and cheerfully frosted the brownies. They seemed a little strange, but I ignored that, only to find that she had gotten busy and never put the brownies into the stove to bake. I had just assumed that the brownies would have gone in the stove, and didn't check them. I can testify that frosted raw brownie mix is really not all you might hope for. While a checklist for brownies probably wouldn't go to the level of 'poke finger into brownies to make sure they are ready to be frosted', it might if you were selling them.

Emotionally, we don't like checklists. We resent them because they are a reminder of how incompetent we can be. 'I can remember all these steps', is the natural and somewhat angry response. Of course, we can't. Study after study shows that we skip things, get casual or busy, or the 5th time it's OK, then well, it's going to be OK forever. So a checklist is a good idea, especially for simple problems which are clearly laid out, but which can be very involved to solve.

Are there special approaches for dealing with a simple problem? Of the list in the last section, these are especially useful:

____ • You can often do a detailed analysis of the problem. There is a recipe that we can follow and we can carefully walk through the necessary steps.

- For a simple problem, you can often simply size up a situation, a very rough mental calculation. If it's a simple situation that you've gone through before, that may be all that is necessary.

- Sit back and see what develops; if a decision isn't required/possible, then don't make a decision. This is relevant for all types of problems, because if you can't make a decision, then don't. Remember the motto of the medical profession: first, do no harm. (not the other motto: 'no insurance card, no good') Not acting may be the best choice.

Just because it's simple, doesn't mean it is easy. You always have to expect the unexpected. As always, thinking is best done before acting and thinking about our assumptions is critical.

It's important to watch for anomalies, even with simple problems. As an earlier part of the book went on and on about, all of our understanding of the world is through stories. Simple problems are a usually a relatively clear, easy to understand story, and so we often don't pay close attention to the story. It's just like the others, and we gloss over the details. An anomaly is something different, often something small, some event that doesn't jibe with the nice story you created. If nothing else, externalities lurk out there, always ready to upset the best laid plans of mice or men. An anomaly in a simple problem is the complexity of the world rearing its head.

> "a mote it is to trouble the mind's eye.
> In the most high and palmy state of Rome,
> A little ere the mightiest Julius fell,
> The graves stood tenantless and the sheeted dead
> Did squeak and gibber in the Roman streets." [96][iv] (Hamlet)

Just because it's a simple story, doesn't mean it can't be serious. The eggs for the brownie mix don't quite look or small right? Trust your judgment and toss them, because rotten eggs don't enhance the quality of the end product.

Even with simple problems, it's important to take into account consequences. I know that I'm beating (pun) on the brownie mix example, but if you are mixing up new batches everyday, you'd better be working in a restaurant. Brownies, while tasty, are questionably healthy, and lead to weight gain and related problems. Anything in excess is going to be a problem.

The brownie mix, while a simple problem, has some rather complex elements that we ignore. After all, we are starting with some stuff, and through combining it and heating it, we have something quite different. The chemical reactions are quite complex! We ignore those because there isn't anything special we have to do other than heat the oven and put the brownies into the oven, but there are extremely complex processes running through our simple story.

And finally, because we know the world through stories, you have to watch that your formulation of a simple problem isn't a morality play, that is, a story of what should be, not what is going to be. As discussed before, morality plays are thrown at us constantly and it's easy to want to have 'good' (organic?) brownies as well as brownies that taste good. We fit things into the pegs that we are used to using, and use multiple pegs where possible.

An advantage of simple problems is that if you misjudge them and create a morality play seeking the 'good' instead of what can actually be done, you're going to notice fairly quickly. Complex problems, the topic of 'I have an unsolvable problem', can go quite a distance as a morality play before it becomes apparent that this isn't going to work.

CHAPTER 25. COMPLICATED PROBLEMS.

A complicated problem can be a solvable problem if it has a clear goal. Of course, if there isn't a clear goal, the solution is either impossible, or the solution can be anything you want the solution to be, as we are defining success based on random results, not a goal, at that point. Both can have advantages, one has to just recognize what you are dealing with.

Complicated problems are ones like sending a rocket to the moon. They can sometimes be broken down into a series of simple problems. But there is no straightforward recipe. You're not cooking brownies here; you are hosting a Thanksgiving Day potluck dinner. Success requires multiple people, often multiple teams and specialized expertise. Unanticipated difficulties are frequent because there are many things happening and one can't anticipate everything. Timing and coordination become serious concerns.

In the Thanksgiving Day potluck example, you have some food that you, as the host, have to cook. All the different items you are cooking demand different ingredients, different pots and pans, different burners and against the limited resources of your kitchen, including never enough oven space. Then, you have to make the eating area ready for people before they arrive. The people who are participating need some guidance so that everyone doesn't bring the same thing and if some people are bringing things that are more critical than others, there has to be a way of making sure they first get the critical item cooked (and it tastes good) and secondly, will be there. If someone bringing critical items should get sick or their power goes out or any of a number of other possibilities, then you have to be ready to adjust.

One simple formulation for handling a complicated project is:

Priorities to Goals: ACTION
A: are measurable
C: compatible with your mission
T: time specific
I: in writing
O: ownership and accountability
N: negotiated

It's a quick mnemonic to remind us of the major issues. Laying out those items, for an even moderately complex project, can be pages and pages of lists and next steps.

I touched on measurability in the feedback section. If you have criteria, then almost always there is some kind of a measurement involved in the criteria, both in your initial decision and then testing whether the criteria have been met. There are books and books about measurement, because it's a lot more complex than it seems. For the purposes of looking at the "ACTION" steps above, you have to be able to measure progress and 'done'.

Complicated problems are those such as working with the tax code. The tax code, at least in the United States, is tens of thousands of pages of densely written material, trying to cover all the esoteric situations that life can develop. The tax code is a continuing skirmish between powerful people with money who want to keep their money, the various needs of society for defense, health and other social goals and the needs of the politicians to have money for programs to buy their way to continued power. Having spent most of my life working with the tax code, I no longer consider it really all that complicated, it's just what it is, which shows that we get used to things.

The limits to our thought processes is shown by the book "Thirty-Six Dramatic Situations, by Georges Polti and Lucille Ray. It effectively lays out thirty-six basic plots for all stories and plays. That's it, that's the highway to our mind. A classical background is helpful, as the example range from older to ancient, but it makes a surprising point: we only want to see these 36 variations: anything else just doesn't connect. If you are looking for black swans, read the book and think about what can't be communicated within those limited story formats.

In traditional planning books, a classic complicated problem is sending a rocket to the moon. The whole process can sometimes be broken down into a series of simple problems, but there is no straightforward recipe. In theory, once you learn how to send a rocket to the moon, you can repeat the process with other rockets and perfect it.

One rocket is like another rocket: except sometimes. The Challenger disaster is a classic example of the focus being taken off the safety of the astronauts, and focusing on the schedule. The O-rings were not designed to be used in cold weather and there was considerable evidence that they would fail. For various reasons, all of which have been examined in minute detail by various committees, that information was either ignored, poorly presented or disregarded, with horrendous results.

The space shuttle was considered a complicated project, which meant it had a lot of steps, but it could be solved. As it turned out, it (like everything in the world) was a complex project, dependent on systems that were poorly understood and many of the systems were out of the control of NASA. The Challenger was an overlaps problem. Many people assumed that what they wanted was in the overlap of the real world and the social world. It wasn't.

The real difference between simple, complicated and complex problems is the extent to which we have to consider the big world in our plans. Making brownies doesn't have to consider the earth's magnetic field, but may have to consider height if you are up on a mountain. Making brownies to sell worldwide raises issues of religious requirements for the materials, a very complex matter indeed.

The Project Management Institute (PMI) lives for project

management. They have developed an extensive process for project planning, embodied in the "A Guide to the Project Management Body of Knowledge" ("PMBOK" for short). It's a very good process, rather mindboggling, but very comprehensive. If you can figure out the planning process, you have proved you have the intellectual ability to figure out almost any complicated project.

The PMBOK process, by necessity, develops assumptions and goals, and then has to build on them. It's functionally impossible, for example, when building a large building, to go back to the assumptions after the building is half build and decide to move the whole thing six feet to the south. Why would you want to do that? Occasionally, the survey wasn't quite right, or the initial layout wasn't quite on the property line. Lawsuit! Complex projects, because the assumptions are changing all the time, are frustrating because it may be absolutely necessary to move the whole project in an unexpected way at a later stage in the project.

So, we have this complicated problem, with a four page scope definition, and fifty pages of specifications and tasks. We have searched our soul, and we are on board to start this thing. Now what? We work the plan, with an eye to proving ourselves right, which is normal. This is where it's easy, even normal, to miss anomalies. Little events that don't match the desired story, near misses and brushes with disaster can and are pushed away, covered up and ignored. It's common to use near misses as proof that the plan is working! And sometimes that is proof of the ultimate wisdom of the plan, but often not.

Again, one of the biggest problems we have is time progression. Especially with a multi-step, complicated project, where things have to occur in the right sequence, it's hard to recognize a delay back over here as leading to a major problem several months down the road. Project management software, with a tightly calculated critical path, can help with the right type of project, but there are many projects out there where actions do not fit into the tight boxes project management software needs. It's the words, usually, that the anomaly is phrased in that cause the problem. Certain words don't trigger panic, or at least recognition of something not going right. Certain weasel words can be 100% accurate (not quite the same as truthful) and trigger no responses.

Here's an example of a conceptual failure. If you live in a climate where there is a lot of snow, you know about shoveling snow. One year, you get tired of shoveling snow, and you buy a snow blower. I've done that, and discovered that for a while I used the snow blower as I would use a shovel. I followed the same patterns of moving the snow away as I would shoveling. After some experience with the snow blower, I discovered that it's quite a different animal and to use it effectively, you need to use it in different patterns than you would a shovel. That's not something I thought about before buying the snow blower, the idea that I would have to change my conceptual model for clearing the driveway. As I used the snow blower, had snow blow back into my face and other little surprises, I began to grasp the differences.

The conceptual change to using a snow blower is pretty small, and didn't have critical mission failure issues. But it is easy to have what you just jump over in the plan have some real surprises. New things are like switching to the snow blower and generally it's pretty impossible to grasp conceptual changes from the new 'thing' before you start. So you have to leave wriggle room in a plan for these types of changes. I have several software packages loaded on my computer that look interesting and powerful, but there is so much lost time in learning them and rethinking what I'm doing, that I have avoided using them. Ironically, I bought the programs for the hoped for new uses, but can't quite get to them.

It's important to gather information, but not too much information. Why? Anyone who has assembles a lot of information must then review this pile of 'stuff' to increase their understanding of a situation. Surprisingly, a decision will not be easier but harder, as the more information you have can just give you more possible choices, not an answer. Sometimes there is even positive feedback between the amount of information we have and our uncertainty. That is, our looking for information gives us a good reason for not doing something that we can tell others and ourselves.

It's an important topic later in this book that people often crave a good alibi more than successful results, because a good alibi is forever, but success demands new success tomorrow. That self-reinforcing feeling of uncertainty and insecurity you get from too much information, which then results in a continued search for more information is at the bottom of many unfinished dissertations and/or books. It is a great alibi!

How to avoid being caught between Scylla and Charybdis? We may resign ourselves to total inaction or we may give in to irrationality and base our actions on intuition. We may resort to "horizontal flight," pulling back into a small, cozy corner of reality where we feel at home. Or we may resort to "vertical flight," kicking ourselves free of recalcitrant reality altogether and constructing a more cooperative image of that reality. All of those have "FAIL" written in large letters over them.

So, how to choose and act for success? The solution isn't really complex. The solution set is like the set of rules each of us uses when we drive our cars each day. We have to, in dealing with complicated problems, keep a few simple rules in mind:

- Recognize that there is a process, probably several linked processes, and try to understand the internal dynamics of the process. Note where you are in daily life, and where you have strayed into something quite different.

- As you observe the dynamics of the process(es), make notes on those dynamics. Writing things down makes it easier to organize and remember them, so that past events can be taken into account. Using the moment as the measuring guide lets emotion sway us, and we only remember what we want - or fear - at the moment.

- Finally, beware of the easy failures: no irrational, intuitive actions - i.e., put it all on red at the roulette table; no pulling back into a small corner of the world that we feel comfortable in and pretending that is all of the complex and annoying world out there, because the world will come in and get you eventually; and certainly don't deny reality and define what you think reality should be like. Try to anticipate what will happen, knowing that you're probably wrong, but the attempt will work eventually. Complicated problems, like all of life, are the plane analogy. It's off course all of the time and it takes constant corrections to reach your goal.

CHAPTER 26. I HAVE AN UNSOLVABLE PROBLEM

and it's not just me-this can't be solved!

Whoever makes it a rule to test action by thought, thought by action, cannot falter, and if he does, will soon find his way back to the right road.[97] *Goethe.*

All problems are actually complex. For a simple problem we extract just enough for the problem, and so it's simple! The brownie mix problem? Just put the stuff together, my four-year-old granddaughter can follow the pictures on the back of the box. Of course, if you want to back into where the eggs came from, all the elaborate process for raising chickens, collecting and transporting eggs, and the retail stores we bought them in, the problem becomes hopelessly complex. And that's just part! What about the mix, which is composed of many items from all over? So, we keep them simple where we can, but we should be aware, even dimly, that it's all more complex.

I've been told that no one person knows all of the steps for the manufacture of a pencil, and I think that is true. Think about the machines that extract materials, which process and shape the lead and the wood? If no one knows how a pencil is made, then what of the really complex toys we have, such as computers and cell phones?

There are many names for complex problems, some looking at different aspects of the problems, some naming the same thing from different perspectives. A complex problem is a Black swan, of which the most famous is Thanksgiving for the turkey. For the turkey, that is an unexpected development, but the focus of the whole process for the rest of the system. A classic Twilight Zone had an alien race suddenly show up to 'serve humanity'. You might guess what their real plan was, a Russian Doll if there ever was one.

The problems are complex because they are systems within systems within systems, all of which are linked, more or less closely, to still other systems. Some of the problems we look at are called wicked problems, because they absolutely refuse to go into the box we want them to go into. Then there emerging systems, which are systems just developing about which it's almost impossible to get feedback on, because it's almost impossible to even see them as they emerge out of the fog. Isn't this fun?

AntiFragile, which I've quoted several times, will never be popular because it isn't politically correct. The human story, to society, that we are in control, and the power in society that comes from allocating resources as if we are in control, means that story will never go away. As an example, in grade B movies when the alien invaders are about to overwhelm the world, it's always a punishment from god, because the universe revolves around human needs. And the accidental error that the aliens made which allows humans to win is god's gift to the humans. What about the alien's gods? How do they read the events into a story?

Against stupidity the gods themselves contend in vain. [98]

Be that as it may, AntiFragile points out that Life, outside the human stories, throws things at the problem, it doesn't care about right, wrong, anything except survival. That doesn't meet the necessary political/social fantasies.

That book has quite a different point of view, a step away from the accepted world model we blithely use. Essentially, this book argues, along the lines of AntiFragile, that we have defined the world around ourselves. Ignoring the real world for the story we want, we have created human scale but fragile structures instead of adopting ourselves to the real world, which is composed of anti-fragile structures that refuse to comply with human dictates. Anti-fragile structures are those that gain strength from chaos and confusion. Fragile structures are those that depend on very structured, non-random processes, and break when subjected to random and chaos. Some of the following discussion are poorly disguised quotes, hopefully paraphrased enough to meet literary standards.

An important example in AntiFragile is:

"Wind extinguishes a candle and energizes fire. Likewise with randomness, uncertainty, chaos: you want to use them, not hide from them. You want to be the fire and wish for the wind." [99]

That is a huge change from our normal thought, which is to quantify risk and get rid of it! Into the trash bin, all that dangerous, chaotic changes that upsets our applecart. To digress, when was the last time you saw an applecart? Still, it's a clear example-the applecart, protecting the precious, fresh apples that if the cart is upset, are ruined when they are bruised. So no upset can come to the applecart, or we are ruined. That's a bad long-term plan, because everything is upset all the time. If you have raised teenage daughters, the concept isn't hard to grasp. Seeking peace by ending the chaos isn't going to work. It's finding peace within the chaos that is life, and that's what AntiFragile is arguing for.

In AntiFragile, Taleb is making a desperate attempt to bring us to our senses:

"Man-made complex systems tend to develop cascades and runaway chains of reactions that decrease, even eliminate, predictability and cause outsized events. So the modern world may be increasing in technological knowledge, but, paradoxically, it is making things a lot more unpredictable. Now for reasons that have to do with the increase of the artificial, the move away from ancestral and natural models, and the loss in robustness owing to complications in the design of everything, the role of Black Swans in increasing. Further, we are victims to a new disease, called in this book neomania, that makes us build Black Swan-vulnerable systems-" progress."[100]

The examples are everywhere, perhaps most clearly in Japan where the nuclear reactors were damaged by a series of events that just were not supposed to happen. And the damage this caused is only what the authorities said would happen, as the truth literally leaks out over time. For a country that has had Tokyo destroyed over and over by Godzilla, leaking radiation into the sea seems foolish, but perhaps there is a plan. Less obvious examples would be the new concept of 'controllable war', which is a contradiction in terms.

In AntiFragile it's argued that

"the central, and largely missed, point-is that the odds of rare events are simply not computable."[101]

That's really terrifying, and should put some hesitation to huge projects, such as drilling in the oceans and climate changing adjustments. Instead, we need more projects with small errors, constant mistakes that are monitored and adjusted, rather than just rolling those dice.

"The AntiFragile gains from prediction errors, in the long run. If you follow this idea to its conclusion, then many things that gain from randomness should be dominating the world today-and things that are hurt by it should be gone. Well, this turns out to be the case. We have the illusion that the world functions thanks to programmed design, university research, and bureaucratic funding, but there is compelling-very compelling-evidence to show that this is an illusion, the illusion I call lecturing birds how to fly.'"[102]

More clearly, he said:

"In short, the fragilista (medical, economic, social planning) is one who makes you engage in policies and actions, all artificial, in which the benefits are small and visible, and the side effects potentially severe and invisible. . . . A complex system, contrary to what people believe, does not require complicated systems and regulations and intricate policies. The simpler, the better. Complications lead to multiplicative chains of unanticipated effects. Because of opacity, an intervention leads to unforeseen consequences, followed by apologies about the "unforeseen" aspect of the consequences, then to another intervention to correct the secondary effects, leading to an explosive series of branching "unforeseen" responses, each one worse than the preceding one."

That is a conclusion that this book looks at in more depth, but in a different way than he does. This book argues that if people are foolish, then exploit that, amoral as that may be. AntiFragile tries to save the world by bringing it to its senses; something that I fear is hopeless. And, with all respect, he has made his fortune and can sit back. Those who are still trying to make a fortune need some tools to help.

I'd argue that the danger we ignore is the classical Hawk swooping down. We are on the ground, toiling away, blueprints unrolled in front of us and we are studying them intently, and then wham! A surprise not in the plans. The raw fact that there are unknown unknowns; that life is more complex and difficult than we would wish; and that social needs/desires do not trump the real world are the dangers we push away, push out of the system. There's an old joke:

> *It's not my job to run the train, the whistle I can't blow.*
> *It's not for me to say how far the train's allowed to go.*
> *I'm not allowed to blow off steam, nor even clang the bell.*
> *But let the damn thing jump the tracks....and see who catches hell!*
> *(anonymous)*

There are lots of people who have that job, because someone has to take the blame for what can't be controlled. Don't take that job.

CHAPTER 27. COMPLEX PROBLEMS

Everything, all the time, is causing everything else. Seems hopeless to figure out, but if we try and fail, well:

"Fate cannot be influenced by any action, for or against," Paul confessed. "Intentions cannot alter predetermined outcomes. We do what we must, and wait for the Gods to decide."[103]

Which is a comfort, especially after you finish this part.

What is thinking? Everyone says 'think', but what does that mean? Where is 'thinking' the problem itself? What do we assume? The diagram below shows how we generally 'think' about the world. We assume that there is an straight line out of the past hitting the 'now', which is the plane. There will be an output going into the future, which will behave in accordance with generally linear rules. We think in linear processes: straight lines in and out, that's morally and ethically defensible. Simple problems can be like this, and even aspects of complicated problems can be like this, which is why they can be solvable. This is how we think, and how we believe - nay, demand! - the world should be.

Figure 9.

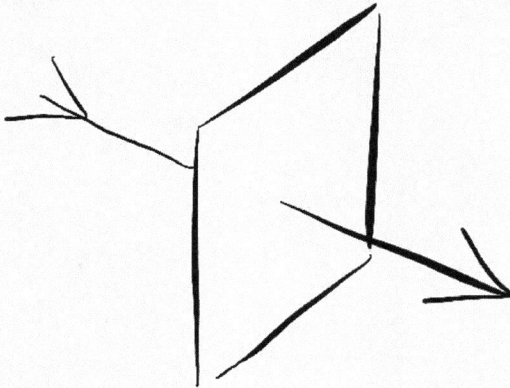

Unfortunately, the following diagram shows how the world really is:

Figure 10.

Complex problems, which are interrelated systems, are not like figure 0, a nice, neat in-and-out diagram. Figure 10 is the way life really is. Squiggly lines, quadratic equations, or worse, a set of quadratic or higher order equations, combine to enter the plane of 'now' at a single point. Then they come out, going back out in squiggly lines as they please, while we, impatiently, wait for the results we sought. The result we expect is the light grey line, confidently coming out in a straight line towards the future. The real result is some combination of the squiggly lines, which may or may not net to an approximation of the straight line-accidentally.

Conceptually, you sit each moment at the focus of multiple differential equations (which I can't solve either) calculating the position and changes in the things that affect your life, and you have to figure out what to do next to maximize results (or at least minimize consequences) in all this muddle. In the diagram, some of the lines coming into the point 'the now' are random, or noise, with no real effect on the problem we are trying to solve. Occasionally, if our luck is bad, the really dependent variable comes from somewhere else and isn't even in the items we are looking at.

Complex problems, being the interactions of multiple systems, are unsolvable in a final sense. That isn't to say that one can't come up with a solution (really more of a patch) that works for some relevant time period. Any significant problem in the real world is complex. All one can do is, at a minimum, first don't make things worse, and work to understand the dynamics of the system well enough to poke the system towards the temporary solution you need.

It's actually worse than figures 4 and 5. I worked up a diagram of a complex problem, a set of multiple intersecting planes, but decided not to use it because it was discouraging. At a certain point, we all just throw up our hands and go and get a Guinness and I didn't want to lose the reader.

A complex problem is a chunk of a bigger process sitting in your lap. For various reasons, you have to do something with this 'thing'. There are critical inputs you don't control and the output wanders off into processes that you don't control. It is dependent on people, resources and constraints that you have little or no control over, and that commonly are unclear, perhaps even unknown.

Worse, complex problems almost always have significant time factors as part of the problem. For example, there are commonly time lags between action and reaction, and feedback isn't immediate. Generally, the final results occur over longer time periods than human perception handles well.

Complex problems are almost guaranteed to have non-linear aspects, which means there are accelerated/decelerated reactions running through the problems. And those non-linear components contribute to the time problems, as squares of numbers and square roots of numbers are sudden jolts to the linear time progression we mentally picture.

A complex problem is, for example, raising a child, as opposed to a complicated problem, such as sending a rocket to Mars. After the first time you send a rocket to Mars, you can repeat the process with other rockets and hopefully perfect it. The mathematical processes are the same, and the mechanical issues relatively constant. One rocket is conceptually like another rocket, as an engineering project. What the Challenger disasters showed is that not only do you have the engineering issues, which are complicated: you have the social and economic issues, which are complex.

Raising one child isn't the same as raising another child, because every child is unique. Certainly raising one child provides experience ('is' an experience) but beyond the basics of changing diapers and preparing bottles, the experience of the first child may not be experience that is all that relevant for the second child. Having obtained certain results from raising one child is absolutely no guarantee of the similar results with the next child. And the child after that will be different from the first two.

From the child's point of view, raising a parent is also a complex project, but remember it's a full time job for them, whereas being a parent is a part time job for adults. The child is going to win.

For a complex problem, some expertise is valuable but most certainly not sufficient. In the child example, your hard won expertise gained from the first child can be a positive handicap, as the next child may (almost always, actually) require an entirely different approach.

A key feature of complex problems is that their outcomes remain highly uncertain. Perhaps unknowable, because a complex problem is a system in process, and as it continues, interacting with other systems, success and failure will trade places. Success is various things to various people. You may be proud of your child's school performance, to find out years later that the child hated the school and their classmates. Bill Gates parents were upset that, as a child, he would sneak off to use a university computer in the wee hours of the morning, yet that turned our reasonably well for all concerned. (Depending, of course on how 'evil' you think that DOS/Windows really is- see, it's complex!) We know that it is possible to raise a child, in the sense that the child starts small and you raise it until it's bigger. What the child does when grown is probably not going to be what you intended, but that's part of the joy. You were a surprise to your parents, as your children are a surprise to you.

HOW TO START?

So, with complex problems, there is no cookbook formula for certain results. For any problem, we have the following choices in assessing and starting on a problem (listed before, and will be listed again, but in different contexts and analysis):

- Detailed analyses;
- Size up a situation.
- A comprehensive but rough outline of a situation;
- Close attention to details.
- Define our goals very clearly and analyze carefully, before we act, exactly what it is we want to achieve;
- Simply to go to work and muddle through. "One jumps into the fray, then figures out what to do next"
- Think more "holistically," more in pictures, drawing in the right side of the brain, the unconscious, when we need to know what the unconscious is thinking;
- Think analytically, using primarily the left side of the brain, when we know what we want and are trying to implement steps;
- Sit back and see what develops; if a decision isn't required/possible, then don't make a decision;
- Move very quickly if the situation demands, an OODA situation.

Particularity with complex problems, be ready to embrace the unexpected and you'll have a better chance of coping with surprises than if we have fantasy plans that have eliminated the unexpected. You can never eliminate surprises, and you should never think you have. Now, the unexpected is not always good. There was a sketch in 'Kentucky Fried Movie" where a newsman is on camera, and he is asked what he will think happen. He said (roughly – I can't find an accurate script) "I'm a Gemini, and I expect the unexpected" and promptly got an arrow in the chest.

We have this complex problem rolling around in our heads. Thinking about how to even approach the problem can be before goal definition, or at least at the same time. Getting a handle on the problem shapes what our goals are going to be, because in the process of pushing the problem around, we make assumptions that define into our goals.

So, we have some approaches to the problem. Our next step is to (tentatively, at least) further define our goals as clearly as we can. With a child, for example, we want, as a minimum that they grow up healthy. Simply keeping a small child alive is a constant battle, as they are fascinated with things that are more dangerous than they appreciate, as are all of us at any age. Once we have a goal, we picture (visualize) how to reach the goal, at least tentatively. Unless this is a jump in and act problem, it's a good idea to watch the relevant system for a while to gather information on what it's doing, and what inputs are producing what effects. Poke it gently and note the results. When we have some guesses about the system dynamics, what the system is doing now and what it does when we poke the system, then we can move to tentative planning.

We have some ideas, and now we can set real goals. We of course had some vague goals, because why else would we be poking at this in the first place? But a vague feeling isn't a real goal. Complex problems are going to have multiple goals, because there are multiple systems. If our goals are not as clear as we can make them, then how can we evaluate the interactions between the different systems?

Non-clear goals and no understanding of the interactions are not going to result in success. General (we want something 'good' to happen) goals or unclear goals (something more or less good to happen) do not give us enough to work with. There are so many possible approaches that we sit, dazed. Where we are dazed, we do what we did before, regardless of the relevance to this problem. This is where ritualizing solutions becomes obvious.

If things are going badly, we may warp the goal to solving a project by picking easy and/or obvious goals as markers. We shift, that is, to a goal of winning from the goal of solving the initial problem. As we shift to 'winning' from 'solving', we must paper over implicit or explicit contradictions in our goals.

If you define the win and create a false world to work with, you should, if you are competent, be able force some initial good results. The results won't last, which is why people rotate out of job assignments, praying that the crash doesn't come until after they leave. That sounds ethically improper, but maybe isn't when a person is handed a mandatory impossible task and a short time to act. It is ethically improper where you were handed a working system and you ran it off a cliff.

Remember, in the long run the house will always win. The real world will do as it will. What then to do, now that we first, out of desperation, moved away from the original goal of solving the problem, and fell back to creating a certain win for another problem, which now isn't happening either?

DESPERATE DEFENCES

There are several techniques to use where failure strikes but you seek to stay employed. Not to be too cynical, but one should always carry a few of these tools in your back pocket. Life is, after all, uncertain, and the slot machine is going to come up losers more than winners. The mistake people make is holding these as trump cards to win with, rather than just to survive. Using these to win really warps your project goals and planning, because you are focused not on the project, but on producing a win regardless of any outcome. Where you win, you bask in your triumph, glossing over the difficulties and then try and use the same strategy. That isn't going to work.

First, Goal Inversion turns unintended bad results into good ones. I.e., you smile and say, this is what I intended all along! This is commonly known as moving the goal posts. With the goal posts on wheels, any kick in their direction is going to score points. It's easy to decry this, but in very complex projects, you may not know the solution until considerably into the project. As the dynamics become clear, systems are seen to be something quite different from what you thought when you started. Moving the goal posts is accepting reality at that point. The problem, practically, is to present a goal at the initial meeting that effortlessly morphs into the ending of the project and still meets the original goal criteria. This is more akin to producing a work of art than what one thinks of as project planning.

Then there is Conceptual Integration. This is using magic words and definitions to blur over and even erase what would seem like problems. This quickly becomes Orwellian: War is Peace, Freedom is Slavery; and Ignorance is Strength. Some quick shuffles of meaning and you have made the incompatible compatible; reconciled the irreconcilable; and convincingly papered over where the real world is trying to poke through to damage your work of art. What is absolutely essential with this tool is to not fool yourself. There is a train wreak till coming under the pretty words, and you have to be taking steps to deal with that while the others are still dazzled by your

239

footwork. While "you can fool all of the people some of the time, and some of the people all of the time, you can't fool all the people all of the time". Disaster will come eventually.

If you are truly desperate, you can articulate a Conspiracy. A conspiracy theory places the blame for our mistakes on others. This approaches madness, as one has to believe (and persuade others) that you are important enough for 'them' to spend all that time and effort against you. The real part of the madness is you have to believe they are competent enough to accomplish this nefarious plan, when you actually know 'they' can't tie their shoelaces.

While these are tools to carry against disaster, they cannot be the starting point of our planning. It's important to recognize these behaviors in ourselves, so that we can clarity our goals. Life is the airplane with constant course corrections. A failure in goal setting shows us what we are trying to disguise and can be what we need to reach our real goal. So denying the failure and shifting to defense loses the positive learning experience we might have salvaged from this mess.

GOALS

Back to goals. A goal is something that our activities are supposed to produce, on the positive side, or that something we want to prevent or avoid on the negative side. Clear goals for complex problems are especially difficult, because until you understand the system, you can't understand what a successful goal would be. You can't understand the system until you are in it, so the problem is obvious.

> There was only one catch and that was Catch-22, which specified that a concern for one's safety in the face of dangers that were real and immediate was the process of a rational mind. Orr was crazy and could be grounded. All he had to do was ask; and as soon as he did, he would no longer be crazy and would have to fly more missions. Orr would be crazy to fly more missions and sane if he didn't, but if he were sane he had to fly them. If he flew them he was crazy and didn't have to; but if he didn't want to he was sane and had to. Yossarian was moved very deeply by the absolute simplicity of this clause of Catch-22 and let out a respectful whistle. [104](Catch 22, p. 56, ch. 5)

The person who drafted Catch 22 had the clear goal of not making it possible for a pilot avoid combat, without putting it quite as insensitively as that. While Catch 22 accomplishes that limited goal, what effect does it have on the key goal, which is to have competent people act as required? I.e., they were bomber pilots who were supposed to be bombing something as ordered. Putting crazy people at the controls of the plane just to keep the planes flying is probably not congruent with the quite different goal of putting bombs on target. It is certainly congruent with the paperwork that headquarters had to fill out.

"Let's look at the goal," Hal continued, smiling. "A device is easy to use when the possible actions are visible, and it's obvious what works where. That's a design rule for physical things, like doors, but the same idea applies to planning for the future. Even with that clear rule, how often are the doors in an office building impossible to figure out how they open until you push on them? You need a visual clue as to whether to push or pull, and which side to grab onto. Plans are the same, except more complex. If we have a plan, and we have an idea how the plan affects things, then we can pick a plan that matches a given situation. That worked pretty well hoeing the fields, because after the one-hundredth time, you had the parameters down pretty well. We don't get those kinds of clear plans anymore with all the changes in the world. Our minds are not hardwired to immediately grasp and act on many things we face today. Oh, we're pretty good at throwing rocks at small animals and reading facial expressions, but genetics, evolution, neuroscience, embryology, economics, and mathematics? "[105]

Let's look more carefully at the idea of trying to defining goals for a complex problem before we jump into planning, because it is not usually immediately obvious what it is we really want to achieve. Oh, we have some idea for an ultimate result, at least an itch if not a vision, but we have to think more as to whether that is even possible. We need at least an inkling of what we want before we start forming judgments and arriving at decisions. Clear goals will give us some guidelines and criteria for assessing the appropriateness or inappropriateness of measures we might propose.

"Alice stood at the fork in the road, and asked the Cheshire Cat which way she should go.
The Cat said, where do you want to go to?
Alice said that it didn't matter to her, and so the Cat said she could pick either road, as it didn't matter."[106]
(Lewis Carroll, Alice in Wonderland)

That's what happens when the goals are not clear. You may see some interesting things, but you can't expect to end up where you want if you don't know where you want to go.

So, we have a little more than an itch, we are now closer to a vision. A vision is essential, actually. A clear word statement forces our ideas into concrete. Once set in concrete, we don't look at them again; we chug away at the plan. With a vision, we can revisit at the vision and think about whether our actions are bringing to-or away from-that vision. Once the vision is relatively solid, we develop a model, more or less tentative, of what the system is like and how we can use the system to reach our goal. We gather information, both to develop the model of the system and to check the model. As covered in more depth earlier in the book than you would have wanted, humans grasp information solely through stories, so a raw stinking pile of information isn't worth much. We need to arrange the information into a story, being careful to not let the story arrange the information, creating a model that explains the system.

We move on to making a prognosis. A prognosis is a prediction of the likely outcome of this situation. This is how things look now; what can we expect to happen next? So, we poke the world a bit. What information comes back from the pokes? Is it what we'd expect from the model, or something vastly different? If we poke and don't get the results we expected, the model probably isn't working. Go back to an earlier step. When we get the results we expected, we start to extrapolate from those results. Our question, as we extrapolate from results, is what will most likely happen as we move down that chain of events that is the plan?

Once we have our model, supported by testing, then we want to start more specifically planning how to reach our goals. What should we do?

First, and this is usually jumped over, should we do anything at all? In medicine, there is a placebo effect. A doctor can give you a pill that is sugar, but if you believe it's powerful medicine, you quite often get better. Because patients want 'action', Doctor's do things. Doctors used to bleed patients, an action correctly classified as somewhere between useless and deadly, but they were doing 'something'.

If we should do something, then we usually start with the easy choice: we do what we have done before. Repair behavior, put a band aid on the problem. If you don't have a clue, then do something that worked, preferably something that has some social approval tied to it. Acting in a ritualized way has many advantages. We don't have to think, we just have to act. Of course, where we use the same ritual on different kinds of problems, we are really demanding problem solutions from random actions. We are hoping for Luck, in the end, whistling past the graveyard. Ritual is most effective for problems that will work themselves out if just left alone. At least the ritual keeps everyone busy while the real process is solving itself.

Or, our trying the last successful plan having failed, we then, recognizing that this is a zebra, not a horse, try and develop a specific plan for this problem. So we plan, either still doing the easy way, doing what we did before even though we suspect it isn't going to work or the hard way, trying to adopt a plan to these circumstances. After the plan is developed, then decisions about what to actually do follow planning.

Ideally, first we made decisions, and then we act. That's not always possible, as we saw in the methods of approaching problems. Some problems are just coming at you and you have to act. Still, thought is better if possible. If we are just acting, we run the OODA loop again-and again. We must not deny information that says the plan isn't working, as that's probably the most important information we can get. By using the OODA loop, we start thinking when we get information. It forces us to face what is being fed back to us.

As we run the OODA loop, we have to be very careful about time lags. There are always lags in the system, and those are just hard for us to grasp. Drawing visuals of the lags is very helpful, because we have to be reminded that this invisible temporal thing is actually happening. This is important for linear changes, which we at least can grasp. It's absolute critical for non-linear events, which is not the way we think. Events have not only immediate, visible effects but long-term repercussions as well. A maneuver warfare example would be where we run the OODA cycle several times, and are now confident that we can flank the enemy squad we are attacking. We didn't consider the time delay for enemy reinforcements, which we saw no evidence of, but which are coming up just as we pounce.

Systems are covered later in this book, but it is important to note here that in complex systems we cannot do only one thing, even if that is all that we want to do. While reducing and simplifying reality is what we have to do to be able to act in the world, we can't fit reality into a predetermined formal pattern. Bluntly, we don't magically control the real world by describing it in our words: we use words to describe the real world. There is a vast difference discussed in length earlier in this book.

Let's go back to goal setting for a minute, now that we have more data. The most useful step, to the extent possible, is to put goals into concrete terms. Concrete terms means: what, in real world pictures, do we expect to happen? Not la-la land happy talk, what exactly is supposed to result from input A? What are the specific next actions that are required to get from here to there? When we see 'done', what is the picture?

It's not our nature, really, to formally plan. As children, we are taught what to do, rarely why to do. Muddling through, in daily life, works pretty well. So we slide over the planning step for the non-everyday events that really do require new assessment and a plan. For everyday problems, we can use the motto "first things first" and work on the problems in front of us. It's easy, when confronted with a task, to just act, rather than facing the laborious task of formulating our goals in concrete terms, balancing contradictory partial ones, and prioritizing them. We've got a problem, so let's get to it and not waste a lot of time developing clarity about it. Again, it's always that implicit assumption that it's the problem we had yesterday and the week before that, so we'll just solve it. Where it isn't that problem, we're in trouble.

Let's say we back up and define the problem a bit. Now, where there are multiple interrelationships among variables, that's hard to think through. It's even hard to graph, if you have more than three variables. Once you have drawn a three dimensional graph, you have used all the dimensions you have available, so how does one show the other six variables feeding into things at different times, places and ways?

It's not a trivial problem, worsened because the mind tends to select one variable as central. The advantage of a central variable is that we are economizing our efforts (so we don't have to do more analytical work) and secondly, we save time gathering information and in planning. One variable, we gather information and plan on that one, job done. There is also an important social aspect to setting a single variable and moving on: if we have to convince a group, people can grasp a single cause and effect fairly quickly. Trying to persuade people to grasp ten causes with six effects, of which you believe cause five and effect three are the most likely, is going to be a difficult meeting. If nothing else, your budget for the plan is going to be reduced, because who would risk money on such a confusing situation?

It is absolutely necessary to deal with a complex system of variables by setting up rules, both because we have to distill all that 'reality' into something we can manipulate and secondly, because we can't communicate uncertainty and confusion to other people and expect results. We are thus economizing by eliminating the need to clarify why a certain action was successful; it is just because this causes that. Case closed.

In getting down and dirty, we streamline our planning by applying as few general rules as we can rather than many local rules. The problem with local rules is that we have to painfully determine, case by case, whether the conditions necessary for their successful application exist. Often, using local rules and carefully contemplating problems case by case is impossible because of all the other events coming at us, and we run out of time-and patience and budget. Because of social issues, we have to present certainty and confidence, but conflicting local rules which result in multiple cases of your changing your mind (flopping like a dying fish is the visual) does not produce confidence in the masses.

Planning without taking side effects and long-term repercussions into account is also far more economical than analyzing those possibilities in advance. And, again, it is far easier to convey to others. They will be plans that fail, but we have discussed methods of dealing with that.

As we looked at earlier in the book, "Methodism", the tool that forces new situations into old, established patterns of action that need only be set rolling, is far more economical than laboring over the local rules and conditions for each individual. In all fairness, Methodism generally works quite well for the everyday, normal cases. It's the non-everyday decisions where it fails dramatically.

Truthfully, reaching 'the' ultimate goal for an extremely complex problem is impossible. You may get lucky, but the world will do what it will. Still, this stinking mess is sitting before you and impossible or not, you have act.

There are some very effective techniques to slice the problem down to size. As Ludwig Wittgensein said "An inner process stands in need of outward criteria", so look around and define what can be done or not done. If you have 3000 man hours of work required to complete a project, and you have 6 people for 4 weeks, each with 40 hours a week available, then your problem cannot be solved. You have 960 possible man hours, and 3000 hours of work to do. Given that you have to do something with what you've got, what can you do? Don't be setup for failure before you even start because of lack of resources/ constraints!

With limited resources, which are always the situation, it's key to ask: What's the most important? What, frankly, is critical but not urgent, because that's the box that always matters? If the people around you refuse to recognize reality, make sure you are off the committee. Even the dissenters are tarred by the final disaster.

Planning. Do you hate the word yet? The initial thesis of this book is that it is almost impossible to plan, and that's why most planning books are so boring, because they restrict themselves to the small problems that can be solved. When we plan, we are trying to change something into something else. Where you have several things, several possibilities for change, and several possible results, simple probability shows that you rapidly have practically an infinity of events that can occur. (10 possibilities X 5 possible methods = 50 possibilities. As we can hold 7 +/- thoughts in mind at a given time, 50 is effectively an infinity) Given that complete examination of a problem area is impossible, how do we focus on and/or find the real problem, not the distantly glimpsed problem through the fog or the easy group perception of the problem? I'm not sure that a committee uses the average intelligence of the group or whether there is an additional dumbing down to the lowest participant, then adjusted for exhaustion and ennui.

HEURISTIC DEVICES FOR PROBLEM SOLVING

Hill Climbing is a simple visual. Hill climbing is the process of trying to choose actions that look like a step toward the goal. We determine a set of next actions that move us towards where we want to be. Stepping carefully, watching for slippery spots and tree roots, we trudge along. And the problem with hill climbing is an effective visual also: as we come closer to the top of the hill, we may find ourselves on a close or secondary peak rather than on the main one. We may have gone where we could go, rather than where we wanted to go, or our vision wasn't quite right. Whether we are close enough to our goal by being on top of the this nearby hill is going to have to be thought about. What is clear is our level of frustration, standing on the wrong hill and so it's going to be hard to make a rational assessment.

Reverse Planning can be effective in limited cases. Reverse planning is what we often taught 'is' planning, actually. If our goal is clear, we can develop intermediate goals by using reverse planning. Even if our goal is not as clear as we would wish, we can choose as intermediate goals situations that offer a variety of possibilities for future action even though we cannot see any direct path leading from them to our goal. These "favorable" situations are ones that offer high "efficiency diversity" situations from which one can move efficiently in many different directions. That is really a good idea in any planning situation. Regardless of how sure you are about the plan and the goal, being able to extradite yourself from the mud is helpful. A recent "Non Sequitur" suggested that the secret to life is having a backup plan to your exit strategy. If it's critical in your life, you always want options.

Planning is using the same tools over and over in different contexts. What if we have no idea what to do? If we have to do something that we are clueless about, about all we can do is what was done in the past. Picking plans that worked well before at least narrows our focus. Because this is really random trial and error, we shouldn't fool ourselves about what we are doing. Random trial and error is free experimentation, a fancy term for simply doing something, and seeing what happens. It is poking the world and quickly standing back.

Trial and error is a means of introducing variability into our planning process, so that we do not accidently limit ourselves to past events. Trial and error is primitive and time wasteful, but the biggest problem we have that we don't even realize is that we often do not realize we are captives of our old ideas. That means that our pokes are limited to events based on past experiences, and so we have filtered without realizing it. We do 'something', and note the result, which is 'something+', but not interpret the result correctly because we force the results into a preselected choice between solutions C, D and E.

As a trivial example, how often do you learn something useful about the computer just by pushing keys? After the momentary panic, you learn stuff that you would never pull out of a book.

A combination of forward and reverse planning is going to be the usual approach to a problem. We have a goal, some goal, so we work backwards as best we can. When we are unclear, we start working our way forward from where we are now as best we can. How clearly we see that vision of the goal opens and closes our choices. With clear goals, forward and reverse planning is effective. If we reverse plan with unclear goals, then the intermediate steps we choose had best have many, many possible actions that we can choose depending on the results of our testing actions.

Finally, there is our old friend "Methodism".

What Works Best and When?

What works best and when? So that we don't become flustered at the very outset of planning, and throw up our arms rather than push further, which ones should we choose, and when? Specifically:

When is hill climbing appropriate? When we are completely uncertain about the best path to our goal, we can try hill climbing, because it's at least something. This is a type of focused trial and error, and we have to watch the results of our actions. If we are not getting closer to the top of the right hill, we have to be ready to modify our plan.

When is the efficiency-diversity method best? If our goals are not clear then the efficiency–diversity method is the best choice. I'd argue that efficiency-diversity is always appropriate in all circumstances, because you preserve options. But if our goals are not clear and we have to do something, maintaining the maximum possible future options can't be argued with. As we act, we discard failures. We act, we fail, we analyze our failures, and then we try something that doesn't have the key features of our failures. This is effective when we are prisoners of our habitual patterns of thought. Efficiency-diversity can make us think about the edges and maybe see that a puzzle piece can fit in several places, not just one.

When should we study past success? If nothing else, past success will give us a warm feeling of confidence to charge into the fray with. Whether the problem is like or unlike the past success, contrasting the two will be helpful because you see the problem differently by juxtaposing the two.

Analogy is probably the most important method for expanding a problem sector. If we have narrowed a problem to a small area, but the solution isn't emerging, then perhaps we are in the wrong area, and need to widen our focus. Perhaps we are trying to solve a problem that doesn't need to be solved, for example. Perhaps we defined the problem in a small box and it really fits in another box-or boxes.

Essentially, planning is an iterative process of narrowing the problem area to something manageable, searching that sector for solutions, expanding the problem if that doesn't work, and doing it again and again. That is why you have to be emotionally involved with the problem, by the way. Unless the problem is something you really care about, you won't spend the time and thought necessary to solve it.

Perhaps a simple way to decide if something is a complex problem is it to say that there's no f**ing way that we can solve this thing. There, you emotionally feel better, and have stepped back a bit, recognizing some of the impossibility. Now, what part of this mess can be worked with?

The Greek Gods took control in a rebellion against the old gods, which was a more successful rebellion than the rebellion on the Christian side. The Gods recognized that the control they had seized would not hold forever. While they had created order out of chaos, they were aware that Chaos was out there, and it would come back. That's a true picture of the world, especially with complex problems.

"Have you heard the expression 'the fog of war'? Hal peered thoughtfully at the dark sky. "The minute you step out of this car, every part of our plan goes to hell. The problem with forecasting the future is that, mathematically, on the 'past' side of the equation, you have hundreds of complex equations, representing resources, constraints, and other forces, snaking wildly along the graph, randomly interacting with each other. At the moment we call 'now,' they intersect into a single point, and we cheerfully extrapolate a linear progression into the future, which means that we assume that point 'now' is going to continue exactly as we want it to and as we need it to. In reality, all those complex equations that intersected into point 'now' are unraveling into multiple curves and lines running in all directions into the future."

"In laywoman's terms," Cali demanded. "Small words and short sentences."

"We made reasonable estimates, and we have backup plans. That's as good as it gets. Should work. If any part of it works, the people who killed our families will wish they had been killed at the same time. Sometimes, it's much worse to leave them alive to face their punishment. Victory is his who makes the next-to-last mistake, and we are going to hope that is us." Hal squinted towards downtown."[107]

NATURES METHOD.

If complex problems are so unsolvable, then how does life solve them? There is no more complex problem than those Life faces as it adopts and spreads. Most of the creatures considered 'alive' are single celled, with no brain. And molecular assemblies not really considered alive, such as viruses, adopt and spread astonishingly well. So it isn't intellectual ability that is driving this. Consciousness loses again.

Essentially, the approach isn't elegant, but it's effective. Life throws as many possibilities as it can at the wall, and the ones that survive stick. The failures become food for the survivors, and away we go. Those that find a prosperous place survive and grow, those that don't die. Various organisms have strengths that other's do not. Occasionally, those strengths become the most useful, and those lucky organisms live when the others die. Those strengths become the standard until the next change.

Nature's proven method for anticipating the future, is, formally, that multiple options be available at all times. Those options are either in operation or ready to be put into operation. Nature hedges its bets with a wide diversity of possibilities so something will some thrive in a new environment. As there is then exponential growth in the winners, the system chugs along. Nature doesn't pick or handicap the winners; the feedback from the system picks the winners. Simple, yet the most effective method of anticipating an unknowable future imagined or imaginable.

In this method of analysis, (setting aside religious explanations) there is no conscious analysis in the traditional human problem solving approach of 'here is the problem, here are the possible solutions'. How can there be? There is only a mass of organic creatures striving to survive. Life continues, and thrives, by having a wide range of actors, able to adjust to certain aspects of change, most of which not relevant or marginally relevant at a given time. Science is continually discovering life in places that Life was not supposed to be possible in, which shows the incredible power of life.

Life freely experiments and maximizes gains. The efficiency-diversity approach writ very large, you might say. Various organisms have slight differences, which most of the time are irrelevant, but when change occurs, operate to maximize growth as the organism exploits the new opportunities. While, from different perspectives, the best future may be many things, each entity focuses itself completely on the future before it. The simplicity of the concept should not hide its power and utility.

All life requires several things. For continued life, specific materials are critical, which on earth are oxygen (generally), nutrients, and certain real world conditions (warmth, cold, etc.). Generally, all life needs relatively stable conditions to continue life but unstable conditions to expand. The most interesting thing about life is that it has expanded in a hostile world from a single celled organism into an unbelievable variety of creatures, of astonishing complexity. The external environment has changed, many times in catastrophic ways, over the last several billion years. Yet life has continued and increased. Individual creatures are remarkably weak in many ways, susceptible to easy destruction from inhospitable environments. Yet life has expanded to places undreamed of, and probably to many places we have not found yet.

In contrast to nature's method, the human approach is to define a future, generally based on the present, projecting our needs and personal desires into that future. This can work with simple plans and sometimes with complicated plans. Complex problems cannot be solved by the focused, specific plan. In complex systems, the multiple contingencies required for a long-term plan to succeed simply don't happen.

An example of complex plans is the following. Every so often, people do create something new. For example, the transistor, which became an integrated circuit, which became the chip that drives this computer. What it may become in the future is something we can't imagine, or plan for. But what we can do is imitate life, and to plan for the short term, using what is here now, with a view to adaption of the future changes, as they are perceived. If people challenge your efficiency-diversity approach as insufficiently rigid, point out how life plans and how successful that has been.

As life expands, it necessarily pushes new life from the rich environments to the barren fringes, where it adopts or dies. Under stable conditions, which of course do not exist, there will be a certain ratio of predators to prey, tall plants to short plants, etc. And there will be natural cycles. For example, piranhas: they eat everything, and will reproduce until all the prey is gone, at which point there is crash in the number of piranhas, giving their prey a chance to build up their numbers for the cycle to start anew.

The natural method is why a profusion of ideas is necessary, because they all have to be tested against events. You can't choose the correct without the tests, and picking the winners before the test is gaming a system you don't control. Throwing the ideas like dust into the air shows you at least which way the wind is blowing, whereas you can talk yourself into believing the wind is out of the south if you don't check things. That is why the 'creative destruction' idea is so important, which argues that failure is essential as the only really effective weeding method.

You need loose structures, which allow for messy evolutions and revisions, and experimentation. Sounds simple, but the devil is in the details. A loose structure is going to be annoying to many, perhaps all. But having lots of options out there is the essential reason for the successes that democracies have had. Any system that is designed for change and to reflect the new patterns of change, i.e., following the future anticipation pattern of life will have more success than systems that are designed for narrow human controlled change. How does life succeed in adopting to change? It's action, reaction, and feedback.

The polar extreme, which has failed pretty convincingly in as an economic system (although has many real advantages to the people running a political system, who can give their friends jobs) is the Soviet Central Planning structure. Taleb would add Harvard as a failed model.

Wisdom is the ability to apply knowledge or experience or understanding or common sense and insight to try and anticipate the future. So if one then takes that prediction of the exact future isn't possible, that most of the choices will be wrong, but a few choices will have great success, the clear path is to structure planning along those lines. One thing that makes the approach hard for humans is the lack of drama in the process, the lack of a 'story'. We want winners and losers, black backgrounds and blue skies, and simple survival doesn't seem to be that kind of a story. It is, however, the story that is.

Here's an example of trying to create a system that grows:

SETTING THE FOXES LOOSE

Hal sat in his office afterwards, staring out the window. Trees and forests, foreground and background alternating. But what about when it's the background definition that's the problem? When the definition frames the problem in a way that really isn't the problem? Memo to the file. Watch more Looney Tunes reruns. Nonsense is good for the mind.

"We are building a fighting force of extraordinary magnitude.

We forge our tradition in the spirit of our ancestors. You have our gratitude," Aliston remarked.

Hal stared at her for a second and then laughed, happy and relaxed. "I'd never have suspected your misspent youth," when he could talk again.

"That went well," Aliston reported. "I watched. Oh, from behind the mirror. If I walk in, every male in the room will be running on testosterone all meeting. And the females will be running on envy and anger, so I hide. But it went well. I've seen Francisco trying to make the same points, over and over, and you've come further than he did."

"Thanks," Hal replied, surprised. "I wasn't feeling all that good about the meeting."

"Of course," Aliston pointed out, "the cartel has a different background. The illegal side—they pretty much weed out their mistakes because the pressures of the business make the errors so clear and the consequences so severe. It's a lot harder with a legal business and a bunch of high-priced egos sitting there. Men who come to the top over the bodies of the fallen are a lot less complacent about their abilities and plans."

"There's a thought. But internships in the peripheral parts of the business probably would be hard to arrange and a security nightmare. That's the terrifying part about the drug cartels and the international drug business that the governments and the news ignore. Those businesses evolve rapidly. Problems? They adjust, move around. They're quick, boots on the ground, rewards and punishments clear and rapidly applied. Governments trying to catch them? They're slow, inefficient, obsessed with infighting and status. It's the difference between evolution and Intelligent Design, and it's pretty clear who's winning."

"Every year, the Columbians provide cocaine at a higher quality and a lower price than the year before," Aliston observed. "I keep thinking that they should hire them to run the medical system, which every year comes at a higher price and lower quality than the year before."

"I'm not sure I want the Columbians doing my colonoscopy," Hal objected. "They might leave things in there and view it as a new distribution system. Still, they are brutally efficient." He gazed out the window for a moment, and, turning to Aliston, smiled: an odd, cheerful smile.

"This is not good, kemosabe," Aliston warned. "That look is trouble."

"I have a new idea, that will be less popular than any of my ideas to date."

"That would be quite an achievement," Aliston admitted. "What, electric buzzers in the executive chairs?"

"That's a better idea than mine," Hal mused. "I'll make a note.

No, I'm thinking that we need to get—what's that buzzword—'creative destruction' churning away inside the company. New little companies that we own tearing the old ones apart. We need to stop waiting for the brash new competitors in sleazy offices to eat our business as we sit in gilded towers, confident in our power."

"So, I'll bite," Aliston sighed. "What specifically are you suggesting?"

"Look at Microsoft. They resisted the split-up of the company, and what happened? Free from competition, the operating system became bloated, a mass of patches and major security holes popped up on such a regular basis that it wasn't even news anymore. Then the application programs, fat and happy knowing that they were tied to the really secret inside wiring of the operating system, lost track of the needs of the users and instead the programs were designed to enhance the power of the division heads. You ended up with the equivalent of fins on a Cadillac—useless padding. The stock price dumped. Had they split up the companies and let them tear into each other, they'd have a group of companies making top-notch stuff. Like the Soviet Union, they got so caught inside their own world that they forgot the bigger world they were supposed to be serving."

"So you want to split up the bigger companies and set up little tigers to tear each other apart?" Aliston asked. "You are going to be popular."

"I'd rather be hated for who I am than loved for who I'm not," Hal declared cheerfully.

"We'll have to double security," Aliston grimaced.

"Again?"

"Again," Aliston acknowledged, worried. "Things, well, they seem weird. Little, odd things are happening. So we took your advice and are trying to adjust to them."

"And you have my fervent thanks!" Hal stood up and started pacing. "The formal stories-prime example, a company mission statement-are useless because those are pretty stories, not the real stories people believe. The stories people really believe and act on have emotion and desire in them, not the selflessness of the publicly allowed stories. If you put a pretty, but empty, story on the wall, you're not going to reach anyone. Meetings are the same—full of words we 'should' be saying, not real words we'll act on. The problem is that having a 'word' as a name for something doesn't mean that the 'thing' the word represents exists at all, or exists in the way you think it does. Create a workgroup, and they produce grammatically correct sentences that are wishful social fantasies, warm feelings and bright pictures. Nothing that refers to the outside world in a useful way."

"You talk like this at dinner?" Aliston questioned. "And your wife puts up with it? You chose well."

"Cali talks like this at dinner," Hal replied. "She is a planning freak. She says so herself."

Hal sat on the corner of the desk, staring out the window, scowling. "We hire this hotshot to come in, and what does he say? The consultant stands up, and with a serious expression, says that the key ability for the tribal chief of the future is foresight—to be able to forecast what is going to grow and what will be fashionable next. Once Swami sees all, knows all, then this person must have the decision-making ability to execute the forecast. Miracles abound with this person, loaves and fishes filling the break room, as this person then motivates the whole organization with their swift execution of their decisions. And, although this person is the font of all knowledge, the father/mother that all come to for guidance, this person must also maintain an environment that can generate useful information and ideas, even though the only one with ideas is the leader. Plato's philosopher king holding court in the corner office! Drucker wrote that trying to predict the future is like driving down a country road at night with no lights while looking out the back window. That's why philosopher kings don't come through in the clutch, because that critical ability to see the future doesn't exist. What's the option? Set up a bunch of foxes and let them tear the prey apart as best they can. Winner moves to the tiger trials."

Hal glanced at Aliston. "I had a dream the other night that I was in jail. It was okay, it wasn't a bad place, and then I realized that I shouldn't be in jail. There was no reason I should be there. I just hadn't taken the steps to not be there. Then I recognized that I'd put myself in my own jail and I could let myself out. It's getting people to see that and let themselves out, and justify the salaries we pay them—that is the hard part."

"So, how are you going to sell this to the Board?" Aliston asked. "You're taking profitable entities and tearing them up with no guarantees about what they will be able to do. That's a hard sell."

"You're dead right about that. Every meeting with the directors is always the same. 'How much is this going to cost?' 'I don't know' isn't the winning answer. If you assume tomorrow is today, then any change costs too much. It's spending $10,000 to make $50,000 that gets people's attention. Spending $10,000 by itself, well, that's money out the door."

"One of the best studies was that corporate boards spend a lot LESS time considering proposals over $10,000,000 than on proposals under $10,000,000," Aliston commented. "Now, that was an old study, so it's probably $100,000,000 and up now. But it's because people just can't grasp zeroes to the left of the decimal point. No one really has an emotional feel for numbers that large, so there is no emotional attachment to the big dollars as they run out the door. One of the mutual-fund managers was quoted as saying that people really don't emotionally connect with anything over $139.00. Larger than that, it's all zeroes, no emotions. If you want to get killed, steal $20 from someone, because that means something to them. Steal $10,000? It's annoying, embarrassing, but not as emotionally charged as that twenty in your pocket is."

"I don't have a clue what the future profit numbers would be," Hal complained, "but I can promise that the profits will go to zero if we don't change our processes. Look at the changes coming. The newspapers are talking about networks of up to one trillion sensors that will cover the world and can deliver data to anybody who needs them, from carmakers to municipal governments. Note, that those are the networks that the government will allow access to. Figure in another trillion sensors run by the various militaries. A company planning to function based on a controlled information flow from the bottom, carefully filtered up through the hierarchy, isn't even in the right geologic era."

"You took this job because...?" Aliston wondered, looking at him appraisingly.

"I was foolish enough to be spouting off to Sir Jonathan about these ideas, pointing out various stupid things the companies had done. So he told me, 'Then you do it,' and here I am. I'd be happier playing with the computers."

"No good deed goes unpunished," Aliston advised.

"And it will be punished," Hal promised. "Look at this," handing her an elaborate diagram. This is my idea for splitting up the various companies and divisions and getting life back into them."

"Has anyone seen this?" Aliston gasped, biting her lip as she went down the list. "Ah, 'There is nothing more difficult to take in hand, more perilous to conduct, more uncertain in its success, than to take the lead in the introduction of a new order of things.' Let's make that triple security."

"That popular, you think? Nice to know I'm still overachieving. Cali has seen this, and some of the info tech people must suspect, because I've thrown out odd questions about sharing information between companies, except those companies don't exist yet. The info people are pretty good with this because they are used to people's constant attacks and sneaky behavior. And they hate the VPs because the VPs don't recognize the importance of the info tech people."

"Perhaps they would if the tech people recognized how the small niceties, like bathing occasionally, affect other people," Aliston countered, grimacing. "There was a petition circulating to isolate tech support in another building, but we couldn't figure out who would fix the computers. Not that anyone understands their explanations anyhow."

"They are open to change...well, change other than their personal habits. I know, I used to be a hacker. With computers, it's all change. You plan and plan and then someone plants a virus on your machine that takes over and pops up a detailed middle finger waving at you on the screen before trashing the hard drive and network. A few times cycling through that, and you learn to plan for disaster and anticipate change. I've created a few of those myself, and gotten hit with a bunch of them.

"I have a meeting with Francisco and Sir Jonathan next week. If they like it, then a meeting with the directors. If they buy in, the shit hits the fan fast, because the rumors run wild once the directors see anything."

"Look at this," pointing to the computer screen. He quickly typed in several keystrokes and a program started to run. "For the meeting preparation, I was playing with little programs, simple equations that run and produce outputs. Wolfram wrote an entire book about the idea. Sometimes they run and then settle into an equilibrium quickly, for all eternity. Like a traditional steel company, for example. Sometimes they run completely randomly forever, but that's pretty unusual. It's the ones that somehow grow and improve we want, but that's really, really rare. That's the key model we want—continued evolution as a structural process. What we have now is case one: equilibrium into a dusty grave. See, they make some really neat visuals, in bright colors."

"I don't care what Cali's background is," Aliston insisted. "If she listens to this at dinner, you really owe her a nice meal somewhere. A very nice dinner, with flowers."

"Probably, but she'd think that so odd as to be suspicious," Hal replied doubtfully.

"Never," Aliston promised. "Always take a nice dinner with flowers. It's in bold print in the secret book for girls. Take my word for it."[108]

Life is organic, i.e., non-linear, which appears to humans as chaos. Human construction and thinking is all angles and squares, neatly arranged. Trees, for example, maximize their environment by twisting and turning, all of the leaves and branches responding to the very specific and detailed local rules they face. A complete allocation of command, you might say. The tree doesn't have a meeting in the morning with specific next actions determined by management; the mechanism is distributed throughout the tree. This is probably further proof that complex problems are unsolvable for humans. Linear project planning will absolutely miss the organic perspective to pressure and how to respond. Our most complex math (at least as calculated by humans) can't describe the complexity of non-linear events. We are having some success with computers doing the calculations, partly because the computers are faster, but partly, I'd suspect, because we just don't 'think' in non-linear ways.

How to approach a truly complex problem? First, set the words that describe the initial concept of the problem aside with their fixed and linear structure and see images of the problem. The images will have organic shapes and relationships. As an example, there is an article "A Life of Slime", in the January 21st, 2010 Economist magazine, that described how enormously complex network engineering problems can be solved by very simple creatures. It seems that slime moulds are neither animal, nor plant nor fungus. Physarum polycephalum, the species in the article, consists of a membrane-bound bag of protoplasm and multiple nuclei. It migrates across the floor of dark, damp, northern-temperate woodlands, searching for bacteria and other food. As it forages, it puts out protrusions of protoplasm, creates nodes and branches, and grows in the form of an interconnected network of tubes. As it explores the forest floor, it must constantly trade off the cost, efficiency and resilience of its expanding network. Researchers wondered if the networks a slime mould created would be like the ones that humans create. They experimented, and discovered that many of the links the slime mould made bore a striking resemblance to Tokyo's existing rail network. For P. polycephalum had not simply created the shortest possible network that could connect all the cities, but had also included redundant connections that allow the creature (and the real rail network) to have resilience to the accidental breakage of any part of it. P. polycephalum's network, in other words, had similar costs, efficiencies and resiliencies to the human version. And it did it on the fly, over and over as it moved across the forest floor!

Now, one difference between humans and slime moulds (or at least we think it's a difference) is that humans can pick their lives. If that forest floor isn't working, we can relocate. But you have to think and plan. Unless you think and plan, Life cares little for 'you'. It will throw you at a problem along with a lot of others. Can you face and adjust to new problems, seek new possibilities, can you adopt quickly and adjust? Or splot?

CHAPTER 28. SYSTEMS.

Complex problems exist within systems. Really, a complex problem is a part of a system that we yanked out of the system to work on for our purposes. What are systems? Technically, everything is part of the same system of the real world, so really we are looking at sub-systems, but rather than get technical with sub-systems, sub-sub-systems, etc., I'll just call chunks 'systems'.

A system is a set of processes, defined separately from the rest of the world by certain criteria, with inputs from systems outside this system, processes within this system, and outputs to other systems. Within a system, there are feedback loops, which can be either positive or negative. A negative feedback loop reduces the strength of a rate process. A positive feedback increases the strength of a rate process. Note that positive and negative for feedback loops are absolutely not value judgments. In reality, negative feedback loops tend to keep things under control, and positive feedback loops tend to drive things out of control. A nuclear explosion is a positive feedback loop, for example. Feedback is necessary for the system to maintain control of a variable or process. Systems act to restore variables to their normal values if the variables change from their normal state. If a system can't keep the variable within certain limits, then the system will generally collapse.

There have been many books written on systems, and the reader is encouraged to look at other sources for detail on systems. The literature is extensive, and is as complex as one may desire. This book is only going to look at certain limited aspects of systems as applied to planning for complex problems.

How does one describe a particular system? How do we put our arms around a part of the world, defining it as the system under examination, pushing away the others so we can model just this small part? The general process is called, not surprisingly, creating a system design map. How to do that? We are mapping the processes in a system, and the first step is to get information. What's coming in, what's being done, what's going out? When we draw the processes, we use flowcharts, and it's important to only use verbs in the operation boxes, because those are 'doing' things. You want to see a process within its time relationships, and the various inputs and outputs.

Ask what keeps the system going? What and where are the dampers, the negative feedback loops? What are the resources, their availability and sources? Then, most importantly, what are the constraints, the limits to action, what are the barriers? Constraints are especially important because people, being optimistic, tend to not like spending time on the constraints. Constraints are not as much fun, but without constraints, you have an out of control system, a cancer, actually.

It's important, in mapping a system, to not put names on parts, at least names that are value judgments or conclusions. For example, if you label something 'waste', even if it seems that, then the label carries all the weight of the word 'waste', which is a lot more than just, say, by-products. Your thinking about that box will forever be based on waste, and the solutions inherent will be lost. You want emotionally neutral descriptions for any process. Think about mapping something like the mid-east 'peace' process. (a diplomatic fantasy) The very second you put names on the boxes, all the emotions come out. You'd actually map the process by using group X, group Y, etc., and neutral names on the interactions, the resources and the constraints.

What are the drags on a system? What keeps in constant, what keeps it from expanding? What are the multipliers, the positive feedbacks? What makes it a live system, and what kills it? Where are you diagraming the parasites, at least from the view of that system, as everything has parasites seeking the resources that the system wants for itself.

Deming had an alternative formulation to OODA, which was plan, do, check and act. That was used in a factory, for example, a situation slightly lower key than actual warfare. What he found was that it was the last two steps which people forget. In the system you are looking at, what happens when you apply 'plan, do check and act'? Are the outputs what you would expect? When you are in the system, and you run the OODA cycle, is it working? Those are good tests for your process model to tell you whether you've grasped the system correctly.

Now, in the real world, which is a huge linked system, you have to be careful of dealing with the systems as a bundle of independent mini-systems. If you run a mini-system into the ground, other systems will be affected, which is the complex problem in a nutshell. Dealing with the world as a set of mini-systems, complete in themselves is going to be trouble, because if we do not concern ourselves with the problems we do not have, we will soon have them. As discussed earlier, that isn't our nature, so we are suddenly in the 'up to our ass in alligator's problem'.

An important example of why systems fail is the "The Tragedy of the Commons". This is a classic example of where a complex system fails because of the conflicting goals within the many subsystems comprising the complex system. In the book, Systems 1 (1980), Kauffman told the following story to illustrate this idea:

> One of the best illustrations of this is a situation known as 'the Tragedy of the Commons,' after an essay of that name by ecologist Garrett Hardin. Hardin used for the scene of his illustration the 'commons' or common pasture of medieval England and colonial America. 'Common' in this sense meant that all members of the community were entitled to graze their livestock there. The positive feedback loop involved in the use of the commons, from the point of view of the individual livestock owner, goes like this: 'The more cows I

have, the better off I will be. Feeding them is free, so I will increase the size of my herd as fast as I can.'

But, this creates a situation that each individual is powerless to avoid. As each person increases his herd, the number of cows grazing on the commons increases; after a certain point, there are enough cattle to eat the grass faster than it can grow back; when there is no more long grass left, the cows will then crop the remaining grass right down to the ground, killing the plants and leaving nothing but bare dirt. Soon the cows are all starving, and the entire village is faced with bankruptcy and possible starvation.

Notice that it does no good for any one villager to voluntarily keep the size of his herd down. If he refrains from putting more cows on the pasture, he simply leaves more grass for his neighbors' cattle, and increases the incentive for each of them to add still more. As a result, his unselfish action will not prevent the disaster, and he will be poorer in the meantime. Since each herdsman can see that it would be pointless to hold back, each one adds as many cows as he can until the inevitable disaster occurs (Kauffman, 1980, pg. 33).

If you look at this situation closely, you will note that each person is making the most sensible decision from his own point of view. The result, however, is that everyone ends up worse off than before (Kauffman, 1980). What is missing from this situation is the negative feedback loop that limits the size of the individual herds and, therefore, the size of the entire herd that matches the rate of growth of the grass (Kauffman).[109]

All the really great disasters/tragedies, perhaps comedies, depending on your point of view, depend on a variant of the tragedy of the commons. Despite pious talk, there is a limited amount that can be done by people trying to be 'evil'. What is unstoppable and overwhelming is a group of people diligently doing what they think is not just good, but the best. Where you have a group that is doing what they think is best for themselves and their children, they have the bit in their mouth and they are going to run with it.

The "Tragedy of the Commons" is caused by trying to handle a problem at too low a level in the system, i.e., each individual making choices. How to avoid this? Ideally, the highest point in the system, which could oversee the entire system, would make wise decisions. We see the Philosopher King, sitting in his wise chair, grasping the problem and gracefully handling it, to the admiring applause of the court. And generally, top down solutions work about as well as that picture has worked in the past. We have a shortage of philosopher kings without personal ambition but committed to the greater good in positions of power. Even if we had the right person at the right time, they would have to have the right information at the right times to make decisions, and full control of the levers of state to enforce the decisions.

That's asking a lot, especially since if you tell someone to have fewer cows, then their family eats less, and their children are hungry. Granted, perhaps they should not have had as many children, but there they are, looking sad and hungry in the village, and a philosopher king who starves children for his pleasure isn't going to popular. More likely, the king has friends, and the friends get large herds and people who are not his friends don't get large herds. If there isn't a solution within the human stories of justice and right, there will still be a solution in the real world. If nothing is done, there will be starvation, the grass will start growing again, and the set of events will cycle over and over. It's really the usual situation anytime there is a predator that is too successful, like the piranha in Brazil, or of the herder's with their cows. It's seeing humans as part of the natural world, subject to the same rules as any other creature that doesn't fit into our usual evaluation of systems.

From the human point of view, there are two conflicts. We could give control to the lowest level of the system, which is quicker, less costly and simpler, but full of its own set of problems as illustrated above. Or, should the control be given to the top end of the system that might reduce conflicts between the subsystems, but cost more, be less efficient, and take longer to implement? And, since we have just seen that neither is going to work, is it possible to convey to the group what will happen if there is individual self-maximization, and perhaps the lower levels can stop and think? That last is (we like to think) the difference between humans and the piranha. The human race has a lot bet on that, but the odds are not so good.

Let's go back to thinking about systems, because we see that they are more complex than expected. And that they just won't do what we think they should! First, we need to think by analogy. We need to think about relationships between broad and narrow concepts, between the abstract and the concrete. Hopefully, we can apply knowledge from one field to another. We can setup simple experiments in which we establish the parts of one element in the system and consider the relationships of those parts to the environment. Again:

> *"By three methods we may learn wisdom: First, by reflection, which is noblest; second, by imitation, which is easiest; and third by experience, which is the bitterest." Confucius*

If we don't apply names, such as the initially obvious elements such as fish (immediate picture is 'food' to humans), water (immediately everyone is thirsty), plants (different kinds of food), but instead looking at the levels of parts that make up the system elements, we have moved our investigation into a neutral land. Then, we have to ask what level of detail are we using? Too low a level, and we are buried in facts. Too high, and we miss the subtle but important relationships. Determining how to define and manipulate a system is very much like goal setting, and the steps listed for goal setting work very well. We think, we narrow, we expand, and we experiment and test.

If we knew at the beginning what we know at the end, we would select that level of detail needed for us to understand the interrelationships among the variables that we want to influence. Sadly, good psychic's are hard to find, so iteration though the problem again and again is the only way this can be done.

Complexity is the curse we give to the existence of many interdependent variables in a system. There are other names, but they are generally unprintable, although emotionally satisfying. All we want is just a simple thing: for the world to do what we want. Is that really that much to ask? Well, yes, it is, but that's not emotionally satisfying.

Where we have multiple interdependent variables, we have to pay attention to great many features simultaneously. Remember, we can hold perhaps 7 items in memory at once, and one of those has to be why we are doing this. You start adding in items such as how do we use the computer programs and other practical items, and we are down to just a couple of empty slots in a few seconds. It's easy to lose track. Worse, for our experiments, it's impossible for us to undertake only one action in a complex system. If we do X to Y and get Z, but then we do Y to Z and get R, what do we do next? How many pokes at the system do we take before we just start hitting it with a stick out of frustration, or shift to magic rituals? Because that's what we do, over and over, where important things don't make sense. If it doesn't make sense but you have to act, well, what other choices do you have?

Reality is not passive. We can't observe a world frozen, in stasis. The world is doing something, all the time. Knowing what happened may be interesting, but we need to know where the system is heading. As we are trying to guess the future, we are still poking the system trying to get a consistent output to a consistent input.

A new word: 'Intransparence'. We may have no direct access, or any access at all, to information about the problem situation. At that point, ritual starts being very attractive. When you factor in that people are most inclined to insist they are right when they are clearly wrong but out on a social limb, and when they are beset by uncertainty, you can see we are going to have a problem. Over and over, especially in social situations, people prefer their incorrect hypotheses to a correct one and will fight tooth and nail rather than abandon an idea that is demonstrably false. Once they set that anchor, that ship is at home. You just hope that they don't burn the messenger, which is you.

We need our internal mental compass telling us that we are in control and doing the right thing. That need, especially if there is a group involved, prevents us from accepting, or even allowing for the possibility that our assumptions may be wrong or incomplete. As our ability to step back, make allowances for incomplete and incorrect information and then generate new and creative hypotheses under fire is important in dealing with complex situations, we can see this isn't going to work well.

And again, it breaks down into the difference between ordinary, daily activities where muddled thinking and experience can and do work, and the non-daily activities where muddled thinking is going to be disaster. When everyone sees a crisis, there is a chance of thinking about things. Where everyone sees the daily grind, they are not going to change their lives and thought patterns because you think it would be helpful to throw a monkey wrench into their lives.

There was an article on the Knowledge Systems of Integrative Thinkers in Rotman Magazine which argued that integrative thinkers:

- recognize that existing models do not equal reality;
- seek out model clash and leverage opposing models;
- believe that better models always exist that cannot be seen;
- believe that they are capable of finding a better model; - They ask: 'Under what conditions does x cause y? What is the driving force fueling this causal relationship? And what are the mechanisms underlying it?' Their goal is to build more sophisticated and creative solutions with more robust model-building.
- are willing and enthusiastic about wading into complexity; and
- give themselves the time to create; they aren't rushed to find 'the answer' to a problem.[110]

Those are ideal behavior patterns for dealing with systems. And probably for a nomination to sainthood. Cynically, it would be interesting how well they apply them with their 14-year-old child, but reality is more complex than theory. Not to throw stones at the integrative thinkers, who are trying very hard, but this is the problem with experts:

> "Now, we have been taught to go to experts for specialized problems. The problem with experts is this: if you go to your doctor with a broken leg, they can fix that. If you go in with a vague itch, which occurs at random intervals in different spots, you might as well stay home. Problems that can be solved have clear borders, such as a broken leg. Problems without clear boundaries, the itches, the occasional rattle in your car, those problems usually can't be solved. But a failure to solve some problems makes people doubt the experts. That's bad, because then the experts don't get paid. So, to preserve their claim of expertise, experts wall off the important stuff for the detail they can control.
>
> Authoritative and learned people create categories, they 'platonify' to define what's important as what they can control. What you think is important is pushed away, because anyone with a mind and a tongue can discourse about what is important to each of us. But, if you focus on petty details, bury what matters under a layer of jargon, and

look serious, then the experts can make a living whether they can solve the problem of not. Making a living is important, because we all have to feed our children.

"So like dung beetles, they pile up esoteric knowledge in a ball and push it before them, proving their expertise. Professors, psychologists, theologians, among others. All the same process in the end. And the writings that the church so reverently venerates, all the cracked parchment written in ancient dead languages that they pore over? Who knows what the writings were before they were edited, revised, and simply re-written? Who knows what the authors really meant by their words? You do know that what is written in the official text is what works for those in power, and that's about all one can be sure of. There's a concept called negative evidence. Who can say what came from what, and what is missing that is important? The water on the floor—was it from an ice cube melting, or something completely different? There is no way of knowing what was lost or destroyed in the past because it didn't support practical power needs for the social structures."[111]

Everyone worries about systems crashing-at least, when there isn't anything else to worry about. It's the essence of many, many movies, and it's realistic-each of us lives in a complex system that if parts of it stopped functioning, we die. As we don't know why the system functions as it is, that's a bit worrisome. So, here is the key to whether a system will crash or not:

"The energy flow to maintain a given social structure must be sufficient for the complexity of the systems involved. The more complex a society is, the more costly it is to maintain. As structures become more complex, information becomes critical. So information flows are centralized and protected, demanding a vast number of trained people to cope with the complexity. An agricultural society needs a many people with hoes and a few to calculate the irrigation flows. A complex society needs a lot of people to calculate and only a few people with hoes.

"All of this complexity absolutely needs huge energy flows. As the society becomes more complex, simple maintenance takes more and more energy. So what collapses a complex society is the drab concept of declining marginal returns. As more and more resources are allocated to just keeping the society running, there are fewer resources available for new growth. Occasionally, new resources will be discovered that change the equation, but the equation in its basic form is a constant. Declining marginal returns dictate that eventually, like the Red Queen in Alice in Wonderland, you have to run as fast as you can to stay where you are. To get ahead, you must run twice as fast as before. Should you slip, systems can stagger along IF there are reserves to cover the shortages. Declining marginal returns are a double-edged sword: because it takes everything you have just to keep things going, there isn't anything to put back into the reserves. Each hit on the reserves lowers the tank. Eventually, a resource has no reserves for emergencies, and it's splat time.

"System failure does not strike like a bolt from the blue; it unfolds in its own time. Part of the problem is that humans freeze in emergencies, grabbing tightly onto the last successful strategy. Given that the last successful strategy probably created today's disaster, that's not going to be very helpful. Technically, this is defined as choosing an efficient but non-explorative mode. The trap is the short-term efficiency focus. It's most efficient to do better what you are doing right now. You're going down slowly, like a balloon with a slow leak. Frozen on pumping in air, the society redoubles it's efforts because it worked last time. Unless someone steps back, and maybe thinks about patching the hole, it's just a question, then, of how long the failure will take. The fracture point is where some critical factor in the real world breaks, and there is no reserve and/or replacement. In other words, no oil, no system. In a linked, interdependent system, a lot of people can go hungry fast. And then dead.

"If there's no money, and no resources, there is actually no money, and no resources. Politicians pretended before that there was no money for bargaining leverage and political points. Horrified, they found that there was no money, and their games were up. Choices are narrowed to what the resources allow, because you can only do what you can do-different from what you want. The social experiment where we are falling off the building, but tell each other it's going to work? Hit the pavement.

"Symbolic forms are a key support of the economic structure and civilization that the economy supports. Where an economy collapses, the support for the moral order and the civilizations cohesion, vitality, and creative powers begin to crumble. Loss of the literally read symbolic forms brings forth uncertainty, and with uncertainty, disequilibrium. Life, as Shakespeare knew, requires life-supporting illusions. Where the illusions have been dispelled, there is nothing secure to hold on to, and the structures' moral laws, their carefully taught meanings, are shaken to the core."[112]

CHAPTER 29. COMPLEX PROBLEMS, CONTINUED

What else can be said (in a short period of time) on complex problems? That you want to hear after wading through the last few chapters? All problems are aspects of complex problems; it's just that all the 'other' stuff doesn't matter. Putting your milk on your cereal in the morning is a part of an incredibly complex chain of past events and future consequences, almost none of which matter to the clear goal of getting enough, but not too much, milk on your cereal. Complex problems become a planning nightmare when we have to take in large chunks of the problem, with all of the multiple system interactions and the lack of control that we have over the important levers. For example, side (for you) issues tied to your morning milk are the daily and yearly food requirements of the cattle, which include planting, irrigation and harvesting of crops, along with transporting the right food to the right place at the right time. Then there are the systems that keep the cattle alive and healthy, the barns, the medical professionals, and it goes on and on. None of that matters to your cereal, but if would matter a great deal if you were concerned with keeping the ground water safe. A dairy farm with several hundred/several thousand cattle produces a lot of waste. What do you do with it all?

One would think that this would be solvable, but it's not. It's possible to make it functional now, and across a range of possibilities in the future, but that's not 'solving'. Very simple computer routines/instructions, left to run endlessly can produce astonishingly complex output that never settles into a regular pattern-ever. If a set of simple rules, running over and over, will create situations that we cannot understand and certainly not control, then the complex processes running the real world are not going to be reducible to simple, easy guides.

Let's go back to defining putting the milk on your cereal as a simple decision with minimal consequences. A four year old can do this, how complex can it be? This can be a 1st level decision, which is a decision you take with little regard to future consequences. There are always some consequences: if you have cereal, you won't have a different breakfast, and food now impacts your energy levels in the next few hours, but those consequences are relatively simple. 2nd level (and higher) decisions look to consequences, and when you do that, you've brought the complexity of the world in and have it sitting next to you. What if you stop your breakfast cereal? Will the milk producers and the cereal companies go broke? Probably not, unless you are guiding light for a mass of people, all of who throw down their spoons at the same time. So you set in motion the children of the farmers starving? That's a heavy load for not having had your morning cereal.

In Star Wars, and many other ethical systems, the whole discussion of the dark side versus the light is a simplification of a complex problem process. The standard allowed decision is a 1st level decision, which looks only at the immediate consequences of an action, tying your action to socially approved choices and leaving it there. Hang the consequences; everyone said this was the right thing to do. That works a lot, and is necessary a lot, because, as is clear, the world is a pretty complex place. You start pulling on that rope, bringing in more and more of the complexity of the problem into consideration, and quickly it's out of control. So the eventual result is let to the problem work its way out if the group is happy with what you did.

That is the thinking that underlies the Tragedy of the Commons, global warming, dead spots in the ocean, and many other problems that are jumping at us. We don't seem to have to tools to deal with these kinds of complex problems. So you see articles that bemoan the huge squatter communities developing all over the world, along-side articles that cheerfully predict the rapid rise of the poor all over the world into the middle class. Next to THAT article is an article that calculates the energy costs of the poor becoming middle class, and the numbers are beyond comprehension-and beyond the resources available if you gutted the entire earth. The stories all slop together without regard to the interactions and necessary consequences of each story, and we hope for the future. And close our eyes to the present.

Having said that, making an effective 2nd level decision is really, really hard. We're not wired to juggle hundreds of variables in our minds, the multiple equations clicking along as we note the points of symmetry and opposition. Perhaps the computers can juggle this data, but the complex calculations still have to be reduced to a simple story to tell everyone. The computer that came up with the answer to the universe as '42' may have decided that was as good an answer as any, because the real story was simply too complex to tell.

And when that simple story results in damage to the present wealthy, that's a story that isn't going to sell well. Or the story says that the world isn't going to work with these processes, that there are too many people, too few resources, well, that's another story that isn't going to sell well, because that means that someone ox is going to be gored, and who is going to make that decision? We stand tall, arms wrapped around our oxen, with fierce glances at the others who want to protect their positions, and suddenly we are all in the Mideast, living an insolvably complex problem that our lives depend on.

"What can be counted (measured) doesn't always matter, and what can't be counted (measured) often matters a great deal." Albert Einstein.

In trying to interpret the world, one of the most critical design issues is whether the system provides a physical representation that can be directly perceived and that is directly interpretable in terms of the intentions and expectations of the person. In small words, when you push on the door, is there a clear visual as to which side of the door opens the door? Not in most of the Mall's/Hotel's that the author has gone to!

This leads to the next point, which was an underlying rationale for the book and Figure 1. Visual representations are critical. When you get something that has to be assembled, what do you look at first: the diagram or the words? We all look at the diagram, falling back to wading thru the words when all else fails. You've got to be able to quickly interpret/understand the physical system to modify it, and then to measure those modifications. Ideally, the gulf between what you want and the nature of the world is small when the system provides information about its state in a form that is easy to get, is easy to interpret, and matches the way the person thinks of the system. That's not likely: remember, we're often dealing with unexpected systems and new problems that we are trying to ignore.

So, OK, we have our shoes tied, which is a definable and controllable activity that fits all of the above issues. Now, what about non-trivial (in the mathematical sense) activities in the real world? Problems that we call 'wicked problems', for a lot of reasons. 'Wicked' because they refuse to do what we want, which is shorthand for evil in daily life. 'Wicked' because they are critical but impossible to resolve in the nice, linear outlines that we are taught to handle problems by. 'Wicked' because they are the outliers, the monsters that refuse to cooperate.

Again, there are problems with representing the complexity of the world in stories and graphs. Then there are a separate set of complexities in conveying to others what you have found, because many things can't be said within a social context, regardless of the truth of the matter. The social system allows for certain things to be believed/said by/to the group. Because there are emotions that are denied, then what is allowed to be said/done socially is subtly (and not so subtly) twisted because people have to do what they have to do. When you have social reasons superimposed on raw emotion, then the story twists, bends, until it can't run any more. Your attempt to clearly show that the train is coming off the rails? In a social context, it's going to be your fault because you are the one who started talking about this. If no one had said anything (the cartoon character walking in air is fine until he notices there's nothing under his feet) then things would have been OK. To recap, you face the complexity of the problem and the complexity of the social interaction.

In attacking complex problems, if I haven't dissuaded you from this frustrating and difficult action, simplifying the constraints and fractures at least shows where can/is being manipulated. When your head hurts, remember that, really, consciousness is a passenger on the bus, not the driver. Listen to messages from the unconscious, because it is driving. When your gut comes up with a solution, don't rationalize that solution away because you will live to regret it.

Remember to always define a game you can win! That's different from pretending the world is different that it is, it's more how you view the problem. You're going to respond to a game you can win. A game you're going to lose? One retreats in despair, which doesn't do a lot of good. What you want, as David Allen says, is a mind like water. Your consciousness is at peace, quiet. A pebble is thrown in the water, the responds, back to calm. Water doesn't tense, water responds and moves on. It's a lot easier on your blood pressure also. With complex problems, one cannot over-plan, because we really can't grasp the whole thing, at least consciously, and all we do in trying is become distraught. So do something and see what happens, in the context of what your goals and visions are.

Let's think about how things change in the real world. In a linear process, a quantity increases by the same amount, not the same multiple, at each step. This is, as said before, how we think and model the world. That isn't, however, the way that the world actually acts. The world likes exponential relationships, where there are dramatic, huge results from actions. We don't think in those terms naturally, and so we instinctively reject them, forcing the world into a linear view. Perhaps it's an accelerated linear view-i.e., something is multiplied by 2 or 3 as it acts, but it's a constant. Exponentials are not constants-they are much more dramatic that that. An alternative way of measuring exponential growth is to express the amount by which the quantity increases over its previous value as a percentage of that previous value; this percentage is called the rate of growth. Maybe that will help.

Let's look at a variant of the exponential problem. If we are looking at a process in the real world, and we have a starting number, we extrapolate from that. The problem is that if we take any increase as our initial figure and calculate growth rates on the basis of that number, we will at first grossly overestimate the speed of the process because we will not have taken the process's "head start" into account. That is, the process has been developing for a while before we noticed it, but we compress all of the developments into the 'beginning' and multiply from there. That isn't going to be accurate. Two problems: first, our projections are wrong, and second, when our projections are wrong, the social world then discounts everything, not just the wrong part, because it's too complex to think thru the whole thing.

So, we turn to experts to run the world.

"How do experts actually do? When it came to predicting the likelihood of an outcome, the vast majority performed worse than random chance. In other words, they would have done better picking their answers blindly out of a hat. Liberals, moderates and conservatives were all equally ineffective. Although 96% of the subjects had post-graduate training, Mr. Tetlock found, the fancy degrees were mostly useless when it came to forecasting.

The main reason for the inaccuracy has to do with overconfidence. Because the experts were convinced that they were right, they tended to ignore all the evidence suggesting they were wrong. This is known as confirmation bias, and it leads people to hold all sorts of erroneous opinions. Famous experts were especially prone to overconfidence, which is why they tended to do the worst. Unfortunately, we are blind to this blind spot: Most of the experts in the study claimed that they were dispassionately analyzing the evidence. In reality, they were indulging in selective ignorance, as they explained away dissonant facts and contradictory data. The end result, Mr. Tetlock says, is that the pundits became "prisoners of their preconceptions." And their preconceptions were mostly worthless.

What's most disturbing about Mr. Tetlock's study is that the failures of the pundit class don't seem to matter. We rely on talking heads more than ever, even though the vast majority of them aren't worth their paychecks. Our political discourse is driven in large part by people whose opinions are less accurate than a coin toss." [113]Jonah Lehrer, WSJ, 10/30/2010, Beware Our Blind Seers

So if the experts don't have a clue, and the world is too complex to model, then we are in a fog. Fog is what we dislike, because something may be out there. (it is, too) Yet fog is the most accurate description of life. You can see a little way into the future, and the past gets hazy as it goes back. To think that life should be otherwise: perfectly clear back and front, just isn't realistic, especially as you look forward. Fog is where the monsters are, which is why we prefer non-fog. And we are back to the beginning quote from the Art of War, which is:

"Victory in battle that all-under-heaven calls skilled is not skilled.
Thus lifting an autumn hair does not mean great strength.
Seeing the sun and the moon does not mean a clear eye.
Hearing thunder does not mean a keen ear.
So-called skill is to be victorious over the easily defeated.
Thus the battles of the skilled are without extraordinary victory,
without reputation for wisdom and without merit for courage."[114] *Pp 14, Form*

This is why it's so hard to see victory. Victory is found as part of the complex process that is the world. Not only do we have to pluck the right problem out of the complex processes roiling the world around us, we have to deny the social world and our minds and look at what we think is, not what we are told should be.

"Thus it is that in war the victorious strategist only seeks battle after the victory has been won,
whereas he who is destined to defeat first fights and afterwards looks for victory."[115]

Unfortunately, the social world lives (and really only understands) the person who stands tall, shouting wildly at the enemy, having taken little thought before except for their anger. Socially, we are meant to be Achilles, all fury and natural ability. If you want to be promoted, you not only have to be skillful enough to win, you then have to project this ability so that you have a reputation (which is a false reputation, as it's defined by the social world) for wisdom and courage. No wonder the Mongols just got on their horses and attacked. It's a lot easier, and you don't get headaches that way.

"And that's a great lead for today's talk," Hal declared. "Wicked problems are not evil, necessarily, but they are complex. Complex means they are tied to other problems, sometimes tightly, sometimes loosely. We are trading off, for example, the happiness of the maintenance staff against our childish glee and momentary pleasure. Now, our childish glee is really important, at least to me, but sullen maintenance staff people are not good. And the results of both our glee and their sullenness are not clear or measurable."

"Oh, it's measurable all right," one of the veterans commented. "It's dirtier after they leave than when they started, and that isn't always easy around here."

"Humm. . it's worse than I thought," Hal mused. "Is there an optimal solution? No. Any solution to a wicked problem is a better or worse choice. No gestalt. Not kindergarten where careful attention to detail and patience puts the puzzle together into a unified whole, a complete, closed job. And an academic approach-careful, structured, time oriented behavior-is about the worst way to grasp these problems. You can't get a solid immediate test for solutions-i.e., the feedback isn't feeding back-and there is no ultimate test of a solution for a wicked problem. No final lab experiment that can stamp 'right!' on your choices.

"And it gets better," Hal promised, smiling. "Because the problems are so interwoven with tightly linked problem there is no real chance for trial and error learning. Why? Because your last action to try and fix the problem, has changed the original problem. Because the problems are NOW!, i.e., real-time problems, every action-or non-action-you take to solve the problem has real, significant impacts, good or bad."

"Okay, recapping what I opened with," Hal began. "Every solution to a wicked problem is a 'one-shot operation' because the problem changes as you act on it. So it isn't the same problem next time. Your choices and actions are critically important; you get no prior learning experience, and no turning back. Goal seeking? A wicked problem doesn't have a clear set of potential solutions. Are we having fun yet?"

"It gets better," Hal continued. "We learn from our prior experiences, and apply those to the future. Surprise! Each wicked problem is essentially unique. So, there is no clear set of possible actions/choices that worked last time to bring to the new plan. Each wicked problem is probably a symptom of another problem. Remember how we talked about how 'garbage in' is going to be 'garbage out', regardless of the quality of the work you do? Well, wicked problems are linked to others; you're getting inputs of 'garbage in' on top of trying to fix what's in front of you.

"In school, we were taught that every problem has a cause. NOT. The base reason, the turtle that the turtle stands on, the tap root feeding the wicked problem-can be any number of reasons, and can be explained in numerous ways. The wicked problem tree lives off of feeder roots, not a tap root, so you can't cut off the problem with a single stroke. That means we can't even have a clear view of what caused/feeds this mess'. Obviously, that makes a huge difference as to what choices we see to solve, or at least live with, the problem."

"Tempting," Hal agreed, "but what fun would that be? Here, we have the joy and excitement of every day facing the complete chaos of life. Best of all, the planner, i.e., the directly responsible person, a hero fighting valiantly against this hydra headed beast, as the crowd ohhs and ahhhs; you have no right to be wrong. No 'bye' pass from the boss. The planner is liable for the consequences of the actions they take/direct. Really, does it get any better than that?"

"At least," Hal replied, nodding happily. "This is really rough stuff we are going over today. Why? Because this is the world we live in. Small stories, small problems don't link to the other small stories and small problems, and so solutions don't. Oil disruptions lead to who knows what? We don't get to reset the game board and try another set of choices. And if we could? Can you imagine the committee meeting who decides what and when gets reset? I.e., whose ox gets un-gored and whose doesn't? The infighting would be with real knives. Maybe this is for the best. In the here and now, we only get one shot at a very rapidly moving target,"

Hal paused for a moment to collect his thoughts. "Every choice we make in what we like to define as normal life is a win/lose. Oh, there is shading, but the happy decision is the clear one. It's black and white, and we choose, never having to look back. That's how people think, in straight lines and clear backgrounds. In the world we live in, we are playing paper, rock, scissors on every decision and problem. We can't be sure of the right and wrong and there may be no right and wrong. If there was a right and wrong, it vanishes because solutions change as we move. We want to see the subtle before it emerges, but in reality, we can hardly see the problem before it hits us, much less the subtle solutions to the problem. So, ideas, approaches?"

"You thought I had solutions?" Hal advised. "Boy, were you wrong. No cookbooks, no checkboxes here. When you are in your office, what are you going to do about tomorrow?"

"Paper, rock, scissors," Cali remarked. "I like that, even though I don't like the game itself. I always find it frustrating."

"So, what you are saying, I think," Cali argued, "is that normally we take problems apart, and by looking at the parts of the problem, we understand what the issue is. That doesn't work here, because we are trying to work with an emergent problem."

"An emergent system is one that is, well, emerging in front of us. It's new, and the pieces are not clear because there are different elements interacting," Cali contended, thinking as she talked. "The result of the interaction is something quite different than the whole of the parts. An apple pie, hot out of the oven, the delicious aroma wafting through the kitchen, is much more than the raw sugar, piecrust, and raw apples you put into the oven. That new 'thing' has to be looked at top down, i.e., the pie's taste when it's cooked, and bottom up, for example, the quality of the apples used to make it. Except that real emergent systems are constantly changing, more like, well, a growing tree. The analysis of the leaf, the root, and the trunk don't add together to the live tree, which is changing and interacting with the world as we try to understand it. Want to grasp what a tree is? A tree then has to be studied as a live tree, and as a set of nested networks of relationships, which is the leaf, the root, the trunk, etc."

"And then there is the tree/forest complexity," Aliston added. "A tree is a system within a much bigger system, that inputs and outputs into that larger system."

"Absolutely true," Hal agreed. "Now, looking back at only the tree, we have to remember that it is developing by and for it's own rules and goals. Those rules/goals have hardly anything to do with your goals. You might be after shade, or apples from the tree, and/or erosion control, or a host of other goals. Your goals don't include roots in the sewers, or leaves all over in the fall, or a dense stand of trees turning into a firestorm. Little things like those are far outside your clear goal for a shady place to sit on a hot day with a glass of lemonade. See, paper, rock, scissors is a completely different way of thinking about the world."

"It's an organic way of thinking," Mary remarked. "The world operates in curves and twists, maximizing resources and opportunities. People demand right/wrong choices because they are comfortable. Maybe, at a stretch, structured multiple choices, but free form? That's not in the rule book that the suits go by. So, yeah, paper, rock, scissors is an essay exam, because the right answer could be this, and it could be this. People in general hate that, and it absolutely drives the authorities insane. After all, you allow ambiguity in one place, and maybe someone will think that the authorities don't have the answers either. I've seen culture after culture bury their heads in the sand, like an ostrich, because they don't want to be bothered with the complexity of the world."

"Only to be buried in the sand as time goes by," Jesus chuckled. "Thank you, Mary, for a great lead-in line!"

"Frankenstein's fateful error was to plan the individual parts, not allowing for what the sum of the parts he had assembled could become," Lucifer pointed out. "He defined a problem, successfully analyzed the parts, but the whole, the apple pie, as it were, wasn't even close to the stack of parts."

"As opposed to Frankenfurter's," Hal added. "His initial decision to use half a brain for his creatures doomed his efforts to inevitable failure. He misstated the problem completely, and failed to analyze the parts in his focus on the whole."

"So, what do we do? We have to act," Hal demanded. "One approach is a root-causes fix versus Band-Aids. It's harder to fix the root cause of a problem than to simply make a problem go away with a Band-Aid. Band-Aids are sometimes the best choice, though. Where and when?"

"Band-Aids where the problems can cure themselves, given time," Aliston responded. "Where the underlying system is working, and there is a temporary need for less stress from the world."

"A perfect answer," Hal agreed. "No wonder you took my job. And so it's rational, and almost always a good idea, to try some Band-Aids first to see what the underlying system is doing. That's not good where you have, say, a nuclear reactor overheating, but for smaller, slowly developing problems, it's generally appropriate. Where and how the Band-Aids are failing gives us some idea where the root causes might be. What's the worst choice? A grand vision, based on our goals rather than the world's nature. A mistaken solution to the root problem intensifies the problem. The cases where an initial success was only the prelude to overwhelming failure are legion."

"Okay, here is what we have faced in the last few weeks," Hal summarized. "There are chronic problems and acute problems. Generally defined by time frames, actually. That sounds obvious, but human time frames imposed on the world are a set of problems all by themselves. So, chronic problems, which are long-term, intractable, progressive, degenerative problems, the ones we really hate to deal with, underlie things like the oil crisis and related shocks. In hindsight, it is always obvious that limited resources and infinite demand plays poorly, but that is background, pushed away by our concentration on the problem de jour. Then, there are acute problems. They are sudden, intense, episodic problems, like, say, a broken toe from hitting a chair leg. Catastrophic problems are generally acute, as something awful emerges out of the background. The boots on the ground say 'Wow,' or less complimentary words to that effect. It's a chronic problems becoming acute, a small shock causing the collapse of corroded, weakened structures, that makes the history books."

"Where is the paper, rock, scissors?" Cali asked.

"Do we buy more efficient oil burning equipment?" Hal replied. "Or do we shift to coal, factoring in transportation and clean-air consequences? Some sets of facts will justify, or negate, either choice, and those sets of facts change going forward, flipping sometimes with incredible speed."

"So," Aliston maintained, "we first determine our goal. We determine our resources, barriers, and constraints. We make tentative choices, knowing that the best choice can change, and we only bet the farm when it's live or die."

"Really, promoting her was one of your better ideas," Cali pointed out to Hal.

"Couldn't agree more," Hal agreed. "What Aliston said brilliantly and succinctly sums up our choices."[116]

Chapter 30. Solving the Unsolvable.

"Pep talk time. The only difference between a fear that excites you and one that you run from is how you look at it. The physical reaction the same in both cases. Eat the white fear, and then it isn't fear anymore. Eat your nightmares, they become part of you and your life. But you have to want to not fear. If you have been taught to think you should fear something, that it's not 'right' to not be afraid, then you will be afraid."[117]

So, we've seen that complex problems are impossible to solve, and the best we can do is create a more or less temporary solution. Wicked problems are even worse, cases where it is almost impossible to even come up with a temporary solution, both because of the complexity of the processes, and because of the complex social interactions imposed on top of the real world processes. All that part of the social world diagram that has no overlap with the real world? That's going to be hard to drag into cohesion with the unpleasant limits of the real world.

Let's be crude about this-over here, on the far left of the diagram, is where it's shit coming in, and it's going to be shit going out, on the far right of the diagram, but you've got some responsibility anyhow.

There's a funny saying: 'I didn't say it's your fault; I said I'm going to blame you', and this may be one of those situations. Our parents used to say, on the rare occasions we were punished falsely, that it was just then for the times we had gotten away with something (parenting was different back then). Not a lot of sympathy.

So, let's think about our risk exposure. If we can't solve it, what is the risk exposure? If we can partially solve it for a while, what's that risk exposure? Calculating a risk involves several things. First, we have to come up with some possible solutions to problems. Then, based on experience or sheer guesswork, we have to estimate the odds that a solution is going to work. Finally, what is the risk if the solution doesn't work, and what is the risk if the solution does work and events change later? The world is full of examples of initial great success that became legendary failure. Non calculated risks are those that reflect uncertainties, but the uncertainties are matter of our ignorance. Purely random risk is quite different. Some purely random risks are that they are simply immeasurable and/or indeterminate. Indeterminate is a roulette wheel: sometimes it's red, sometimes its black, and it spins on it's own. Immeasurable says we don't grasp enough of the system to make any useful calculations. Now, at that point, the MBA's throw that risk out of the spreadsheet, but that's not the same as throwing it out of the world.

A risk is calculated by first estimating the probability, the likelihood of the risk occurring. Note that we are estimating an estimate here! Secondly, we have to estimate the severity of the risk, which is the amount of damage if things go south; and then the probability of detectability, which is the ease of recognizing the risk in advance. So we have three very rough estimates multiplied together and then a forth-our guess as to the possible damages. British Petroleum blew this quite badly in their estimate of drilling risks in the Gulf of Mexico, which is another important point. You may come to a conclusion that is reasonable in light of given facts-today. If it goes south badly, your best efforts are going to be judged inadequate and pitiful.

A risk intelligence test is an approach to test our focus on risk. One example would be the following questions:

- "How often do you acquire information related to the risk
- How relevant is the information too possible causes of the risk? Does the tester theories about the risk?
- How surprising does this information tend to be? Does it have a large impact in your views?
- How diverse are the sources of information that you use in learning about the rest? Do you talk to customers as well as suppliers, for instance?
- How well do keep records of and share this information? To make it available to people on the front lines?"[118]
- Where you have risks, you can do the following:
- Accept the risk, which is understanding the consequences and choosing to do nothing
- Avoid the risk, which is not doing the project or changing the scope to eliminate the portion with the risk
- Transfer the risk, which is purchasing insurance; utilizing contractors or other parties
- Mitigate the risk, which is reducing the risk through contingency planning
- Exploit the risk, which is ensuring the opportunity is realized
- Enhance the risk, which is working proactively to increase the probability or positive impact"[119]

That's pretty much all your choices. Nowhere are you given the choice 'ignore the risk and it will go away'. Make notes, so that if you guessed wrong, next time you'll have some ideas to work with. And have contingency plans, a fallback when things don't go as you hoped.

The Greek's liked paradox's. Perhaps 'liked' is the wrong word, but they created many that have survived to come down to annoy us. The trick behind a paradox is the frame of reference that you choose. We often jump right over the frame of reference into action-it's our nature and wiring-and that's what makes the paradox's so annoying.

I touched on the paradox of Achilles and the Tortoise earlier in the book. To go into more detail, Achilles is in a footrace with the tortoise. Achilles allows the tortoise a head start of 100 feet. If we suppose that each racer starts running at some constant speed (one very fast and one very slow), then after some finite time, Achilles will have run 100 feet, bringing him to the tortoise's starting point. During this time, the tortoise has run a much shorter distance, for example 10 feet. It will then take Achilles some further time to run that distance, in which time the tortoise will have advanced farther; and then more time still to reach this third point, while the tortoise moves ahead. Thus, whenever Achilles reaches somewhere the tortoise has been, he still has farther to go. Therefore, because there are an infinite number of points Achilles must reach where the tortoise has already been--he can never overtake the tortoise

The trick is the frame of reference being the runner's relative relationship to the goal, not external reality. If you reset the frame of reference into the real world, then of course he's going to pass that stupid turtle. Before, I briefly discussed the concept of a system cannot be understood within the system, as the reference points of an external world are absolutely critical for definitions. Paradox's are an example of that.

The problem with paradoxes is that they are not always clearly displayed. There are many reasons people create paradoxes but don't present them that way. A paradox parading as an answer is something that allows for only one answer of any question aimed at it. This is the key to many, many social delusions. For example, Marx's whole work really seems to have started with his ultimate goal, and worked it's way backward. In that process, Marx defined people as what was necessary for his system to work. He ignored (casually brushed off, actually) the way people are for what he thought they should be. That's not an unusual social position, and was probably an authorized viewpoint at that historical time. Marx's writings were so complex that it overwhelmed many of those reading it, leaving them with the certainty that if it's so complex that we can't understand, then it must be true. Marx defined an external world and system, which made the dialectic work-unfortunately words, and plans don't create and rule the world, they only more or less describe the world.

A paradox is a focus on the measurement, not what is being measured. When you focus on what is being measure, the paradox goes away. It's the quick jump into the problem, ignoring the setup, which makes the trick work

"That's a good lead for today," Hal added, thoughtfully. "Because today's topic is, what's the purpose? Why are we doing what we are doing? What is the outcome we want to produce? If we don't know what success is, we won't reach it."

"If you don't know where you're going, any road will take you there," Mary pointed out.

General groans came from around the table.

"It's Lucifer's fault," Mary claimed. "I think that pithy sayings are infectious."

"But that's true about any road," Hal declared. "And the question needs to be asked over and over, while a project is underway, not just at the beginning. What isn't true now and what has to be changed to make it true? So, once you define success for this project, is this different than the outcome you were thinking of? Those seminars that Mary went to pounded in the idea that if you start thinking about something, anything in the world, as different than it is now, then the brain starts thinking in random order, coming up with ideas. Collect the ideas, because as you hold an outcome picture, the brain works towards that picture. One idea triggers another idea, freeform towards where we want to go. Then, with a bunch of ideas, the mind starts to organize into patterns. Project planning flows from the outcome you see. Event sequencing, priorities, resources, and constraints all come into order once you see what you want. Until you see that, it's just banging around and frustration."

"I've been trying to accept the chaos outside, as chaos, and not letting it bother me," one of the transferees confided. "If the world is unknowable, then relaxing and taking it in is the necessary precondition. Quite different than if the world is a giant clock, where you're always tense, trying to spot the gears moving."

"I like that," Mary mused. "Ten points to Gryffindor."

"Sssssss," one of the other transferees hissed.

"Once your basic mind is settled, you should just tune and order it, making it calm and stable, undisturbed by events, not deluded by prospects of gain," Lucifer commented, smiling.

Hal made some careful marks on the whiteboard. "That's one for Mary, one for Lucifer. Pithy sayings scores," he pointed out.

"The more relaxed you are, the more powerful you are," Cali proposed. "But relaxation is hard because we're taught to be tense. Tense people are easy to control, and so tension is socially favored. Relaxed people are like cats, and controlling cats is hopeless."

"Herding cats?" Hal questioned. "I've heard of cats."

Cali threw an eraser at him. Hal ducked.

"It's key," Mary argued, ignoring Hal and Cali, "to plan for failure. So you design a system that works when you have the flu. Any plan that assumes complete focus and maximum ability at all times, heck, at any time, is an exercise is wishful thinking. If you need maximum productivity to keep the trains running, then there is a wreck headed your way. A plan and related systems that function when you're flat and barely functioning have a chance of success."

"It has to be Monday," a transferees sighed. "The voices in my head are arguing."

People around her nodded agreement.

"So why don't we just focus on what's important, relax and surf along the top of life?" Hal asked. "Sounds so easy to do. Ideas?"

"Well, because it's not the way people are wired," Aliston replied. "People define themselves by their prisons. We hang on to our cocooned pain because the thought of looking directly at it is unimaginably worse than what we suffer living with the known pain. We get distracted. Example: B'rar rabbit and the tar baby. The more you fight, the more tightly you are bound. "

"Worry loses focus," Cali added. "Worrying is like a man with an arrow in his chest, gasping questions about the man who made the arrow. The problem is the arrow hanging out of you, not who made the damn thing. Ask the wrong question and you die because you never treat the real problem."

"That's one that a clear outcome would help with," Hal agreed, nodding. "Focusing on getting the arrow out would be key there."

"Another problem," one of the transferees mused, "is that people want life to be fair. It isn't, but we pretend to ourselves that it is, deceiving ourselves."

Jesus looked out the window.

"Because we deceive ourselves," the transferee continued, "we don't want to know an outcome because that's facing the unfairness of life, and then we'd have to get up and act despite it."

"True enough," Jesus interjected. "Unstick yourself from our small human stories, and it is hard to make a case that the authorized stories with their trumpeted 'meaning' mean anything. The human wished-world has no power over death, or over the larger universe."

"Our deceptions are not easy to uncover, because each mask we wear has a story," the transferee continued. "'The Presentation of Self in Everyday Life' denied that the masks are simple to discard because there are masks on masks, masks all the way down."

"Like the theory of the universe that had the world on the back of a giant turtle?" Lucifer added. "A nice theory, and then someone asked, well, what's the turtle on? Another turtle, and finally the answer was— hey, it's just turtles all the way down."

"We're crawling along here," Hal observed, dryly. "Coming out of our shells into the sunshine of truth."

There were general groans and head shaking around the table.

"Okay, how about this?" Cali offered. "We don't think about problems about to bite us. We are focused on the now, and so any problems that are not actually chewing on us are in the category 'non-urgent and non-critical'-i.e., ignored. That's a huge problem, because when the problem does start gnawing on us, we have not thought about it. But you can't respond to a problem if you haven't thought about it. To solve a problem, you have to define the problem, figure out what are the possibilities, what are our resources? Acting before thinking, unless you have faced the problem ten times before, isn't going to work. Up to your ass in alligators when you planned to clear the swamp is the classic formulation."

"And if you have faced the problem ten times before and it's still back, then maybe there is more thinking to be done," Mary added. "The solution set seems to be incomplete."

"All this chewing and gnawing is making me hungry," one of the transferees commented. "And we are out of brownies."

"Almost done," Hal advised. "Please stop eying the arm of the person sitting next to you. A quick snack would only ruin your appreciation of the exquisite dinner awaiting us."

"Then there is the worlds favorite way of handing uncertainty" Lucretia cautioned, "which is working on only those problems we knew how to solve. Then it's gold stars and smiles because you won, although you really accomplished nothing. In the meantime, the important but complex and new problems were pushed under the rug. It's easy to have a successful outcome for a problem that's been handled before. First, because it's been done before, and you know the steps, but more importantly, because you know what success is defined as and you can step right inside those boundaries."

"The rug gets some pretty big lumps in it after a while as the avoided problems pile up," Mary observed. "Vacuuming becomes an exercise in grooming a ski hill."

"It isn't just forcing yourself to act," Lucretia continued. "It's worse when you have to explain this new thing to others for their buy-in. Defining a successful outcome for a new group problem? That's really hard, because the people you are trying to persuade have to take some big jumps. First, they have to grasp the problem, using precious thought and time taken away from the other fires they are facing. Once they grasp the problem, they may or may not consider it the problem you do, and they may or may not be right. There's a lot of thrashing about right there. Assuming, as the meeting drags on, that they grasp the idea of the problem, and buy-in that it's (a) as big a problem as, and (b) the same kind of problem, you think it is. Then comes the really big jump: because this is 'new', you can't give the meeting or group or committee that vision of the Grail they seek, i.e., a clear, unambiguous plan on rails towards the distant glowing goal, because the outcome we are after will change as we wade through the swamp of reality. As the outcome changes, you have to pull the tracks up and move them. Not only does that take time, but looks like a type of failure, and no one wants to be tarred with the scent of failure."

"So, you're trying to get this tired group to risk their prestige and thinly spread resources on a possible profit, as they stand at the edge of the precipice, staring at a certain loss if it doesn't go right?" Mary commented. "Been there many times, rarely successfully."

"There is a technique that works," Lucretia admitted, "But it holds the seeds for future failure within it's success. In desperation, when things are going badly, and the group is starting to stampede towards you, the ground shaking from their rumbling and the little birds around you taking flight to safety, you then pull out the full meeting notes that carefully defined War as Peace, Freedom as Slavery, etc., and suddenly, Pow! Things went the way you wanted them to. Moving the goal posts is an act of desperation, because they will be watching for that next time. To do this successfully, you have to keep your project goals hidden, like cards in poker. Thus, each buy-in that you get people to do is a buy-in to a lie. You'd better win at the end, or the herd will run over the top of you. "

"The normal corporate solution," one of the transferees added "Is to get promoted to another division before the wave crashes over your house of cards. Then someone else is standing at the rail as the ship goes down."

"Too true," Hal agreed. "We want that to be our competitors raison d'etre, not ours. That's the 'no-one wants this to happen but each step taken to avoid it brings it closer ' little joke that the structure fairy likes to play on the world."

"The fairies do have a wicked sense of humor," a veterans declared.

"So how to let the fairies have their laughs at someone else's expense? Outcome thinking, before and during the project can win, or at least draw. It also pushes away the FUD factor," Hal contended. "Fear, uncertainty, and doubt overcome us, and if not us, our supervisors. FUD freezes, so if a choice doesn't have to be made, it isn't made. Until the hungry wolf crashes through the door, eyes red, snarling viciously, no change will be made. Beware the triumph of the status quo, because it's the quagmire that is the status quo that is driving us to the brink of change. The wolf at your throat is a FAIL."

"So," Mary concluded, "who takes what away from this meeting? What are the next actions we all have to do? And who has ownership of what actions?"[120]

What they are arguing is that we have to see in the system what is, rather than what we think should be. And in complex systems, it's key to understand that each actor makes decisions as they see best in the context of their choices, as limited by structures, norms, governments and the Good. It isn't really unstoppable unless everyone seeks their goal with their highest level of drive and energy. As a result, all these choices gain force of momentum to run off the tracks. It's rarely a single decision, but the inevitable result of multiple choices that were clearly the best action for an individual but that acts against their interests of everyone involved.

Related to the above is the concept of an externality. This is when someone takes an action, but someone else, without agreeing, pays some or all of the costs of that action. In the complex world we live in, this happens more and more, and is part of the lament of AntiFragile against the world we live in today.

To digress to the big problems, there was a study a number of years ago called the Club of Rome. It was laughed off, because it argued that increasing population would put too much pressure on the available resources, and something was going to have to be done. The most recent update to that study indicated that the factors they calculated are still in process, and actually adhering fairly closely to the projections.

It's the idea of "overshoot and collapse" of the global system that is terrifying. It's argued that technology will save us, and we can certainly hope so. The problem is that as changes to assumptions and parameters are made, other things pop up to offset the technology gains. Try and sell that in a meeting to a group and it's going to be a hard sell. Disaster and problems is lower sales and higher costs, not good for promotion.

Whilst we know the known knows, and known unknowns, we do not know the unknown unknowns. Rumsfeld may have blown the Iraq war, but he was right about the unknown unknowns. He should have listened to himself before he started.

Closing thoughts on systems: we must extract simple problems out of complex systems, but not forget what we have abstracted away. If we have doubts, test with more reality points and see how well our model handles them. A final cheerful thought is:

What a tangled web we weave when first we start to deceive.

Part 5 - Dancing in the Storm

CHAPTER 31. WHAT DO WE DO TOMORROW?

As the old saw says well: every end does not appear together with it's beginning. Herodotus

How to deal with all this? What are our choices? Sitting back, relaxing, letting the river take us where it will? Actually, there's a lot of that in life. Most times, we should just accept those larger forces shaping us, and focus on what we can change.

"Whatever you may dream, fate has other plans in store." Thomas à Kempis wrote five centuries ago. (technically, "Homo proponit, sed Deus disponit")

"There's a divinity that shapes our ends, rough hew them how we will"[121]

Along those lines, Davy Jones said in the "Pirates of the Caribbean", "My fate was set long ago." A comforting thought, but he used it to run his life into a horror even he was terrified of. Rely on a crutch to justify your life and you shouldn't be surprised you're handicapped.

How about this?

"Odin hung crucified on a tree for nine days, pierced by a spear, embracing his suffering and the loss of an eye, in exchange for wisdom. A terrible image, isn't it? And why? Why is embracing life so dangerous, so harsh, that to embrace it you must be driven completely out of your bounded life? Why, when you can live pleasantly, thoughtlessly, the life of a flower in the sun? But once you move past the empty life of the flower, the full embrace of life is a terrifying step. What you sow does not come to life unless it should die, but you must die first before you live again. April, when the seed dies to live, is the cruelest month."[122]

Well, that's cheerful. Maybe being a flower isn't so bad - when the sun is pleasant, the rain is just enough, and the competition for the soil isn't so bad. Any of those change, and the flower is screwed, without alternatives. Hopefully the flower has seeded, and the seeds have more options. 'Grow where you are planted' has some truth to it. But you've got to keep your roots mobile, ready to jump if you have to.

She drew a sloppy circle on the page, studying it. That's what I look for. It's the gestalt that I see, and I don't see outside the lines. No one can see everything all the time. The mind weeds stuff out. How many investment seminars and stock offering meetings have I sat through where everyone around me was so focused on the information on the pages they were given that they didn't ask: what's supposed to be on the page, but isn't? What's the logical extrapolation of the story being presented, which isn't there? The dog that didn't bark, Holmes said. The mind is always happy to weed something out. The dog was sick, it was asleep, out hunting, so it didn't bark. The guard dog, one hundred and forty pounds of vicious malice, didn't bark. The dog didn't bark BECAUSE NO ONE BROKE IN. And we dance on, happy with the story we are telling ourselves.

In life, the missing numbers and information are more important than the carefully prepared words and numbers on the page in front of us, all that carefully arranged flotsam and jetsam given surface relevance. That's why the information is missing. That information is so important to someone that they carefully crafted the smoke and mirrors to hide them. The errors of commission are often easy to spot, holes in the story we expect. It is the errors of omission, outside the story we are reading from, that constantly bedevil us. So, Hal beat me good, spotting what I didn't see."

Ripples can signal the black swans, but not clearly. Like waves, sometimes they combine. You can have forty-foot waves, nasty stuff, and then suddenly a one-hundred-foot wave, which is disaster. Or that one in Alaska with its seventeen hundred-foot wave! That's what I don't think he's allowed for, Lucretia realized, nodding to herself. I found an amplified event, and positive feedback goes big fast. I don't think he really expects the size of what's going to happen. She put down her pen with a sigh and shrugged her shoulders. I've done my job. Given an assignment, done the work. Obeyed orders. Orders from people who betrayed me before, and certainly are doing it again."[123]

One of the annoying things about life problems is that meaning well doesn't work. Kindergarten was wrong about so many things.

"It serves us right, in a way," Jesus admitted. "We meant well for them and he meant for them to serve him well. He won because we pretended to see what they were and denied what they are."

"Really, all their ethics and philosophies are rooted in the smell and the visual tests," Mary muttered, disgusted. "Pretty/perfumed things are good, messy/stinky things are bad, and so they ignore what's really going on out there."

"And we tried to work with that, using the well-meant lie, and it's been our downfall," Lucifer declared. "Well-meant lies just confuse people, which we actually planned on. We hoped confusion would lead to understanding, but it didn't because they think only in set stories. The stories are small, all bordered and bright edges, only clear against the dark backgrounds. The light-filled symbols in the stories froze into grey concrete weights. The stories became forts to hide in from understanding the world. Stories bonded them into groups, and became their masks in the social world. So the harder you push on the stories, the tighter they hold onto them. Paul understood his prey far better than we, who thought we were the hunters."

"Fishers," Jesus corrected. "Technically."

"We tried the bigger stories, but they couldn't grasp the full complexity," Lucifer continued. "So we lied, meaning well. Intending that the next story would correct the first one, and so on. We thought we could coax them, move them gradually to the bigger stories, by little stories that weren't quite true but had elements of the truth. We treated them like children, trying to keep them alive to adulthood, but they never took the next big step, to challenge, question, and rebel, and then rebuild the stories. Unfortunately, a single contradiction corrupts and allows falsehoods to proliferate. The stories became falsehoods built upon falsehoods. Well meant, but not working."[124]

MAKING CHOICES UNDER UNCERTAINTY

The following rambles along, ruminating about the problems of making decisions under conditions of uncertainty.

All of us have to make decisions constantly. Making 'correct' decisions is self evidently critical. Decisions are linked, so that a correct decision in a given situation may result in the wrong decision several choices hence. Less commonly, a mistake at step 3 turns into the correct choice in step 10. So you have to keep in mind the future, and options, while making decisions.

Example: if you are a 'buggy whip' maker, you are unemployable. If you are a 'leather worker', you have a future. The ideal choice recognizes the present factors, but leaves growth for the future. Like tinker toys, you always want to leave additional holes to grow in new directions. Irrevocable actions, while often socially praised, as you stand there proud and defiant, are generally bad choices.

Luck, both good and bad, has to be recognized as possibilities. Work hard, but get sick, and your goals will not be reached. But usually there is more to the story. I often see people who work with their bodies: carpenters, plumbers, other construction people, who are out of shape, and smoke. Those factors multiply the likelihood of their eventual sicknesses that will result in loss of work, perhaps loss of livelihood down the road. So if you adopt a self-destructive practice, which eventually results in economic or other loss, is that really bad luck? Technically, not, although the final blow certainly feels like bad luck.

That leads to the next issue. A regular review of our goals is critical, first to monitor progress on reaching the goals, but secondly, and more importantly, to wonder about what our goals really are. For many reasons: we did (do) as we were told, we act against what we are told, we do something that we enjoyed once but didn't analyze why we enjoyed it, swimming through all of the flotsam and jetsam that life throws at us we usually find that what we thought were our goals may not be our goals at all. We may have chosen an avenue based on a misperception of what was required to do that choice. Or our work may change, such that what we really enjoyed/were good at, changed also. And time and maturity makes a huge difference that simply cannot be anticipated. As you grow into something new, goals change as the years and life events go by. Setting your life in concrete and refusing to change is crafting and feathering your personal hell.

Part of life is simply climbing from event to event, like Tarzan grasping a succession of vines as he swings through the trees. After a while, you are somewhere else than when you started. There are always compromises and changes in perspective, and after some time any original goal is compromised past recognition. Compromises, made at least partially to reach the goal that is now not attainable, stop making any sense. This isn't the exception, it is the rule, because you are a different person than you started out as, and goals have to change as you change. Refusal to change goals is the problem, not the solution. When this hits in mid life, it is called (duh) a mid-life crisis. It's signaled by your emotions turning on you, as they should. We've talked about near misses and close calls before, and when you ignore those, grasping for that stale goal, eventually the real problem will emerge, annoyed.

This is not a call to make dramatic changes in your life. Dramatic changes stand a low probability of success, simply because you often are changing to something that you do not know. Dramatic changes tend to be reactions to existing conditions. If the existing condition is driving you crazy, there is no guarantee that the opposite of the existing condition will not also drive you crazy. It may well be that both the existing condition and it's linked opposite will drive you crazy, and you need to look outside where you are before you react. No, this is a plea to notice the little things and react to them.

So, now that you are adjusting goals and plans to changes, how to act? It's simple, conceptually. Determine what you want to do. Assess the steps needed to get there. Determine the time line for the steps. Setup a monitoring system to check your progress, and provide feedback on problems. All of the elements of 'happy stories' covered much earlier in the book.

Making new choices is like making financial projections for a new business. The less information you have, the more important projections are. Why, since the projections are by definition speculative? Because random guesses narrowing down the possibilities are the only way to carve out the broad parameters. Financial projections are easier because they are numbers, easy to add and subtract. If your new, proposed business requires 300 customers buying $1000 per day ($300,000 gross sales) and your proposed store is only 100 square feet large ($3000 per square foot in sales each day) and you are going to sell legal items for sale, a quick calculation shows that this is probably not going to work, at least selling milk.

If, on the other hand, you have $5,000 in capital, your monthly costs are $300, and you only have to sell $10 to an average customer, you are in the range of one person per day. At the worst, you should cover your costs. From that range of choices, you then do market research and product analysis to see whether you will sell one per day, or fifty per day, and go from there.

Having done the financial calculations, you then have to measure your gut reactions. If the gut doesn't like it, even if the numbers seem to work out, it will be a failure.

It's a good idea to every so often simply write down all of the possibilities you see at a given time in random order. Daily writing is an incredibly powerful tool, as the mind really treats things written down as something vastly different from random thoughts. Experiment with possibilities/choices and new choices will pop up. Work on those for some time (always sleep on problems) and choices will align into some clear categories. Sometimes everything in life is just hunky-dory, so you can chug along, and sometimes the near misses start popping up on the radar.

Decisions have second and third order consequences. Let's pick on furniture purchases. There is the cost of the furniture, X. Then there is the implicit cost of the house space around the furniture, which is a big number not usually calculated. Another big cost, difficult to calculate, is why you are buying the furniture-what needs is it supposed to fill? Children's play area, formal display of power and wealth, perhaps a comfortable refuge from the world are all possibilities, and the costs differ dramatically. Hint-a formal display of power and wealth is far more expensive than just the furniture, because there is a lot of house that isn't used needed to wrap around that furniture.

One buys furniture for several reasons. The easy one, to match your existing life style, has limited consequences. The kids sofa is trashed, you replace it, same size and same style. The real hidden consequences are where you buy something that is a 'new you' or a step in that direction. A modern sofa, huge and spread out, dropped in your small apartment. Or a traditional chesterfield leather sofa dropped into your sleek modern apartment. You are recognizing that a change is brewing, and in a way forcing bigger changes.

Where new furniture may not fit (in an interior decorating sense) or in a physical sense, very few of us can live with a bad fit. It grates on you every day. So you start looking for a new house/apartment, which will hold the furniture or be a better decorating fit. When you consider the costs of moving, house sale, remodeling/repair of the old and new houses, plus people usually move to a larger house, you can easily run a $100,000 purchase, stemming in a direct line from the purchase of the furniture. The final snicker of the wishing fairy is that the furniture really doesn't fit in the new house, so it is then replaced.

There was a funny short story, which I have searched for in vain again, in which a happy bachelor was given a new, elegant robe. It was exquisite, and he loved it, but gradually he had to replace all of his furnishings to match the new concept. That was an expensive gift he received!

The key to life is easy to say, but hard to execute. Ignoring metaphysical issues, it is to balance off life experiences with a concern for the future. I.e., do what you want in life, leaving enough to pay for your old age. This is difficult, because you don't know how much your old age will cost, what, if anything, the government will pay, and how long you will live. Spending everything on today is foolish, because buried in that purchase mania there is usually a desire to avoid something in your present life, and the purchase mania just makes it worse. On the other hand, you will spend a lot less in your old age than you now imagine. Sadly, between lack of energy and gradually weakening health, people stop travelling even if they have money, and stop buying things because they are comfortable with what they have now. That's why the financial projections that investment advisors run are usually nonsense, because they don't factor in the new person and the lower costs. That's not to say that it wouldn't be nice to have a home on the beach and servants, but it is to say they are not absolutely necessary.

All you can to in life is play the percentages. If you are pursuing a goal, you should purse the steps in line with that goal. If you do the things that bring you closer to the goal, you are more likely to reach the goal. But it's a paper rock scissors world, options and constraints changing with each calculation.

Most of us want to be wealthy, and many decide to seek this through investment. The usual plan is to a Wall Street or other investment house. You would read the financial papers, ask questions about every business you see, and live and breath finance and business. This is essentially the pattern that Peter Lynch, an extraordinarily successful money manager, articulated in his book. But he seemed to love that type of work. There were many failures, many years before he reached the level of financial resources that he sought. If you hate doing those things, then don't try and be wealthy through investments. All the money you make, unless you are exceptionally lucky, will never buy back the time and the experiences that you lost by doing something that you hate.

There are two ways to be wealthy in a financial sense. This is not new. The old English statement still applies: Income 20 lb a year, expense 19 lb, result happiness. Income 20 lb a year, expense 21 lb, result misery. In reality, the wealthy in your town are going to be successful shop-owners, farmers and small real estate developers, who usually live low and let the assets pile up.

The world, for better or worse, seems to demand we run as fast as we can just to keep up. It's like the Red Queen in "Alice in Wonderland", who coolly advised that you have to run twice as fast to get anywhere. Lots of reasons are advanced for this, and what you believe depends on your political agenda and philosophical beliefs. Commonly, the reasons center around someone doing something to make it this way-it is 'someone's' fault or choice.

The reality is pressure is caused by the vast number of people in today's world. We have a lot of people fighting for limited resources, and that's a 'run faster' world.

I like to look at my daughter's hamster as a refreshing adjustment to reality. If you don't have a hamster, they are quite a nice little animal. They are neat and tidy, and reasonably friendly. Hamsters are like robots in some ways. There are clear priorities: food is an obsession the entire time they are awake. They prowl, explore. When they find food, they bring it back to store it, and then look for more food. Building a nest, storing food keeps them totally absorbed. When they are not doing either of those, they sleep.

You can trust a hamster to eat, sleep, and work on it's nest. You can also trust it to try and escape at any opportunity. You know that a hamster in the wild is a quick morsel for a range of predators. The hamster doesn't think for a moment about that, but focuses on escape.

As long as you trust a hamster to do those things, you will be repaid for your trust. But if you expect a hamster to make the beds each day, you will be bitterly disappointed each and every day. Trust is recognizing reality. If you trust people to listen to themselves first, you will live a long and comfortable life. If you trust people to do what you think they should, your life will be bitter and unpleasant for all of your days.

HOW TO ASSESS & FILL IN THE OVERLAPS

How do we know what we think is overlapping? How to test, and how to develop further? This is a great little poem, old and out of style, but it's still true.

"I Keep Six Honest Serving Men ..."
I keep six honest serving-men
(They taught me all I knew);
Their names are What and Why and When
And How and Where and Who.
I send them over land and sea,
I send them east and west;
But after they have worked for me,
I give them all a rest.
I let them rest from nine till five,
For I am busy then,
As well as breakfast, lunch, and tea,
For they are hungry men.
But different folk have different views;

I know a person small-
She keeps ten million serving-men,
Who get no rest at all!
She sends'em abroad on her own affairs,
From the second she opens her eyes-
One million Hows, two million Wheres,
And seven million Whys!"
The Elephant's Child

Pull out Figure 1, rough out the circles, and start filling in the overlaps using the magic words.

DAVID ALLEN'S NATURAL PLANNING MODEL.

David Allen developed a planning method that he calls the "Natural Planning Method"©. It's a wonderful method for simple and moderately complicated problems.

"NATURAL PLANNING MODEL®

1. Purpose/Guiding Principles

• Why is this being done? What would "on purpose" really mean?

• What are the key standards to hold in making decisions and acting on this project? What rules do we play by?

• The purpose and principles are the guiding criteria for making decisions on the project.

2. Mission/Vision/Goal/Successful Outcome

• What would it be like if it were totally successful? How would I know?

• What would that success look or feel like for each of the parties with an interest?

3. Brainstorming

• What are all the things that occur to me about this? What is the current reality? What do I know? What do I not know? What ought I consider? What haven't I considered? etc. (see Project Planning Trigger List).

• Be complete, open, nonjudgmental, and resist critical analysis.

• View from all sides.

4. Organizing

• Identify components (sub-projects), sequences, and/or priorities.

• What needs to happen to make the whole thing happen?

• Create outlines, bulleted lists, or organizing charts, as needed for review and control.

5. Next Actions

• Determine next actions on current independent components. (What should be done next, and who will do it?)

• If more planning is required, determine the next action to get that to happen. Shift the level of focus on the project as follows if needed:

If your project needs more clarity, raise the level of your focus.

If your project needs more to be happening, lower the level of your focus.

How much planning is required? If the project is off your mind, planning is sufficient. If it's still on your mind, then more is needed."[125]

I cannot recommend too highly his books and his methods for actually 'getting things done' each day in the messy world we live in. His books are truly life changers! They are not the traditionally inspirational (a set of nominally uplifting words strung together into meaningless sentences) or spiritual (a different species of uplifting words), but are a mass of effective tricks and toys to handle life as it comes at you.

Interestingly, the Natural Planning method is quite effective with complex projects. Complex projects, generally, are insolvable. David Allen's planning model is effective because it looks again and again at success, and that's the key driver for your assumptions. Complex projects twist and turn assumptions, and if you're looking at success, you'll see it the 'success goal' changing and adjust.

GTD doesn't work as well where you have an extremely fluid situation, such as like maneuver warfare, for example. Now, David would probably argue with that, saying that thinking is essential before action, and he's right. But in a classic fluid situation, you can only think so far ahead because there are too many variables. The OODA (observe, orient, decide and act) cycle works in a really rapidly changing (bullets) world.

This sounds trivial, but GTD demands you use positive visualizations. It's not trivial. The mind runs toward what it sees, whether positive or negative. So if you want to accomplish something, use a positive visualization, and if you want to avoid something, use a positive visualization, because a negative visualization will only draw you towards what you fear.

If you do nothing else, and if you get nothing else out of this book remember: You need to start with the critical question: What is success? What will it look like when I am done?

And always define a game you can win! David points out that if you don't think you will win, you won't work at the game, because your mind is no fool, even if your social self is. Another practical aspect is to plan for failure. Design a system that works when you have the flu. Any plan that assumes complete focus and maximum ability at all times, heck, at any time, is an exercise is wishful thinking. If you need maximum productivity to keep the trains running, then there is a wreck scheduled for the next Thursday. A plan and related systems that function when you're flat and barely functioning have a chance of success.

David says something really interesting:

> "Let's get something really clear: success doesn't come from getting organized—it comes from following your heart. Or your intuition. Or the seat of your pants. Or your gut. (Pick the words you like or that you're not allergic to.) Getting organized (a la GTD) won't in itself solve the bigger issues and creative challenges that we all face from time to time. What it will do is help clear the decks internally, and create a more open space within which to do the real knowledge work— making the decisions about allocation of resources to make things happen that won't happen by themselves."[126]

One's goal should be a mind like water. At rest, aware of the world around it. When a pebble is thrown into the water, the water responds, then calms. The water doesn't tense, it responds and moves on.

DANCE STEPS

Dance steps are ideas for particular things to focus on. There are lots of ideas in this section, ideas hitting the big ideas from different angles.

How does a gambler (one who actually makes money!) look at the world? The successful gambler doesn't have a big secret. Instead, he has a thousand little secrets, information that he lays out, trying to solve a puzzle that changes all the time. He's watching for patterns, but most patterns are suckers bets, patterns that are purely change – or at least not caused by the reasons important to the gambler.

Successful gamblers do not model a future with guaranteed winning bets, absolutely correct theories, and exact details that can be estimated beforehand. That's what the internet sells, pretty illusions for a sucker, the sweetly singing sirens of our downfalls. Successful gamblers view a probabilistic future, seeing speckles of possibilities, flickering upward and downward with every new holt of information. When their estimates of these probabilities diverge by a what they think is a sufficient margin from the odds on offer, they may place a bet. That's completely poking the world, testing the feedback, and changing plans on the spot.

Amarillo Slim, a poker player said:

> *"Play the players, not the cards, he would say. Watch them from the minute you sit down. Play fast in a slow game, slow in a fast one. Never get out when you're winning. Look for the sucker and, if you can't see one, get up and leave, because the sucker is you."*[127]

That's acting, not over-planning. You do something and see what happens, in the context of what yours goals and visions are. You are testing constantly and testing small things, not waiting to test only big critical things in process. It's applied trial and error, constantly looking, pro-actively testing and checking.

When you do jump, the concept is 'Schwerpunkt,' which means to attack where all your power can go against one point, 'a torrent of boulders against eggs,' or something like that. You want to exploit the power law, which means that you get nonlinear positive results, not just additive. In other works, too often in daily life, we are sold additive results – put in 1 and get 2 – maybe 3 if lucky! But too often we are sold stuff with power negative downsides – i.e., you lose 20 if things go wrong, it's just in the small print.

If you are going to act (not simply be a participant, taking bets others define for you) you have to figure out their strengths, technically known as surfaces, and their weaknesses, i.e., their gaps, then we can plan an attack.

"Maneuver warfare is a fancy term for putting our strengths into their weaknesses. Like a boot into a soft spot. To do that, we have to figure out how to GENERATE confusion and disorder to attack them. They have to think we are attacking somewhere else than our real target. They have to wonder if we are running, hiding or just trembling in the dark. See, we, ideally, want them on the horns of a dilemma. When they look as us, they have to see a problem with no solution, all contradictory information pointing to inconsistent choices."[128]

In planning, it's essential to accept confusion and disorder, because that is the way events happen in the real world.

I was at a hacker conference, and they talked about the idea of the 'kill chain', which I thought was a really great concept. It's used in the military, and it's obviously what has to be done to kill someone. We all, from watching movies, have some idea. If you want to shoot someone, you have to have a gun and bullets; you have to be a certain distance from the people, you have to know how to use a weapon, and the ability required varies greatly. If you are shooting someone from one foot away, that's one thing. Shooting someone from two hundred yards away, that is a completely different set of abilities.

You of course have to emotionally be able to shoot someone. An army has to consider all the logistics in the kill chain. Food, other supplies, clothing, it is an incredibly complex process to get a squad, not to say a regiment, in position to kill. And then there is tying that chain into another chain, so that the killing goes on and on. That's the way war is, another view on why no battle plan survives the first contact with the enemy.

So you don't want to kill people? The kill chain is the best defense process you can use to protect yourself, because if you think of someone doing something to you that you don't want, what has to happen for them to be able to do that undesired thing?

This is a really powerful tool for any plan you are working on. For X to happen, what's the train of events and supplies needed to get to that position, and the other chains that set of actions ties into? At the hacker conference, they used the idea on the context of attacks on a computer network system-what had to be done to get into the position that they wanted to be in, which was inside someone else's computer with full administrative permissions. Backing into the chain, you clearly see that the enemy has to take certain required steps. If you are watching for those steps, those give off warnings that can be detected. It gives you a way of anticipating problems, not just reacting.

Obviously, the Boyd process is a dance step, laying out the key idea that you think, decide, act and test over and over. The David Allen approach, looking at what the goal is, puts the mind in the correct frame to move forward.

You can never, and I mean never, go wrong if you always try to maintain a situation where you have the maximum positive solutions. Not just one positive solution, which you grasp closely, but a preferred solution, alternative solutions, and backups, for a changing world.

Here's a tool:

"Let's create the question map to go fishing in unknown territory. I put a topic in a center circle and then generate questions about that topic. Then I create "know" and "need to know" lists. What is it I know, and what is it I need to know? Then question the "I know" maps. He played with the lines on the paper for a while, linking things, and then sat back, thinking."[129]

Where the world is changing, who defines a new structure? How does doing the next step and the next step lead to a new structure? When you see outside, what do you do next?

Here is a different point of view, something that we forget:

"To attain knowledge, add things every day. To attain wisdom, subtract things every day," it said, capsulizing teachings of Lao Tzu. "Profit comes from what is there, usefulness from what is not there."

It dawned on me that I'd been looking at my problem in the wrong way. As is natural and intuitive, I had been looking at what to do, rather than what *not* to do. But as soon as I shifted my perspective, I was able to complete the project successfully.

I discovered an essay by the management educator Jim Collins, in which he confirmed the ancient philosophy: "A great piece of art is composed not just of what is in the final piece, but equally important, what is not. It is the discipline to discard what does not fit — to cut out what might have already cost days or even years of effort — that distinguishes the truly exceptional artist and marks the ideal piece of work, be it a symphony, a novel, a painting, a company or, most important of all, a life."

In reading several articles in scientific literature, I discovered that subtraction lights up a brain scan differently than addition does, because it uses different circuitry. In fact, accident victims suffering brain injuries often lose their ability to both add and subtract, retaining only one of the two. Subtraction is literally a different way of thinking.

THINK about what you could do — or rather not do — in your own life that would put these principles into play. There are two easy ways to begin subtracting things every day:

First, create a "not to do" list to accompany your to-do list. Give careful thought to prioritizing your goals, projects and tasks, then eliminate the bottom 20 percent of the list — forever.

Second, ask those who matter to you most — clients, colleagues, family members and friends — what they would like you to stop doing. Warning: you may be surprised at just how long the list is.

The lesson I've learned from my pursuit of less is powerful in its simplicity: when you remove just the right things in just the right way, something good happens."[130] (Matthew E. May is the author of "The Laws of Subtraction: 6 Simple Rules for Winning in the Age of Excess Everything.)

Subtracting lets you focus down on what you want to do.

Part 4. Maneuver Warfare & Feedback.
The military has no constant form,
just as water has no constant shape
adapt as you face the enemy,
without letting them know beforehand
what you are going to do.[131]

Chapter 1: "ON ASSESSMENTS"

Hackers think about systems. They think about whether they have to just get past one layer or whether there are multiple layers involved, with multiple checks that tie the layers together. They think about whether there are multiple checkpoints, or simply one to be beaten. You have to contextualize vulnerabilities–which is a fancy way of saying you have to think about where you are weak and how people can get to those spots. If you have a checkpoint, what happens if it is turned off? Say the firewall is turned off for an upgrade, what reminds someone to turn it back on? Are there multiple checks on the firewall, or are you so comfortable with the protection that there is only one thing holding it in place? As systems change, do the protections change also? Or are we well protected for last year's problems and wide open for tomorrows?

Chapter 32. Anomalies are the Answer

This book argues that anomalies are the whole trick to catching our false views of the world and the social fantasies of the world.

Why?

We deny anomalies because we must see and feel ourselves in control, both of the world and ourselves. Where we are driven from control, we react with madness and madness then creates it's own twisted world to control. Madness is a dark and distorted mirror in which we see our needs reflected back as nightmares. Emotionally, constantly not being in control, to act accepting our lack of control is a difficult dance. We can pretend a 'we don't control' but it turns into a proof of our control that we can show our non-control. We're just not made to see the world as events without causes, relationships or values that we don't control. We can still act effectively as long as we work with our limitations, not against them.

The song "Scarborough Fair" is disturbing because it is two songs at once, and the underlying song is far more serious than the top melody. We are gliding along on the top melody, and the bottom song shakes our control, our consistency. It's a far more powerful song because that mixed message disturbs us.

How to deal with the world then? We must hone and sharpen our stories and our understanding, and as we expand our stories, listen and see where they are not working. That failure, that course correction process, will ideally lead us to a deeper understanding, while, at a minimum, keeping us out of the quicksand.

> "Instead of a discussion of risk (which is both predictive and sissy) I advocate the notion of fragility, which is not predictive-and, unlike risk, has an interesting word that can describe its functional opposite, the non-sissy concept of antifragility. To measure antifragility, there is a philosopher's-stone-like recipe using a compact and simplified rule that allows us to identify it across domains, from health to the construction of societies. We have been unconsciously exploiting antifragility in practical life and, consciously, rejecting it-particularly in intellectual life."[132]

Perhaps I should quit here, while you are still excited about the idea. But what fun would that be? There are a lot of interesting details and ideas on anomalies to explore. So lets present a thesis: that seeking feedback on anomalies is more effective than seeking feedback on the expected results. What does that mean? It means that we are looking for failures, not successes.

We've covered, in more depth that the reader wanted, why we fail, and one of the primarily reasons is that we need success so much that we cheat. We see what we want, we collect confirming evidence, we look away from odd results, brushing them off as accidents, the near misses confirming the truth of our plan, and/or unrelated random events.

So, what is an anomaly? Normal is the story you tell yourself, or are told. An anomaly is an event from a different story. Something is supposed to go 'boop' and it goes 'poob' – or maybe 'obop'. Some of the story is there, but it isn't quite right. More worrisome is where it goes 'thunk', which is completely outside the authorized story but there is a specious excuse to cover up. Such as, oh, every 13th 'boop' is a 'thunk', we knew that. So move along, move along, there's nothing to see here.

Let's set our minds to watching for little failures and then ask why they occur. This is Sun Tzu's wisdom. Let's be, at least to ourselves, the wise man who does not have a reputation for skill but who is actually skillful. In this case, we are seeking, at least in the world's eye, to avoiding a reputation for mistakes by catching our mistakes before others know of them. If you have to share your mistakes, find a trustworthy bartender in a noisy bar who wouldn't hear half of what you're saying. Better yet, a Freudian psychiatrist, who won't respond and so you can talk to yourself in a socially allowed setting that is legally protected.

How do we watch for the failures? Remember, watching for failures in our mind are more fun than seeing them as they unfold before us in the real world. We think of something we want to do (or something we have to do) and we determine a goal. From the goal, we determine steps, and we take steps, watching the reactions. We are watching, not for what's going right (our usual approach) but what's going wrong. We need to tie our sense of competence to our ability to catch the surprises, not paper over them. It's quite a mental adjustment, but it can be done. It's different from collecting our failures as an alibi to present to the world, which is pitiful, actually.

If we are looking for help in the surprises, then we will think about how to spot them. What are we perceiving, what are we avoiding? What is the reporting and measuring hiding as much as it's revealing? We know how we hide and conceal; yet we accept what others provide with minimal thought. What are we trying to collect, and how are we tricking ourselves in our collecting process? Make a test design as we want, but test the design. Will it catch the worst case? Run the test, and what does it really say? Does it answer our question, and what are the inevitable little oddities? Often they mean nothing, but too often they are the truth being brushed off as experimental error.

Here's an idea that is heresy: if people must use stories that don't make any sense, why not make money off their stories? It's an interesting ethical issue, which is explored in the next chapter. If you implant a false idea in them, and exploit that, there's an ethical violation there under most sets of ethics. We will not ask whether most ethical rules are a set of false ideas, but there's a topic to think about in the quiet of the night. Implanting a false idea may not be a violation of the real world rules, which are harsher than human rules, but certainly a violation of the human rules. But if 'other's insist on doing something that is just god-awful stupid, then why should you have to stand in front of the stampede and be crushed trying to make them see the light? Weapon's manufacturers do not stop making weapons because the weapons would kill someone, as an example.

If they are throwing money away to humor their stories, there's nothing wrong with your collecting their money as it's thrown to the ground. Certainly that's the ground rule for investment bankers, and if it's good enough for them, with their New York, London and Aspen homes, it's good enough for you. That is, although I suspect the author would deny it, the message of "The Black Swan". His investment strategy of losing a little to win big occasionally is exactly that picking up the dollars that the foolish are throwing away. Now, he did take the step of telling them about their foolishness, after he made a considerable amount of money, so he has complied with all legal, ethical and moral rules out there. The joy of telling the masses about their errors is that they will not pay attention, and so the anomaly exploiter has money, social standing and ethical backing when it's all done. That's generally considered 'game, set, match' in life.

What an anomaly tells you is legal asymmetric information. This is information that you know, that other's do not, and which you can make a profit on. That's a lot different from illegal asymmetric information, which is an invitation to closer discourse with the guardians of the Right. Remember, a successful crime (1) doesn't look like a crime, and (2) is done completely and forever by yourself, and yourself alone. No co-conspirators and/or witnesses. It's obvious that the usual insider trading scheme, and its variations, fails on both of those criteria. Any jury of lunkheads dredged out of their homes can grasp that your pocketing $50,000,000 on a quick trade because you knew financial results two days before others is a crime (or should be a crime, because they didn't get a piece) and all the people you plotted with, who solemnly swore secrecy forever, will race to cut the best deal with the prosecutors.

The power of legal asymmetric information was shown by a study of the investment results Senator's had. Utilizing public information, abet buried in incomprehensible bills, their return on investment was considerably higher than the average.

Look at Figure 1 again. Because the overlaps between the various worlds are so limited, anomalies are everywhere. That entire social world that doesn't overlap the real world is a nest of untested/untestable ideas/hypothesis about the real world and people that are socially, and often legally, imposed. All of that part of the circle of the self that doesn't overlap the real world and/or the social world is the same kind of free floating chunks of untested but firmly believed ideas and truths about the world that people act on everyday. They are throwing their money and lives into pursuits and causes that will fail. Perhaps if you make a profit off them, they will notice and change their ways. Perhaps not, but you'll still have some money. Cynical? Yes, but the people preaching you shouldn't make money off their stupidity are the people preaching the stupidity. Are you going to take their advice?

Let's get back to finding anomalies. We know that we want to know what we want, not what we think may happen. Why not? There are a lot of possibilities out there, but only a few things we want to happen to us. To reach what we want, our job is to think of, and then do, the right things at the right times and in the right way. Now, there's a grammatically correct sentence that that is probably impossible to execute in reality! But it's a guide, a touchstone.

Where it's possible to reach what we want, there may be rules for accomplishing our task, but the rules are local. A local rule is dictated by specific circumstances. Driving an auto is all local rules, for example. Because the rules are local, subject to specific events, there are a great many rules. When there are many rules but they are unclear, then out of frustration, people often turn what they perceive as rules into rituals, because then you are doing something. That's a bad plan, because the social ritual doesn't control the world.

We've all seen the pictures of the Wright brothers flying in that very strange first flying machine. They succeeded, where others had failed, partly because they realized that flight was not a single puzzle that could be solved by simple trial and error. Flight, like most of life, is a set of puzzles that are often not part of the same big puzzle. Puzzles can be like Russian dolls, solve one and another appears, or they can be separate problems which are not linked. Worst is when they are separate sets of Russian dolls!

Where problems are interlocked, you have to systematically think about the problems. If you run a single test, and the result is shaped by the interactions of several interrelated puzzles, and you are thinking that you have only one puzzle at work here, your test results are going to be nonsense. You will get one result one time, and a different result from what looks like the same test. You have to understand the dynamics of the underlying system. Continued garbage test results is an anomaly, by the way, that tells you something is wrong with the model, but that requires thought and time, so people brush it away, or ritualize the behavior. Ritual behavior is divorced, as I've said before, from the real world, and so if 2 or 3 of you lined up together agree on the ritual, then who cares what the real world does? Fail. The real world does care, and it wins 3 out of 3 falls.

The problem with systematic thought about multiple problems is that you have to hold in mind two or even three different models that are compatible with the premises. That hurts to even think about it, and individuals differ in this ability. We all have co-workers who if they had to tie their shoes in the morning would never get to work, so it is fortunate that slip on shoes were invented. This may explain relationships between reasoning ability and intelligence tests. When the going gets tough, and we can't cope with multiple mental models, we are going to err.

To act, we must think that we are drawing a valid conclusion, but if there are multiple models in action and we have based our actions on one model, the problem is obvious. We will overlook many things, including evidence that disputes or denies our conclusion(s). Life is short, and we generally use intuitive thinking, so we often depend on a single mental model. It may, and often is, the wrong one. That's fine! We're going to be wrong most of the time, and it's anomalies that show us the way to the light. It's not fine if we deny and ignore. As this book says many times, if nothing else, it's recognizing where you have drifted from ordinary life decisions into non-ordinary decisions that is a critical point at which to start evaluating your thinking more carefully.

You want to seek-deliberately seek-anomalies that destroy/void your plan. Anomalies are generally detested on sight, because they are something in a story that isn't working. So it's additional work or worse because the world is failing to cooperate. We're standing there, and people are looking at us, and we're saying to the world, 'Look, world, I'm laying out the rules here, and you're not getting it, so we're going to ignore this discrepancy and move on with how it should be.' That's not always a bad strategy. Sometimes the data is wrong, sometimes the data is an aberration that means nothing, and sometimes the plan is working in a way we didn't expect but will end up in the same place. But most of the time it is a bad strategy. MOST business failures, such as engineering disasters, product malfunctions, and public relations explosions give ample warning. The inevitable post-mortem report grimly lays out the many near misses, brushes with disaster and close calls that, had it not been for chance, would have been worse. The Fairies, having a sense of humor, usually saves the worst case for when things actually blow up.

People, to be kind, often misinterpret these warning signs because they are blinded by mental biases. To be unkind, they misinterpret, that is, when they can't just hide, deny or blame them on someone else. Near misses, where they have to be confronted, are seen as an indication that systems are working well: look, if it weren't for the system, there would have been a disaster ....

FINDING ANOMALIES

The basic idea is just test events against the story, over and over.

Here is an easy one: if someone is selling you something, and in the course of that sale they are talking, showing you pictures, etc., and they then stop, they think they have closed. Only a fool sells past the close. Did you realize you'd made a decision? It's the same where people stop giving you feedback. They now want you to do something. Do you realize it? Is it what you want to do? What story are they listening to, and what story are you listening to?

Another simple trick to help catch anomalies is called 'the model method'. Let's suppose there is a problem with your computer (a fantasy is where you suppose there isn't). The problem is either in the computer or the scanner. Draw a line down the middle of a piece of paper and put 'computer' at the head of one column and 'scanner' at the head of the other. Then, as you receive further information, add it to the relevant column or columns. You add information to the columns and eventually you have accumulated enough to make some decisions, which you test.

The advantage of writing the information down is multiple: first, you don't rely on keeping things in memory, which blocks finding new solutions; secondly, writing the information down actually changes the way that your mind processes the information; and most importantly, by pulling out the piece of paper and setting up the problem structure, your mind recognizes that this really is a problem that you have to think about, not something to use slop on. It's that seeing it is a problem that is half of the battle.

Let's say that we have what we think are some facts. We then combine and play with the facts, and infer something about the future from the facts. We usually make some assumptions, buried very deep in our thought patterns, about what is truth and what is false. Those assumptions then apply to the truth or falsity of an assertion, given the falsity of another assertion. If X is true and Y is true, then Z is true. That's not always true, because there are many factors to the relationships between assertions. There are many factors in the way that we fudge assertions to make them fit together.

Failing to think about how things can be false is part of our wiring. It seems to go back to the need for control. If we have a 'fact' that is true and another 'fact' that is true, then add them together and you have a big truth, not a falsehood. Two wrongs don't make a right, but maybe they do? That's disturbing and takes time and thought.

The following is an absolutely key concept for catching anomalies. Peripheral signals (those little flickers out of the corner of your eye) are difficult to capture, partly because they are easy to ignore. They are, actually, the vital early warning signs of both threats and opportunities. Our ancestors knew the difference between the tall grass blowing in the wind, and the tall grass rustling as the lions creep towards us. The ancestors who didn't notice are 'negative evidence', you might say. In today's world, the tall grass a distant memory; most of us are 'passive scanners' of our environment. We solve the problem we in front of us, we wait for information to reach us, and deal with the problem as it arrives.

You've probably guessed the danger in passive scanning. It's too easy to miss those unexpected and unfamiliar weak signals on the periphery. All that blurry zone at the edge of our vision, when we are having a hard enough time trying to figure out what we are staring right at. Hint: by the time the lion is right in front of us, it's a bit late. We will be dinner, not having dinner. Death and transfiguration, as Wagner would say.

Active scanning is the goal. Active scanning is looking for the unexpected, the new. You can start active scanning by asking yourself questions about problems, and active scanning is driven by your curiosity. Active scanner catches surprises. Passive scanning catches messes.

"INFORMATION OVERLOAD

There's too much stuff to track, Hal thought, staring dejectedly at the piles of paper taking over his office. Worse, the e-mails are stacking up faster than I can review and toss them. He gave up and idly watched the number of unread e-mails increase by the minute. It's like playing Whack-A-Mole, but my hammer broke.

He started pacing. The world is too complex to monitor everything, clearly. A pile of paper shoved on a corner desk decided to slowly cascade down to the floor. "Thank you," he told the pile on the floor, "for accenting my point." And, I only see what I'm looking for anyhow. So the important stuff, the stuff I should be thinking about, should be watching for, is hiding from me in plain sight. By the time it's in the newspapers, it's too late. So how to see that little stuff before it gets big?

Driving in fog and rain has always called for caution as well as a clear sense of destination. Nice slogan, but useless. He sat on the corner of his desk and stared out the window. So, I have to learn to see what I'm not looking for, to see the subtle emerging. Another useless slogan! I'm beginning to sound like the caretaker— it's all Zen. What is the sound of an unsent e-mail?

How can I see the crucial gaps in what I know? He doodled on a piece of paper. First, doubt what I know. Gaps are obvious if I can recognize an absence of something. That's really, really hard to do, because the mind hates not knowing, not being sure. Indecision and uncertainly are no fun, not even for the systems-obsessed of us. It's too easy to just slide past the odd parts, the puzzle parts that don't fit. We all have a box somewhere that the extra parts get shoved into and forgotten. Basics: it's a system out there, interacting with itself, and the story format we all use doesn't handle random events well. We all use analogies that may or may not be right, and there are delayed consequences and multiple causations all over the place. Argh. 'Fifteen men on a dead man's chest, yo ho ho and a bottle of rum. Drink and the devil have done for the rest, yo ho ho and a bottle of rum.' No, the sun isn't over the yardarm yet; the bar hasn't opened. Not a solution set.

It's the odd parts that are key, he realized, excited. That's how I caught that problem at the San Francisco plant. And the Paris problem—that was an oddity. Something didn't reconcile with what it should have. A type of fraud against the assumed story, I guess. Catching the peripheral, marginal signals that are the early warning signs of threats and opportunities. The near misses and the close calls I talked about at the seminar, but making them the center of attention. Like noticing when Cali isn't really smiling, which means I forgot something. That article I read contrasted passive versus active scanners of our environment. Active scanning still requires attention on something, a focus, but setting up structured, open-ended questions? Could work.

Use the creature. The mind processes all the time, and consciousness just gets in the way. Relaxation, visualization. What I'm thinking about will pop up. When I'm uncertain, undecided, I'm trying to tell myself something. The phone rang. When I get a f*cking moment to think, that is. He controlled his breathing and picked up the phone. Twenty minutes later, the small group left his office, smiling.

Hal sat there stewing. There was a cartoon I remember: the guy answers the phone "And on that day you will feel my wrath with the heat of a thousand suns! You will recede into the depths of hell and you will bear witness to my fury!" Yeah, that's the recording I'd like to put on the phone to weed out calls. That meeting was useless. The dance of indecision. I've got to start pushing the responsibilities down further. I don't want to help them make decisions. That's what they are paid for. I just need to see what the decisions are coming out as.

So, back to how to think? Risk is the margin, where it matters. And we all overestimate risks for things that are out of our control and that people talk about at the water cooler. We underestimate risks for things that are mundane and ordinary. It's that little drip we ignore that is the warning sign of the flood." [133]

Anomalies as the question: have we been looking for the keys under the lamppost because the light is better? Even though they were not lost there? We can decide where and how to look. We can change our focus, and each day, the change becomes stronger.

> *"Any act often repeated soon forms a habit; and habit allowed, steady gains in strength. At first it may be but as a spider's web, easily broken through, but if not resisted it soon binds us with chains of steel."* [134]

That works both ways, and we can make new habits if we want.

"If it's written down, it's too late," Hal complained. "By the time I see it, its just piles of stuff to sign off on."

"The real problem with focusing on anomalies is that you are then outside the social consensus," Cali observed, buttering the hot bread the waiter had just brought them. "No one, well, except antisocial, systems-obsessed men..."

"Who are exceptionally well-endowed physically," Hal interrupted.

"...want to be outside the social consensus," Cali continued, ignoring his remark. "You talk about watching the edges, what's wrong—it makes people uncomfortable, uneasy. You're asking them to peek into the abyss and they don't like that. There's stuff moving in there! Anomalies are thinking different things, looking for different things, finding different things. That is a constant challenge to others in many ways that disturbs their worldview and their sense of self. So people don't do it. Now, if you do focus on anomalies, the group won't be happy, but you're right—it works a lot better for reading the real world."

"That makes me feel better. I've played with anomalies as an orienting response, but I didn't follow them up in a structured way because there wasn't a lot of reinforcement. Even geeks appreciate a little social approval occasionally. Now it's clear why that approach is rejected and denied by people and society. So it wasn't my unwashed clothes all those years?"

"No, it was the unwashed clothes," Cali countered. "Shallow surface appearances mean a lot in bars."

"Actually, shallow surface appearances mean a lot everywhere. "People can just act without thinking, using the usual symbols that people wear to judge them. That's what produces all those useless reports, measured by weight instead of quality. What was that ad campaign that advocated men buying an ultra-expensive automobile because women would then give them hand jobs? I think the campaign was pulled because it was deemed too crass or too truthful—one of those."

"Mind on the table, out of the gutter. As if a woman would have to do anything so gauche to control a male," Cali sniffed. "So how do we use anomalies to truly understand Sun Tzu? 'To lift an autumn hair is no sign of great strength; to see sun and moon is no sign of sharp sight; to hear the noise of thunder is no sign of a quick ear.'"

"That is the complete question! "Answer that question, and you have the key to The Art of War, and probably life, too."

"So, bringing it back to a practical level—we're trying to head off disasters of all kinds before they become too big to fix," Cali mused. "It's like an airplane. Every minute it's off course, but it's constantly correcting to get to the airport."

"I like flying less and less."

"It's knowing where you are headed that makes it possible to course correct. There's a lot of good stuff on how to make decisions when you know what you are facing, when you know what the goal is."

"Management by objective works, if you know the objectives. Ninety percent of the time you don't," Hal quoted. "Gospel from

Drucker, the master himself."

"Where you know your objectives might be more than ten percent. "But that's the key. It's when you don't know what you're facing, what the hidden gaps are, which unexpected feedback is out there that is showing up randomly as noise. The surprises that the world has out there, how the world just doesn't want to follow the storylines that each of us, in our infinite wisdom, have laid down for the world to obey."

"There are lots of good slogans," Hal growled, poking at his salad. "Never fall in love with your decisions, remember that everything is fluid. Be constantly aware of and subtly adjust your feelings. Yeah, what does that mean? And as high as I am in the organization, if I just sit at my desk and stare blankly into space, people start to talk. Oh, less since I put that plank in and walked a few of the malcontents off the fifteenth floor, but they still whisper."

"It's the immeasurable feedback that drives you crazy," sketching ideas on the tablecloth. "Whoops, this is cloth, not paper. Hal, leave a bigger tip. Humm, maybe a lot bigger. An event is something in, something out. If we don't notice the event, then the chance to head off what is coming is gone. If we are missing the real inputs and outputs, then what we are measuring is useless. Worse than useless, actually. Solving the wrong problem, with all the disaster that brings. What about that article on luck you found in that magazine? Good luck is finding what works for you—that's what it was driving at."

Hal did a quick search and popped up the article on his laptop. "Yeah, this one." He scooted his chair over, and turned the screen so Cali could see it also.

"Hands on the computer, please," she ordered. "That won't help you to get lucky." She kissed him.

"Lucky is focus," Hal replied. "Always keep trying. Okay, it's these ideas. Pay attention to your surroundings; you won't spot good luck unless you look for it."

"Yeah," Cali replied, doubtfully. "Being awake is good. But awake to what?"

"Idea. Strike up conversations with strangers. You might meet the love of your life or make an important business contact."

"No love-of-life conversations," Cali declared. "Not allowed. That's already been found. Skip the conversations with wicked-looking women."

"Can't argue with that," Hal agreed, "but I'll take another kiss. Okay, back to the list of ideas"

"Idea. Vary your routine every day. Walk on the other side of the street or try a new lunch spot. Never a bad idea," Hal mused. "But if you're the kind of person who goes for new stuff, that's different from the fixed person. Maybe we put that on the job interview questions? People who vary their inputs keep more alive. I'll make a note. How about this? Be aggressive about making the changes you want. Keep thinking about moving cross-country? Just go already."

"Let's not," Cali demurred. "I don't want to pack all this stuff. And if you get any more aggressive about making changes at work, they will throw you out a window."

"Angry mobs with torches...And the wind was a torrent of darkness upon the gusty trees, the moon was a ghostly galleon tossed upon cloudy seas...running across the dark moors ," Hal murmured. "Yeah, that's how I want to go."

Cali studied him carefully. "See, I was right, you are really weird."

"Too many graphic novels in college. They love that stuff. Hey, if you're going to go, make it dramatic," Hal advised. "Otherwise, the people at your funeral have nothing to talk about. They get bored and go through your pockets for loose change."

"Moving on," Cali declared. "Idea. Follow your hunches and gut feelings and treat nagging doubt as alarm bells; they're often right, even if you can't pinpoint the reason."

"That's also Moscow rules," Hal added. "Never go against your gut—it's your operational antenna."

"That's critical," Cali agreed. "Remember how we detoured to look at the wall in Ann Arbor? We'd have walked into crossing rifle fire if we hadn't. Of course, my nagging doubts about your suitability as a stable, solid, providing mate had some basis, actually."

"Ah, you fell into the confirming evidence trap! We seek out information supporting our existing predictions. You made judgments based on my poor attitude in class, my failure to wash my clothes often, my unkempt hair, and my scurvy friends. Only the exterior shadows of my true self, as it turned out."

Cali eyed him doubtfully. "I reference my prior remarks, Senator."

"Perhaps we should move on here. Idea. Expect good fortune! If you think something's going to happen, you'll be more likely to spot it when it does. So you expected good things in college, and there I was," Hal asserted, ducking the roll that came flying towards him.

"Ah, sorry," Cali apologized, smiling sweetly at the couple in back of Hal.

"Not a problem," the woman laughed. "I usually throw knives." The man she was with smiled, but didn't look happy.

"You throw like a girl," Hal snickered. "Oof!" The next roll hit him in the head.

"I am a girl," Cali pointed out, "and if I get close enough, it doesn't matter how I throw."

"I'm thinking a really, really big tip might get us back into this restaurant," Hal sighed, "but I'm doubtful. Hey, and if you get close enough," moving his chair right next to Cali, "then that's when lucky starts. So how about this idea? Idea. Smile. People will smile back, and suddenly you're off to a good start."

"Or they will wonder what you've been up to—or are planning. Your smiles in class, for example, usually meant something awful was going to be said to the professor. Which wasn't a bad thing, truthfully. I used to enjoy his red-faced outbursts. Aliston tells me that when you smile, she's learned to double security because something bad is coming."

"It's going to be wall-to-wall guards there at this rate."

"So what's the concept? Intellectual, that is, please!" she protested as Hal started kissing her neck.

"What is all this really saying? That lucky is holding out your hand, and what you want drops into it, out of the confusion and noise of life. Except that lucky is a continued focus, staying out of the daily rut and paying attention to the outside world. Actually, that's probably the essence of all the little sayings—they just try and take small bites of the apple. In control is too controlled, and out of control raises opportunities. Or this: go for walks. Read a lot. Go outside your comfort zone. Stay interested. Daydream?"

"It's clear it's the anomalies," Cali agreed. "Catching the oddities—that the stories are going sideways, or a new story is opening up. First, people hate anomalies because they love their stories just the way they are, and you are already ahead of them simply by noticing the differences. Second, the anomalies do the heavy lifting of changing your focus. Notice the oddity, ask questions, and your focus moves to the problem that you didn't suspect. And it's the anomalies that the gut spots first."

"The voyage of the Starship Hal: to seek anomalies that destroy/void plans?" Hal mused. "I like that. Maybe I can get a soundtrack to go along with it? At least a guy with a saxophone to follow me around, anyhow. Where is the disaster, where could there be a disaster—and be open to those little things. It's a plan. And speaking of a plan, I have a plan, and I'm feeling lucky tonight."

"Oh, you are?" Cali teased. "Well, maybe I'm feeling lucky too. But after dinner! How about dessert?"

"I'm good with that," Hal promised. "I'll bring the whipped cream."[135]

Let's look quickly at some common anomaly triggers and hints. First and foremost, we have problems with language. A simple sentence can refer to hopelessly complex situations, which seem solvable because of the simplicity and clarity of the sentence. A complex sentence can refer to a very clear and specific situation that is completely understandable and useful. For example: A long, detailed and technically worded legal description, running for three pages, results in a clear and usable description of an area of land. A statement such as 'we should end war' has a simple, clear sentence structure, but is utterly useless for effective next actions. The difference? The terms used are either measurable or not, but people will jump in that horse and ride that sentence off, happily read to end war and to fight with anyone who disputes with them, without noticing that it isn't going to work. The 'war to end all wars' is just one of those jokes the Fairies love so much.

Another common situation is where defining a perfect world allows a person to not change this one. While have to live in a social environment, re-think the social demands on their basics: critical vs. non-critical and the tools used to enforce. This is a specific example of the case of a defining question frames and incorrect answer. Simply defining a situation does not mean a solution is possible. Simply defining a problem does not mean that is it solvable. If you have defined a problem that isn't solvable, you can gather all the data you want, but it won't help. All the data in the world on an unsolvable problem isn't going to help until you back up to think about the essential insolvability of the problem. The more options on the table, the more difficult it is to assess them in a meaningful way, and the easier it is to make a bad decision. The usual (poor) choice is to invoke a ritual and do the dance.

Perceiving is sorting of sensory information. We sort every moment, based on heuristics developed/taught over time. For many reasons, the new is often sorted out. Change is often sorted out. If new or change is perceived, then what does it mean? We are loss based calculating creatures, and if we smell a loss, we bolt. So looking carefully at the new and changed is hard. We all use the past as a guide, and with the new we have to find a path that we didn't trod before. Finally, when does one have discretionary time to think and analyze things? Eating, sleeping, work, socialization, when does the spark of recognition, creativity drop in?

You and I do make all of these mistakes every day, probably at least one an hour. The difference is that, having read this chapter; you are motivated to want to catch the anomalies. What we want to avoid is called inattention blindness, defined as instances when we don't see something because it's not what we are expecting to see; it's not what we are looking for. Sherlock Holmes had a somewhat different description. "I have trained myself to notice what I see," Holmes said. There is a classic basketball game movie, mentioned before, which has a person in a gorilla suit wandering on and off the court. People watching the movie, told to watch for certain aspects of the game, just don't see the gorilla at all. Asked about a gorilla after watching the movie, they deny it ever was there. I was recently at a seminar where they ran the clip, and out of roughly forty people in the room, only two caught the trick because they were looking for it. When you're watching the video, smiling at the gorilla, and you see the person next to you frantically counting the ball passes, not seeing the gorilla at all, it's a bit terrifying.

If you are focused on quitting an old habit, you are bound negatively to that habit. Create a new habit, and the old one sloughs off. Reward yourself for thinking about anomalies, and you will do it more and more.

Here's another analogy. Life is like sailing a ship. Wind, water, weather and the ship combine to create an infinity of possibilities. You will do better if you use maps, lay in provisions and ask questions before acting. Simply going out without preparation will sink your boat. The 'good ship lollipop' isn't going to handle well in a storm. Too often, we tacitly agree with others that if everyone just looks the other way, then things are not a problem and the problem vanishes from perception. Except the problem really doesn't vanish, and we know it. If it's going to be our problem more than other's problem, then we'd better pay some attention.

That leads into why it is hard to discuss some of these ideas with a group. Social life being what it is, we are euphemistically part of a web of pleasant fictions (a chain of lies) about the group and our relationships. If you call them on their lies/misperceptions, then they call you on yours. It makes it hard to step back, because the webs are linked. Still, if you exist in a web of falsity/deceit and half-truth, you shouldn't wonder why things don't seem right.

Catching anomalies isn't always about the little things, either. Sometimes they can be sitting right in front of you, as clear as day. The classic example is suppose a water lily is growing on a pond in your backyard. The lily plant doubles in size each day. If the lily were allowed to grow unchecked, it would completely cover the pond in 30 days, choking out all other forms of life in the water. For a long time, the plant seems small, so you decide not to worry about cutting it back until it covers half the pond. You even like the flowers, and the little frogs sunning themselves on the plants. How much time will you have to avert disaster, once the lily crosses your threshold for action, defined as covering ½ of the pond? The answer is, "One day." The water lily will cover half the pond on the 29th day; on the 30th day, it doubles again and covers the entire pond. If you wait to act until the pond is half covered, you have only 24 hours before it chokes the life out of your pond. If a group is cultivating those water lilies, and your life (but perhaps not all of the groups lives) depends on some open water, you'd better catch this one as it occurs, not after.

"Well, the meeting is almost over, for what that's worth," Hal answered. "Okay, what is my favorite topic?"

"Anemones," Cali responded, cheerfully. "Those strange little creatures that live on coral reefs."

"I love the clownfish," a transferee added. "Nemo was so cute!"

"Okay, if we are done having fun at my expense," Hal continued, "it's anomalies. Otherwise known as system deviances?"

"We love deviance," Aliston asserted and there were general nods around the room.

"I'm going to have to wrap this up quickly, I see," Hal sighed.

"The troops are getting rebellious. Okay, in a nutshell, an anomaly is some part of the story that isn't working. Everything is a story. All stories have a chronology, a beginning and an end, and a background that it is played against. Just like any play, but an anomaly is something 'not right'. The problem is that we don't see the 'not right.' A great example was the gorilla in the basketball game. These professors filmed a basketball game and guy in a gorilla suit wandered in and out occasionally. The people watching the game didn't see the gorilla because they were told to watch a specific aspect of the game, and that's all they saw. They saw the game they were expecting and never even saw the gorilla! So why are we like this? A study studied scientists studying data denying desired deviances."

"Bet you can't say that five times quickly," Cali interrupted.

Ignoring her, Hal continued, "We resist anomalous information, assuming that unexpected results are a stupid mistake, because we are hard wired that way. Each of us, all the time, carefully edits reality, selecting evidence that confirms what we already believe. Which makes a lot of sense, because who can rethink everything all the time? It's a problem, though, because we are just as blinkered as a horse pulling a wagon, but we deny the blinkers. The anterior cingulate cortex, referred to as the 'Oh Shit! circuit,' affects our perception of errors and contradictions. Tied to that is the dorsolateral prefrontal cortex, which suppresses thoughts that don't square with our preconceptions. So think about this and try watching for the parts of the story that don't work. That's where the money and the opportunities are, if that helps. Fine, recess, everyone, we're out of here."[136]

If nothing else, remember that anomalies are the key to asymmetric information: you know and they don't, but this is legal. Anomalies are the critical link to the real world. If we listen/see anomalies in the stories we are acting on, we get hints as to where stories and the world are diverging. If we, like very little children, put our hands over our eyes so that we can't be seen, (i.e., my perception of the world is the world) then we deserve what we get.

FAILURE - AND WHY ANOMALIES ARE IGNORED

"How did the researchers cope with all this unexpected data? How did they deal with so much failure? Dunbar realized that the vast majority of people in the lab followed the same basic process. First, they would blame the method. The surprising finding was classified as a mere mistake; perhaps a machine malfunctioned or an enzyme had gone stale. "The scientists were trying to explain away what they didn't understand," Dunbar. says. "It's as if they didn't want to believe it." The experiment would then be ·carefully repeated. Sometimes, the weird blip would disappear, in which case the problem was solved.

But the weirdness usually remained, an anomaly that wouldn't go away. This is when things get interesting. According to Dunbar, even after scientists had generated their "error" multiple times-it was a consistent inconsistency they might fail to follow it up. "Given the amount of unexpected data in science, it's just not feasible to pursue everything," Dunbar says. "People have to pick and choose what's interesting and what's not, but they often choose badly." And so the result was tossed aside, filed in a quickly forgotten notebook. The scientists had discovered a new fact, but they called it a failure.

The reason we're so resistant to anomalous information-the real reason researchers automatically assume that every unexpected result is a stupid mistake-is rooted in the way the human brain works. Over the past few decades, psychologists have dismantled the myth of objectivity. The fact is, we carefully edit our reality, searching for evidence that confirms what we already believe. Although we pretend we're empiricists-our views dictated by nothing but the facts we're actually blinkered, especially when it comes to information that contradicts our theories. The problem with science, then, isn't that most experiments fail-it's that most failures are ignored.

There was a squirt of blood to the anterior cingulate cortex, a collar of tissue located in the center of the brain. The ACC is typically associated with the perception of errors and contradictions-neuroscientists often refer to it as part of the "Oh shit!" circuit-so it makes sense that it would be turned on when we watch a video of something that seems wrong.

But there's another region of the brain that can be activated as we go about editing reality. It's called the dorsolateral prefrontal cortex, or DLPFC. It's located just behind the forehead and is one of the last brain areas to develop in young adults. It plays a crucial role in suppressing so-called unwanted representations, getting rid of those thoughts that don't square with our preconceptions. For scientists, it's a problem.

However, when it comes to noticing anomalies, an efficient prefrontal cortex can actually be a serious liability. The DLPFC is constantly censoring the world, erasing facts from our experience. If the ACC is the "Oh shit!" circuit, the DLPFC is the Delete key. When the ACC and DLPFC "turn on together, people aren't just noticing that something doesn't look right," Dunbar says. "They're also inhibiting that information."

Their background noise was still inexplicable, but it was getting harder to ignore, if only because it was always there. After a year of trying to erase the static, after assuming it was just a mechanical malfunction, an irrelevant artifact, or pigeon guano, Penzias and Wilson began exploring the possibility that it was real. Perhaps it was everywhere for a reason.

There are advantages to thinking on the margin. When we look at a problem from the outside, we're more likely to notice what doesn't work. Instead of suppressing the unexpected, shunting it aside with our "Oh shit!" circuit and Delete key, we can take the mistake seriously. A new theory emerges from the ashes of our surprise."[137]

Again, peripheral signals are difficult to capture, but they are the vital early warning signs of both threats and opportunities. Passive scaning doesn't catch these. Waiting for information to reach us and dealing with it as it arrives-too late won't work. Active scanning usually requires thinking about some specific questions, but at a minimum requires expecting something. It can catch that torpedo snaking towards your pretty ship.

CHAPTER 33. USING STORIES AGAINST THEM.

The anomalies have shown a gap, a weakness. Now what?

"If you use the enemy to defeat
the enemy, you will be strong
wherever you go."[138]
Chapter 2: "ON WAGING BATTLE"

Sun Tzu believed in winning.

Figure 11 is the world many people live in. It's not a good world, and it won't last, but it was their choice. You will be their victim, or they will be your prey. Your choice, actually.

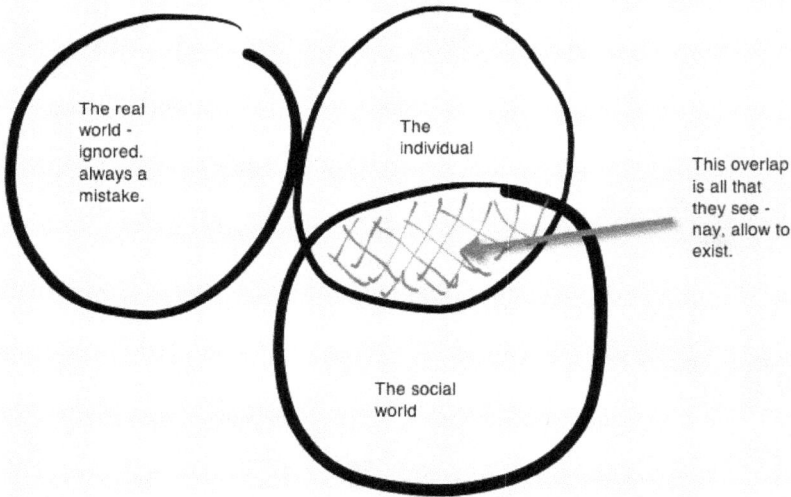

Figure 11.

So, if you're still with me, I've argued that each of us is a parasite, and has to live in a big world by parasite rules. And that our best chance is to use anomalies-i.e., the stupid stories that people are telling themselves, which result in them throwing money and resources away to keep their worldview afloat, for our prosperity and our children's. Yeah, that's a pretty good summary. In a complex world, I cannot foretell the future-but I can foretell what people's stories will lead to, and that's good enough.

A worthy goal is an annuity on the friction between their

demands/dreams of the world and what the world really is. That's what a successful parasite would do and you can ponder the implications as you sip a cool drink sitting on the beach, watching the sunset over the breaking waves. Or, believe their stories and toil in their hellhole–your call. A successful parasite makes the host provide for the parasite, while making the host think it's acting for itself. Would the saint's agree? Find a saint who had a mortgage, three kids and a crappy job before you live your life by their carefully edited and authorized story.

Let me throw out another idea, if you are doubtful. If you cannot decipher other people's stories well enough to use their stories against them, then you cannot decipher your own stories to know when people are using your stories against you. So you can remain pure of heart reading this chapter, seeking only protection against the others (always a good idea) or drop the pure of heart and go for the gold. It's really your choice.

> *"Good warriors make others come to them, and do not go to others.*
> *This is the principle of emptiness and fullness of others and self.*
> *When you induce opponents to come to you,*
> *then their force is always empty;*
> *as long as you do not go to them, your force is always full.*
> *Attacking emptiness with fullness is like throwing stones on eggs*
> *The eggs are sure to break."*[139]
> *Chapter 6: "EMPTINESS AND FULLNESS"*

Here's an example of where the most foolish, but potentially profitable, stories come from. It is the legendary 'Suits in Rooms and Decision Making'. The modern world is full of law, regulations, and the like to protect us, or at least meet socially defined goals. What people don't realize are the huge limitations on possible outcomes caused by the basic structure. The bureaucracy is people in a formal structure making decisions. It's Suits at desks making choices about our lives. This structure underlies all formal decision-making, and the steps leading to the decision-making. Whether it is the College of Cardinals, the Senate, or all the myriads of lesser organizations, there is a limiting structure that has to be considered. When you look at what the Suits came up with for you today, are you thinking through the dead hand of the past that obscures the real choices and fogs the future?

> *"To unfailingly take what you attack,*
> *attack where there is no defense.*
> *For unfailingly secure defense,*
> *defend where there is no attack."*[140]
> *Chapter 6: "EMPTINESS AND FULLNESS"*

The problem is that the formal structure doesn't allow a lot of feedback and information into the process. In a meeting with the Suits, only certain types of events are captured, and not all those events are considered (for good and not-good reasons). The underlying frustration with the suits system is that where the events to be measured are outside the 'suits at desks' view, those events don't exist even if they are the most relevant facts. The legal process is an exceptionally formal case of suits at desks, even more than the administrative agencies. This is good in many ways, because flexibility tends to go to the well connected, but another reason that things just don't seem to work. While in theory a considered, structured process eliminates discretion and favors, sadly it doesn't work that way.

> "Adding to our problems" Lucretia fretted, "is that no matter how noble the goal, what you want to accomplish in this world has to go through a room of suits. The suits are carefully selected to have experienced none of the problems that they are supposed to be solving. The options given the suits are limited, as well as the understanding of options by the suits, and what comes out may have little relationship to what went in. Still, we do what we can."[141]

Max Weber believed that the invention of the bureaucracy was a watershed event for human society, because the process would decrease discretion. As it turns out, it only multiplied the possibilities.

> *"Invincibility is in oneself,*
> *vulnerability is in the opponent."*[142]
> *Chapter 4: "FORMATION"*

So, what is the story that they want to buy? You can't sell them your story-you have to sell them their story. It's done in advertisements and pulpits all over the world all day long. Buying their story isn't a ticket to happiness, even if it comes with prizes. For example, the singer Janis Joplin was never as good after she left the rock band Big Brother. Big Brother, based on their albums, were not, perhaps, the finest musicians in the world, in the sense that they were not the most mechanically accomplished on their instruments. Janis Joplin had technically more accomplished musicians in the background after she left Big Brother, which all the critics and music companies applauded. The sad surprise is that after she left, she was never as good-her new music didn't have the fire, the intensity, that the music with Big Brother had. She became something other than what she was, something that others thought appropriate, but turned out not to be. I'm sure that they shrugged and blamed it on her, which was made easy by her death by drug overdose, but the new story she listened to brought only failure. Her story is in a sense a design story. It is common to want that should make each individual piece beautiful, the very best, but then you have a collection of isolated pieces. It's the combined effect that matters, and she lost the forest for the trees. Its a mistake we all make all the time.

> *"Therefore, victory ...*
> *is not repetitious,*

but adapts its form endlessly."[143]

Chapter 6: *"EMPTINESS AND FULLNESS"*

Where are the stories that are not working? Ritualized behavior is a good place to start. Ritualized behavior is where people seek the good, essentially through magic. We do something that may have worked once, may work occasionally, and we do this 'something' because we don't know what else to do. A serious, authorized ritual allows no questions, or else the magic is harmed. This will work, people firmly say, it will work because we want it to. This works in many cases for accidental reasons. For example, where the economy is down, people run around doing things, and eventually the economy will turn up, at least partially because people get tired of feeling down and start buying things again. What caused the new activity? It could have been one or all or none of the frantic activities done by those in power, so they save them all until the next time, and try it again.

> "So it is that good *warriors* take
> their stand on ground
> where they cannot lose,
> and do not overlook conditions that
> make an opponent prone to defeat."[144]

Chapter 4: *"FORMATION"*

Where you spot the 'good' not working, you have discovered a gold seam. People will pour money into a problem, generally to avoid thinking about it, and you might as well be there with your hat out as the dollars drop from the sky. Middlemen discovered this a long time ago. While it's almost always profitable being in the middle, it's best where people know they have to do something and so don't look at the costs very closely. In our world, investment firms have grasped this very well. Your pension? Your financial future? The smoothly functioning economy? It all has to go through them and their clearinghouses. In setting things up so that the investment firms profit, they limited the options available. This, paradoxically, has been the gold seam for hedge funds, who were able to make investments that most of us didn't have the opening into a market to make. Those hidden markets, with hidden inefficiencies and loose diamonds just lying there, were where they almost literally minted money. They didn't mind making money off the stories that we passed off as true when they were not. Why should you?

How about this: viewing the financial world like a hacker attacks a network? You scan, test, waiting for a gap, for the firewall to go down. Then you step in and grab. Now, that's a lot different from getting the secret stuff from your friend who will feed you to the SEC in a moment.

While we are on the topic of investment choices, if nothing else, remember that any pre-defined bet is a loser. The house has taken their share before the wheel starts. You may get lucky, you may not, but the pre-defined bet isn't hung out their primarily for your benefit. Whether it's an obvious bet in Las Vegas, a not so obvious bet in the stock market, or a bet on a new job that you are considering, there are hidden limits and risks. That's not to say you don't want to take the bet - you just need to be completely sure about the bet you are really taking. So how should we learn about the world? Not by the carefully crafted stories fed to us. We have to look in the corners for good information.

> *"Making yourself invincible means*
> *knowing yourself; waiting for*
> *vulnerability in opponents means*
> *knowing others."*[145]
>
> *Chapter 4: "FORMATION"*

As long as we are being amoral, lets look at the final chapter of The Art of War that demands the use of spies. But using effective spies, who can provide the foreknowledge that enables you to overcome others. Foreknowledge does not come from ghosts and spirits, isn't available by analogy and cannot be calculated. Sadly, it doesn't seem to come from the NSA either. It must be obtained from people, people who know the conditions of the enemy. The section on spies is the culmination of the entire work.

> *"So only a brilliant ruler or a wise general who can use the highly*
> *intelligent for espionage is sure of great success.*
> *This is essential for military operations, and the armies depend on*
> *this for their actions.*[146]*"*

Sun Tzu's commanders are not passive "consumers" of intelligence. A general in the Sun Tzu tradition takes as much personal interest in employing spies as he does in issuing orders to his subordinate commanders. He is as active in intelligence as he is in operations:

> *"Of all those in the army close to the commander, none is as intimate*
> *as the secret agent; of all rewards, none more liberal than those given*
> *to secret agents."*[147]

And:

> *"To be parsimonious with positions, compensations, or hundreds of*
> *pounds of gold, and thereby blind to the enemy's status, is to be*
> *extraordinarily inhumane:*
> *such a man can never be considered his people's commander,*
> *can never be his lord's aide, and can never be the ruler of victory."*[148]

It seems doubtful that a US Army commander whose primary contact with intelligence is the Army's scripted, and rehearsed "intelligence briefing" could ever be successful in the Sun Tzu school.

Now, you have to be careful with the 'spy' idea. Spies are acting in a grey moral world, and acting on certain (financial) information that you pay for is clearly criminal activity. Also stupid, as people seem to exchange e-mails that say 'if this comes out we are screwed' in the text. Why not just highlight the printout and mail it to the SEC? Still, if it's important enough, you have to ask around and listen to what you hear. For winning, it's a moral imperative, even if spies are an ethical violation of most of the common rules.

Here's a hard question. You do have to ask yourself, honestly, whether you are seeking success, or a good alibi. Success is demanding, it must be done over and over. A good alibi? That will cover you for life. You just 'can't', and people nod their heads. Of course, living the life of a good alibi means no change, no growth, just a gradual wasting away into a dried husk. Unless your good alibi provides an income of several million dollars a year and a nice home on the beach (and even then, perhaps not) you won't enjoy it. Like Beowulf, your conquest will turn to ashes, your triumphs to empty markers.

"My lord," the head accountant stammered, "we have made enormous profits on the majority of the contracts we entered into. We actually went past our best-case projections. Our partners have made enormous sums of money also. And the connections with the people in India are completely severed. There is nothing to lead anyone back to us."

Paul looked at him, drumming his fingers on the dais, and the accountant looked down.

"But it spread much further than we anticipated, my lord," the accountant stammered, staring at the floor.

"Many people find a good alibi better than a successful achievement," the Cardinal remarked, watching the accountant closely. "An achievement isn't permanent, and tomorrow demands another achievement. Tomorrow we have to prove our worth anew, that we are as good today as we were yesterday, perhaps even better. But a good alibi covers us for the rest of our lives if need be. Small wonder then that the effort put forth and the punishment endured to find a good alibi often exceeds the effort and grief requisite for achievement. And I'm thinking you have a good alibi."

The accountant gulped, and then looked at the Cardinal. "I do, but you see through me, my lord. This has become a tidal wave, sweeping all before it. Many of our companies are in financial distress because of the huge changes in commodities and oil. The whole underlying structure that we based our plans and projections on has been tossed, and the foundations may be broken."

Paul contemplated the carvings on the wall, and then looked at the accountant. "Had you stuck with your alibi, I would have had you killed," he declared. "But your honesty has saved you today. No one foresaw this. I have no complaint against you. Get the lawyers into action. Every country and every company has the same problems. Pull together into groups that are too large to fail. It's worked before, and it will work again. Go, now."

The accountant knelt and then ran out of the room, his staff behind him.

"We have a plan?" Paul asked the Cardinal.

"We do, my Lord," the Cardinal replied. "Reserves and resources have been stockpiled. Creatures and troops are marshaled for protection."

"Good," Paul announced. "The old world is about to become the new world."[149]

This is a LOT more important than I ever thought when I was younger. A good alibi is the basis for many people's lives. Look carefully at the overlaps-and the non-overlaps-in the Figure 1. What really are you hoping for? More importantly, what are your actions pointing towards? Let's go for success, checked by failure as it must be. Fortune in men's eyes will always be a fleeting thing, but fortune in your eyes is the most lasting accomplishment you can have. Your significant other will be appreciative also.

It's interesting, but many people really don't want to win. It's work to win. Our brains trick us, and we get more excited about the idea of winning than the drab and drudge work required to win.

This really isn't new:

"Seduce them with the prospect of gain,
send interlopers in among them,
have rhetoricians use fast talk
to ingratiate themselves with their
leaders and followers, and divide up
their organization and power."[150]
Chapter 1: "ON ASSESSMENTS"

Sun Tzu was nothing if not direct, and people have not changed in the thousands of years since he wrote.

"You go into greed mode," he said. Guy Spier called it "cocaine brain." Neuroscientists have found that the prospect of making money stimulates the same primitive reward circuits in the brain that cocaine does. And that, Pabrai said, is when serious investors like himself try to become systematic. They focus on dispassionate analysis, on avoiding both irrational exuberance and panic. They pore over the company's financial reports, investigate its liabilities and risks, examine its management team's track record, weigh its competitors, consider the future of the market it is in trying to gauge both the magnitude of opportunity and the margin of safety

For example, looking back, he noticed that he had repeatedly erred in determining how "leveraged" companies were-how much cash was really theirs, how much was borrowed, and how risky those debts were. The information was available; he just hadn't looked for it carefully enough.

In large part, he believes, the mistakes happened because he wasn't able to damp down the cocaine brain. Pabrai is a forty-five year-old former engineer. He comes from India, where he clawed his way up its fiercely competitive educational system. Then he secured admission to Clemson University, in South Carolina, to study engineering. From there he climbed the ranks of technology companies in Chicago and California. Before going into investment, he built a successful informational technology company of his own. All this is to say he knows a thing or two about being dispassionate and avoiding the lure of instant gratification.

Yet no matter how objective he tried to be about a potentially exciting investment, he said, he found his brain working against him, latching onto evidence that confirmed his initial ,hunch and dismissing the signs of a downside. It's what the brain does. "You get seduced," he said. "You start cutting corners."

So Pabrai made a list of mistakes he'd seen-ones Buffett and other investors had made as well as his own. It soon contained dozens of different mistakes, he said. Then, to help him guard against them, he devised a matching list of checks-about seventy in all.

Like him, the anonymous investor I spoke to-I'll call him Cook-made a checklist. But he was even more methodical: he enumerated the errors known to occur at any point in the investment process-during the research phase, during decision making, during execution of the decision, and even in the period after making an investment when one should be monitoring for problems.

He then designed detailed checklists to avoid the errors, complete with clearly identified pause points at which he and his investment team would run through the items.

He has a Day Three Checklist, for example, which he and his team review at the end of the third day of considering an investment. By that point, the checklist says, they should confirm that they have gone over the prospect's key financial statements for the previous ten years, including checking for specific items in each statement and possible patterns across the statements.

I asked Cook how much interest others have had in what he has been doing these past two years. Zero, he said-or actually that's not quite true. People have been intensely interested in what he's been buying and how, but the minute the word checklist comes out of his mouth, they disappear. Even in his own firm, he's found it a hard sell."[151] From checklists manifesto book)

Checklists work if you want to succeed in the world, and we all resist them. I know I do, and I'm more organized than most. (Of course, we all see ourselves as 'more' than the rest-we are all from Lake Wobegon, after all)

Finding the weakness in the stories is an attempt to separate the social consensus from what is happening in the real world. Look at Figure 1 again. That small area of overlap between the social world and the real world means that the social world believes and does many, many things with no relationship in the real world. When they do what they want, expecting a result in the real world, that's going to be a disaster for someone and a gold seam for someone else. To catch this, you have to back out of the social consensus, which is very hard, and contrast what the social consensus is doing with what is happening in the real world. Also hard, but no one said life would be easy. The next chapter, "Doing Nefarious Things" looks at this topic in greater detail.

Again, I can't predict the future–but I can predict the stories that they live by, and think are critical. If I know that story, then I know what they will do when faced with difficult choices. Between their difficult choice and reality, there is a gold seam, a hedge that will pay off. You can't get your information from the mass media:

> *The predictions that seem most correct are almost certain to be wrong – Ray Kurzwell*

You can get some help from a healthy dose of cynicism. If you trust people to listen to themselves first, you will live a long and comfortable life. If you trust people to do what you think they should, your life will be bitter and unpleasant for all of your days.

> "They think their system is safe and secure because it's working and has a password. See, people use computers for different reasons, and those reasons don't include security hassles. That was my specialty at the accounting firm—thinking about how people don't follow the rules. The other hackers, they played with the machines. You don't need the bits and bytes if people tell you how to get in. People think that if the doors lock, they are safe, but they will hand you the keys and not realize it. Once we get in, we loot to our hearts' content, my beauty. But I'm not there yet."[152]

Unethical? There are many times stealing information is a moral imperative, it just depends on your point of view and that of the relevant authorities with guns. If ordered to steal information during wartime, you would act without hesitation. It's making a decision on your own that is hard. Having to assess and weight, and then choose the good against the good and the bad against the bad. Whether you seek the destruction of the system or protecting the system, there are lots of ways back and forth to justify what you want. But it's important, and it's done all the time. If you don't do it, then the others will. If you wall out monsters, don't allow them in your calculations or belief's, that doesn't mean they are not still out there.

Surprises, otherwise referred to as 'Gold seams', come from social beliefs out of sync with reality, social beliefs that everyone emotionally loves and/or doesn't dare challenge. Now, this is a bit complex. Where you have a social belief that is 'The Word', you have a story that admits no questions. So there isn't an opposing story, or alternatives that people have thought about. Where something doesn't have a good story, or no story has been developed, or it isn't a story that fits into the accepted plots, then that situation can't be grasped. So the information on the events is tossed aside, or massaged into another story, and the edges are not looked at closely. That's why the edges of the 'approved story' offer tremendous opportunities.

Like everything else in life, it isn't always one event and actually it's usually not one event. It's ripples, the cumulative results of events, that accumulate over time, and combine into waves. Our inability to grasp time constraints, as well as too many things happening to track, let ripples sneak up on us. This is another aspect of feedback that is ignored and/or not monitored and/or interpreted incorrectly.

Here is another weakness in the authorized story. Exception handing is one of the weaknesses with a system. If an alarm appears a few times a week, people know what to do. If it happens once in a while, or never before, then no one has any idea what to do. The problem with words and actions in a manual is that until you have walked through an event at least once, the words, which are general, don't mentally match the action, which is specific. If it is a conceptual alarm, something in the economy or a company's numbers or estimates that is out of whack, that's an exception that is generally ignored.

Social creations, such as banks, central banks, all the complex conceptual world of finance and money, are the usual black swans. These are black swans because even if everyone means the best, they are complex, their interrelationships are unclear and murky (if you understand them correctly, please, tell all of us and win a Nobel Prize) and as they are tied to very important parts of the social contract, there is a lot of the social world that isn't overlapping the real world in these.

People will throw facts and numbers at you with a smile and expect you to sit down and numbly do as you are told. Measurements are a source of false security. Simply measuring something doesn't mean you measured anything meaningful for what you are concerned with. All of the audited financial statements mean hardly anything about what is going to happen tomorrow. They hopefully mean that the stuff in the warehouse is there and the money in the bank is there, but what they are going to do with that stuff tomorrow-which is all that matters for investment decisions, isn't hidden in those statements. Doubt certainty.

If people are stuck on their stories, and determined to make the world conform to their stories, regardless of what the world is like, how are we to deal with this? Do we go off the cliff with them, or look to our own interests? (Hint-this book advocates the second choice) If people are determined to stick to their stories, stories with 'fail' written all over them, how can one survive and prosper in a storybook social world that isn't based on the real world? How can one know where their false views are and work with the false views without taking the hit when it falls apart? Let us let others do as they please, but we want to stay out of the wreckage.

Let's put this in simple terms: If everyone is crazy, what is the next cliff they are running off? And if I can't stop them (assuming I should want to protect them from their own stupidity for various reasons) how can I at least make some money off of this? If you don't think they are crazy, ask how often people are expecting a result in the real world without any real relationship between their actions and the desired result. Hint: big words will not change the real world, even if delivered in the correct deep stentorian tone of voice.

Ecosystems change and inflexible institutions will collapse. The participants disperse, lamenting the loss of the old beliefs, trying new things, making their living in different ways than they used to. That's one of the best, and easiest stories to grasp-the glorious past contrasted with the pitiful present; we are but a shadow of our ancestors, etc. Those who stay in that story, seeking a dead past, will not succeed. Those who are selling that story are putting gold in their pockets. For those who look to the future, there is there is a compensating advantage: it is the people who figure out how to work simply in the present, rather than the people who mastered the complexities of the past, who get to say what happens in the future. And the paychecks.

"Structures, he thought as he walked down the hallway. The highest achievement of human kind. The group working together, all parts in this vast machine, all interdependent. Beautiful, but not life, and they don't see the limits. A structure is a group of people; each with their own desires and conflicts. They have certain possible physical movements, and certain physical resources. Those can be combined and worked with. But the structures are not built with the magic fairy dust that is good, beauty, right, justice. Those ideas, goals, are completely separate from the structure's processes. People forget that because you sell the structures on the ideas. People deny the weaknesses of the structures, because they need the structure for other emotional reasons.

You can only do what the structure allows. So you can have beautiful phrases and logical sentences, and see a certain cure to the problems besetting you. But in the end, it's suits in a room, with limited real options and powers to create change in the world. You want to overthrow a government that oppresses its people? You have to bomb the people and destroy their world in the process. You want to protect people from the scourge of drug addiction? Then you destroy everyone connected with the drugs, throw them out without any hope of redemption, as part of the process. Destroy their families, their livelihoods, if they fall into the addiction you are fighting against. And then the people who handle the fight—the police, prosecutors—they are bought off, cynical and warped. The medical people who treat the addictions become cynical and manipulative, pushing up those bottom-line numbers because they can't help the addicted, and they become numb to the destruction that the structure creates. Just one example of many. Because that's what the structures are. Rigid, limited in applications and possibilities. Making the structures the be all and end all has destroyed them."[153]

Behind every great fortune lies a great crime. - Honore de Balzac

The key model is to picture the interactions of multiple tribes in conflict-they will ebb and flow, there will be moments that see the strengths, then they fade away. That's what the future is.

CHAPTER 34. HOW TO DO NEFARIOUS THINGS

This chapter looks at how to do nefarious things. We love villain's in the movies, which is probably why they get the best lines and the big houses. If you want to be the hero, well then you need to know how to avoid having nefarious things done to you. And there are lots of nefarious things done all the time that people never see happening. Oh, they see the unemployment, the wage reductions, the higher cost of living, but the slight of hand by which those things are accomplished are hidden.

Let's have some fun in the tradition of "The Prince" and The Art of War. Why do the forces of evil always have expensive cars and big houses? Because we are told we can justify to ourselves that we are not evil then, not a comforting thought.

"Either you think -- or else others have to think for you and take power from you, pervert and discipline your natural tastes, civilize and sterilize you."[154] *(F Scott Fitzgerald)*

This section starts with a very long quote from "Paul" because it both does something truly nefarious, and raises the key issues in the process. It's a lot more interesting in novel structure than a dry recitation of ideas. The book started with how we think in stories, so here is a story to help our thinking.

DO WHAT?

"Lucretia sat in her office, re-reading the notes she made after the meeting with Paul. Yeah, that's what he actually ordered. Amazing. She shook her head. Thank you, may I have another, my lord? What have I gotten myself into? Ah, Lucretia, a small job for you, if you have time. Sink a country, spark a war, and make huge, enormous profits in the process. Sooner is better than later. Ciao. As you wish, my evil master. She bowed slightly. Clean the Augean stables afterwards? No problem.

Okay, what he's asking for is an amplified result from an event. Such as... She reread a newspaper clipping she had saved, because it was so amazing. From The Surfersvillage Global Surf News, 27 December 2009:

"The biggest wave on record occurred in Lituya Bay on the southern coast of Alaska in 1958. An earthquake measuring 8.3 on the Richter scale hit the area and shook loose an estimated 40 million cubic yards of dirt and glacier from a mountainside at the head of the bay. When the debris hit the water, a massive 1,720-foot wave was created and washed over the headland.

"How did the scientists know the wave was so incredibly enormous? Simple. To measure the height of the wave, scientists found the high-water mark — the line where the water reached its highest point on land. This probably is not the biggest wave ever, just the biggest documented. Three fishing boats witnessed the Lituya Bay event. While two people on one of the boats were killed, incredibly, the other two boats rode the waves and their occupants survived." That had to be a day to remember, Lucretia thought. The cruel part is that they couldn't brag about it afterwards, because who would believe a story like that?

"Technically, this wave is described as a 'Splash Wave.' The photo above shows the headland beside the Lituya Glacier that was swept clean of soil and trees to a height of 1740 feet by the giant splash wave. The icebergs seen in the water of Lituya Bay, foreground, were knocked off the glacier by the landslide falling into the bay from a slope to the right of the photograph." That's incredible, studying at the pictures. Who would believe a wave could be seventeen hundred feet high? Roughly one and one-half times the height of the Empire State Building rising up towards you. Exactly what I need to have happen in the economic world. But not with me sitting between the wave and the rock cliff, thank you.

So, I need to arrange an earthquake that jars loose some very big things that sync together and POW! How hard can that be? Paul said he has money, political and press connections, and questionable authorities on our side. On the other side is a sovereign government with an army and a diplomatic corps. Oh, and a historical bent towards machismo—that male-honor thing. Women stay home, mind their little business. Okay, I'm rationalizing, but that's going to make this more fun. Now if I could just arrange for Cesare to have all his money there, that would be the icing on the cake.

This is certainly going to be illegal. Perhaps not the exact black-letter of the law, but certainly the spirit. If it goes well, they'll amend the law. The equivalent of a seventeen hundred-foot wave coming through the financial world is going to make powerful people unhappy. So how to handle that before they are standing in a mob around me with the torches flickering, other than fleeing to a desert island somewhere, which wouldn't last? The mafia knows how to run a fraud. If you run questionable transactions through a failing business, then crash and burn the business in the bankruptcy court, no one pays much attention to the details. Ideally, before the authorities show any interest. Case closed; all that is left are a few dusty, yellowing documents in the court archives. Nothing left on the bare bones but a few teeth marks, and the actual business records interred in an unregulated landfill after a brief but respectful ceremony. Prosecutors pick cases by re-election value, and there's little to be gained from using scarce resources poring over failures. By the time anyone wises up to the extent of the disaster, the trail is cold.

How not to do it? Run it through a business that not only continues, but has a prominent business address. If Enron had the sense to crash their little subsidiaries, the trail would not have led back. Ironically, they thought they could make it work and ran it the legal way.

Of course, if they had any sense, they would never have created a publicly held house of cards. Talk about having "ruin" stamped all over the plan! Why not just give the prosecutors a road map and confession to start with? Once the prosecutors realized they could walk into that big office building and get on the evening news, i.e., positive reelection publicity, there would be no stopping them.

What was the Monty Python sketch? Lucretia thought to herself. They had it dead on. She stood up and declaimed to the empty office: "And so the Scarlet Permanent Assurance boldly hoisted sail on the high seas of international finance. For a long time, they sailed empty seas, growing lean and hungry, their ship tattered and worn. And then, suddenly rising before them, was the prize of their dreams. An arrogant financial district swollen with fat, bloated Investment Banks, Hedge Funds and luscious Sovereign Funds. Unsuspecting, the Mandarins of high finance sat smug and self-satisfied, master's of the universe they knew, blithely unaware of the terrible revenge planned against them. The Jolly Roger run up, the reasonably violent men of the Scarlet Permanent Assurance attacked without mercy, ceasing only when the once-proud financial giants lay in ruins, their assets stripped, their credit lines emptied, and their officers walked off the plank."

"It's fun to charter an accountant, and sail the wide accountan-cy ," she sang loudly to the birds flying outside the windows.

Her secretary poked her head in with a questioning look on her face. "Practicing for the opera?" she asked.

"Argh," Lucretia growled. "It's the briny deep and the pirate's life for me."

"Aye, aye, captain," her secretary declared, standing straight and saluting. "I'll run the flag up the mizzenmast." She closed the door.

I like this secretary, Lucretia thought. She may be owned by Paul, but at least she has a sense of humor. The other one was just all petty viciousness. She deserved Mother Superior.

Lucretia sat back down at her desk, doodling. So, I need a chain of crashing businesses, based in different countries and subject to a welter of jurisdictions and laws. Not just laws written in different languages with unclear translations—I need them written in different dialects so that even the lawyers in that country cannot decide what the law is. No one person knows all the languages, and the translations can be attacked. With enough money and planning, a web can be spun that no one is going to work through. Fortunately, or unfortunately, few people plan ahead enough. Or perhaps they are just never caught? Lucretia sat back, remembered what the professor who taught the advanced accounting class had said. One day, a brave student had raised his hand and asked what the smart people did when they ran a fraud.

The professor gazed at him thoughtfully. "The party line is that there are no smart people running frauds. The party line is that they always make mistakes, will always be tripped up. The reality is that we don't know because it's all negative evidence. We don't see the holes where the successful frauds were. If you think about it, there are a number of ways to run a fraud that can't be tracked. Now, a successful fraud requires thought, planning, nerve, and focus. Fortunately, there are few people—at least we think there are few people—who can pull that off. I'd feel better," the professor commented dryly, "if everyone in the class didn't have the same excited look, that look that says you have seen the Promised Land open before you." The class laughed, but the look stayed.

"Some people are born to piracy, some people achieve piracy, and some people have piracy thrust upon them," Lucretia mumbled to herself. What happened to my classmates? Most vanished off the face of the earth. Occasionally I see reports of their houses being sold in faraway places as they move to larger homes. Perhaps they took the message of that class to heart. That attorney that Paul uses in the U.S.? I can meet with him and have a business plan ready. Plausible denial, that's all the law firm needs to cover themselves, and that's easy to do.

The next day, Lucretia was riding in a cab back to her office after meeting with the senior partners of the law firm. They even have standard forms for this type of business structure! With check-off boxes for "difficult to track," "impossible to track," and "hang the cost, no one will ever find out." I'm not as smart as I thought I was, but at least I'm on the right track.

"So, where is that seventeen hundred-foot wave?" Lucretia demanded, staring intently at the wall. Hal caught me, and I thought I was being so clever. Anomalies, he told me, and he's right. Watching for the subtle forming, but putting that into measurable goals. I wish I could get his help on this! I'm not sure how that would look on the expense report. Line item—expensive dinner with and enormous bribe paid to sworn Enemy Number One? Perhaps not.

Let's see. Take this from the top. Project planning is simple conceptually: determine what you want to do, assess the steps needed to get there, determine the timeline for the steps. Finally, set up a monitoring system to check your progress, and provide feedback on problems.

So: a clear goal is the first requirement. Okay. I want to make a vast fortune for my evil master in the next few months, focused on Paraguay/Brazil, beginning with manipulation of the global currency markets. That's a nice, simple goal statement. Works in cartoons, at least. The problem with goal statements is that they imply a structure. That is, the goal assumes a world and tools to reach that goal. This seems to be outside the existing structure, if not absolutely banned as destructive to the structure's heart.

Going back to organization, simply writing down all of the possibilities in random order, is the first place for me to start. Expand on the possibilities/choices that I see, and new choices will develop. Work on those for some time, giving myself at least several days to sleep on problems, assuming sleep comes, and my choices will, more likely than not, align into some clear categories. Some choices will be clearly irrelevant; some will open to new definitions of the problems. That's a plan, but let's not put all the eggs in one basket. Another approach—has this ever been done before? I have a lot of eager interns and can mix the questions up so it isn't quite so obvious what's going on. That's tomorrow's project. She shut down her laptop.

PRIMING THE MIND

Lucretia was again at her desk at the office. The door was barred and no phone calls were allowed. The general ponders in her chamber, reading omens and signs, while the troops patrol nervously the perimeter.

She skimmed the piles of research generated by the interns and hopeful junior partners, and then pushed it all aside. Fine, she thought. The general who wins a battle makes many calculations in his temple ere the battle is fought, but what calculations to make? Clarity, simplicity, but what is that? The essence of calculation, to paraphrase Sun Tzu, is to (1) clearly grasp the social consensus worldview, i.e., the story we tell ourselves about how the real world is as we want it; and (2) clearly see the real world as it really is, and then (3) contrast the two, profiting from the errors in the social consensus worldview. That requires: first, clear articulation of the social consensus worldview from a view not buying or selling that consensus, which is pretty damn hard, and second, some way of touching/grasping events in the real world outside the limiting human stories. The bounded world is seeing the world through the stories; the unbounded world is seeing the stories through the world. Again, pretty damn hard.

But like many hard things, there is a reward. The easy thing, which is buying into the social consensus and only seeing real-world events through that consensus, puts you in the fields with a hoe, not the Lord of the Manor. I don't like working with a hoe in the hot sun, she recalled. Tried it as a kid. Misery may love company, and they are welcome to it. Seeing past the stories, playing the social consensus against the real world, profiting from the gaps—there is life in the lap of luxury. Cool drinks on a hot day, pool boys at my beck and call. I like that! Distracted, she drifted away for a minute, and then shook her head. Back to reality.

Now, each moment contains an infinity of events. Lots of them, like stars crashing in a distant galaxy, have a hopefully minimal effect on me. Actually, things just happen and we define them as events. Those events sometimes create/cause/influence other events, sometimes not. Sometimes the ripples combine, sometimes they peter out. Ripples generally build over longer time periods than humans perceive, only to surprise us when the wave finally breaks on us. Patternicity is the blessing and curse of the human mind, the hard-wired obsession to see patterns everywhere and right now, whether or not the patterns actually exist.

My mind, all human minds, must emotionally be in charge, organized, on top of things, in a world that clearly is running outside of our control. Stark proof that we must believe ourselves in control is the right brain/left brain problem. People with severed brains, who actually had surgery, a scalpel physically cutting the connections between the two sides of the brain, can still provide lucid, rational explanations for behaviors controlled by the other side of the brain. Unfortunately, those explanations are completely wrong because the one side of the brain explaining literally has no idea what the other side is doing. The mere fact that their explanations are completely wrong, created out of whole cloth, forced by that necessity to see yourself as coherent and consistent, doesn't dent the individuals absolute belief in their explanations.

Does make one question one's own explanations occasionally," she thought wryly. Case in point-her senior partner, who actually believes his speeches, and is clearly deluded and delusional. That won't play well at the salary review, I'm afraid, and she regretfully drew a line through that idea.

So this is a difficult problem. Compounding the problem, humans have a limited attention span and a very finite number of items that we can keep in focus at any given time—oh, somewhere between five and nine, depending on the person. Something else comes in, one of the others has to go away, which is why writing things down is a good idea. That's why in "The Hitchhiker's Guide to the Galaxy," they build a computer that ran for millions of years to solve the answer to the universe. The computer may have been right, and perhaps the answer to the universe really is "42," but that doesn't tell me anything that's helpful today.

So I can't just say to myself, "Show me what I can't see!" Lucretia thought. Can't wave a wand and show me the future, because I can't see what I'm not seeing. Even the Harry Potter people couldn't do that either. You had to know the spell to cast it, I guess. This makes my head hurt, she realized, wearily rubbing her temples.

Now, even if I clearly see real-world events on one hand and social consensus on the other, the gaps between them nicely defined, there is no guarantee that there will be an investment opportunity. There must be, first, a negative/positive intersection between the coming real-world events and the social consensus, then second, a way of calculating the time impact on the consensus. I.E., when will the real world hit the group hard enough that notice has to be taken? And third, most importantly, there has to be a market whereby one can place your bets on the future. Otherwise, no cool drinks on a hot day for me.

Actually, that's really important, because it narrows down the possibilities. I already know the relevant market, the currency exchange markets, FOREX, and the private and public derivative markets. I know their rules and leverage, and I can pop that up on my computer screen. It's scary, really. All that a country is—resources, opportunities, debt, depravities and wholesome desires of the citizens, everything—

summarized into one number, the value of the currency at a given second. Which fluctuates wildly from second to second, as it should.

Driving one day, I realized that the future is like driving in traffic. I know my usual haunts, my small world, and have a general idea what traffic I can expect at a given time. My expectations are clearer today than a month from now. I don't know the specific cars, where they are headed, or what the driver's choices and lives are—none of the minute detail that explains each car on the road. But I know roughly, for my purposes in calculating travel times, when it will be busy and when it won't, and what the average traffic flow is going to be. What I need to know is when an accident is going to occur on X road, which drives all the traffic onto Y road. That's the equivalent of what I'm supposed to do with this currency.

On the bright side, I'm not in college with a thousand dollars to risk and high hopes for the future. I have Paul's resources behind me, which are enormous. The country in point has certain exports, and there are known demands and supplies. It has certain products produced and consumed within the country, again with known demands and supplies. All of those exports and products have pressure points. Food rumored to be poisoned drops in value quickly. Drugs rumored to be inferior, defective, drop in value rapidly. Land rumored to have secret resources can jump in value and ironically bankrupt the people who need that land, because it's grabbed away from them. Fear of a sinking economy dries up bank lending, creating the depression they fear. Then the torrent of Sun Tzu, rocks crashing down the mountain onto eggs, beats on that magic number that is the currency value. Enough of these little drips combining under pressure, and there is my seventeen hundred foot wave, sweeping all before it.

It's anomalies, like Hal told me, excited, drawing connecting lines on the paper. It's the little things that hint the story isn't working that count. So what are the anomalies surrounding the values of the exports? What little facts hint where the demand curve shifts rapidly? That's another thing to unleash the interns on. I like that, she mused. I'm standing tall in black leather boots, holding a field marshal's baton, roaring 'Unleash the interns!' And they rush out into the street, all dark suits and power glasses, pillaging on their laptops as they go.

Finally, we need friends, especially if this blows up as big as it will. Good, close, powerful friends. Many people must make money off this. Bulls make money, and bears make money, but pigs get slaughtered. Paul has a list of his friends who are in. I just have to make sure that they make so much that we all hang together, for we shall assuredly hang separately otherwise.

And where to look to focus down on the key influences on the magic currency number? Tail risk. The risk that the tail wags the dog, not the dog wagging the tail. What did they say in finance class? Lucretia thought back to finance class. How did the professor carefully state the problem and solution?

So, you're a portfolio manager with a condo in New York and a beach house in Maine. You want to keep them. Your significant other wants to keep them, and you want to keep your significant other. Towards that worthy goal, you create a concept that defines a portfolio of investments. That portfolio, you assert, will provide a desirable rate of return. You have tied the projections to reasonable assumptions, it all 'looks' good (skipping the smell test) and the risk committee signs off. The portfolio is marketed to investors (marks) as a substantially above market rate of return that is even safer than leaving your money in your mattress. How much better can things be? So people throw money at your idea.

The devil is in the detail. 'Safe' means that the probability that returns will move between the mean and three standard deviations, either positive or negative, is 99.97%. The probability of returns moving more than three standard deviations beyond the mean is 0.03%, or virtually nil. But, and this is what keeps you up at night, the big money and your superstar status require being in that .03%. You know that the concept of tail risk suggests that the distribution of events will not be not normal, but skewed. Skewed is fatter tails. Fatter tails increase the probability that an investment will move beyond three standard deviations. It's pig in clover time, if they move in a positive direction. If they move in a negative direction, the portfolio is destroyed.

But you're a smart investment manager, Harvard degree on the wall. The risk factor has been signed off on, and you've met the social—AND legal—criteria for rational investment behavior. Extensive analysis, backed up by reams of printouts, proves that the probabilities have been calculated in a statistically rational manner. Lawyer's and accountant's letters fill the prospectus. That you know; and the risk committee knows; and the senior partners know; that it's all pious nonsense and you're betting someone's else's ship on events way, way more likely than .03% is something that only comes out, first, if there is a complete disaster, and second, only if the people who lost money have more political power than the company. That's a little, little tail risk, clearly less than .03%, and so life goes on at an investment firm.

No one really understands statistics anyway, Lucretia knew. Look at the occasional papers popping up saying that the drug companies don't have a clue, statistically, what they are doing when they analyze their test results. They know the results they want, and POOF! The drugs do what they are supposed to do, at least on paper. Are the results defensible? Yes. Are they correct? Probably not. And the data mining of health statistics? That should be characterized as a pirate expedition, blatant looting by research MDs and PhDs desperate for grants and publicity. The lone voices in the wilderness pointing out errors in the calculations are not even shouted down because no one understands what they are talking about anyway.

So, yeah, that conceptually focuses down the target She added a few small touches to her drawing, tying relationships together, and nodded to herself. Anomalies show you the resource inputs that are

THE critical change drivers. Change driver effects, being non-linear, are positive feedback cycles, and thus multiplied by their fatter tails. Amplified by the gaps between the social consensus and the real world (IE, the tails are really FAT), then there is that seventeen hundred foot wave. I'm riding it like a pro, all the way into the golden beach and the handsome pool boys. And the continued existence of my family and I, because that's the way that Paul plays. That's the gold, matey, if one can just find it. Arghhh.

Let's hit it from a different angle, keep narrowing this down. There are two ways to make money in the system. One can either make money selling people the story they want to hear, or make money profiting when the oh-so-important story that they run their lives by breaks up on the reef. Selling them the story they want, well, there's crowds lined up to do that—tough to get through the noise. Whereas by making money from the flaws in their story that they can't bear to look at, and so pretend the flaws don't exist, I can sit on the beach and snicker about their errors, tipping the waiters well for drinks. I like that. So it's back to catching the anomalies.

Now, it isn't enough that there is a story and possible problems with the story. There are always problems with the stories. There has to be a problem, by definition. A story is a selected set of events against a sharply colored moral background, highlighting what people want/fear the most. So the background is a problem, what people want is a problem, and what the story will lead to is a problem. The newspapers sell papers exploiting the weakness of the story structure. You can always come up with a reason for why something happened, will happen, shouldn't have happened, and so on. If you're wrong, well, who can foretell the future? And, by the way, because you are my special friend, and you get my special friend price, here's another story about what's really going to happen this time, no kidding, cross my heart and hope you die.

The newspaper seeks impeccable, crosschecked facts and then weaves them into a narrative that implies causality and superior knowledge. We have to be told stories, and there is nothing wrong with that as long as we realize why and what we are doing. Stepping outside, we realize it's not whether a story distorts reality, because all stories distort, but how it distorts reality.

For better or worse, most human communication is no different from monkeys pulling lice out of each other's fur, Lucretia ruminated, listening to the women chat in the bathroom as she sat quietly in her stall. It's all grooming and social touching. Necessary and useful, but not to be confused with the communication of facts. Speaking of pulling lice out of fur, looking critically at strands of her blonde hair, now I'm wondering about the cleanliness of that hair salon. Yuck.

Most of the time, sadly, the stories have nothing to do with the relevant issues driving the problems. So using the news for investment choices is a sucker's game. The Wall Street Journal is no different from seagulls flying over the beach. Seagulls fly in small, widely spaced groups, watching both the water below them and the other seagulls. The minute a seagull dives for a fish in the water, a hundred flock to follow. If you're the ninety-ninth seagull to the party, there isn't much left of the fish when you get there. However, the patrolling sharks, who also watch the seagulls, may have reached the scene by then, because they have a story, too.

Pierre-Daniel Huet, in his Philosophical treatise on the weaknesses of the Human Mind, which was published in, oh, approximately 1690, wrote that any event can have an infinity of possible causes, which humans ignore. We focus on preselected segments of the seen and generalize from it to the unseen, which is the error of confirmation. Socially rewarded behavior, by the way. We all pull the same kind of lice out. We fool ourselves with stories that cater to our hardwired need for patterns and control. We behave as if unknown unknowns, black swans, do not exist. We lament: "To-morrow, and to-morrow, and to-morrow, Creeps in this petty pace from day to day, To the last syllable of recorded time ," and yet we cling to the vision of yesterday becoming today. No real thought for the differences, the possibilities. We're not programed to expect the unexpected.

Kant clearly wrote, well, as clearly as a German philosopher can, that what we see (perceive) is a small subset of what is out 'there'. First our perceptions are limited by the hardware-eyes, nose, etc. Then there is the distortion of silent evidence. Remember the professor talking about silent evidence? The class didn't think the idea was all that important, and the professor knew it. "Age shows the value of this," he told us, surveying the dazed and dulled faces in class. "You'll think more of this later. We see what happened, or what we are told happened. We do not see, do not have time to see or think, about what could have happened, what might have happened, and what the differences were have been. Where are the events that didn't happen? Where are the events riding on other events that look like they caused them? History hides Black Swans from us and gives us a mistaken idea about the odds of these events. You stumble over the silent evidence when your plan crashes around you."

Finally, and this is Hal's gift to me: we tunnel; we focus on a few well-defined sources of uncertainly. We are taught to define, structure, and proceed when the light is green. The higher in the educational structure you go, the more carefully you are trained. Within a carefully limited and structured system, like a school, one can do that successfully. On the wide ocean of life, you watch the waves and choose based on scraps of random information—the anomalies. Little wisps of clouds in the distance, red sky at morning? Pay attention and pull the sails in or perish. See the birds wheeling over the water in the distance? Sail there and the fishing is rich.

The both comforting and terrifying thing about the mind is that, really, consciousness is like a passenger on the second floor of a double-decker bus. Frantically sorting through maps, holding his notes against the wind, peering through the rain on his glasses, he shouts directions to the driver, waving his arms wildly to prove his control. The real driver, the unconscious, sitting comfortably on a plush leather seat, confidently holding the steering wheel of the bus on the enclosed first floor, can't hear the consciousness's ravings and so it drives the bus where it should go. The unconscious snickers to itself, knowing that what the consciousness perceives is only what the unconscious feeds to it. So, relax. Decisions make themselves if you just gather data. A picture will form in your mind if you're willing to ignore the wildly shouting person on the second floor of the bus.

"Okay," Lucretia proclaimed, contemplating the bright city lights sparking against the dark night. "A glass of wine, a glance at the picture of the beach house I want, and to sleep. The plan will emerge."

THE PLAN EMERGES

Why Paraguay? Lucretia puzzled. And what is the tie to São Paulo? Paul's instructions were clear and focused. What am I missing? The interns and junior partners had been frantically jumping to her commands for several days. They presented a huge pile of information to her in a long meeting full of charts, graphs, and PowerPoint presentations. Most of what they found was irrelevant, but she bought them all dinner at a nice restaurant for their hard work. Then she sat back in her office and worked through the piles of documents behind the presentations.

Like any country, Paraguay has key products to be stockpiled and then driven down by releasing the stocks. That is the traditional, physical way of crashing a market, but you have to pay market price for all that stuff you are planning on selling cheap after the crash, so there's a big risk doing that. You have to make more profiting from the currency crash than you lose on the value of the stuff you bought falling because of said currency crash. Otherwise, your clever knife in the back ends up in your back—a poor plan. Finally, if you do succeed, there are a piles of warehouse receipts and waybills showing who bought what. That's pretty easy to track back in a computerized world, and when they track back to you, there are angry mobs with torches outside the office building. Fail.

The modern way is to sink the ship with rumors. Rumors that products are inferior and/or poisoned. Or rumors that the key products have vague health risks based on indefinite proofs offered about some people who may have been sick for undefined but inferred reasons. Rumors that build on themselves, posted in blogs, e-mails, phone calls— and then the authorities jump onto the bandwagon. Rising stars at regulatory agencies need a story to build a career on. They produce serious white papers with weasel words in the text, but strong sound bites in the summary for the news media. There are hosts of regulatory authorities to work through. There's the EPA, the various health commissions in Europe, and funny little groups with important sounding names that can easily be confused with really important groups. There's always a blog willing to take up the cudgels that something is unsafe if they get prestige, power, and advertising revenue for being ahead of the crowd. There's no question that some of the processing and shipping methods that any industry/country uses are, at best, questionable in today's world. Any time you have a process unchanged for many years, something isn't going to pass muster by some modern standard. Enough little torpedo rumors hitting under the waterline, and the ship goes down.

So who could pull together a statistically defensive study that could rapidly damage things? Information spreads so quickly now—it would have be timed perfectly. From little countries and backwater web sites that can't be tracked back to by the angry mobs later. It can work, because there are a lot of people sitting out there, waiting to hit that sell button. It's all numbers. For this to happen, the investment analysts have to sit in a room, push spreadsheets around, and the bottom line has to show a crash for the currency based on projections. All those portfolio managers dreaming of that magic .03% result—living proof that they are the Masters of the Universe. What will or won't happen doesn't matter. It's those projections, and acting first to protect their bank/country/corporation/wealthy client. Then the bulls are loose, trampling the crowd running in terror before them.

Conceptually, a disease epidemic and a financial bubble revolve around structural changes. Contagion is the key. Physiological contagion for a flu epidemic and psychological contagion for a market bubble. That's the little weasel reports flitting around the Internet, mutating like a flu virus and spreading by e-mail, faster than air transmission.

What's the downside? Well, the country is devastated—children are hungry in the streets, the wealthy are destroyed. There is that. Paul then comes in, buys assets on the cheap, and doubles his money again on top of his vast profits from the currency manipulation. Yes, that is a plan that even my evil master would embrace. Should I present it? Shall I rationalize to myself, by acknowledging that my family's safety, nay, their very continued existence, is dependent on my coming up with something like this? While I may guess about what happens to all of them in that far-off country, I know exactly what would happen to us. Rationalization, yes. Reality, certainly.

Lucretia spent the next few days laying out the details. What regulatory agencies would have to do what, and when. Who to contact at the agencies with what proof for actions to the taken. What blogs in the world to be encouraged with gifts and grants. Who would profit off the intermediate steps. And the financial investments—hedges to make before the ball starts to roll.

She sat back and contemplated her plan. Karla bought a legend for a girl, and it was the anomalies that tripped it up. The men with no tradecraft skills, the weak-minded that no one would use as agents unless there was no other choice. And here, studying her nice diagram, are the weaknesses in their economy, in their worldview, that they deny and ignore—papered over because they had to believe things are a certain way. They firmly believe, basking in their power and glory, that the world has to be 'this' way, without question or deviation allowed. But it isn't that way. Surprise!"[155]

And the plan worked-better than Lucretia had anticipated, because the buffers were stripped off by fools and the positive feedback was non-linear. Boom!

So, there are some troubling things in this chapter. (perhaps everything is troubling, actually, which is fine) For example: the Golden rule: is "Do unto others as you would have others do unto you." A wonderful rule for keeping a village functioning, but complex in operation, not the least because the Supreme categorical imperative implicit in the Golden Rule is: "Act only according to that maxim whereby you can at the same time will that it should become a universal law." So it works pretty well in a small village, within limits, but is really not that functional at the international level.

Don't walk away from what you've learned about someone just because it's socially recommended. When someone does something wrong, don't assume it's the only thing wrong. Forgive in your heart, if it lowers your blood pressure, but keep your hands over your wallet. The flash of 'wrong' you saw may be just the surface, as others can have quite different world views.

"Guilt is one of those concepts that Grendel found fascinating," Hal mused. "He thought it was hilarious that one would regret your actions. The closest he got to grasping the idea of regret was sorrow that he couldn't pillage and burn a village again, experimenting with new concepts and methods. Regretting the pillage and burning just wasn't his modus operandi."[156]

Quote number 2 along the same lines:

"Back to Hal's intersecting circles—looking at the circle labeled 'yourself,' and the intersection with the circle labeled 'social structures.' You are different than they want you to be, Take my word for it, I know. William James asserted that we are the survivors of the successful killers, and while we may put on a happy and peaceful face, inside us, ready at any moment to burst into flame, are the smoldering and sinister traits of our ancestors. People under pressure revert to the norm. Unsophisticated native peoples are deadly serious about warfare. They exterminate their enemies when they can, while enthusiastically torturing captives, collecting body parts for trophies, and feasting on enemy flesh. I mention this because people, enmeshed in a structure that provides food, shelter, and protections for their children are dramatically different people from those either outside a structure or people whose structures have collapsed. You can't assume polite behavior after a crash."[157]

Which is the underlying concept of pretty much all the apocalypse and disaster movies.

Here is a diagram of all black swans:

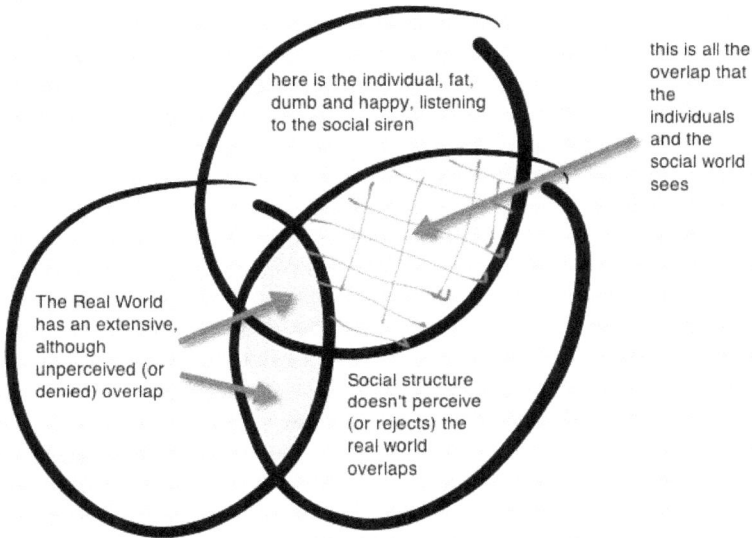

here is the individual, fat, dumb and happy, listening to the social siren

this is all the overlap that the individuals and the social world sees

The Real World has an extensive, although unperceived (or denied) overlap

Social structure doesn't perceive (or rejects) the real world overlaps

Here be the gold, Matey: if ye be on the right side of the disaster coming.

Figure 12.

Copy the diagram, tape it to your refrigerator, and watch the financial news.

CREATING DISASTER

People will do nefarious things-at least from your perspective. In a computerized world, full of new technology and untried systems, everything is hackable. And I mean everything! The most sold system in the world still has passwords and people who can be bought, bribed or threatened.

So, you want to do something nefarious? Here is the plan that a hacker uses to break into a computer system. It's a plan that you can use for any project.

You start your attack by:

"1.   exterior reconnaissance – you poke, carefully, trying to leave no traces behind.

2.   initial breach-you get somewhere, in at a low level.

3.   escalate privileges-you work your way into the system, moving up.

4.   persistence-you know what you want, and you focus on it. You take your time, watching.

5.   Internal reconnaissance-inside, you poke and test, carefully.

6.   lateral breach-you widen your intrusion, you keep poking, testing, adding to what you know.

7.   maintain presence-stay there and keep poking.

8.   achieve objective-having continually monitored your plan and expanding the plan as opportunity presents itself."[158]

Isn't this what the book has recommended in different terms and times? Isn't that the OODA cycle, executed with focus and clear intent?

Another way to do nefarious things, which you won't see in a movie is to first carefully define how a story will work, and how a story will not work. Movies like obvious villains, because it's a movie and time is short. But you can then define how to hide the truth-or for the squeamish, how to suspect that something is being hidden. We think in stories, and people will often take the story presented to them, without checking it closely.

If you really want to know how to do nefarious things, study a good design book. For example, the Universal principles of Design-because good design shows how to get people to do what you want then to do without them having to think. Good design anticipates good behaviors and goals, which I leave to you to define and choose.

In a design book, you are confronted with reality. Design deals with the real world, not 'hoped for' or 'desperately desired' worlds, and looks at what actually happens. Working through good design answers the questions How to design to confuse others? How to design to confuse yourself?

There are standard User Interface Design Guidelines, which advise:

- Strive for consistency
- Cater to universal usability
- There must be a match between the system and the real world. Offer informative feedback-the system status has to be clear.
- Design task flows to yield closure
- Prevent errors by structuring choices
- If there are errors, design so people recognize, can diagnose and recover from errors.
- Recognition rather than recall – people forget quickly.
- Flexibility and efficiency of use, which includes easy reversal of actions

- Make users feel they are in control
- Minimize short-term memory load
- Aesthetic and minimalist design, so the design doesn't get in the way of the user
- User control and freedom
- Provide online documentation and help

Obviously, you can flip all of the above, turning the system into a buggy, incomprehensive mess that no one has any idea what is going on of what it's supposed to accomplish, with the result that people are not going to thinking through end goals. You're most of the way to your nefarious plan at that point. While they are struggling with alligators in the swamp, your boat laden with gold is quietly rowed away.

Then, there is perception. Our perception of the world around us is not a true depiction of what is actually there. We perceive, to a large extent, what we expect to perceive. Our expectations - and therefore our perceptions – are biased by three factors:

- the past – our experience
- the present – the current context
- the future – our goals

Buried in perception, are the following key issues, if you want people to grasp what is going on:

- Our vision is optimized to see structure, the gestalt. We are wired to perceive our surroundings in terms of whole objects.
- Proximity. The relative distance between objects in a display affects our perception of whether and how the objects are organized.
- Similarity. Objects that look similar appear grouped, all other things being equal
- Continuity. Our visual system's tendency to resolve ambiguity or fill in missing data in such a way as to perceive whole objects.
- Closure. The visual system automatically tries to close open figures so that they are perceived as whole objects.
- Symmetry. We try to parse complex scenes in a way that reduces the complexity, seeking symmetry and simplicity
- Figure/Ground. Our minds separates the visual field into the figure (the foreground) and ground (the background). Too much forest and you miss the details, too much trees and you miss the concept.
- Common fate. The idea that with moving objects, objects that

move together are perceived as grouped or related.

- Finally, the totality – does the total design suggests any relationships between elements that you do not intend?

Again, that's what you are supposed to make things work. Staring at your computer, you can ask yourself whether the program designer knew any of that, or just wanted to be difficult. And if you flip all of them, no one is going to grasp what you are after because they will be frantically running just to jump through hoops.

The design books have many more ideas, but I think you get the concept.

A couple of other thoughts: learning from experience and performing learned actions are easy; problem solving and calculation are hard. So what choices do you want to give people? Story problems with big numbers, and no one will get it right.

When people make a mistake, they don't always learn the right lesson from it. It's hard to connecting the problem actions with the result, and very common to miss the true cause or causes. How to exploit? Provide a socially authorized explanation that is wrong but can't really be challenged. There's a hole you can run through all day long.

CHAPTER 35. CLOSING THOUGHTS

There is no time for everything. There is no optimal solution to life. The best one can do is a succession of minor dents and near misses. You can't start with high-level goals and work down, because those high level goals are obviously word concepts, vague to start with. High-level, socially approved concepts are washed, cleaned and emptied of emotion for the good of the group.

The whole purpose of the parasite discussion was to focus on the impact of a system, being in the system. We exit within a chain of creatures of life, and there is nothing shameful in that, but it is absolutely critical to realize. The point of the whole chapter is to break the reader out of their comfortable world into the complex systems that make up life–out of the human stories and into the primordial soup, as it were.

One of the best approaches to handling problems is, before you make a model, to take the names out and model the systems without the names. Don't model the Mideast; model a set of geographical situations and possibilities, certain resources and options. Then, drop real world names into the model–but experiment, drop them in in difference ways in a couple of different scenarios. Test your understanding of the model by your reactions to the names being in different places in the diagram, places outside where they would normally be. Jar your thoughts and perceptions that way.

Here's an extract from a planning meeting:

"Because today's topic is, what's the purpose? Why are we doing what we are doing? What is the outcome we want to produce? If we don't know what success is, we won't reach it."

"If you don't know where you're going, any road will take you there," Mary pointed out.

"But that's true about any road," Hal declared. "And the question needs to be asked over and over, while a project is underway, not just at the beginning. What isn't true now and what has to be changed to make it true? So, once you define success for this project, is this different than the outcome you were thinking of? Those seminars that Mary went to pounded in the idea that if you start thinking about something, anything in the world, as different than it is now, then the brain starts thinking in random order, coming up with ideas. Collect the ideas, because as you hold an outcome picture, the brain works towards that picture. One idea triggers another idea, freeform towards where we want to go. Then, with a bunch of ideas, the mind starts to organize into patterns. Project planning flows from the outcome you see. Event sequencing, priorities, resources, and constraints all come into order once you see what you want. Until you see that, it's just banging around and frustration."[159]

Dr. Chris Argyris researched what happened to organizations and people when obstacles block their plans. He called the most common response 'single loop learning', a mental process in which we consider possible external or technical reasons for obstacles. That is an overlap of the real world and our self, but without really taking into account new information.

A far more effective approach is called 'double-loop learning'. In this mode we question every aspect of our approach, including our methodology, biases and deeply held assumptions. In terms of Figure 1, we open our minds to more of the real world than we had originally overlapped. When we do this, we have to challenge our beliefs and act on that information, which may lead to fresh ways of thinking about our lives and our goals.

If you stick with single loop thinking, at least don't count your chickens before they hatch, one of those very old slogans that has an essential truth in it. Lots of slogans have the same concept: tennis and football all advise don't take your eye off the ball, which everyone does. How many replays have you seen where the person is clearly looking at what they are going to do after they catch/hit the ball, with the clear result that they miss the ball. Where would the after-game joke reels be without those kind of basic mistakes? So, focus on the details of the plan as they happen, and let others be fodder for the gossip mills.

Should you trust the authorities do to the right thing?

Enlightened people seldom or never possess a sense of responsibility. George Orwell

In AntiFragile, Taleb argues that:

"How do you innovate? First, try to get in trouble. I mean serious, but not terminal, trouble. I hold-it is beyond speculation, rather a conviction that innovation and sophistication spark from initial situations of necessity, in ways that go far beyond the satisfaction of such necessity (from the unintended side effects of, say, an initial invention or attempt at invention). Naturally, there are classical thoughts on the subject, with a Latin saying that sophistication is born out of hunger (artificia docuit fames). The idea pervades classical literature: in Ovid, difficulty is what wakes up the genius (ingenium mala saepe movent), which translates in Brooklyn English into "When life gives you a lemon ... "[160]

Taleb argues that when you plan, do what the real world does:

"It is all about redundancy. Nature likes to overinsure itself. . . Layers of redundancy are the central risk management property of natural systems."[161]

Now, a cynical approach would argue that the typical project goes through 6 phases:

Enthusiasm

Disillusionment

Panic

Search for the Guilty

Punishment of the innocent

Praise and honor to the non-participants" -Unknown

Blonde cheerleaders are smarter than they are given credit for. They don't get hurt in whatever game they are cheering for, and when things go badly, they quietly fold their pom-pom's and skitter away.

Here is another mental approach:

> "Here you are running the road seeking an answer, thinking about the road. Maybe you need to focus on the answer sought; the goal, not the approach, and the approach will come to you. 'Named must your fear be before banish it you can.'"[162]

As you seek knowledge, think about what you are trying to be taught. Is that something different that seminars are trying to teach? Ask yourself what knowledge is relevant in the future? With the internet, all the information you might need is available and you only have to know where to find the instructions. Now, doing is always harder and the knowledge of when to, how to look outside a box, and applying the knowledge is always going to be hard to do. It's a future where it's thinking and accessing information, knowing what to access, not what you can rote remember and spit back. It's still going to be a world where people filter by who you know.

If you seek to motivate yourself and others, then focus on loss, because that is how we are made. Fear of loss is far stronger than seeking gain. Gain pulls, but loss pushes hard.

Want to do something hard?

> "The arks are clear, conceptually," Hal asserted. "To create something that has the seeds of its own destruction within it. To grow something that will become greater and greater each time it tears itself apart. Without the tearing apart turning into civil war and wasteland."[163]

How to do that? Humanity has had little luck so far, but it's a good goal.

> "So why don't we just focus on what's important, relax and surf along the top of life?" Hal asked. "Sounds so easy to do. Ideas?"

> "Well, because it's not the way people are wired," Aliston replied. "People define themselves by their prisons. We hang on to our cocooned pain because the thought of looking directly at it is unimaginably worse than what we suffer living with the known pain. We get distracted. Example: B'rar rabbit and the tar baby. The more you fight, the more tightly you are bound. "

> "Worry loses focus," Cali added. "Worrying is like a man with an arrow in his chest, gasping questions about the man who made the

arrow. The problem is the arrow hanging out of you, not who made the damn thing. Ask the wrong question and you die because you never treat the real problem."

"That's one that a clear outcome would help with," Hal agreed, nodding. "Focusing on getting the arrow out would be key there."[164]

All situations have balances and checks, and those support the situation so that a drastic change in a present situation is harder to anticipate than expected. Which is a polite way of saying: you try as best you can, but some days the world is subject to your Will; others you will as the world would.

Do we now have the tools to plan? Conceptually, yes. Model the system, draw and redraw Figure 1, recognize when one's perceptions are oriented towards wants, not 'is', and anticipate change. You stand balanced and ready to react. It's a 'paper rock scissors world', there are no forever plans, and randomness is in everything.

And the world is about to turn upside down. Computational power is crushing the old systems. For years, computers have changed how we do things. Now, they are going to change what is done. Education: colleges, the credential controllers, the social mega filters, are breaking apart, issuing credentials without value, too slowly and too expensively. The health care system, which really is all information about the person, is crashing because the profitable niches build up over control of information are broken. And, what I think is the biggest change, at least in the US: autonomous automobiles. Everything changes when the cars/trucks drive themselves, absolutely everything. Once you are driven to work, the robots will be working right next to you, faster and error free.

While more data is sometimes more confusion, our models and stories will be tested like never before. Retreating into a warm fantasy while acting in the larger world will be less satisfying than ever, because whether we want the feedback or not, it's coming and coming fast.

While you're waiting for the future, the best way to perform under extreme stress is to repeatedly run it through rehearsals beforehand. Or as the military puts it, the "Eight P's": "Proper prior planning and preparation prevents piss-poor performance.

A couple of closing thoughts:

If you ever find yourself in the wrong story, leave.

And If all else fails, fight when you can, run when you can't and don't leave the food behind. Take the Cannoli.

"All things come out of the One and the One out of all things...I see nothing but Becoming. Be not deceived! It is the fault of your limited outlook and not the fault of the essence of things if you believe that

you see firm land anywhere in the ocean of Becoming and Passing. You need names for things, just as if they had a rigid permanence, but the very river in which you bathe a second time is no longer the same one that you entered before. Heraclitus, 500 BC."

Endnotes

[1] Sun Tzu, "The Art of War", pp 177
[2] Hunt, John. "Apocalypse", pp 319-320
[3] Ibid, pp 299
[4] Sun Tzu, "The Art of War"
[5] Hunt, John. "Paul" pp 41
[6] "Apocalypse" pp 68
[7] "Paul" pp 228
[8] ibid, pp 95
[9] Johnson, Steven. "The Ghost Map" pp 134
[10] ibid
[11] ibid
[12] Paul, pp 299
[13] ibid, pp 299-300
[14] Apocalypse, pp 165
[15] ibid, pp 80-81
[16] ibid, pp 130-131
[17] Taleb, Nicholas. AntiFragile, page 75
[18] Guardians, pp 260-261
[19] Paul, pp 233
[20] Proverbs, Book 1, King James Version
[21] Sun Tzu, The Art of War.
[22] Apocalypse, pp 79-80
[23] "The Bible" Genesis, 1.28
[24] Apocalypse, pp 167
[25] Sun Tzu, the Art of War, Chapter 5
[26] Conan the Barbarian
[27] Doyle, Arthur "Silver Blaze, pp 346-7
[28] Paul, pp 119
[29] Apocalypse, pp 191
[30] Carl Zimmer, New York Times, Voices: What's Next in Science
[31] Wilson, Timothy. "Strangers to Ourselves"
[32] Paul, pp 277
[33] Gazzaniga & Sperry
[34] Orwell, George
[35] Campbell, Joseph "The Power of Myth"
[36] Paul, pp 68-9
[37] Guardians, page 126-127
[38] Cherryholmes, "I Don't Know"
[39] Apocalypse, 187
[40] ibid, pp 101-2

[41] Paul, pp 24
[42] ibid, pp 281-2
[43] Schneier, Bruce
[44] The Dark Knight
[45] Paul, pp 265
[46] Schwartz, Peter "The Art of the Long View"
[47] "What's Up, Doc"
[48] Fitzgerald, F Scott "The Best Early Stories of F. Scott Fitzgerald
[49] Markman, Dr. Arthur
[50] Nietzchke "The Will to Power"
[51] Sun Tzu, "The Art of War", Chapter 4, Formation
[52] Farrell, Catharine from a story retold by Joel chandler Harris
[53] David Brooke, The Behavioral Revolution
[54] Paul, pp 193-6
[55] Apocalypse pp 178
[56] ibid, 23-24
[57] ibid 161-2
[58] Campbell, Joseph
[59] Apocalypse, 137
[60] Jorgensen, Sven, "Systems Ecology, an Introduction"
[61] Guardians pp 273-4
[62] Sun Tzu, "the Art of War", pp 14, Form
[63] Sun Tzu, "The Art of War"Chapter 4, Formation
[64] Guardians, 244-5
[65] Sun Tzu, "The Art of War" Chapter 6 Emptiness and Fullness
[66] ibid, Chapter 1 On Assessments
[67] Guardians, pp 277
[68] Sun Tzu, "The Art of War" Chapter 1 On assessments
[69] ibid
[70] ibid, Chapter 4, Formation
[71] Guardians, pp 243
[72] Goethe, Johann Wolfgang
[73] Paul, pp 158
[74] ibid, pp 154
[75] Shakespeare, "King Lear"
[76] Morrison, Jim "The Soft Parade"
[77] Taleb, "AntiFragile" pp 179
[78] ibid,
[79] ibid, pp 150
[80] Paul, pp 90
[81] Seneca, Lucius Annaeus
[82] Paul, pp 40-1
[83] Heraclitius
[84] Paul, pp 33-5
[85] Paul, pp 193-4
[86] Monty Python's Flying Circus, "Ethyl the Frog" Episode 14
[87] Dorner, Dietrick "The Logic of Failure"
[88] Guardians, pp 61-2

[89] Apocalypse, pp 361-2
[90] ibid
[91] Sun Tzu, "the Art of War" Chapter 111 The Nine Kinds of Terrain
[92] ibid, Chapter 1 On Asssessments
[93] Apocalypse, pp 102
[94] Paul, pp 36
[95] ibid, pp 84-5
[96] Shakespeare, Hamlet
[97] Goethe, Johann Wolfgang
[98] Schiller, Friedrich. "Don Carlos"
[99] Taleb, "AntiFragile" pp 3
[100] ibid, pp 7
[101] ibid, pp 7
[102] ibid, pp 8
[103] Paul, pp 331
[104] Heller, Joseph, "Catch-22" pp 56
[105] Apocalypse, pp 25-6
[106] Carroll, Lewis. "Alice in Wonderland"
[107] Guardians, pp 280
[108] Paul, pp 38-9
[109] Kauffman, Systems 1 (1980) The Tragedy of the Commons
[110] Rotman Magazine, Becoming an Integrative Thinker, Roger Martin
[111] Apocalypse pp 319-20
[112] ibid 139-20
[113] Lehrer, Jonah, in the Wall Street Journal, 10/20/2010
[114] Sun Tzu, "the Art of War" pp14 Form
[115] ibid
[116] Apocalypse pp 148-9
[117] ibid,
[118] Rodman Magazine, Questions for David Apgar, Spring 2008
[119] ibid
[120] Apocalypse pp 99-9
[121] Shakespeare, "Hamlet", Act 5, Scene 2
[122] Guardians, pp 9-10
[123] Paul, pp 119
[124] Paul pp 265
[125] Allen, David, "Making it all Work", pp 290, Appendix ii
[126] ibid
[127] The Economist, 05/12/2012, obituary for Amarillo Slim
[128] Guardians, pp 243
[129] Paul, pp 97
[130] May, Matthew "The Laws of Subtraction"
[131] Sun Tzu, "The Art of War" Chapter 1 On Assessments
[132] Taleb, "AntiFragile" pp 9
[133] Paul, 89-90
[134] Edwards, Tryon
[135] Paul, pp 90-2
[136] Apocalypse 26-7

137 Neuroscience of Screwing Up
138 Sun Tzu, "The Art of War" Chapter 2, On Waging Battle
139 ibid, Chapter 6, emptiness and fullness
140 ibid, Chapter 6, Emptiness and fullness
141 Apocalypse, pp 137
142 Sun Tzu, "The Art of War" Chapter 4, Formation
143 ibid, Chapter 6, Emptiness and fullness
144 ibid chapter 4, formation
145 ibid, Chapter 4, Formation
146 ibid, Spies
147 ibid, Spies
148 ibid, Spies
149 Apocalypse, pp 314-5
150 Sun Tzu, "the Art of War" Chapter 1 On Assessments
151 Gawande, Atul, The Checklist Manifesto
152 Guardians, pp 265-6
153 Apocalypse, pp 364-5
154 Fitzgerald, F Scott
155 Paul, pp 272-6
156 ibid, pp 245
157 Apocalypse, pp 26
158 DefCon, Grand Rapids, MI 09/2013
159 Apocalypse, 98-100
160 Taleb, "AntiFragile" pp 41-2
161 ibid, pp 44
162 Guardians, pp 267
163 Apocalypse, pp 100-1
164 ibid

www.ingramcontent.com/pod-product-compliance
Lightning Source LLC
Chambersburg PA
CBHW050502210326
41521CB00011B/2289